A Separate Little War

The Banff Coastal Command Strike Wing
Versus the Kriegsmarine and Luftwaffe in Norway
September 1944 to May 1945

ANDREW D. BIRD

GRUB STREET · LONDON

Published by
Grub Street
4 Rainham Close
London SW11 6SS

This revised and updated edition first published 2008

Copyright © 2008 Grub Street London
Text copyright © 2008 Andrew D. Bird

British Library Cataloguing in Publication Data
Bird, Andrew D
   A Separate Little War: The Banff Coastal Command Strike Wing
   versus the Kriegsmarine and Luftwaffe in Norway, 1944-1945
   1. Banff aerodrome – History 2. Great Britain – Royal Air
   Force. Coastal Command – History 3. World War, 1939-1945 –
   Aerial operations, British 4. World War, 1939-1945 – Aerial
   operations, Norwegian
   I Title
   940.5′44941

ISBN 978-1-906502-13-3

Formatted by Pearl Graphics, Hemel Hempstead

Printed and bound in Great Britain by
MPG Ltd, Bodmin, Cornwall

Grub Street only uses FSC
(Forest Stewardship Council) paper for its books.

CONTENTS

FOREWORD

To have been a member of the strike wings was an unforgettable experience. They were momentous days, over sixty years ago. I was greatly honoured when asked to contribute a foreword to this book. It was such a privilege as a young flight lieutenant to be led into battle by experienced wing commanders of the highest order and to fly with fellow airmen of skill and great courage that I readily agreed. This book commemorates the men and women who served with the multi-national squadrons, which formed the RAF Coastal Command, Banff Strike Wing at RAF Banff, known locally as Boyndie between September 1944 and May 1945, and our neighbours the Dallachy Strike Wing. Sometimes elements of the two wings operated together.

The Banff wing, under the command of Group Captain the Honourable Max Aitken DSO DFC, made up of mixed Mosquito and Beaufighter units, mounted concentrated attacks on German surface vessels and U-boats in the North Sea and along the Norwegian coast. Their success in the closing months of World War II was significant in the defeat of Germany and strike wing aircraft operating from the aerodrome inflicted heavy damage on enemy shipping and supply routes. Many thousands of tonnes of vital iron ore and other supplies were lost to the German forces as a result of rocket and cannon attacks carried out by this gallant strike wing. Losses amongst RAF commonwealth and Norwegian squadrons were high. More than one hundred aircrew gave their lives flying with the RAF Banff Strike Wing. Nevertheless, with resolution and courage we carried on *Per Ardua*.

Group Captain Angus McIntosh DFC
Formerly of No. 248 Squadron.

ACKNOWLEDGEMENTS

I am indebted to the survivors of the anti-shipping squadrons, all exceptional people, who have contributed their time and expertise and above all, generosity. A large selection of scarce photographs and material, mainly from personal collections, have surfaced since the first publication of this book six years ago, including two exquisite diaries of survivors from the anti-shipping strike campaign, making this edition one of the most comprehensive books on the Banff anti-shipping strike wing based in 18 Group Coastal Command. It would be wrong to assume that their 'strikes' were a mere side-line. All have a story to tell – a story of courage, camaraderie and endurance and a team spirit which made them feared by the enemy coastal convoy men – but casualties were often severe. My object is to give the reader a feel of what it was like as events were unfolding, even if this has meant that regretfully I have had to exclude some actions for want of space and others for dramatic accounts. Perhaps readers whose relations took part in anti-shipping strikes that have been omitted will send me their accounts, thereby enabling me to cover them in subsequent editions of the book. The following survivors delved into their memories – I hope I have remembered all of you:

18 Group Coastal Command: LAC John Peck (235 Sqn), Wt Off Alex 'Coggie' Cogswell CdeG (235 Sqn), Cpl Joyce Sherlock (née Trovey) WAAF, LAC Ron Brooks (248 Sqn), Flt Lt Alec Williamson (235 Sqn), Flt Lt Des Curtis DFC (248 Sqn), Wt Off Jim Hoyle (248 Sqn), Flt Lt Aubrey 'Hilly' Hilliard (248 Sqn), Wt Off Ron 'Ginger' Burton (235 Sqn), Sgt Tom Wilkinson (235 Sqn), Cpl Les Taylor MID (235 Sqn), Flt Lt 'Jimmy' Rogers DFM (235 Sqn), Flt Lt Lawie Shields DFC (235 Sqn), Flt Lt David 'Jack' Frost DFC & Bar, Flt Lt Basil Quelch DFC (235 Sqn), Agnes Shayler WAAF, Sqn Ldr George Lord DFC CdeG (235 Sqn), Flg Off Ray Hall (235 Sqn), Flt Lt Norman Carr (143 Sqn), LAC Ray Tucker (Armour), Sqn Ldr Norman 'Jacko' Jackson-Smith DFC & Bar (235 & 248 Sqns), Air Chief Marshal C. Foxley-Norris KCB, CB, DSO & OBE (143 Sqn), Sqn Ldr 'Bill' Clayton-Graham DFC (235 Sqn), Flt Lt Ken 'Ginger' Webster (235 Sqn), Flt Lt Tom Armstrong DFC (235 Sqn), Sqn Ldr 'Paddy' Wright DFC (235 & 248 Sqns), Flt Lt 'Pat' Ross DFM (235 & 248 Sqns), Flt Lt Ron Hawkins (143 Sqn), Flt Lt 'Paddy' Tuhill (143 Sqn), Flt Lt Geoff Mayhew DFC (235 Sqn), Flt Sgt Bryan Woodier (235 Sqn), Flg Off Geof Hinde (235 Sqn), Flg Off Sid Saeer (235 Sqn), Grp Cpt Angus McIntosh DFC (248 Sqn), Flt Lt Brian Beattie (248 Sqn), Flt Lt Wallace Woodcock DFC (248 Sqn), Sqn Ldr David Pritchard DFC & Bar (143 Sqn), Flt Lt Arthur 'General' Jackson (235 Sqn), Flg Off George Quinton (235 Sqn), LAC 'Jobby' Jobson (235 Sqn), LAC John 'Jock' Raymond MID (Armour), Wg Cdr Tony Gadd DSO DFC (144 Sqn), Flt Lt Charles Corder CGM CdeG (248 & 404 [RCAF] Sqns), Flt Lt Geoff Rouse (235 Sqn), Plt Off Tom Scott (248 Sqn), Wt Off Harold Corbin CGM (248 Sqn), Sqn Ldr Don Rogers (144 Sqn), Sgt Joan Lewis (WAAF), Wt Off Andrews (144 Sqn), Flt Lt Bill 'Puppy' Calder DFC (235 [RCAF] Sqn), Wg Cdr 'Bill' Sise DSO DFC (248 Sqn), Flt Lt Raymond Price (248 Sqn), Flg Off S.T. Faithfull (404 [RCAF] Sqn), Flg Off Norman Earnshaw (248 Sqn), Flt Lt Ron Simmons (143 Sqn), Flg Off Les Parker (143 Sqn), Flg Off Bill Knight (143 Sqn), Flt Lt Ken Jackson (235 [RAAF] Sqn), Ray Hannaford (143 Sqn), Flt Lt Raymond Holmes (248 Sqn), Flt Lt John Bell DFC, CdeG (58 Sqn), Group Captain Raymond Price (248 Sqn).

Great Britain: Wg Cdr John Yonge (daughter Charlotte Leadbeater and Ian Yonge), Flt Lt Richard Young (248 Sqn – relative Richard G Young), Flg Off 'Syd' Hawkins (235 Sqn – widow Grace Mayne), Wg Cdr Roy Orrock DFC (248 Sqn – widow Anne Orrock), Wg Cdr A. H. 'Junior' Simmonds DFC (235 Sqn – widow Mrs H Filton and daughter Susie Burrows), Tony Craig, Air Marshal Ian Macfadyen CB OBE, Lady Joan Foxley-Norris, Paul Hutchinson, Colin Jeffery, Flt Lt 'Wally' Webster (235 Sqn – son Martyn Webster) Maureen Quelch, Dr David Findlay Clark, Sydney Legg, Alex Crawford, Chris Goss, Vicki Morgan – Aberdeen City Archive assistant, National Archives Kew, London.

RAF Peterhead: Flt Lt 'Dan' Nowosielski DFC AFC (315 Polish Sqn), Flt Lt Peter Banks (65 Sqn), Flt Lt Arthur Doley (19 Sqn), Wt Off Bronislaw Skladzien (315 Polish Sqn).

Coastal Command Air Sea Rescue Fraserburgh: Plt Off Duthie (279 ASR Sqn), Wt Off Don Mabey (281 ASR Sqn), Tom Jackson RAF (HSL 1210 Fraserburgh).

Overseas: Alan Scheckenbach who interviewed Bill Herbert (445 [RAAF] Sqn), Flt Lt Ken Beruldsen (235 Sqn – brother Jim Beruldsen), Klaas Timmer U-843 & Dolfijn researcher (Netherlands), David Burrowes, Karen Parkinson, Sqn Ldr 'Bill' Mullen (RAF Dallachy – son Gerry Mullen) (USA), Lt Frederick Alexandre (143 Sqn – sister Mathidle Zara) (USA).

Luftwaffe Jadgeschwader, 5 Eismeerjåger: Staffelkapitän Werner Gayko, Rudi Artner, Heinz Orlowski.

Kriegsmarine: Gunner Karl Werner, Lt Oskar Herwartz (Commander U-843).

Germany: Horst Bredow (U-Boat Archive), Frau Orlowski, Frau Herwartz.

Scandinavians: 333 (NorAF) Sqn, Sten Stenersen (publisher), Halvor Sperbund (Norwegian aviation historian), Fohannes and Gudmund Helland (rescuers), Mr J. Helme, Ingebrikt Melingen, Nils Olav Hufthammer, Bjarne Agdestein (rescuers), Svein Ove (aviation historian), Oyvind Ellingsen, Arne Enger (Norsk Aviation Historical Society), Sverre Rødder *(Austri)*, Olav Larson *(Austri)*, Nils E. Skovheim (Norwegian diver), Andreas Brekkon, Jan Olav Flatmark, Øisten Thomas Berge, Hans Olav Henanger, Kurt Nuav, Cato Guhnfeldt, Rune Rautio, Olve Dybvig, Soren Flensted, Flemming Melin Christiansen.

Thank you to my wife Carol for your support, patience and understanding. Also to my daughter Jessica and son Nicholas, thank you. To my parents and sister for their encouragement, to my wife's parents especially for their time and help translating the German text. Sadly neither of our fathers saw the finished article.

Chapter 7 Psalm 69: Verses 1-3

Save me, O God!
For the waters have come up to my neck.
I sink in deep mire where there is no foothold;
To have come into deep waters, and the flood sweeps over me.
I am crying; my throat is parched.
My eyes grow dim with waiting for my God.

RAF Bible, Revised Standard version, 1946

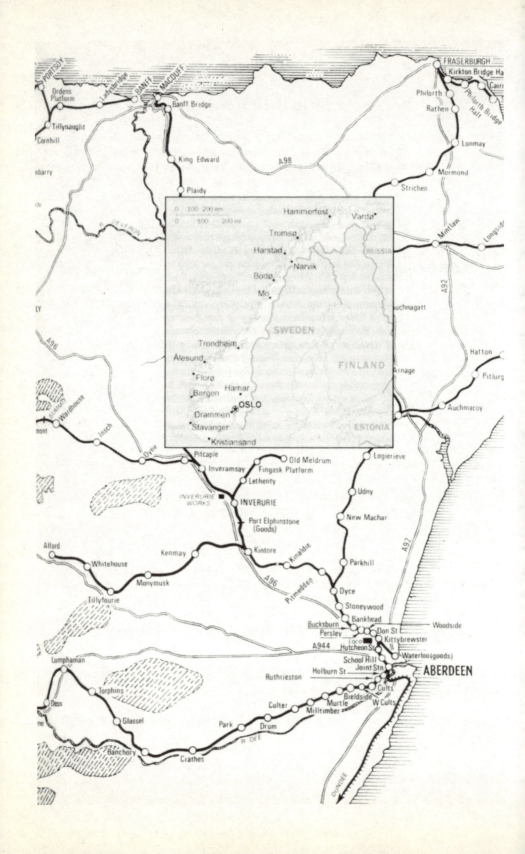

INTRODUCTION

Germany invaded Norway on 9 April 1940, an operation codenamed 'Weseruburg'. The occupation of Scandinavia had begun. The British landed troops on 15 April but after several weeks of fierce fighting the men were forced to withdraw when the German Blitzkrieg left Britain isolated in Europe. One of Hitler's desires after conquering these small nations was to guarantee Germany's ore base, as her armaments and munitions factories were largely dependent on the high quality iron ore which was mined in northern Sweden. It was then transported to Germany's industrial centre in the Ruhr by two routes, the most important of which was over the mountains using a rail link to the ice-free port of Narvik in Norway. From the port it was shipped along a route in between the numerous islands, down the rugged Norwegian coastline, then directly across the North Sea to the well-equipped harbours in the Netherlands. Self-propelled barges then carried the ore up the Rhine to the various factories located in the Ruhr and Saar. In return, Germany exported vast quantities of coal and coke, by the same shipping routes.

There were other natural resources to be found in Norway. Nickel, used for armour plating and armour piercing rounds, was mined in the country, further supplies coming from Lapland in Finland. Norwegian molybdenum for hardening steel, iron pyrites for sulphuric acid, and aluminium produced by the power from the Norwegian hydro-electric stations were all invaluable to Germany's bid for world domination.

With Germany's occupation of Europe after the Blitzkrieg, her coastline was extensive, from the Artic Circle to the Franco-Spanish border. Its length was vast. The Norwegian coastline alone was 2,100 miles long, if the Leads and islands were included, the extent was 16,500 miles, half the circumference of the globe. Along the whole of this coastline Germany plied captured merchantmen from France, Holland, Denmark and Norway, almost with impunity in 1940.

Responsibility for attacking enemy vessels from the air resided mainly with RAF Coastal Command and the Fleet Air Arm. In September 1939 the Coastal Command strike force consisted of two squadrons of obsolete bi-planes, in addition there were eight Avro Ansons, which were quite unsuitable for the role as strike aircraft. There were also two squadrons of Lockheed Hudsons, a twin-engine monoplane, which assumed the assignment of bombing enemy surface ships.

With such an inadequate strike force in the early part of the war, Coastal Command were given three squadrons of Bristol Blenheims by the Royal Air Force, also transferred was a Swordfish squadron from the Fleet Air Arm. In 1940 the Bristol Beaufort, designed for low level bombing, was introduced into frontline service, and Coastal Command thus began a more aggressive role against enemy merchantmen. The Avro Ansons were replaced with Hudsons or Beauforts, while the Handley-Page Hampdens also began to appear.

The crews of Coastal Command served with valour between 1940 and 1942 but results were disappointingly meagre. Post-war analysis has revealed that between the periods 1940 to March 1943, all commands in the Air Force sank only 107 enemy vessels, with a tonnage totalling 15,076 at sea by direct attack for the loss of 648 aircraft. These enemy losses did not affect Germany's coastal traffic and supplies of iron ore and other minerals continued to reach Dutch and German ports.

Nevertheless, Hitler worried about Norway and the possible Allied invasion and also about Germany losing the supplies of Swedish iron ore. It would be impossible to execute a full scale war once her reserves had been exhausted. In February 1942 two schlachtschiffs, the *Scharnhorst* and *Gneisenau*, left Brest and eluded the British forces for three days. They were bound for Norway in order to help the defence of Norwegian coastal waters. British air and naval attacks failed to stop them and this highlighted their limitations.

In the first four months of 1942 Coastal Command only sunk five ships for the loss of 55 aircraft. Germany was also increasing defensive measures on merchantmen and their escorts with the positioning of anti-aircraft guns on raised towers to give a better field of fire against air attack, and this improved armament began taking out Coastal Command aircraft. Between July and September 1942 it was estimated that Coastal Command were losing one in four aircraft in low-level attacks.

A plan favoured by Winston Churchill codenamed 'Jupiter' for the invasion of Norway in 1942 was shelved after it was rejected by Roosevelt in preference of the Anglo-American invasion codenamed 'Torch' in North Africa. It is unresolved whether Jupiter would have been a success. In the absence of direct attack the British sought to hit the merchantmen plying to and from Scandinavia from the air. Some of the problems were solved by a concept based on the experiences in Malta where strike wing tactics had evolved. Experiments had been carried out using anti-flak aircraft and torpedo bombers with excellent results. The idea was for the anti-flak cannon and 500lb bombs to subdue enemy anti-aircraft fire. These escorts would also defend the torpedo bombers against enemy fighters at the critical moment when the torpedo bombers made their straight and level run in to the targets.

The strike wing tactics were perfected in Coastal Command with the Bristol Beaufighter. An anti-flak aircraft and improved torpedo bomber were both found in the versatile Beaufighter in 1942 when Coastal Command began to receive the Mark VIC, the first version to be used by the strike wings. This mark has a dihedral tailplane instead of a straight one and could fly long distances at low level. Two 1,650 hp Hercules radials powered the Beaufighter Mark VIC (C denoting Coastal Command) and it was armed with four 20mm cannon mounted under the fuselage, firing through the nose, and six .303 machine guns, four in the port wing and two in the starboard wing. A single backward-firing .303 machine gun was mounted in the mid-upper cupola above the navigator. With a top speed of 350mph, the Mark VIC Beaufighter was adapted for torpedo carrying to destroy enemy merchantmen and was named the Torbeau. It carried four cannon as well as the torpedo.

The first strike wing was formed in 16 Group in November 1942, at North Coates on the Lincolnshire coast. It consisted of 236 Squadron armed with cannon, machine guns and bombs, and 254 Squadron armed with cannon and torpedoes. In early 1943, 143 Squadron (which had reequipped with the Beaufighter Mark XIC, a version of the Mark VIC with two 1,772 hp engines, used in the anti-flak role) joined these two squadrons. The Air Officer Commanding Coastal Command, Air Chief Marshal Sir Phillip Joubert de la Ferté KCB CMG DSO, recognized the potential of this aircraft. He wrote: 'My ambition was to form a strike squadron of Torbeaus supported by two Beaufighter squadrons armed if possible, with rockets and cannon. With a wing of this sort I felt that real damage could be done to German coastal shipping.'

In February 1943, forty-seven year old, Air Marshal Sir John Slessor, KCB DSO

MC succeeded Joubert as Air Officer Commanding-in-Chief Coastal Command. Two months later after training, the command had a specially trained Beaufighter strike wing. When the North Coates strike wing flew on a strike, two single-engined fighter squadrons of RAF Fighter Command protected them. This limited the range to the Dutch coast as far as the Frisian Islands. The primary task was to destroy enemy merchantmen and their escorts along this very important coastline.

One authority, the Reichskommissar for Schifffahrt based in Hamburg, controlled the entire merchantman fleet totalling 506 vessels in north-west Europe. Their tonnage ranged from 1,000 to 10,000 tons, the average being 3,000 tons carrying petroleum and lubricants to the occupying forces in Norway. All vessels were armed, the defences being manned by well-trained naval gunners. The Kriegsmarine (German Navy) protected the merchantmen. The escort vessels were often converted fishing trawlers or whalers, usually about 500 tons, packed with weapons of all calibres. These *Vorpostenboote* had obvious gun positions that distinguished them from fishing trawlers. The RAF referred to them as TTAs, 'trawler type auxiliaries', or flakships. Then there were the purpose-built minesweepers or escorts that sailed ahead of the convoy; *Minensuchboote* to the Germans and 'M-class minesweepers' to the RAF. There were other smaller minesweepers called *Raümboote* or 'R-boats' to the RAF. Sometimes the defences might include German destroyers or armed coasters.

Prior to April 1943, strikes to the Norwegian coast by that 'maid of all work' – the Hampden – were accompanied by Beaufighters as escorts, which certainly saved the Hampdens when attacked by Fw190s and Bf109s. The Hampden retired in the December, replaced by the Beaufighter which was becoming available in ever-increasing numbers to Coastal Command. In 1942 18 Group (Norwegian Detachment) had formed at Woodhaven, a year later the unit became No. 1477 Flight and reconnaissance patrols in Norwegian coastal waters were added to their repertoire in March. This proved dangerous in the slow Catalinas and by the end of the month Coastal Command managed to obtain six Mosquito IIs for the flight. On 16 April, the crews commenced operations from Leuchars in the first armed de Havilland Mosquitoes in Coastal Command. Using these six Mosquitoes was an immediate success and they were soon flying armed reconnaissance off the Norwegian coastal waters, the flight was then made into a unit designated 333 (Norwegian) Squadron on 1 May. 236 Squadron at North Coates usually carried 500lb bombs but had their aircraft modified to carry 3-inch rocket projectiles, but special techniques were required and these took time to develop. The first operational use of the rocket projectile was made by the unit during a detachment to Predannack, Cornwall. By mid-June all the pilots of the North Coates wing were trained in its use.

Slessor agreed to establish two additional strike wings which went ahead despite the shortages of trained aircrew, which delayed the build up. The Wick wing had been formed earlier in March 1943, but its first official strike took place on 22 November against a convoy off Stadlandet in Norway.

The Mosquito Mark VI employed by Coastal Command had two Merlin 25s of 1,635 hp and carried four .303 machine guns in the nose and four 20mm cannon in front of the bomb bay. It could also carry 2,000lbs of bombs, two 500lb bombs in the bomb bay and two under each wing, although this was changed to depth charges when flying on anti-U-boat work.

Coastal Command now had three strike wings completely equipped with Beaufighters based at Wick, Leuchars, and North Coates. By the end of 1943 the newly formed wings had sunk 21 merchantmen and damaged 23. The tactics were right and moral was high together with Coastal Command headquarters' expectations.

CHAPTER 1

OPERATIONS BEGIN

There are wars within wars. Although they are all part of the same whole, sometimes important aspects of a war are not as well-known as others. One of these wars, the battle between Coastal Command squadrons and German shipping, began eighteen months before the end of the Second World War and intensified during the last nine. It was a 'separate' war not normally covered in news columns, and the last phase of Coastal Command's war.

Attacks by the Beaufighters and Mosquitoes of Coastal Command's strike wings on German vessels must be classified as some of the most dangerous and ferocious encounters during the war. 333 (Norwegian) Squadron, formed from 1477 Flight, was the first Coastal Command Mosquito unit, except for the Photographic Reconnaissance squadrons. 248 Squadron was part of 19 Group and converted to Mosquito Mark VI (fighter/bombers) in mid-December 1943; as the conversion took place operations continued using the Beaufighter MkXs. At this time they were based at RAF Predannack in Cornwall. 248 Squadron received a detachment of five crews from 618 Squadron. They flew Tsetse MkXVIII Mosquitoes, so named because of their fearsome 57mm Molins automatic weapon, installed in the nose in place of the four 20mm cannon. The arc-shaped magazine held 24 rounds of 57mm armour-piercing HE shells which weighed 7.1lbs, were tipped with hardened steel and capped with tracer. After some modifications, fitting 50 gallon drop-tanks to give greater range, excess weight had to be reduced to compensate and some of the armour plating was removed. After extensive trials at Ashley Walk Range in the New Forest the rate of fire was fine-tuned. In all, 17 Mk XVIIIs were built of which 13 saw active service.

Having declared themselves operational on the 3 November an order came through to be airborne at 08.00 hours the next day. Two Tsetses – HX903 and HX902 – headed south to a grey point in the ocean. Sighting a trawler HX902 attacked, getting off two rounds. Smoke was then seen coming from behind the Mosquito's port wing and seconds later it hit the calm sea. It had probably been struck by a ricochet. Three days later HX903 went out to a potential rendezvous with a returning U-boat. Much to the crew's astonishment, at 09.45, flying at 300 feet over the Bay of Biscay, they found a surfaced U-boat. The IXB Type U-boat U-123 was approaching St Nazaire after U-boat Control ordered the captain, Horst von Schroeter, to return, having been depth charged by allied naval vessels near Cape Finisterre. On the first run in Canadian Flying Officer Al Bonnett opened fire at 1600 yards and at 200 feet. Eight rounds of 57mm were fired and strikes were observed on the foredeck, which struck between the conning tower and the deck gun, then aft of the conning tower. The gun crew returned fire, one hitting the oil tank. A second attack was made, but the Molins jammed, so Bonnett fired with his machine guns. Von Schroeter reported he had a hole in the conning tower that prevented diving and he requested air cover. U-123 reached St Nazaire that day after a fruitless patrol of 84 days.

On 16 February 1944, 248 Squadron was transferred across the Cornish peninsular to RAF Portreath, an already busy airfield; another of its functions was the Overseas Aircraft Dispatch Unit, from where aircraft and personnel were moved to and from

Gibraltar and North Africa. Also operating from the aerodrome was 235 Squadron with Mark XI Beaufighters mounting anti-aircraft and convoy patrols. 235 Squadron departed for St Angelo in Northern Ireland on the 20th. The first operational sortie with 248 Squadron Mosquitoes took place on the same day their sister squadron departed, just three days after their move. 248 began attacking all types of surface craft and engaged Luftwaffe aircraft escorting their naval vessels. Flight Lieutenants Doug Turner and 'Hilly' Hilliard in their respective Tsetse sank U-976 off Ile d'Yeu. 235 Squadron rejoined 248 at Portreath in April 1944 and further achievements came to both squadrons. These months were hectic in the Biscay area leading up to D-Day, hampering both air and surface craft, and subsequently aircraft went missing.

For example Flight Lieutenant 'Paddy' Wright DFC and Flying Officer Pat Ross of 235 Squadron shot down a Junkers 88 while flying anti-aircraft patrols off Ushant. Such patrols and engagements continued until June. A Mosquito strike wing was formed at RAF Portreath during early June 1944, when 235 Squadron started converting to Mosquitoes. On D-Day, 6 June, 248 Squadron flew anti-shipping, escort and blockading sorties on the Normandy, Brittany and Biscay coasts, including one operation acting as fighter escort for Beaufighters of 404 (RCAF) Squadron and 144 Squadron. On the way home a Mosquito shot down a Junkers north of Ushant. 248 Squadron flew 274 sorties in June; and despite 235 Squadron's conversion, it flew 117 sorties. 9 June saw Wright and Ross claim another Junkers 88 off The Lizard. The last operation in a Beaufighter was flown on 22 June, while the first squadron Mosquito sortie had already been flown seven days earlier. The month of July was quieter, as Allied forces advanced and the Germans began to be driven from the west of France. 4 July saw Wing Commander A. Phillips, commanding officer of 248 Squadron, killed with his navigator as they attacked shipping at Penfoul Cove and the Kercreven dock. Despite this loss the strike was classed as a success.

Aircrews found themselves flying air umbrella patrols against Luftwaffe aircraft with glider bombs. Two such crews consisted of Wing Commander John Yonge and Flying Officer 'Jack' Frost of 235 Squadron who provided an aerial 'umbrella' for a naval escort group off Ushant. In foul weather they flew towards their patrol area at 13.20 hours on 21 July. They had not found the enemy aircraft or the destroyers, then half an hour later they opened fire on two Dorniers carrying Henschel 297 glider bombs and in a one-sided air-battle shot both down into the sea. Yonge saw several of the German crews in dinghies and spotted the destroyers they were defending at the same moment. Between them, the two squadrons flew 339 sorties in the month of August, mainly attacking shipping in the Gironde estuary during the Biscay patrols and were either responsible for, or shared in, the sinking of seven vessels between June and the end of August.

Flight Sergeant James 'Jimmy' Rogers DFM, a navigator with 235 Squadron, kept a diary which captures the mood and the tragic losses:

Monday 14th August
I spend the morning reading and get information on Dobson and Millar's ditching on 12 August, which we watched. It seems that 'Dusty' Millar was knocked out on ditching, and when he came to, Dobson, his seat and Gee box had all disappeared through a hole in the floor – it's not a good idea to ditch...!

The crew's nerves are on edge at present and cigarette consumption has risen rapidly. My own feelings are of apathy. If one goes on too many strikes, only good luck will save you.

Strike-briefing at 17.25 hours and worse luck, it's the Gironde once more. As Sise and Maurice [from 248] are both airborne at the moment on reconnaissance,

Hal Randall will lead. Our aircraft will carry depth charges. No one seems at all keen, especially on learning that Beaufighters will go in half an hour before we do. We set course at 19.15 hours and crossed the coast at 20.50 hours.

Russell and ourselves are caught in some pretty murderous crossfire from flak and we cannot afford to stop and prang it. We are evidently south of track and cross over a small lake before reaching the Gironde. Flak at first is negligible and then we see our target, a Narvik class destroyer and a large merchantman or *Sperrbrecher** of about 3,000 tons. We take on the *Sperrbrecher* and although our master switch is not on at first, we manage a long burst with many hits and our depth charges are a very near miss. We are caught in the destroyer's light flak and see one Mosquito explode and spin in and another ditch in flames.

'Taffy' Stoddart (248) and 'Jeff' Harker are the ones who explode and Genne made the ditching which was a good one.

We cruise back most of the journey alone but join up with Noel Russell off Ushant and after half an hour on the circuit we land. We have been well plastered with hits on the spinner, the starboard, and port mainplanes and on the nose and tail unit on both starboard and port side – so we have had someone looking after us today. We think Cookie and Corbin may have made Vannes. On the way down to the target, I managed to receive Maurice and Sise's first sighting report on the enemy shipping by radio. They were pleased that it had been picked up. Official report; three aircraft from 248 and one from 235 lost.

Tuesday 15th August
At midday, the wireless announced the invasion of Southern France between Nice and Marseilles. This is good news. The cry 'on to Gironde' is heard from the aircrew.

At that point, with elements of General George Patton's Third US Army in Brittany driving hard towards the Biscay coast, Kriegsmarine maritime operations in the Bay of Biscay were clearly at an end. A brief concentrated period of operations came towards the end of the month and then orders were given to 235 and 248 Squadrons to move base at short notice as enemy activity had lessened. The final sortie flown from Portreath was over Biscay on 7 September 1944, when three 248 aircraft, hindered by poor visibility, searched over the mouth of the Gironde for U-boat activity.

RAF Coastal Command had been formed on 14 July 1936 at RAF Northwood, Middlesex, when Air Defence of Great Britain (ADGB) was replaced by fighter, bomber, coastal and training commands. When it formed Coastal Command had a strength of three groups, No.18 based in Scotland, No.16 in south-east England and No.15 covering western England and the Irish Sea. As early as 13 June 1944, Northwood had prepared an assessment of the importance of Norwegian coastal shipping in view of the altered strategic situation resulting from Operation Overlord. Planning was based 'on the assumption that... at least 150 U-boats would be based in Norway, of which about 30 would operate against Russian convoys from bases in the extreme north'. In an effort to restrict German shipping even further, the Allies asked Stockholm to stop all trading with Germany. The Swedes, however, were as yet unwilling to initiate a complete break and would only agree to withdraw marine insurance from vessels sailing to Dutch and German ports lying west of the Kiel.

Sperrbrecher – blockade breaker. A specially strengthened ex-merchant vessel between 1,500 tons and 8,000 tons. Heavily armed with 88mm, 37mm and 20mm guns and machine guns, their armament was for self defence, as their task was to keep the shipping lanes open by mine-clearing.

Within days the Allies issued a reminder of the hazards Swedish vessels would face, timing their words to coincide with the reopening of the mining campaign in the Baltic and Kattegat, plus an air raid which added three more vessels to the Swedes' mounting losses.

Consequently, on 18 August, the Swedish government withdrew marine insurance for all the vessels sailing to Axis ports. Germany suffered another setback when Sweden reluctantly closed its ports to German shipping on 27 September. The Russian-Finnish armistice of 4 September 1944 was also to deprive Germany of 363,000 tons of Finnish shipping and ports.

Norway saw the arrival of 200,000 Wehrmacht mountain troops, en-route from Finland to Germany. These retreating troops devastated the Finnmark area. During the retreat, buildings were burned to the ground, the infrastructure demolished, and anything of importance or value that the Germans came across was destroyed. The Norwegians were worried that they might suffer a scorched earth policy on their own territory. As well as her internal lines of communication, Germany still relied heavily on sea borne traffic and merchantmen under escort still passed along the Norwegian coast daily. They transported large quantities of fuel, iron ore and other urgent supplies imported from Norway into Germany at a rate of nine million tons per annum, carried in 700,000 tons of merchantmen via Danish ports which were closer to the Ruhr than the more secure north German harbours. This route assumed a higher degree of importance from September 1944 as the Ministry of Economic Warfare estimated that 1,218,000 tons of shipping was trading regularly between the two countries and was now at full stretch. 60,000 tons was engaged in carriage of military equipment, 85,000 tons was estimated to be engaged in routine movements of personnel, (this figure catered for the Wehrmacht divisions usually based in Norway, plus naval and Luftwaffe personnel) while tankers totalling 152,000 tons operated a shuttle service to Norway. Of the remaining merchantmen some 221,000 tons were used to carry consumer products, typically fish and timber goods from Norway. With the increase in traffic through ports like Emden, the process strained enemy canal and rail links.

The first phase of the invasion of Europe was over by the end of August. Therefore in early September the bulk of 19 Group switched from their duties along the French coast and Channel area and went north to Scotland where the foundation for a new strike wing was being created in order to re-open 18 Group's offensive against Norwegian coastal traffic. This began to gain momentum because of the German shift in strategic emphasis to Norwegian waters. With the French and Italian ports having fallen into Allied hands Norwegian raw materials would be making a greater contribution to Germany's supply position following the loss within Europe of substitutable materials. One of the airfields chosen was RAF Banff, near Moray Firth, known locally as Boyndie. The airfield, originally built for coastal operations, was used for flying training. The base was hastily made ready during August to allow deployment of 153 (GR) Wing to this region.

CHAPTER 2

RAF BANFF AERODROME

Banff was first mentioned in aviation circles in 1913 when this sparsely populated village was featured in the *Daily Mail* water-planes circuit of the Great Britain Race. Banff was one of the stages during the 1,540 mile race, as rivals competed for the £5,000 prize money, on their way to Cromarty in Moray Firth. H.G. Hawker in a Sopwith, and F.K. McClean in a Short both strived to win the race before heading south. During the First World War a Short Seaplane No. 185 was involved in mine-spotting duties from Macduff and Banff Harbour between 17 and 23 August 1915, flown from HMS *Campania* and commanded by seaplane pioneer Captain O Swann. Sopwith Babies from HMS *Campania* were then engaged in spotting duties during 1917 from Banff to Portsoy. They were severely taxed by their war load whilst covering the area, which in addition to fuel and oil for $2^1/_2$ hours, included a Lewis gun and ammunition, two 65lb and one 112lb bomb, carrier pigeons and a sea anchor, which was a lot for a little Sopwith seaplane. It did not feature in aviation for the next few years until the Second World War when the Air Ministry Lands Board visited the north east counties of Scotland to find suitable sites for bomber airfields.

One of the proposed areas was a 280-feet-high plateau called Boyndie, lying between the Burn of Boyndie and Moray Firth. Engineers from the Air Ministry Aerodrome Board examined the selected vicinity and walked field by field, paying particular attention to the soil type, drainage characteristics and potential obstructions to flying. Apart from a slight hump to the north-east, it seemed a good position, despite being exposed to the often bitterly cold winds, frequently more north than west. On the debit side was the fact that fogs and mists tended to gather coming in from the sea and it was also sited near two fishing villages, Banff and Macduff. After a few days of examination it was deemed suitable for development and in excess of 600 acres were requisitioned. Officers from the Air Ministry Lands Branch performed the complicated legal and administrative responsibilities relating to this acquisition. The Defence Regulations made under the Emergency Powers (Defence) Act, 1939, permitted the act of immediate possession of land and buildings when approved by a competent authority. The land was owned by one estate and had been in The Earl of Seafield's family since the 16th century. The cost for purchasing this vast expanse of land was £32,000 and the agreement between the Air Ministry and the Earl of Seafield for the requisition was made using Air Ministry Form 1553. Civilian contractors were invited to tender for the construction contracts. Boyndie had always been a farming community where the majority of men worked on the land. The 1939 electoral register shows a population of 918. Most of the land to the north of the road, where the airfield proper was to be constructed, belonged to the Earl and was regularly used in the pursuit of pheasants and grouse; this was bought together with the land to the south, where eventually dormitory units were to be built.

1941 saw cities and counties across the United Kingdom compete in a race to form their quotas of local squadrons of the A.T.C. – the new air training corps for boys. Banff was allocated one squadron. At the same time the neighbourhood heard gossip that an aerodrome was to be built the following year, but just passed it off as a rumour.

Subsequent events the following year proved it to in fact be true. Before the nine-month construction project started it was clear that the eleven people registered at Moor of Rettie, were going to be severely affected. The Moor of Rettie dwellings would have to be demolished, and their unfortunate occupants were given a month's notice for resettlement. Nine crofters were given notice from their landlord to relocate. Lorries arrived to move belongings and, in some instances, live stock to their new accommodation which had been hastily found despite accommodation of any kind being in short supply. Once tenders had been accepted, the job of clearing the land quickly got underway. Machinery started to arrive in the district that had never been seen before, their first task the demolition of the crofts. One crofter had chosen to stay and labourers gradually began deconstructing his croft from the top down, finally he begrudgingly moved to his new dwelling on the Seafield Estate. The removal of tree stumps, generally using explosives, began at the same time with a local man having been contracted to carry out the work.

Sydney Legg lived at Thriepland cottage, earmarked to be demolished:

'Our house was quite new, about five years old. It had to be flattened to make way for the main runway run-off area. I was transfixed watching the bulldozer come up the valley towards our house. It picked up speed, belching black smoke, slicing through our former home like a knife goes through butter. It was gone in minutes. The roof trusses and roof tiles crashed to the ground as the bulldozer carried on its merry way. My father found our family a place to live at Wester Whinty cottages on the farm where he worked, one was empty and we moved in straight away.'

Construction then commenced. The main contractor for the work was George Wimpy Construction. Creating the aerodrome itself began in the middle of 1942 using Irish and local Scottish labourers. A number of small local contractors were also involved, and where they had insufficient tools and equipment of their own, machinery was loaned to them by the Air Ministry Works Directorate so that they could all play their part in the airfield construction programme. It was built at great speed and in Banff itself, amongst the 2,190 inhabitants, there was now a sense of involvement with the offensive and the push for victory. This had grown with every lorry load of shingle laboriously dug up by American-supplied caterpillar scrapers and bulldozers on the shores of Palmer Cove, Sunnyside Bay, Boyndie Bay at Cullen, Banff and Macduff and the men worked continuously to provide raw materials between the tides. The shoreline never recovered. For months on end the roads to the Boyndie site were like mud tracks, as lorries busily transported shingle to the site up to eight times a day. Four Koehring scrapers levelled the expanse and rollers and mechanical spreading and compacting machines planed down the earth so no gradient was more than 1 in 60 prior to laying the runway foundations. Hundreds of navvies laid down the concrete runways and pipes to the main drainage system. Mixed concrete was forever being spilled and ran into the remaining farm land.

The runways themselves were of conventional three runway layout: the main strip of 290° was 2,001 yards long and aligned roughly east-west; the subsidiaries were of 180° and 1,409 yards, and of 236° 1,409 yards, laid out in a triangular pattern. The NE-SW runway had an unusual narrow extension of about 200 yards to give an extra safety margin. Once Banff's runways had been completed, the area between them was sown with grass seed. Three enormous steel T2 hangars were erected for major servicing, then high priority was given to the completion of the domestic sites. Dozens and dozens of corrugated-steel Nissen huts were erected for accommodation units, stores and offices. Concrete-framed offices and workshops were built and miles upon miles of underground services were laid. Completing the layout were 40 circular concrete hard-standings where the aircraft would be dispersed, one to each hard-standing and arranged off the perimeter track, though some of these later became bases for 13 blister hangars. Instead of the pleasingly designed brick structures of the pre-war aerodrome, Banff had prefabricated utility buildings of steel, brick, concrete, timber, plasterboard and asbestos. They combined ease and speed of erection with low cost and durability, with a life of just a few years at the most. The bomb store, grouped in neat rows between bomb blast walls, was situated as far away as possible from the camp buildings, amongst woods on the north-east perimeter. The airfield had several Link Trainer buildings and a bomb teacher installed. The flying control tower and the technical buildings were clustered in sites further south among trees and open fields, while the firing range was in the north-east corner. Ground staff and aircrews lived in Nissen huts, scattered amongst the fields, in seven dormitory groups providing accommodation for 2,000 men and women. The women of the Women's Auxiliary Air Force (WAAF) lived on two separate dormitory sites opposite Crow's Wood. It would be some time before it was all completed and a while before the camp reached the capacity for which it was planned.

An inspection of the airfield in March 1943 stated that although the airfield and camp were far from ready they were progressing. The aerodrome was offered to Bomber Command but was refused and Banff was taken under the control of 21 Group Flying Training Command on 5 April 1943. Officially opened on 21 April 1943, it was a more extensive site than originally planned, rivalling Lossiemouth and Kinloss in area. 14 (Pilot) Advanced Flying Unit, which had been moved around Britain every consecutive year since 1939, was ordered to move straight away. As personnel started to arrive at their new base they found conditions were still primitive, not all the dormitory sites being completed due to slackness and the inevitable time-wasting. While the half-finished huts were bad enough there were times when even the basic amenities of life were in short supply. During the next few months work continued. In the midst of all the frenzied activity there was often much confusion and it took a tremendous effort to get the aerodrome operational.

Corporal Joyce Trovey volunteered for the WAAFs although she was in a reserved occupation. After her training she was posted to Ossington, and in May 1943 the move to Banff was duly carried out. All personnel, including WAAFs, were marched with full kit from the base to Retford railway station for the long journey. Each person was issued with a food parcel containing a pork pie, sandwiches, and a slice of cake; both the pork pie and the cake were inedible and many were thrown into the Clyde when crossing the Forth Bridge. Finally after two days the personnel arrived. Corporal Joyce Trovey reflects:

'We had been sunbathing in Ossington and were now in blizzard conditions, our kit was thrown in a massive heap in the snow and we were marched to the mess hall for a hot meal and a mug of tea. The camp was in fact not finished, there were hardly any toilet facilities other than a few in the living quarters, one of the hangars had no roof, and was nicknamed "The Sunshine Hangar". The lack of toilets in the early days was a nightmare. I was taken aback when I was asked to include in the Daily Routine Orders "Airmen must refrain from urinating on the tailplanes of aircraft" as this was rusting the controls.'

Aircrew had ferried their twin-engine Oxfords from Ossington, Nottinghamshire. As the aeroplanes joined the circuit, heads turned skywards and young children raced to the airfield boundary fences. Lorries and tractors pulled trains of trailers piled high with engine gantries, tools, and accompanying kit along the narrow country roads from Portsoy and Banff railway stations. When all the equipment had been transferred the ground crews settled into their huts near the dispersals and for the next few months lived rough in their gumboots while the camp was completed. From now on the local children would spend a lot of time near the aerodrome, sometimes playing football with the lads and getting treats of sweets and chocolate.

This unit was a large one having three flights affiliated to it – No.1532 (Banff), No.1542 (Dallachy) and No.1518 (Edzell), while the airfield at Fraserburgh served as a satellite. All four were under the command of Group Captain A H Peck DSO MC, affectionately known as 'Daddy Peck'. The year was an extremely busy one for 14 (P) AFU, and despite the incomplete accommodations, an enormous amount of flying was achieved. The fuel complex work for the two 78,000 Imp gallon aviation fuel tanks had been speeded up and completed. No one had installed a telephone cable connection between the flare path caravan and the flying control office so take-off was laboriously signalled back to the flying control officer with the aid of an aldis lamp. Of the three T2 hangars one and two had been erected and the electrics and painting was in progress, while the steelwork for number three was on site and partly completed. The spring sunshine of 1943 shone on the bright yellow livery of a host of Oxfords, together with a few support aircraft including Avro Anson MkIs and a De Havilland Moth. For a short time the airfield had two Horsa gliders in preparation for operation 'Tyndall'. 3 (Coastal) OTU was supposed to have transferred its Wellingtons from RAF Cranwell to the Scottish base but this never materialised and the unit moved to Haverfordwest instead. The airfield was seldom quiet when the weather allowed and training and diverted aircraft were always in the circuit. Frequent visitors at night were BOAC Hudsons carrying Norwegian SOE agents. Emergency landings were commonplace, with Wellington bombers, Spitfires and an early Mosquito Mk II crashing outside the airfield perimeter. Walrus aircraft often landed on the River Deveron between Banff and Macduff above the bridge. The crew would walk to the airfield and request information about the tide and forecast. Although the early Oxford was not the most forgiving of aircraft, considering the amount of hours flown by the pupils, the accident rate was not exceptionally high.

Flight Lieutenant 'Smudger' Forbes explains: 'Our Ox-box's at Banff were well-used, there were several recorded cases of them just falling out of the sky with fatalities.' Throughout 1943 men and women on the base continually suffered health problems because the disinfectant plant stopped functioning. In December 1943, a severe frost caused the electrical supplies to fail due to ice on the conductors three miles from the base. Water froze in all the water pipes, causing extensive damage.

The invasion of Europe in June 1944 forced the Air Ministry and RAF to rethink how they were going to use Banff and other local airfields. High level meetings were held during the first weeks in August 1944 at which representatives from 18 Group, 21 Group and 14 (P) AFU were in attendance. It was agreed that the transfer of RAF stations, Banff, Dallachy and Fraserburgh to 18 Group Coastal Command would commence and that 14 (P) AFU would be closed down or disbanded. The station headquarters were also responsible for the administration of 8 and 9 HSL (High-Speed Launch) Air Sea Rescue Units operating from Buckie and Fraserburgh. During this 12-month period 14 (P) Advanced Flying Unit's output was 1,516 pupils and 113,896 hours of flying completed. Instructions were issued by Flying Training Command for aircraft to be dispersed, which were flown to destinations by trainee pilots. All administrative ground staff and other ranks, on the strength of headquarters at Banff and satellites, were to remain together with nominated personnel from other branches while the remainder were posted to other RAF stations.

A poem was written by WAAF Corporal Joyce Trovey on hearing all personnel were to be posted away from Banff.

Today, I have heard that Banff we are leaving,
It is strange how everyone's started grieving,
There was a time I seem to know,
When south of the border we yearned to go,
But now time has come to part,
We find we've a soft spot for Banff in our hearts.
It's strange how quickly we find we've forgotten,
The rains, the gales, all the things we thought rotten,
We remember the two days the sun shone,
Memories of ten months of winter are gone,
We have visions of hills that are purple with heather,
We've forgotten the mists and filthy Scotch weather.
Whenever I go there will always go with me,
The scream of the seagulls, the blue of the sea,
Skies that no beauty on earth could surpass,
Thistles that grew amongst the long waving grass,
Breathtaking sunsets I'll never forget,
Scot's hospitality, kind friends we have met.
Dancing at Whitehills on Saturday nights,
Doing Scottish reels – we surely looked frights,
Cycling through BAT flights without any lights,
A thing you dare not do on other raff Camps,
But this is Pecks Air Force, Britain best AFU,
You could do almost anything...
I'll remember the good times we had in the Mess,
To forget them I'll never be able to guess,
The roar of the Cheetahs, a guy named Sanger,
The fun we had at No. 3 Hangar,
The 765B, and lost flying hours,
The way we picked raspberries and gathered wild flowers,
Mac with the man-hours and the nominal roles,
The people detailed for flare path – poor souls,
The way 'C' Flight got off the deck,
"Afternoons'off" if your trade was 'Flight Mech',
The days we played baseball with Flying Officer Barnes,
Flights on defence day without any arms,
Camp night on Tuesdays – Oh, what a din!
The night Ray was detailed to clean the coal bin...
Pilots who shot a horrible line,
The way hundreds of kites and thousands of sheep,
These memories of Banff I shall always keep.
If you've read this epistle, you'll think I adore,
This desolate, wild and lonely shore,
But as Faith I am told, our lives can order,
I pray that she'll post me 'South of the Border'

CHAPTER 3

SEPTEMBER 1944

The airfield was duly handed over to Coastal Command on 1 September 1944 at 12.00 hours. Group Captain A H Peck DSO MC officiated a short marching in and out ceremony. Peck had formed the outgoing unit at Kinloss in May 1939 (originally 14 SFTS until November 1941) and it had been in his command since that date. RAF Station Banff was, as of 12.15 hours, under the complete command of Group Captain the Hon J W Max Aitken, DSO DFC, son of Lord Beaverbrook, the newspaper proprietor and former Minister of Aircraft Production. Aitken was 34-years-old and had flown in the Battle of Britain. Three months after Air Marshal Sir William Sholto Douglas had taken over Coastal Command as Commander-in-Chief he had arranged for Aitken to come back from the Middle East. Returning from a posting in the eastern Mediterranean commanding 219 Group, Aitken had asked to serve directly under Sholto Douglas' command again for the third time. Douglas knew from experience of Aitken's ability as a pilot and also knew that as a commander he was one of those upon whom he could rely to produce results, and he arranged for him to form this new strike wing. In time, his wing would consist of six Mosquito squadrons, the largest in Britain during the Second World War and one which went on to become famous as an elite unit specializing in rockets and the world's first all-rocket wing.

Corporal Joyce Trovey recalls the first meeting with her 'new' boss:

'We were strolling across the almost deserted airfield wondering what the future held for the few remaining ground staff, not realising at this time that I would stay at Banff. A twin-engined aircraft joined the circuit and landed taxiing to a dispersal area near the Watch Tower. The side door opened and out jumped a very handsome young man clad in khaki. He grinned at both of us and acknowledged us. As he walked by we realised his cap had gold braid on the peak, and we found out later that it was our new station commander!'

On 29 August two Beaufighters from 144 and 404 Squadrons landed at Banff with their respective commanding officers to view the new station and to make accommodation arrangements. On 1 September, the station began preparing to receive more aircraft and personnel from Stubby. The rather pedestrian radial engines of the Oxfords gave way to the more powerful radials of the Beaufighters two days later. Prior to the shift, 404 Squadron's English Wing Commander Ken Gatward DSO DFC was replaced as commanding officer after completing his third tour by Wing Commander 'Ed' Pierce, who had been one of the unit's first RCAF aircrew in 1941.

Canadian 404 Squadron's stores were unloaded from the railway coaches at Portsoy and the personnel settled in their Nissen huts. The Canadians were impressed with the splendid meals served up in the messes and of the foresight and patience of WAAF personnel who had planted a garden of flowers in front of the station headquarters. They remarked: 'The colours are startling and the variety enormous. When the rain pours down this bright spot is a welcome sight from the otherwise drab outlook.' With this arrival, 404 RCAF Squadron comprised 34 of the 36 pilots and all but three of the

131 ground crew. 144 Squadron's main party had also arrived during the day. The Norwegian contingent of 333 (Norwegian) Squadron was a dual-purpose unit operating a section of Catalinas from Sullom Voe in the Shetlands and Mosquitoes from Leuchars. Commander Lambrecht arrived with two Mosquitoes at Banff. New aircrew for 333 Squadron 'B' Flight detachment were ferried in and then briefed by senior Norwegian fliers on likely operations – using knowledge gained from their experiences. In the next few months these young pilots and navigators would work their socks off and it was largely due to their daily efforts that any strike action could be planned. Hours completed for the month of September amounted to 12,009 by day and 2,691 by night.

For a few days there were air tests and then on 6 September, three days after moving, operations commenced off the Norwegian coast. Half an hour before sunrise two Norwegian Mosquitoes took off on the first recorded operational flight. Searching the coastal waters of southern Norway, which was a comparatively long hop across the North Sea, the crews sighted several convoys and then returned safely to the airfield to report back. At 14.45 hours, 24 Beaufighters took off for a proposed strike near Utvaer, north of Bergen. As they approached the Norwegian coast the weather began to close in making it unsuitable to continue. The formation was led by the ubiquitous Wing Commander Tony Gadd DFC, who was rarely away from the action. Having joined the RAF in 1935 he became a 'tin-fish' (torpedo) trainee and had made more than 1,150 torpedo drops up until this time. Gadd gave the order to return to base, and sweeping in over the Scottish coast both squadrons tightened up their formation flying, approaching low and fast over the airfield, which set the control tower window panes rattling. The aircraft broke formation; the return then developed into individual shows of airmanship as they began to perform aerial stunts. This attracted a crowd on the ground and everyone enjoyed the flying display, including those in the control tower! Then they landed one by one.

MT Driver WAAF Agnes Shaylor, a native of nearby Portsoy, served at RAF Banff:

'As the wing was being formed, it needed all the available electricity. So the local people made do with paraffin lamps in the surrounding villages for their illumination. This continued until the war ended.'

In northern Cornwall, there was talk of postings to the Azores, Iceland or the windy northern coast of Scotland and of their prospects. On Sunday 3 September, just after the Fifth Sunday after Trinity church parade, RAF Portreath received instructions from HQ Coastal Command that the two Mosquito squadrons should be ready to move north to Banff. 235 Squadron would be first to move. Wing Commander John Yonge, commanding officer of 235 Squadron, began working out the route north and when the air party and main party should leave. Preliminary arrangements began and the squadron photograph was taken at 2.15 pm so that Squadron Leader Richard Atkinson could attend as his wife had just given birth to a baby boy in Redruth hospital. Personnel watched Squadron Leader Barnes and Flying Officer Clayton, the advance air party, fly off on 5 September, but both were diverted to Ronaldsway on the Isle of Man owing to the deteriorating weather. At Portreath the Air Officer Commanding Air Vice-Marshal Baker arrived in a Domino for lunch. Most of the afternoon was spent packing. All the equipment, tools and accompanying kit were piled high and transferred by lorry to Redruth railway station. Everyone going by steam locomotive assembled outside one of the piquet posts. After an inspection they proceeded by road to Redruth, where tea was provided. Their journey had begun. The Mosquitoes departed in two flights, the first nine leaving at 11.30 hours and the remaining nine following a quarter of an hour later on 6 September. Before their departure, ground crew loaded equally between the aircraft 235 white toilet rolls into the bomb bays ready to drop over RAF Banff! A farewell pass over Portreath village school made the children scurry inside. The aircraft flew into heavy rain over the Irish Sea then cut across from Prestwick to Edinburgh, finally landing at Banff after a flight of two and a half hours. Flight Lieutenant 'General' Jackson recalls:

'When we left Portreath to fly to Banff we were under orders not to "shoot up" the harbour or airfield. Nevertheless, we were in high spirits. Needless to say we shot up both and flew up in loose V (Vic) formation with Flight Lieutenant "Butch" Jacques leading the second flight. Nearing our new aerodrome, Jacques called up and we went down for a low pass over the main runway, dropping the 235 toilet rolls, some landed on the control tower. "Two Thirty Five" had arrived!'

After getting out of their flying kit, the aircrew had a late lunch in the messes, Yonge met Group Captain the Honourable Max Aitken DSO DFC and introduced him to his officers. On 7 September, Yonge and Wing Commander Cross, the equipment officer, together with the aircrew went around the station gathering up all the furniture and flying lockers they could find, with enough for 248 Squadron as well. Operationally three Norwegian Mosquitoes flew between Obrestad and Skudenes experiencing heavy flak. No further flights were carried out from the base. During the evening five officers from 235 Squadron ventured into Banff village by bus and had a few drinks. Unfortunately one of them, Flying Officer Godwin, put his right arm through a window. Wing Commander John Yonge, who had managed to borrow a Morris van from Wing Commander 'Ed' Pierce, arrived at Portsoy station at 01.00 hours to meet the train together with Flight Lieutenant Richardson who had come in one of the seven three-ton lorries to help. For warmth they both sat in the signal box with the signalman in front of a blazing fire chatting until the train arrived. For those on the train the trip was tediously prolonged by unexplained stops on their passage northwards, the last being at Huntley. Finally, after passing Tillynaught at 02.30 hours on 8 September, a Great Northern Class 'T' locomotive pulled into a dimly lit Portsoy railway station. Personnel stumbled out onto the platform from the stuffy blacked out coaches to be met by their commanding officer. They then climbed aboard three-ton lorries provided by the motor transport section and moved off to their new station. Yonge took the squadron adjutant officer, Flight Lieutenant Harding, and two others in the van. In the darkness they lost their way, having taken a left turn too soon, the van's engine then caught fire. Once it was extinguished they eventually found their way back. Upon arrival breakfast was served in the airmen's mess and after blankets had been drawn from the main store, everyone was pointed in the direction of their sleeping accommodation – damp Nissen huts, scattered among the fields on site three. The metal construction of the huts attracted condensation and clothing left in front of the stove soon filled with steam. They rose for lunch at 12.00 hours and afterwards a parade was held outside the airmen's cookhouse. 8235 Service Echelon went off to inspect the Mosquitoes in readiness to prepare the aircraft for re-commencing operations against the enemy from their new home. The remaining personnel left in lorries for the conveyance of kit and equipment from Portsoy railway station.

Other units were moving into place in readiness for the support of operations from northern Scotland. Tom Jackson who was 21-years-old, and a wireless operator onboard an RAF High Speed Launch at the time, recalls:

'As an experienced crew we had participated in the D-Day excursion acting as a beacon for the airborne forces, well in advance to the beach landings. In early September 1944 our two launches and crews were sent to No. 9 Air Sea Rescue Unit based in Fraserburgh harbour replacing the crews and boats already there. Wearing the 1939-1943 Star medal, which was an indicator of being experienced and had the D-Day identification markings on our launch. We made a stopover on our journey up the west coast from Plymouth to Fraserburgh. A very memorable occasion, with great hospitality at all our moorings, especially when celebrating my 21st birthday in Douglas, Isle of Man. Once at our Fraserburgh moorings, both launches began to cover the Coastal Command strike wings and other Allied Air Forces operations as each raid's return stragglers and flak damaged aircraft attempted to recross the North Sea to their bases.'

Flight Lieutenant George Nicholls, together with Flight Sergeant Alan Peters from 248 Squadron, departed at 10.00 hours from RAF Portreath as an advanced air party. Landing at 12.30 hours they were met by Group Captain Max Aitken who remarked 'the station's not ready for another squadron yet.'

Domestic life in the officers' mess at Banff caused some concern with the sudden influx of so many officers; it soon became apparent that the bar was not long enough to accommodate everyone. Moreover Group Captain Max Aitken had inherited a poorly run bar with no beer and no money in the mess account. Squadron Leader Don Rogers of 144 Squadron and the engineering officer were asked by the station commander to help make some improvements. With this in mind, Group Captain Aitken picked out the biggest room in the officers' mess, the billiards room. There were two full size tables, one of which was put in the under-used table tennis room, while the other was moved to the airmen's mess. Aitken decided it would make a splendid bar and lounge, with the bar across one end of the room and another adjoining it, for storage of beer barrels and whisky. Everything proceeded quickly and soon a respectable bar was taking shape, even though it was described as 'rustic'. Above the bar the four squadron coats of arms were displayed in panels with the squadron honours; swastikas representing victories against enemy aircraft and a sunken ship for enemy shipping sunk.

By an extraordinary coincidence, a signal was dispatched from Coastal Command Headquarters Northwood, copied to all Coastal Command stations, stating that too much money and resources were being spent on the building of new bars in officers' messes and this practice was to cease. Aitken was not the least bit concerned. Squadron Leader Rogers was able to get the brewers at Elgin to supply and deliver 20 barrels straight away; by putting the beer up by one penny a pint the overdue brewers' bill was soon cleared. Later two former bar stewards were court martialled for stealing the mess funds.

All three service echelons worked hard but there was a severe shortage of petrol bowsers, but the Mosquito fuel tanks were finally refuelled by sun-down for the big strike. On 9 September, two 333 aircraft out on a 'Rover' returned with sightings between Kristiansund and Stavanger. 235 Squadron aircrew took the chance to familiarise themselves with the area. Flight Lieutenant Basil Quelch was first off. The Air Officer Commanding No. 18 Group, Air Vice-Marshal S Simpson and the Air Officer Commander-in-Chief of Coastal Command, Sir Sholto Douglas arrived by Hudson FK745 to discuss the wing's first strike in the operations room with the station and squadron commanders. 43 aircraft took to the skies and made for Stavanger but when they encountered heavy rain they decided to head back. After landing everyone was ready for the 'ops meal' of two fries eggs in the airmen's messes. In the evening Sholto Douglas opened the bar, while the flamboyant Group Captain Max Aitken paid for everyone's drinks! Every officer took full advantage of his generosity and had a good time. The morale on the station could not have been higher. As they quenched their thirst, Sholto Douglas, Simpson and Yonge went to the station cinema; Simpson fell asleep and snored very loudly throughout the picture. In the interval Yonge learnt from Douglas that two of his men, Warrant Officers Chew and Couttie who had ditched on 14 August, were now fighting with the Maquis. After the cinema the three went to Aitken's accommodation for some whiskies and the remainder of the evening was spent discussing the wing's new roles and the RAF in general. Douglas was also introduced to the distinguished Canadian war artist Flying Officer Don Anderson who was visiting the airfield making sketches of the different phases of station life while attached to 404 Squadron.

Corporal Les Taylor, a member of 235 Squadron said of his arrival:

'When I was told I had been posted to Banff, Scotland, a warrant officer assured me that it was a wonderful place saying, "The air up there is worth a guinea a breath". I often recalled his remarks when battling to reach the mess or Nissen hut in a 100 mph gale or blizzard!'

Another mixed force flew out on 10 September, but no shipping or fighters were seen. Just before the force returned 248 Squadron's air party arrived. The main air party was led by an 'old hand', New Zealander Wing Commander 'Bill' Sise, DSO DFC. He had flown Beaufighters with 254 Squadron from North Coates continuously for two years and was highly respected within the strike wings. At 28-years-old he had already been awarded the DSO and DFC, and he was able to pass on his experiences in the coming months. The newly arrived aircrews were shown to the airmen's mess for their meal, those not flying heard that £180 of mess funds at Portreath had been spent on a big party because everyone thought it would be closing down now that the Mosquitoes had departed.

During this period senior staff decided that aircrew should improve their marksmanship and provided each squadron with a number of single barrel 12 bore shotguns and all the equipment for clay pigeon shooting. Quite often the local pheasants were the targets as the countryside around the airfield in the autumn of 1944 was teeming with game, resulting in the officers often dining in the mess on pheasant, partridge or hare!

Only 333 Squadron 'B' Flight flew the following day, the remaining three squadrons were released until 18.00 hours when they were to return for briefing on the forthcoming operation. Just before the aircrew were about to go into the briefing they heard that the North Coates wing had attacked vessels off Mandal on the very southern tip of Norway. Operations continued for the Norwegians, a reconnaissance by strike wing aircraft spotted various vessels including the Swedish *Drottningholm* near the Naze with an escort. Shortly after 07.00 hours on 12 September, a strike wing consisting of 24 Beaufighters and 13 Mosquitoes was mobilised and began rising into the air. 235 Squadron was the only one without any failures. One Beaufighter had a tyre burst on the perimeter track, a second swung violently prior to take-off and held up those awaiting clearance, while a third was hit by a seagull just as the pilot brought the wheels up and had to make an emergency landing at Fraserburgh. Once the force had circled the aerodrome in formation Flight Lieutenant Christison of 404 Squadron led them off across the North Sea. During the flight, two aircraft were forced to turn back with engine defects and Flight Sergeant D Reeves of 144 Squadron was forced to ditch after the starboard engine failed 25 miles south of Aberdeen. He made an excellent ditching with no injury to the crew, and they were then rescued by a small fishing vessel. Both pilot and navigator returned to base on 13 September. The rest of the force returned without sighting a convoy. A U-boat patrol followed. A single Norwegian Mosquito carrying 250lb depth charges arrived in the circuit and landed. Its pilot Lieutenant Plyhn quickly briefed those who had been brought to readiness. A U-boat was known to be exercising between Svino and Ytterøyane. Group Captain Aitken shouted "scramble" over the tannoy system; eight Mosquitoes from 235 Squadron took off together with 'P' 333. Flight Lieutenant Geoff Rouse led with the Gee box, Yonge led the remaining seven. Warrant Officer Matthews in 'R' 235 had fuel consumption problems and had to return to base. Unfortunately nothing was sighted except three fishing boats, the occupants waving frantically. Near Ytterøyane light flak hosed up into the sky but luckily no one was hit. All set course for base at 20.29 hours, landing at 22.30 hours. Fresh eggs and bacon in the airmen's mess and a quantity of beer in the officers' mess went down very well. Shortly before everyone turned in for the night Squadron Leader Atkinson, officer commanding 'B' Flight, arrived from Portreath in 'Q' 235. His wife and son would join him shortly.

Agnes Shayler WAAF of the MT Section recalls the effect of the start of operations:

'The RAF crews needed beds so I drove to a local prison to pick up extra beds as the Air Ministry could not supply them for those on camp. Whilst I was living at home, the camp's butcher, his wife and baby used my old room, and I had the spare!'

'Operations begin' was written at the time by Leading Aircraftman Ron Brooks, a radio operator serving with 'C' Flight 248 Squadron:

'A burst of activity came with the arrival of the aircrews at their flight hut. The whole place was bustling with vehicles, with aircrews checking round their aircraft, Mae Wests on or slung over one of their shoulders and ground crews waiting for last minute problems in readiness for engine starts.

'The aircrew climbed the short ladder leading to the cramped cockpit area, the crews would then settle in their aircraft; the ladders were drawn in and fitted into place. A strange silence would fall across the aerodrome with the aircraft from all the squadrons of the strike wing awaiting the signal to operate engines.

'A Very light was fired off from the control tower and immediately the propellers would commence turning slowly, firstly on the battery and then faster as the plugs fired and spat smoke and flame as they picked up. Once one propeller was going well then the other engine was started, both running steadily to warm the engines. Once warm they were run at full revolutions to check them. (The noise and fumes from this was tremendous.) If the aircraft was satisfactory the pilot would then commence taxiing from the flight dispersal point to the take-off position. The air would then suddenly be full of aircraft, gaining height and getting into formation behind the lead aircraft. Finally, they would fly over the control tower, where Group Captain Aitken would be talking into a hand held microphone telling them to tighten up. They would then turn and head out to sea and peace would return to the aerodrome with the ground crews carrying out routine maintenance or waiting for their return.'

Even with little enemy action in the first fortnight the hard-working Norwegians could not cover the entire maze of islands and fjords on their daily reconnaissance flights. Not only were there about 2,000 miles of coast line to cover, there was also a lack of manpower. But it was on an armed Rover off the Norwegian coast on 14 September that the wing was to have its first success with 25 Mosquitoes and 19 Beaufighters, led by Squadron Leader Bob Schoales DFC from 404 Squadron. Soon after leaving the Scottish coast, Schoales brought the combined force down to almost sea level. Flight Lieutenant Rollett, piloting 'B' 248, drew up alongside Warrant Officer 'Bill' Parfitt and waggled his wings, before turning back with air pressure failure. At 16.35, the wing made landfall at Egero, searching between Egero and Stores Torungen Light for a suitable target. Three Swedish merchantmen were sighted at 16.53 hours, they started to attack but broke off quickly when the leader discovered they were neutral; however Beaufighter 'P' 404's radio failed and the crew, not hearing the strike leader's call not to attack, unfortunately did so, hitting one of the neutral merchantmen with 50 rounds of cannon. As the formation approached the southern end of the patrol area the strike leader then sighted vessels in position 58.00N/08.55E. The convoy was proceeding 18 miles off Kristiansand, comprised of two motor vessels protected by two flak ships en route to the Skagerrak. There was a further convoy of three merchantmen with UJ 1104 as escort south of Mandal. Schoales duly reported seeing six enemy vessels steaming along only feet apart, which from the air might have been viewed as one convoy. At 17.20 hours, Schoales ordered an attack; coming in with the sun behind them opposition was extremely heavy.

All the escort vessels were heavily armed. Vp.1608 and Vp.1610 fired off each of their four rocket dischargers. Called 'Raketen Geschoss' (Rocket Projectile, known as RAG), their intention was to fire in front of the attacking aircraft, so that the hanging wires cut off a wing or damaged the aircraft. The aircraft split either side of these objects; the crews watched the yellow parachutes descending slowly, with the yellow mines dangling from the cables. 235 and 248 Squadron Mosquitoes assigned as anti-flak went in to silence the fire. In a matter of seconds a wave of Torbeaus and rocket-firing Beaufighters swept in, hitting both escort vessels and merchantmen as Mosquitoes strafed the decks, cannon shells exploding on the decking and the hulls as they went in at mast height. In one of the leading three 404 Beaufighters, Flying Officer Joseph Baribeau, flying No. 3 to the strike leader, followed him in, targeting the largest merchantman Iris of 3,323 tons. At 250mph Baribeau opened fire at 1,000 yards, the cannon fire spraying the deck, and at 400 yards he released his 60lb rockets in salvo.

Iris was first to be hit and was holed in compartment six, which rapidly filled with water, but she remained afloat as German seamen battled to save the vessel, plugging the underwater holes. On deck, a fire took hold belching out thick smoke. As other aircraft converged onto targets, Baribeau's aircraft 'O' 404-NE341 broke away and a violent jolt sent it out of control. Baribeau, wrestling with the controls, managed to straighten out, but with the Beaufighter barely flying he pushed the nose down. He radioed that he was going to ditch. Schoales' navigator transmitted an 'SOS, aircraft ditching' with the aircraft's position to the Group Headquarters. With ditching only seconds away, five miles south of the convoy and 15 miles out from the coast, Baribeau jettisoned the top hatch. Upon impact, the port engine burst into flames; after a few seconds water was coming in and he quickly unclipped his Sutton harness and scrambled out of the top hatch. His navigator, Flight Lieutenant C H Taylor had got out and water covered him as he inflated his lifejacket and began to swim. The two seat 'L' type dinghy had automatically opened from the trailing edge of the port wing, activated by an immersion switch. Sliding down onto the wing Baribeau hauled himself in. 150 feet away from where NE341 sank he saw Taylor swimming. Several aircraft flew over the dinghy at less than 50 feet. Baribeau waved frantically and fellow Canadians reported, 'One member standing up in the bright yellow dinghy waving'. Below in the freezing water Taylor waved to Baribeau. The young Canadian navigator failed to reach the dinghy and presumably became exhausted because of the conditions and drowned. Both Squadron Leader Atkinson and Pilot Officer Douglas of 235 Squadron radioed a message on the emergency frequency to the patrolling Air Sea Rescue Warwicks but the messages went unheeded; they would not venture into the location without fighter protection, which was unavailable. Eventually Baribeau was picked up by the Germans. Notification reached the Air Ministry of him being a prisoner of war on 16 September 1944.

The former German fishing trawler *Hamburg* of 264 tons, renamed as Vp. 1608 *Sulldorf* had been repeatedly hit in quick succession, exploded and sank; a Beaufighter broke away steeply to avoid debris. Another merchantman, *Pompeji* of 2,196 tons, burned furiously some five miles behind; water poured into the forward holds, but nevertheless the crew managed to keep her afloat. Badly ravaged, they beached the vessel at Justøya. Still burning and with a list it was then towed into Lillesand where it took two weeks to repair. In 1946 *Pompeji* sailed to England and was renamed *Empire Black-Water*. *Iris* was also towed into Lillesand for repair. As the dispersed strike aircraft wheeled round the convoy was enveloped in smoke as they swept past Lindesnes Light on course for home. German anti-aircraft fire had been effective. Pilot Officer Douglas in 'P' 235 had a large hole in his starboard aileron. Schoales' Beaufighter NE766 was struck in several places by cannon fire but it was the starboard engine which had suffered the most. After taking photographs he nursed his crippled aircraft 400 miles back home on one engine, making a hurried landing at the first available airfield, Crimond, which was still under construction.

Flying Officer H E Hallatt from Hamilton, Ontario, flying a Beaufighter had made a rocket attack on *Iris*; he recalled: 'There was an explosion and a short sheet of flame from the vessel and we were gone.' Another member of the strike force was Warrant Officer Harold Corbin CGM, a 23-year-old pilot flying one of the anti-flak Mosquitoes, who said:

'It was beautifully clear, and we attacked out of the sun. I went for the leading trawler but after the rocket attack all I could fire at was a patch of smoke and flame. I passed over the trawler and found myself in line with a large merchant vessel, on which I opened up with cannon scoring many strikes.'

As the strike wing aircraft began to join the circuit Group Captain Max Aitken became increasingly impatient with flying control over their slowness in dealing with the aircraft in distress on VHF. A Canadian Beaufighter, 'C' 404-NE793, was one such aircraft. It had been struck by flak while attacking the second vessel and had a damaged starboard propeller, severed intercom cable and shattered windscreen. The aircraft lurched sideways. The pilot, Flying Officer Arthur Menaul, was stunned and wounded in the right arm, shoulder and breast by flying glass. His face was peppered with Perspex fragments which were embedded in his skin. Only when he had finished his attack did he turn for home. Navigator Flying Officer John Tomes came forward and with great coolness helped to regain control of the stricken aircraft, and after returning to his seat to get a Gee fix he came back to help his pilot. He cut off his sheepskin jacket sleeve and administered relief to the deep wounds in Menaul's shoulder. Barely able to see through the shattered windscreen and despite intense pain Menaul flew back to Banff with Tomes giving valuable assistance. Menaul tried to conserve his energy to make a safe landing on the runway. They were newest crew on the squadron. Menaul collapsed and was hoisted out of the top hatch and taken to the station hospital. Both were awarded the Distinguished Flying Cross for the outstanding ability displayed in the handling of their aircraft under hazardous conditions during and after the attack.

Aircraft were needed for operations the next day so the ground crews had to re-service them in the dark, with only the uncertain light of a torch. With the limited number of petrol bowsers available replenishing the aircraft's tanks took until sunrise, while in the officers' mess pilots enjoyed an evening of liquid refreshment. In the morning more probing Rovers were flown, though squall showers caused operations to be aborted for two days as visibility was poor. This gave the squadron commanders a chance of catching up with their administration duties. On 16 September Group Captain Max Aitken took delivery of his personal Mosquito, serial number HR366 from a member of the ATA. Wing Commander Yonge, as well as getting on with the paper work, showed the group captain over his Mosquito explaining the cockpit layout and instruments and Aitken did 50 minutes local flying. 8235 Service Echelon then began painting on the markings 'MA-01' in burgundy. Aitken's aircraft was on 235 Squadron's strength as he intended to fly with the squadron on operations.

During the early evening atrocious weather blew in. Heavy rain, thunder and lightning lit up the sky and the intelligence office was abuzz with activity. News had come in that U-boats were making their way to Bergen unescorted. So far the other Coastal Command squadrons had failed to catch them. Aitken planned for a number of U-boat patrols to try and hit them outside Bergen. 235 Squadron was designated fighter protection. After a brief talk with the squadron commanders about the forthcoming operations they went to a drinks party in the WAAF mess. Their host was Flying Officer Taptiklis. Later they took all the WAAFs to the officers' mess bar and had supper. On 17 September at 06.27 hours Flight Lieutenant Stanley 'Baby' Nunn led an armed reconnaissance of eight Mosquitoes in search of a U-boat. Half way across the North Sea at 07.55 hours the leader, flying 'S' 248, experienced engine problems due to a faulty petrol feeder and turned back for base. On his port side his No. 2, Flight Lieutenant Lewis Bacon DFC, took over and the remaining seven Mosquitoes pressed on down their patrol route. Five miles from the Norwegian coast Bacon led the formation in a climbing turn and finally ordered a return to base. 235, 248 and 333 Squadrons' Mosquitoes kept up the pace with further reconnaissance patrols during the day but visibility was poor and all aircraft returned having sighted nothing.

That afternoon, 28 Beaufighters of 404 and 144 Squadrons in company with eight Mosquitoes of 235 Squadron for fighter escort took off at 13.44 hours. Also with them were four Torbeaus led by Squadron Leader Duncanson. The Torbeaus were an adapted Beaufighter, which carried four cannon as well as a torpedo. Later marks were modified to carry rocket projectiles under the wings together with the torpedo. The wing leader for this sortie was Wing Commander Tony Gadd. As he led them away from Banff aircraft 'G' 144 left the formation and returned with undercarriage trouble. The formation adjusted, and navigator Duncan Marrow gave Tony Gadd the course for Lista, who turned on a setting slightly north. After a short time Gadd's aircraft suffered engine trouble so, having handed the leadership to Lieutenant 'Freddie' Guyott, he turned back and landed at Fraserburgh. In the hunt along the Norwegian shipping lanes from Lista to Homborsund Light nothing was sighted, except for a small vessel run aground off Lillesand.

Flying Officer S T Faithfull DFC served as a navigator and flew with Lieutenant Freddie Guyott (USAAF) on 17 September with 404 Squadron:

'We led a section on this sortie, no sighting was made, we then flew due east. Freddie Guyott took a great deal of persuading to turn the formation about for home. At debriefing there were a few words said about the shortage of fuel!'

No further sweeps took place that day because of low cloud, with patches of fog;

visibility worsened at sea level. A second U-boat search came on 18 September, when shore-based HF/DF had picked up a good fix on distress signals being transmitted and Coastal Command were alerted. Ten Mosquitoes from 248 Squadron carried out fighter escort duties jointly with two aircraft from 235 Squadron. Airborne at 06.33 hours they searched along Utvaer, Ytterøyane and Flora then back on a reciprocating course, led by Wing Commander Bill Sise. The formation made landfall from over the rough sea and under 10/10ths cloud just north of Ytterøyane Light, then banked to starboard and keeping one mile off shore searched the empty wastes for enemy vessels. Sise, flying at 300 feet, spotted a U-boat on the surface off Utvaer at 08.20 hours, two miles ahead. U-boat U-867 was a type IXC-40 from Deschimag AG works and was commissioned in December 1943. It was commanded by Captain zur See Arved von Muhlendahl, who had celebrated his 39th birthday the previous month. The U-boat had begun her first war cruise on 9 September 1944 from Kiel, later sailing from Norway. Her assignment was to place another automatic weather station on Labrador.

Flying in a 248 Squadron Tsetse was Warrant Officer Jim Hoyle: 'Flying in the vicinity of Utvaer Lighthouse we came across an unescorted U-boat. The order of attack was given and "Hilly" Hilliard claimed a number of hits with the 57mm gun.'

A heavy barrage of opposition came up from batteries on a nearby island. Sise immediately climbed the sections to 500 feet and gave the order 'Attack, attack, attack'. Each aircraft wheeled to port attacking in turn from either stern or broadside at the conning tower in a shallow dive and made short sighting bursts followed by a longer burst of cannon and machine guns. Striking all around the hull, two 248 aircraft ('B' 248 and 'U' 248) dropped depth charges but a third aircraft failed to get its bomb doors to open on the first run. Aircraft 'B' 248's depth charges fell astern but the crew of 'U' 248 saw their depth charges enter the water 20 feet from the conning tower and along the water fore and aft of it. The U-boat appeared to be forced out of the water by the exploding charges. It later began to settle, turning to port and listing by 15°. With U-867's diesels out of action and the battery completely dead, von Muhlendahl radioed for a tow back to Norway. A rescue attempt was mounted by other U-boats to get the crew and the weather equipment, but it failed. A Liberator of 224 Squadron piloted by Flying Officer P Hill hit one of the rescue boats, U-1228, commanded by Friedrich-Wilhelm Marienfeld, aged 24; it had sailed from Bergen the previous day, returning damaged on 20 September. Photographs later showed it with a heavy list and making for Utvaer seemingly badly damaged. Harold Corbin, CGM wrote in his dairy: 'Went on a U-boat hunt near Bergen. Sighted U-boat on surface, strafed it with cannon 20mm, and straddled it with my two depth charges. Claimed as sunk. I hope this is kept out of the newspapers as my wife and parents had had so much worry with me being reported missing in August together with my navigator Maurice Webb.'

Two armed reconnaissance patrols failed to locate U-867 after this encounter. It was in fact in grave peril. Von Muhlendahl struggled on until the next afternoon when a Liberator of 224 Squadron sighted her at 16.25 hours. Still on the surface and unable to submerge, she put up flak as the Liberator crew headed in. The front and mid-upper gunners opened up at 1,000 yards and the flak ceased. The aircraft's depth charges mostly overshot, but the U-boat captain decided to abandon her as this further sighting would bring more aircraft. After the explosions U-867 remained afloat for a few minutes, then sank on an even keel. 'Q' 224 completed a second circuit and its pilot Flight Lieutenant H J Rayner reported '50 survivors in dinghies'. Photographs showed seven small and one large one with about 50 crewmen, floating in a pool of oil left by the sinking submarine. Other debris littered the area. The attack took place west of Stadlandet, not far off the coast but none of the 50 crewmen were recovered. The reason for this is unclear, but most likely the radio operator was unable to get a signal off to his command centre giving his position so that a rescue could be mounted.

Whilst this operation was taking place Flying Officer Driver accompanied his commanding officer in 'P' 235 to Portreath to retrieve 'G – George' only to find that one of 248 Squadron pilots had already taken it earlier in the morning. However one of 248's Mosquitoes would be arriving from the maintenance unit and Driver stayed to collect it. Thick fog enveloped them on their flight to Banff forcing them to land at an aerodrome near Sheffield. Industrial smog prolonged their departure until the morning of 21 September.

On 19 September, Mosquitoes from 333 Squadron took off at 04.00 hours on the familiar daily reconnaissance. These were proving quite invaluable for the wing. Flying over Fedjefjord one crew picked out in the twilight three merchant vessels travelling at an estimated speed of nine knots. On their flight back the pilot of 'F' 333 was detailed to land at Fraserburgh and plans were finalised at 12.00 hours for an immediate strike. A mixed force of 21 Beaufighters and 11 Mosquitoes laboured into the sky and circled around the base in a wide sweep, passing over the villages below to form up and disappear. Crossing the North Sea, hugging the wave tops, the Beaufighters' engines throttled back to 1,950 revs with 1lb on the boost gauge, giving a cruising speed in the region of 180 knots. Wireless silence was preserved but a number of aircraft kept a listening-out watch. A 404 Beaufighter developed a serious engine problem and dropped out to return and land early.

On they went mile after mile; enemy lookout posts near Stongfjord heard the rumble of their engines and notified coastal batteries which brought an assortment of weapons to bear. There were two merchantmen with one escort vessel, the D/S *Lynx* of 1,367 tons and the larger 3,080-ton D/S *Tyrifjord* with flakship Vp. 5101, sailing from Hamburg via Bergen, and travelling north to Tromsø and Hammerfest. Wing Commander Tony Gadd wheeled around to attack and came up against intense flak from the escort and shore batteries. Onboard the vessels the alarm sounded at 18.30 hours (German time). The anti-flak Beaufighters of 144 picked out the escort vessel. All aircraft pressed home their attack from 3,000 feet to 150 feet. One vessel disappeared in the smoke of bursting explosives, and a few hundred metres from another of the vessels a Beaufighter was hit by return fire. Its crew was Flight Sergeant Ernest Hossack of Enfield, Middlesex and his navigator Warrant Officer Bernard Wicks. The Beaufighter, 'L' 144-NE437 was seen suddenly to go into attack and climb to 500 feet then nose dive into the sea near Stavenes. Both crew perished.

It was a furious exchange between vessels and their attackers. A seasoned 'shipbuster' said: 'As I went in after the vessel there was a brilliant red flash of flame and clouds of thick black smoke.' On board the *Lynx* a fire was raging, its cargo of military supplies now loose above and below deck in precarious positions. Her captain Harry Evensen and Norwegian crew struggled to manoeuvre into shallower water to beach the vessel and get the cargo off. The Norwegian pilot onboard, Charles Enoksen died during the attack. An hour later the *Lynx*, having been beached south of Stavenes lighthouse sank. D/S *Tyrifjord* with its cargo of wheat and other perishable supplies was also hit and set on fire. It remained afloat, although seriously damaged, and her crew succeeded in stopping the inrush of water to number one hold with no casualties. D/S *Ursa*, the escort vessel, came under cannon fire but missed being sunk. An orbiting Mosquito piloted by the experienced Flying Officer David 'Jack' Frost DFC, with navigator Flying Officer Fuller was taking photographs with an F24 camera of the mayhem below. Suddenly a 37mm shell peppered their aircraft, resulting in a fire breaking out; orange flames billowed out from its port engine with flames licking the paintwork. Inside the cockpit Frost pressed the extinguisher and feathering button, and the engine packed up. Frost was injured, struck by dozens of shrapnel slivers in the left hand, thigh, and ankle. There was also a large tear on the starboard side fuselage in front of the navigator's position. Hurricane winds howled through the shattered wooden structure. Despite suffering from intense pain Frost eased the throttles forward, tugged the control column back and the aircraft began to gain height. Fuller was on the radio sending out a distress call and minutes later he shouted: 'There's a Warwick coming up' into the intercom as the 281 Squadron aircraft came alongside. The remaining Beaufighters and Mosquitoes broke away and made off for Banff, some singly, and some in small sections in loose formation.

Frost gave his Mosquito adequate trim from the rudder tab to hold it straight and level, flying at a reasonable speed. The Warwick crew give words of encouragement, although he thought it funny that their escort could not go fast enough to keep up with the Mosquito flying on one engine!

Fuller pulled open the first aid box: assessing Frost's injuries he found in wiping the blood away that the little finger on his left hand was only attached by a thin piece of the remaining bone and the fourth finger was broken with splinters embedded in the palm. With a large swab Fuller tried to suppress the bleeding, then despite the Mosquito's cramped interior he succeeded in putting the arm in a sling. His navigator then offered him morphia which he declined – Frost wanted to stay awake, but ate all the barley sugar they had between them. Fuller was unscathed. The Mosquito held altitude and after 2 hours 30 minutes, the aerodrome came into view. Fuller managed to rouse the control tower operator. 'We've got a wounded pilot; we'd like a straight-in approach.' The reply was 'Come straight in and good luck'. At the same time Fuller from his right hand seat dismantled the swab and sling for Frost to control the throttle and pitch; the wheels locked into place and, although suffering severe pain, Frost made a perfect single engine landing, but then immediately passed out at his dispersal point. The station medical officer gave Frost a sedative in the 'blood wagon' (ambulance) on the way to the station hospital. He was then moved to Royal Infirmary Hospital, Aberdeen, where surgeons amputated the remains of his left little finger. While he was recovering from his injuries, the hospital received a visit from Her Majesty the Queen, the young flying officer on Ward 8 being introduced to her. During the conversation she asked if there was anything he required. Frost said he was to be married shortly on 21 October in Essex and did not have a car for the occasion. Her Majesty duly arranged one. The wedding to Miss Betty Ackroyd, a member of the Women's Land Army went ahead as planned with his arm in a sling; the happy couple then honeymooned in Cornwall. Frost was put forward by Group Captain Max Aitken for an immediate bar to his DFC for his bravery, which was duly awarded. Aitken wrote: 'This officer has at all times shown great gallantry and a keen desire to engage the enemy. On his last sortie after a determined attack he brought his aircraft back to base on one engine, although severely wounded. Recommended for a Bar to DFC.'

In Norway the D/S *Tyrifjord* crew were able to sail her back to the nearest convoy harbour, Askvoll, where the ship burned for several days and eventually sank. The German sea commandant in Bergen ordered the tugboat *Willy Charles* and the diving boat *Seehund* to Askvoll in the hope of salvaging the vessel. They were unsuccessful.* The team on *Seehund* also tried to salvage the *Lynx* but it slipped down a crevasse into deeper water. Future attempts to rescue the vessel were also abandoned.

Paul Hutchinson was a schoolboy living in a nearby village and explains local interest in the activities at the station:

---

*On the vessel's return voyage it was to have carried iron ore. In 1948 the shipwreck was bought by Coox in Bergen and D/S *Tyrifjord* was broken up.

'When the aircraft began to arrive we watched excitedly as Beaufighters and Mosquitoes circled in formation, then broke and landed one by one. We noted the different squadron lettering, which we were to learn by heart in the coming months and we stayed until the last aeroplane had taxied to its allotted dispersal and the propeller blades came to rest. The ground staff where remarkably tolerant, answering our endless questions and allowing us to wander (with an escort) near the parked aeroplanes dispersed near the control tower. Soon, notebooks had these jottings, the continuity of these records only halted by the hours we were obliged to spend at school.'

On 21 September, three Mosquitoes took off at separate intervals across the North Sea, 'white horses' breaking just below, and their propellers leaving a wake behind them. At the correct time they broke, separating to patrol individually. 'E' 333 sighted three merchantmen sailing at six knots near Lista, a single Mosquito flying over was reported at 08.48 hours (German time).

In Scotland a strike force was standing by, but the weather intervened and the operation was postponed until 12.00 hours, with take-off an hour and a half later. Pilots and navigators were left wondering why they had been woken at 06.00 hours to take off in the middle of the day!

During this lull a single Beaufighter, NE436 from 254 Squadron, piloted by Squadron Leader Arthur 'Junior' Simmonds and his navigator Flying Officer Murphy landed short of fuel. Unbeknownst to them they would soon both be flying from the 'desolate wind swept drome' described in Simmonds' flying log book. Airborne between 13.34-13.45 hours, 21 Beaufighters with 17 Mosquitoes led by Squadron Leader Don Rogers flew out. Two returned shortly after take-off with engine trouble. Just off Kristiansand near Lista, two small Norwegian freighters were sighted: *Vangsnes* was sailing from Stavanger to east Norway, at the same time *Hygia* was on a passage from Randers in Denmark to Bergen. When they crossed each other a quarter of a mile south-east of Lista they were targeted. The leader's VHF stopped working and no one heard the order to attack. He turned in and opened fire with cannon. Every one else soon followed. *Vangsnes* immediately caught fire. Second mate Jens Bårdsen Nernæs was killed in the first pass. With a cargo of 52 tons of ammunition and barrels of fuel onboard, the vessel exploded; two German soldiers together with two Norwegians were badly injured though they managed to survive the blast. One was Jens's brother, Edvard. The remaining crew put the vessel aground on Rudna. *Hygia*, with a cargo of 98 tons of ammunition, sustained serious damage and sank in two minutes; of the crew of four, the engineer Stonghaugen died. Regrettably, a local fishing vessel was also sunk. The whole action was over within five minutes. A flight sergeant recalled: 'I pushed the switch to remove the protection flap over the lens, to take photographs of the strike. I didn't get a single picture although I had used all the film. The G-45 camera lens was covered in sea spray!'

En route back to base, the crews saw a tanker and noted its position. No enemy aircraft were sighted at Lista aerodrome but there was heavy flak. Two Beaufighters sustained damage: Flying Officer Maurice Exton's aircraft 'U' 144 suffered a hole in the nose and the port airscrew was pitted and Flying Officer D C Lee in 'K' 404 made a single engine landing, after the other packed up 60 miles from the Scottish coast.

The remaining crew on *Vangsnes* left in the lifeboat and were put ashore at Lista lifeboat station. The Germans sent crew members from one UJ boat to try to stop the fire spreading but the dynamite on board blew up, killing one of the Germans. Squadron Leader Don Rogers said: 'My mother was delighted when she opened her local newspaper *The Sussex Express & County Herald* to read that Squadron Leader

Don Rogers of Lewes had led a successful attack against a convoy.'

The next day, 22 September, the aerodrome was shrouded in rain. Canadian aircrews from 404 were rested, but some were later required for a strike. Briefing was at 11.00 hours with take-off at 12.30 if they could still see the main runway! Aircraft staggered into the air and set course for the Norwegian coast; there had been reported sightings of targets inside the Leads, half way between Bergen and the southern Norwegian coast. Squadron Leader Don Duncanson from 144 Squadron led a mixed force with 404 Squadron's rocket-armed Beaufighters. 235 and 248 Squadrons provided additional cover. Mosquito 'V' 248 sighted a flakship, which fired off star cartridges. With a low cloud base and in poor visibility Duncanson led the formation up to 5,000 feet and above the clouds. No targets were seen and the adverse weather continued all the way back across the North Sea. Upon nearing the airfield, the leader called up the control tower to check conditions over the base (Banff). 'It's poor and the cloud base is practically on the deck!' was the reply. While some landed without mishap, nine Beaufighters landed away at Dallachy. Group Captain Max Aitken became irritated that the nearby homing station did not seem to function correctly whilst the aircraft were airborne. A visit was quickly scheduled once the weather cleared.

The weather intervened again on 23 September, giving personnel a welcome respite. Wing Commander John Yonge, using the time to deal with his administrative duties, recommended Flying Officer David 'Jack' Frost, for a Bar to his DFC. Others relaxed in the messes or at the rural public houses, while some went off for a spot of salmon fishing or went to local farms scrounging eggs. Later Yonge journeyed via Fraserburgh to Aberdeen with WAAF Section Officer Plumbridge and one other WAAF officer. Here he visited Frost in Ward 8 of the Royal Infirmary Hospital, who was quite happy with a pretty nurse. Just after midnight heavy rain began to fall and it continued till first light. At dispersal points ground crews worked in the abysmal weather – the only orders being to 'get the work done as quickly as possible!'

On the morning of 24 September and once the skies had cleared searches commenced with a number of sightings in the Hjeltefjord area made by the Norwegians. German radio location detected these early flights and this information was sent to Hjeltefjord Coastal Artillery Group, which sounded the alarm. All guns were manned in readiness for an air attack. Between 12.03 and 12.33 hours six Mosquitoes took off led by Squadron Leader Maurice, DSO, DFC, CdeG and Flying Officer 'Jimmy' Orchard, to carry out a Rover from Utvaer to Marstein Light. They thundered over Utvear Light at 14.05 hours; gunners on an anchored coaster (merchantman) fired into the air as the six swept over at mast height. Seven minutes later crews observed a flakship in position between Hjeltefjord and Sognefjord – it was Vp.5502 *Biber*, an old Norwegian whaler named *Veslefrikk*, protecting the merchantman *Storesund*, of 563 tons, which was about to head south. Maurice gained tactical surprise by climbing to 6,000 feet above the cloud. In attack formation the crews received the order: attack, attack. The pilots opened their throttles, increased speed and in a shallow dive broke through the clouds; they went straight in lining up a vessel. Four aircraft attacked. Anti-aircraft batteries onboard and shore batteries put up a wall of fire through which the Mosquitoes flew to go down the narrow sound, using cannon, machine guns and 500lb bombs. Tsetse Mosquitoes from 248 Squadron's 'C' Flight fired off 57mm shells into the superstructure of Vp.5502 which sank immediately. Strafing with all available weapons, both received heavy damage during the attack. Norwegian vessel *Storesund* was left burning off Hjeltefjord. However, the German fire had also been effective. Mosquito 'R' 248 slowly turned away hit by cannon, causing a fire extinguisher to be set off. A distress cartridge was used; two aircraft appeared shadowing it back to base. Mosquito 'R' 248 landed safely minus a large section of its leading edge.

Less than an hour later two patrol vessels were discovered in Sognefjord by a separate force of seven Mosquitoes, NB.07 *Bison* and NB.14 *Hornisse*. NB.07 took several hits on the bridge, and was fully ablaze as it grounded. Three Germans lost their lives and 27 were wounded. The Germans thought they had shot down one of the attackers but the aircraft all broke away and made it back to Banff, in loose formation or singly. Upon inspection, when the aircraft were safely down by 15.46 hours and back at their dispersal points, all had suffered some battle-damage, and one airman needed hospital treatment.

Wing Commander R H McConnell DSO, DFC now arrived to take over his duties as wing commander flying at the station. McConnell had formerly been 235 Squadron's commanding officer between July 1943 and April 1944. He has memories of firing the (6lb) 57mm Molins:

'At about 1,200 yards or thereabouts, slight pressure on the gun button resulted in a simultaneous blast and flash visible from the cockpit. My navigator, sitting on my right and slightly to the rear, looked stunned. Dust and debris from the floor, mixed with blue-grey fumes, sprang into the sunlight. The spring-mounted flight instrument panel danced against its stops. The instruments were unreadable. The aircraft seemed to pause in the air and I was thrown forward against the safety harness. The mayhem was multiplied many times as the feed mechanism shovelled in the shells at a rate of one every 1.5 seconds. I thought that the "Wooden Wonder" would never stay glued together.'

On 25 September, three Norwegian aircraft carried out separate dawn searches off southern Norway. 'F' 333 covered Ustira and Ytterøyane sweeping over Askvoll. 'N' 333 surveyed Utsira, Kristiansand and Mandal area, spotting a single vessel sailing between Mandal and Kristiansand. Beyond Kristiansand they passed over little fishing boats. Mosquito 'F' 333 detected a laden merchantman near Leirvik where a convoy of five was being prepared but, short on fuel, discontinued its operation making for Sumburgh then onto Banff. After this early operation, 20 Beaufighter and 16 Mosquito aircraft where made ready, but inclement weather postponed the operation. Link Training and dinghy drill took its place for aircrew, the squadron commanders again returning to their paperwork. Wing Commander John Yonge spent most of his time with Wing Commander Evans of 18 Group discussing 235 Squadron's aircrew situation, having seven tour-expired crew and another two nearing 200 hours. Group Captain Max Aitken informed Yonge that his squadron would remain purely a fighter squadron so that they had first priority on the drogue-towing Miles Martinet JN541. Flight Lieutenant Dommoi, the pilot, received orders that he was to be attached to Yonge's squadron for flying duties. Unfortunately high winds forced the cancellation of the proposed operations on 26 September. During a thunderstorm in the early afternoon an Oxford landed, aquaplaning to a dispersal with Wing Commander Stubbs of Air Training Coastal Command headquarters on board. He discussed the aircrew output situation with Aitken, Sise, Yonge, Pierce, and Gadd. After a whiskey with Aitken and despite the appalling weather Stubbs flew on to Leuchars. Wing Commander Evans from 18 Group informed Yonge that headquarters had given authority to allow his aircrew to extend their operational tours by 100 hours or two months, whichever was the shorter. He then set about getting volunteers, noting; 'It is noticeable that those about to get married are reluctant to continue.'

Two days later, on 27 September, with a dozen de Havilland representatives from Hatfield in attendance and under the direction of their squadron engineering officer and the station servicing wing, commanded by the station chief technical officer, the Mosquitoes began to be modified to carry eight under-wing rocket-projectiles on rails using a blueprint to show where the new rail units were to be mounted. 20 Mosquitoes took part in Rover patrols throughout the day making a number of sightings. Three Norwegian Mosquitoes armed with 250lb depth charges and eight from 235 Squadron were tasked with anti-flak/anti-fighter duties and took off at 14.31 hours on a U-boat patrol, the object being to attack U-boats and their escort between Lista and Kristiansand. They were led by Wing Commander John Yonge. At 15.52 hours they had reached Lista and one Norwegian caught quite a bit of light flak from their ground defences, a minute later it was behind them. As they neared Kristiansand Yonge spotted three small ships not worth attacking because of their size. The visibility then deteriorated. Through a heavy rainstorm the shape of a vessel momentarily appeared. Jettisoning their drop-tanks Yonge gave the order to prepare to attack, followed by 'attack, attack'. The 235 Squadron Mosquitoes opened up with cannon and machine guns. The *Rossfiord* received hits outside Kristiansand at 16.40 hours. 'Riddled with cannon fire' said one of the pilots afterwards, 'we left it burning'; however only slight damage to the wheelhouse roof was recorded. As they broke away another merchantman three miles behind opened up, wildly shooting rounds into the air. Yonge tried to re-gather the force but only the Norwegians heard his calls, they had missed the first target which had been obscured by the heavy rain. 'A' 235 and the Norwegians swept in but broke off when they realised that it was too small, falling below 1,500 tons. Flight Lieutenant Noel Russell had already strafed it himself. Three minutes later the Mosquitoes were on their way home, flying through extremely rough weather. Yonge was experiencing problems with 'A' 235. The radiator cooling shutters continued to open and shut, and he had to continually change the trim and speed of the aircraft. Yonge recalled; 'it was particularly annoying.'

The next day non-operational activities included the transfer of individual Beaufighters of 144 Squadron to Bircham Newton by way of Leuchars and North Coates. A total of 44 Banff aircraft took part in separate patrols, only one was successful. A convoy of two vessels had sailed from a Dutch marine factory flying the German ensign bound for Norway; minesweeper NK.02 *Dragoner* and former Norwegian torpedo boat *Kjell* were beyond Ryvingen heading for their next halt. Both carried two 105mm guns, one 37mm anti-aircraft gun, one quadruple-mounted 20mm anti-aircraft gun, four twin-mounted 20mm anti-aircraft guns and four rocket dischargers. At 17.28 hours on 28 September they were making good time, and sailing south of Mandal. Flight Lieutenant Lewis Bacon DFC led six aircraft on a Rover patrol between Lista and Kristiansand South, taking off at 14.53 and reaching Lista at 16.14. Bacon in 'S' 248 saw the two vessels at 16.26 hours. One by one they swooped down and Tsetse 57mm shells first ripped into the hulls while MkIVs used cannon and 500lb bombs and the crew of 'K' 248 released their depth charges. 17 rounds of 57mm out of the 24 fired penetrated the harbour defence vessel. *Dragoner* was hit amidships and 500lb bombs and the depth charges detonated on the starboard side caused a large explosion throwing a column of spray and debris into the air. Belching thick black smoke *Dragoner* began to sink on an even keel. Bacon said; 'I watched the vessel disappear below the surface.' Clinging to floating debris were some of the 25 survivors with 18 perishing in the blast. The aircraft returned to Scotland, landing at 18.41 hours. A navigator who took part recalled:

'Ignoring everything but the target, we went straight for the vessel and opened up with cannon, scoring hits freely. Our speed was now over 300mph as we broke away nearly at mast height. During these few seconds I was busy with the camera, at the same time alarmingly sick with excitement and /or fear.'

At the end of the month, this newly-formed wing finished with a combined operation of 17 Mosquitoes and 23 Beaufighters on 30 September, from Utvaer to Statlandet but sighted nothing. The Germans had been warned the force was coming and dispersed in the morning.

A delegation from the station departed in an Oxford to visit Tain to see the ranges. At midday Group Captain Max Aitken assembled all the aircrew in the station cinema and congratulated everyone on their excellent work, saying the AOC was very pleased. A flight from 281 Squadron with Vickers Warwick aircraft moved to Dallachy in readiness to support the strike wing, sharing the aerodrome with 838 Squadron of the Fleet Air Arm, which flew anti-U-boat patrols with Fairey Swordfish. In the evening Flight Lieutenant 'Royce' Turner acquainted himself with the Crown in Banff accompanied by his Wing Commander John Yonge. They returned with Flight Lieutenants Jacques, Rouse and a young WAAF wireless operator. As a result of an ENSA concert taking place the bar remained open until after midnight.

It was not all work on the station during the month. Recreational facilities were good. Personnel were treated to three ENSA concerts, one called *Lucky Strike*; two station dances and occasional parties and an RAF *Gang Show*. The station had its own small band. Twenty WAAFs from the station attended the local Battle of Britain parade in the village of Banff and before setting off a collection was taken by Wing Commander Tony Gadd amongst the WAAFs for Wings Day. Group Captain Max Aitken made time to support local RAF occasions and took the salute during the march past commemorating the Battle of Britain on 17 September 1944. A local 'RAF Night' was held which Aitken attended. Two hours of wonderful entertainment by show-business personalities were rounded off when Aitken took to the stage. He remarked; 'I've never seen such a large gathering of airmen and women before except on pay parades.'

September 1944 proved to be a time of explorations along the Norwegian coast, and the new wing completed 2,207 hours of operational sorties. Coastal Command notes on 'The Employment of Coastal Command Anti-Shipping Strike Forces During the Winter 1944-1945' illustrates the difficulties faced in attacking vessels along this coast:

'Our knowledge of enemy movements on the Norwegian coast south of Kristiansand North has always been very much less complete than in other areas. This combined with the greater distances from our bases and the topographical difficulties, has resulted, according to recent statistics, in less than half the interceptions per sortie which we have been accustomed to obtain on the Dutch Coast...

'In spite of these difficulties, our operations against Norway have not been without effect. Already the enemy sails south of Stavanger by night only, lying up in narrow fjords like Farsund and Egersund most of the day. However, because it is difficult for him to get in and out of these places in the darkness, it has been a habit to sail before nightfall and wait for the dawn before entering these anchorages.

'North of Stavanger, the position is reversed. The channels through the Leads are so narrow that night sailings are avoided and shipping is found moving in small convoys of usually not more than three or four merchantmen with three or four escort vessels. Here the enemy has a good warning system and it is his practice, as soon as the presence of our aircraft is detected, to move into the nearest anchorage where the steepness of the coast or the land defences makes attacks unprofitable. Because of this large strikes preceded by reconnaissance aircraft in this area have been largely successful.'

CHAPTER 4

OCTOBER 1944

Two uneventful searches took place on 1 October, and a Norwegian crew had a lucky escape. Shortly after spotting Kristiansand fjord full of vessels, the aircraft and crew encountered heavy and effective opposition from several emplacements. Badly shot up, and its tail hanging on by a few strips of wood, the crew nursed their Mosquito back. The hydraulics and brakes were unusable, but the pilot managed to get his wheels down and landed from north to south. The lack of brake pressure and flaps kept him running at high speed towards the officers' mess bar, but the hydraulics gave way on the grass strip between the mess and the end of the runway.

That afternoon 11 Beaufighter crews where briefed for night operations, 'Moon Rovers', between Oberstad and Kristiansand South. Flying at hourly intervals throughout the night, the wing tried to close this section of water where vessels lost the cover of coastal islands. Frequent rain showers meant only three aircraft became airborne out of 11; the third returned shortly after take-off having collided with a flock of seagulls. The impact damaged the port wing, which became plastered with blood and feathers. Another Beaufighter returned after flying in the darkness for two hours. When the pilot landed in the light of a bright early morning sun a heavy landing was made causing damage to the stern frame.

Other early reconnaissance flights on 2 October over Stavanger, Lindesnes and Husvegg located visible targets. Throughout the morning patrols closed the stretch between Ytterøyane and Bremanger by permanent sweeps. The leader for one sortie was Squadron Leader Bob Schoales, who had 11 aircraft from 404 and nine from 235 acting as fighter escort; they thundered down the runway, taking off at 12.00 hours. Rising quickly, they began to form up in the circuit of the aerodrome but an unfortunate accident occurred five minutes after take-off. Two 404 Beaufighters, LZ189 and LZ444 collided at 1,000 feet. Both aircraft were so badly damaged that the pilots were unable to maintain control of them, they spiralled out of the air one and half miles west of Banff, both crashing vertically into the ground at Wellhead Farm. Wing Commander John Yonge had just become airborne; 'No sooner had I taken off when I saw two large fires in a nearby field with a thick black column of smoke rising to 100 feet. I realised there must have been a collision. A quick count of Mosquitoes assured me that the accident was not in my squadron.'

Exploding ammunition and bits of aircraft covered a wide area and a plume of thick back smoke hung in the air as the remaining aircraft flew on. Both crews in the collision perished, Flying Officers Davey, Robinson, Flight Lieutenant Long and Pilot Officer Stickel dying from multiple injuries. Their objective had been to sink a 2,000 ton merchantman in Sognefjord, sighted by Flight Lieutenant 'Paddy' Wright DFC just an hour and a half before the main force was due but the vessel had sought shelter and they returned to base. That evening while the men and women went to a NFS dance in Macduff a note was pinned on each crew room notice board reminding aircrew to keep a careful look out at all times. The following day all that remained was the burnt out shell of the machines. The bodies were recovered, however. Ernest Davey, Louis Robinson and Fred Stickel were buried in New Cemetery, Banff on 5 October at 15.00

hours, with full military honours and their comrades as pall-bearers. An RCAF chaplain Rev Squadron Leader S M Inman and Rev Squadron Leader Lockhart, the station padre, read the lessons at this solemn occasion. The weather stayed clear for this moving ceremony. A few relatives of Flying Officer Ernest Davey attended and afterwards had tea in the officers' mess as Wing Commander Ed Pierce's guests, they also raised their glasses to congratulate Captain Johansen at the announcement that he had received the Norwegian St Olav medal with silver leaf. The citation read 'for you have shown great keenness and courage as a Mosquito pilot, and successfully carried out several attacks on U-boats, sinking one.' Originally from Trail, British Colombia, Flying Officer George Long's remains were accompanied by Flight Lieutenant Johnsson to his wife's house in Hull, and buried in Hull Eastern Cemetery, Kingston-upon-Hull at a private family funeral service at 13.15 hours on 7 October which his wife, Gladys attended. This was a tragic loss for the squadron. Warrant Officer Jimmy Hoyle, a navigator on Tsetse Mosquitoes remembers: 'I still recollect the shock at seeing the two Beaufighters crash to the ground when their wings touched as one formatted on the other in preparation for setting off to Norway.' Flight Lieutenant 'Webby' Webster wrote: 'My navigator and I arrived at dusk on 4 October having been posted to 235 Squadron. A Bedford van was waiting at Portsoy railway station to take us to base, it had the coffins onboard – after signing in and getting our accommodation and bedding sorted, I went straight on two weeks leave as my navigator was getting married.'

In the evening on 2 October, two 144 Squadron Beaufighters made a quick attack on a vessel; but were unable to observe any visible results. A Beaufighter pilot recalls:

'We were to take off at hourly intervals, fly along the Norwegian coast at 1,000 feet on a moonlit night, navigating by Gee (this was an RAF navigation aid that gave a fix from pulses transmitted by three ground stations and had a range of about 300 miles), and looking for merchantmen. It was vainly thought by Coastal Command 18 Group Headquarters and Max Aitken that we would catch sight of a vessel silhouetted between the moonlight and the sea, and attack it. The operation was postponed because of bad weather, only three aircraft managed to get airborne. A dawn search would take place instead. The on-duty crews were normally called at about 2.00 or 3.00 a.m. As we were half awake and waiting, we stayed up!'

These coastal patrols had the desired effect of increasing the amount of vessels that now took refuge in secluded anchorages in small fjords and then made their passage along the Norwegian coast by night. Moon Rovers kept up the watch at night covering the area between Egero and Kristiansand in southern Norway. Due to the limited period the moon was in the right quarter and to the changeable weather, these night-time operations had their drawbacks but the dedicated crews persisted, often landing in the morning sun.

The wing flew three patrols during 3 October. First off were two aircraft from 235 Squadron and a number of vessels were sighted near Utsira, approximately 18 km out to sea west of Haugesund. Warrant Officer Ian Martin spotted the merchantman seen the previous day near Sognefjord. Mosquito 'Q' 235 reported being fired upon from a German radar station at Vall; the pilot returned fire with a short burst, expending 100 rounds of 20mm cannon but broke off the attack to avoid hitting the brightly painted Norwegian homes nearby. Its pilot, Flight Lieutenant Basil Quelch, feathered the starboard engine as glycol began streaming from it and landed back at base on one engine. Another incident occurred when the brakes failed while taxiing around the perimeter track in Oxford T1192 causing it to collide with a Beaufighter of 404 Squadron. Both occupants from T1192 were unharmed. Two Norwegian aircraft and a single 235 aircraft kept under observation vessels between Kristiansand and Ålesund. 'G' 235, short of fuel due to a faulty petrol feed, landed at Crimmond. The last operation with 18 Mosquitoes was uneventful. The Beaufighter crews were not required to fly during the day and a party of Canadians, led by Schoales, requisitioned an aircrew bus which they drove into Aberdeen, reporting upon their return that a successful reconnaissance without casualties had been made.

Constant sorties were flown over Kristiansand during 4 October but they found nothing worth attacking. The flak was heavy at Lista aerodrome, one Beaufighter dropped out with engine trouble and the patrolling Warwick guided him to base. Moon Rover patrols were aborted during the evening as strong northerly winds battered the airfield. The weather deteriorated, resulting in only two aircraft, 'N' 333 and 'H' 333 taking to the air the next day. It gradually improved but no further operations took place. Although a conference was held with all COs and the group captain about the possibility of a night operation against shipping near Kristiansand this was cancelled at 1900 hrs. This was a good thing as the serviceability state of aircraft had dropped on all squadrons. The most some could make ready was six.

On 7 October all squadrons were released for ground training. The serviceability state of aircraft soared to 12 each from the three squadrons. The various trades had worked throughout the night with torches at the dispersal points or in the blister hangars. The wing began searching in earnest on 8 October. Individual sorties took place: Squadron Leader Stanley 'Baby' Nunn led one between Marstein Light and Bommelfjord, sighting several small vessels, and Flying Officer C H Foster in 'R' 144 LZ538 led a formation composed of eight Beaufighters and two Mosquitoes into the air at 12.45 hours. Foster took off, then circled to let the others gather formation.He found his bearings from the Bommelfjord to Utvaer Light just west of Sula and searched for possible targets along the coast. At 12.48 hours (German time), *Boknafjord* and *Süderpip* reported being strafed by two Mosquitoes. Further north in Leirvik, one hour later, convoy NK.21 was found by a pair of Mosquitoes, and a U-boat was sighted, which was soon identified as U-483, a Type VIIC commanded by Hans-Joachim von Morstein, aged 35. One of his U-boat colleagues, Rolf Nollmann, commander of U-1199, had left Bergen on 14 September. Nollmann, once off north-eastern Scotland, spent 31 days patrolling the waters between Peterhead and Aberdeen, quite possibly sending reports back about the strike wing's activities.

Continuing on, Mosquitoes led by Flight Lieutenant George Nicholls started patrolling at 13.45 hours and began investigating leads, as three vessels had been seen in a distant fjord. A minute later, at 13.46, a merchantman was seen and three armed trawlers came into view. All opened fire. A hail of accurate anti-aircraft ammunition caused the fire extinguishers on 'F' 248, flown by Nicholls, to operate. He turned westwards believing his aircraft was hit. At 13.51 the engines appeared all right, and he continued the patrol. Further vessels were sighted at 13.55 hours, apparently a 2,500 ton tanker being led by a small vessel, possibly an armed trawler, followed by two more astern. Three minutes later Tsetse pilot Flying Officer 'Wally' Woodcock flying 'H' 248, shouted 'Bandit'; one duly appeared, fired a two second burst and then disappeared. At 14.10 hours one small merchantman and flakship was spotted while searching for targets, convoy NB.17 was evidently proceeding from Hjeltefjord towards Bergen. Black clusters of flak surrounded the aircraft as they swept in amid anti-aircraft fire from vessels and shore batteries. Nicholls opened up with cannon and machine-gun fire at 1,000 yards, rounds hitting the bridge and amidships. 'F' 248 received a jolt as it flew through a hail of light machine-gun fire which smashed into the tail. More damage was inflicted on the vessel as the Tsetse Mosquito 'H' 248 followed behind and pumped it with 57mm cannon shells. Four rounds were fired and then a stoppage occurred. Hits were claimed on both vessels, and fires started. The Mosquitoes broke away and made their way back to Banff. Nicholls wrote: 'I could hear the cannon shells hitting us for a good half minute; the steering was bloody awful afterwards. Some of the tail was shot away.' With light damage, the boat limped along. The attack left five wounded and killed two German sailors. Once in a safe harbour the five wounded seamen were taken to a local hospital.

A new system was tried by those at Banff when 18 Group adopted a technique known as the Drem system (after the Scottish airfield where it originated). The idea was to position the strike wing off the enemy coast at first light, in order to attack the convoys before they turned into a defended anchorage. Drem was most appropriate because of the open stretch of water between Stavanger and Kristiansand South, and it was first used on 9 October 1944 adopting 16 Group's tactic at Banff of a dawn strike, a method developed and perfected by the North Coates Wing during the previous August. The Germans realised the strike wing could not fly in tight formation in the dark so there were a few hours before 'first light' when the convoys could move whilst the aircraft were still flying over the sea towards them.

On a dark and cheerless morning at 04.17 hours, a Warwick of 281 Squadron, piloted by Flying Officer Jenner took off from Banff to lay the Drem flares, disappearing into the blackness ahead of the main force. Wing Commander Tony Gadd then led a force consisting of eight Beaufighters from 404 Squadron, armed with armour-piercing rockets, six of 144 Squadron's with cannon and four with torpedoes and eight 235 Mosquitoes acting as fighter escort and armed with cannon and machine-guns. They started with a briefing at 03.00 hours. Wing Commander 'Ed' Pierce and his Essex born navigator, Flying Officer Charles Corder CGM, CdeG, who was on his second tour, were tasked to lead the formation. All took off singly between 04.56 and 05.29 hours and flew 'in loose order' to the rendezvous at various heights with navigation lights on. On the way across six illuminated neutral Swedish merchantmen were nearly mistaken for the sea markers.

At 06.10 the Warwick dropped the markers made up of seven MkII and MkVI marine markers, 17 flame floats and 50 drift lights; all in a circle of a radius of three miles in a position off Skudenes Fjord, a hundred miles west of Stavanger. At 06.27 and thirty miles on from the Swedish vessels the formation sighted the Drem flares and circled them while forming up into battle order. At 06.49 hours in faint dawn light the wing set course south at an altitude of 100 feet. Reaching the designated position of 59.00N x 05.00E at 06.55 hours, they climbed to 2,500 feet in the twilight. The intelligence proved correct, a merchantman convoy was twenty miles ahead in the distance, very close inshore off Egersund. The strike leader announced that he could see three vessels. Yonge, leading 235 Squadron, broke in by saying he thought there were several. Being top cover at 4,000 feet he was in a better position to see. Yonge then counted eleven exactly and gave this over VHF. The convoy consisted of five merchantmen and six flak-ships in three columns travelling at six knots. Indication of this strike force on the German radar screen was given at 07.01 hours. There followed a brief debate with the Torpedo Beaufighter leader as to whether the target was too formidable for them to attack. Nine minutes later the aircraft pounced through an intense barrage of light and heavy flak.

At 07.10 hours six cannon Beaufighters engaged the largest merchantman and an escort nearby, then turned and attacked the rear merchantman and escort. Seeing the size of the targets and failing to observe any hostile aircraft Yonge took three Mosquitoes into the mêlée as anti-flak. Almost simultaneously these Mosquitoes attacked the three leading vessels and escorting flakships with their cannon, reserving their 0.303 ammunition for hostile aircraft. Between these two sweeps they smothered the vessels' surfaces to good effect neutralising incoming flak. Three other Mosquitoes stayed aloft as fighter protection. Seconds after the cannon attack, a wave of eight 404 Beaufighters went in, releasing their rockets at ranges from 700 to 450 yards and at heights between 400 and 500 feet. They hit the leading escorts, then the remaining vessels. The Canadian crews claimed 34 'dry' and 16 'wet' hits, on both escorts and merchantmen. Four Torbeaus attacked the largest two merchantmen, their aircraft skimming low just above the water; they skilfully dropped the torpedoes from 150 feet and at a distance of 1,000 yards, which resulted in at least two hits.

Once the Germans had recovered from the surprise of an attack at that early hour in the morning, intense flak was directed at the incoming aircraft from both merchantmen and their escorts and nearby coastal batteries. Tracer, rocket and cannon splashes and torpedoes exploding made results difficult to observe. Under billows of black smoke the crewmen of the 1,953 ton merchantman *Rudolf Oldendorf*, which was transporting building material, thought they could see torpedo tracks running towards them. In the wheelhouse Captain August Rach tried evasive action, but at least one torpedo hit the vessel, others narrowly missing. But the cannon and rocket fire was devastatingly effective. Four gunners on the forecastle perished and one gunner was wounded when cannon rounds smashed into the gun platform. *O.N. Anderson – UJ. 1711* of 485 tons was badly damaged – the submarine chaser was hit by torpedoes to her boilers and the main engine room and steering gear were put out of action as she circled out of control, burning furiously and making water. Cannon shells raked her. One seaman was thrown into the water and seven men were wounded during the attack. Armour-piercing rockets struck below the waterline of *Rudau*, a merchantman of 2,883 tons. Her crew struggled to save the cargo of smoke screen dispensers bound for Narvik, aided by some sailors on shore, who made frequent attempts to fire a cable to the stricken vessel. The Norwegian vessel *Norgat* was holed below the waterline, and one-compartment floods made the vessel weak. The German crew worked desperately against time; aided by water pumps they succeeded in repairing her port side. The 1,116 ton Norwegian *Sarp* was damaged, stopped and reported one civilian killed. At 07.28 hours tugs came out to attempt to tow *Rudau* to shallow water. The flakships suffered casualties: onboard K.02 one was dead, one missing and ten seriously and 16 lightly wounded; on the training boat *Stolpe* three sailors lay wounded.

At 07.15 hours, five minutes after engaging the convoy, the entire wing was on its way back to Banff, leaving the enemy in confusion. Only three aircraft were damaged. The port wing of 'J' 144, piloted by Flying Officer Maurice Exton, was perforated by flak and there was a line of cannon holes along the length of the fuselage. He was unhappily making 160 knots and hardly had the strength to hold his wing up. Yonge escorted him home while the Warwick 'Plainsong' failed to answer the distress calls. In sheer exhaustion, Exton nearly ditched ten miles from the Scottish coast. With Yonge's encouragement the young officer bravely continued and finally made base and did a good landing, as did Squadron Leader Duncanson of 144 Squadron who had been wounded in the foot with shrapnel. Group Captain Max Aitken was impatient again at the slowness of flying control in getting the damaged aircraft down. Everyone safely touched down between 08.30 and 09.43 hours, however. One of the last 235 Squadron Mosquitoes to land had been delayed due to undercarriage trouble. Flight Lieutenant Richardson had overcome the problem and had eventually arrived at Egersund 19 minutes after the attack. His navigator, Flying Officer 'Red' Godwin, counted eight vessels remaining. A single 248 Squadron aircraft was then dispatched to confirm this information. Flight Lieutenant D Crimp was airborne at 10.16 hours, making landfall at 11.36 hours under a dense barrage of anti-aircraft fire. While sweeping over Egersund the navigator, Flying Officer John Bird, assessed the damage. Below the recovery had already begun. Minesweeper M.1 went to the assistance of the stricken K.2 flakship whilst the tug *Lom* slipped its moorings and went to help *Norgat* and *Olwe* sail into Egersund harbour. Medical personnel brought first aid equipment to the jetties. *Rudau* was beached in Lundevikbukt, south Egerøy, but it would be a week before it was repaired. The merchantman *Sarp* put aground in Hovlandsvik, east Egerøy, and was sunk. Later the vessel, after being salvaged and refloated, was sighted under repair in February 1945 in Sarpsborg.

Still photographs taken during the strike showed that two merchantmen had been fatally damaged, and that serious damage had been inflicted on three other vessels, and although this verdict was accepted at the time, post-war records show only one merchantman of 1,959 tons and an escort vessel were sunk and another merchantman of 1,116 tons seriously damaged. Strike crews were joyful on learning of a successful strike. A de-briefing report reads:

'Torpedoed two merchantmen, setting them on fire, and seriously damaged another merchantman and two escort vessels with rocket and cannon fire.'

The German account of the strike of 9 October, which was made public the next day on Berlin Radio stated:

'Escort vessels and flak of a German convoy off the south-west coast of Norway yesterday morning brought down nine enemy aircraft in seven minutes. Further aircraft were probably destroyed. 22 [*sic*] had attacked the convoy with torpedoes, bombs, and machine guns. The first four aircraft were brought down at long range, thanks to the defensive fire immediately put up by the German guns. In fierce battles with the aircraft, which attacked in several waves, five or more aircraft were brought down and two German launches were sunk. Some of the remaining aircraft were set on fire and were last seen flying low over the sea, so they may be presumed to have been destroyed.'

German claims for shooting down aircraft were grossly exaggerated, since none were lost, but this tends to suggest that there was at least some element of genuine belief among the German crews that gunners were finding their mark. This is likely to have arisen from a feature of the Beaufighter's performance. When the aircraft was operating at full throttle at low level, as it would have been attempting to get away after the attack, a thick dark brown exhaust trail was left behind. This gave the impression that the engines were on fire.

An extract from a letter dated 9 October 1944, sent to Banff from Headquarters at Coastal Command, Northwood reads: 'Your strike this morning seems to have been extremely successful, and it looks as though you sank two or more ships. The rendezvous at first light with the aid of flares seems to have been a very good piece of work, and I think that the chaps ought to be congratulated on carrying out this difficult operation so successfully.'

On 11 October, Group Captain Max Aitken left Banff in his personal plane 'MA-01' for a coastal patrol off Stadlandet near Vågsøy. On this brief flight one merchantman and a number of fishing boats were spotted. Shore batteries opened fire, so they turned back, but navigator Flying Officer 'Micky' Potts noted the position for future reference. They landed back after a trip of four hours and ten minutes. With persistent rain and poor visibility continuing from the previous day all the squadrons were given a brief respite from operational flying which was then extended to 12 October.

333 Squadron ground staff were able to finish off their new crew room, while Aitken gave a lecture on beam approach to aircrew. A small celebration was held in the officers' mess at lunchtime. After an announcement that the King had granted awards to a number of aircrew on the base, the whole of 235 Squadron had a big party in the upstairs dining room at the Seafield Arms in Chapel Street, Whitehills.

The following day Canadians helped in welcoming eight journalists from Scottish based press, representing 11 newspapers. The correspondents came to Banff to see Aitken and his 'gang' at work and report back on the way the battle was being conducted. Flight Lieutenant Harold Mitchell, one of the public relations officers and former proprietor and managing editor of the *East London News Agency*, gave them a briefing and programme and showed them to their accommodation. The air was buzzing with activity as air tests were carried out while the journalists stowed their baggage and had tea. They then saw a strike film in the station theatre, the same one the aircrews had seen earlier during the week. Afterwards they boarded a three ton lorry and went to the far side of the aerodrome where a tethered Beaufighter fired cannon and rocket projectiles into the sea. A talk was then given by the armaments officer on the torpedo and rocket projectile. The WAAF driver then dropped them outside the officers' mess for drinks at the 'Strike Bar' after which they enjoyed a three course meal with cheese and biscuits with brandy or whisky. Just before midnight they turned in.

Operations re-commenced at 05.55 on Friday 13 October. The Drem system was used again. The press correspondents were awoken at 03.00 hours by the duty ordeal officer and Flight Lieutenant Harold Mitchell and after a meal of egg and bacon at 04.30 they listened to the briefing of operational crews by Squadron Leader Maurice, 'A' Flight commander from 248 Squadron. He was in fact a Frenchman, Lieutenant Max Guedj, who had requested permission on 26 March 1942 to adopt a *nom de guerre* to protect his family as he had received reports that his father had been imprisoned in Morocco because of pro-British sympathies. He had selected the name Jean Maurice on joining the RAF. His operational flying commenced with 248 Squadron in February 1942 with his navigator Flight Sergeant Charles Corder. Maurice was the first French airman to receive the DSO in March 1943. By the spring of 1944 he held the rank of squadron leader. He led the force of 20 Mosquitoes and 16 Beaufighters away at 05.13 hours, briefed to patrol from Utsira to Kristiansand searching for merchantmen and U-boats. The correspondents stood watching the departure from the flying control tower. Afterwards they had tea. Group Captain Max Aitken DSO DFC then gave a talk on the new method of attack by his 'ship busters'. One reporter wrote: 'he lives, talks, and works at the tempo of a rocket projectile.' 'He had a constant interest in the well-being of his crews', wrote another. As Squadron Leader Wilson and Flight Lieutenant Harold Mitchell conducted the tour, miles away the force was running into quite a bit of difficulty.

Low cloud base and drizzle greeted the force 15 miles from where the marine markers were due to be dropped by 'V' 281. The appalling weather, quiet contrary to the meteorological office forecast, prevented forming up; nevertheless, several crews carried out lengthy individual searches along the Norwegian coast. Flying Officer Ross DFC ran into a very turbulent cloud and was tossed about. Unable to control his Mosquito it finally flipped onto its back. His navigator, Flying Officer Hollinson DFC, persuaded him not to bail out. Eventually control was re-established. Flying Officer J H Symons flying 'F' 404 mentioned at de-briefing seeing a large orange flash at 07.43 hours at 59.19N/04.07E, which may have been 'K' 248 which was posted as missing. Maurice ordered a search for the missing aircraft but they found no trace of crew or wreckage, and other searches by 18 Group aircraft proved fruitless. Sadly, the crew of the aircraft, Flight Lieutenant George Nicholls and Flying Officer Anthony Hanson were presumed to have perished in a crash. It seemed the tumultuous cloud that Ross had trouble with could have been responsible. Flight Lieutenant Turner in 'E' 235 also sustained damage to his tailplane from flak fragments which were embedded in the plywood.

The eight correspondents from the press were then invited to watch the interrogation of aircrew upon their return from an operational strike, see a Mosquito being prepared, then listen to a lecture on escape and evasion. After a general tour of the airfield they completed their visit at the officers' mess having watched a mock attack on smoke floats in the water off Portsoy by all serviceable aircraft. According to one journalist writing on 14 October – 'It was a fantastic sight finally seeing these coastal Mosquitoes.' Unfortunately the visit was marred by 248 Squadron's first loss of a crew (Nicholls and Hanson) since August 1944 when the squadron had lost five crews in operations over the Gironde.

That evening the station cinema was packed, with all aircrew called together and given a pep talk by Group Captain Aitken about the local police curfews and, among other things, plans to visit their respective crew rooms regularly in order to receive verbal and written notices. Earlier during the day quizzes had taking place on aircraft and shipping recognition, the winning squadron won a round of drinks at The Seafield Arms, paid for by the station commander.

In the afternoon of 15 October, 21 Beaufighters, with 17 Mosquitoes engaged as anti-flak aircraft took off at 12.40 hours crossing the Scottish coast. Twelve of the Beaufighters carried rockets. The force went down to 50 feet above the waves. Squadron Leader Christison led them again, together with Atkinson leading the Mosquitoes. This trip was over new territory and somewhat longer than normal. Landfall was made just off Denmark, and the formation then turned towards the southern Norwegian coast where landfall was made at Homborsund. Readjusting to battle formation at 15.16, they found a 1,202 ton tanker, the German *Ingeborg*, sailing between Justøya and Lillesand, south-east of Kristiansand on a voyage from Oslo to Kristiansand with a cargo of petroleum. With its single escort, the steamship Vp. 1605 *Mosel* of 426 tons in position 58.08N-0817E, the *Ingeborg* was now sailing under the Norwegian flag as *Inger Johanne* also known as *Nachschubtanker Norwegen 15*. The *Mosel*'s captain was ordered to escort *Inger Johanne* only between Kristiansand and Arendal.

As the attack began two sections of Mosquitoes were directed to shoot up the flakship as 88mm flak came up to greet them, followed by rounds from *Mosel*'s 37mm and 20mm anti-aircraft guns and RAG. Led by 404 (Canadian) Squadron, their Beaufighters worked in pairs firing salvoes of rockets and cannon helped by the Torbeaus of 144 Squadron. Columns of spray rose into the air; the tanker's cargo caught fire and engulfed it in flames with a plume of black smoke. A concentration of rounds found their mark and exploded, the debris from the explosion caught 'A' 404-NE699, causing serious damage to the flying surfaces. A large area was a mass of flames. Only burning oil remained on the surface with the floating debris, the remnants of which later washed ashore at Ågerøya near Lillesand. On board there had been a crew of 16. Several survivors were seen bobbing in the water after the explosion; 15 were recorded as having been killed, and only one survivor was pulled from the sea near Lillesand by a rescue craft. He was heavily burned and later died in hospital. Today what little remains of the *Inger Johanne* rests at a depth of five to 40 metres at Skaarebøkslene.

As the tanker exploded Vp. 1605 *Mosel* was damaged by 25lb rockets that hit the hull and boiler room. But the crew fought on. When the Beaufighters and Mosquitoes cleared the area at 15.37 hours Vp. 1605 was alight from bow to stern, and with the last rounds fired bursting above it, it too exploded and sank with 21 crew perishing.*

Black smoke from the tanker was in sharp contrast to the grey sea below and was visible from over 50 miles away. The strike wing suffered no losses although a few aircraft sustained light damage. Warrant Officer W J Jackson from Winnipeg, on his fourth strike brought his Beaufighter back with a threadbare tailplane, and was promptly christened 'Lucky' Jackson. Flight Lieutenant George Lord DFC CdeG, of 235 Squadron reported: 'One minute the tanker was there, erupting in flames, then only a large plume of smoke and a ring of fire on the sea.' Another Beaufighter pilot on this operation said in an Air Ministry Bulletin: 'As we passed over, we fired our cannon into the smoke and flames.'

The following day 235, 248, 144 and 404 Squadrons were released for training. 235 Squadron practiced air firing against targets towed by the Miles, which had flown over from Leuchars. Meanwhile, six crews of 333 (Norwegian) Squadron were briefed in the operations building to carry out searches for enemy shipping. Shortly afterwards they flew out via Sumburgh. One of the Norwegian crews, including Captain Erling Ulleberg Johansen, reached the patrol area without incident; en route over Åalsund Johansen saw merchantmen through a break in the cloud, anchored in the southern and northern harbour of the town. He then turned south-west, pushed open the throttles and continued checking the Leads. Vessels were sighted at Maløy, Rovdefjord and Asknoll, and his navigator reported back their discoveries as they turned west for Banff. Further roving sweeps along the Norwegian coast were flown at intervals throughout the day.

At 11.30 on 17 October, Banff Mosquitoes had landed at Sumburgh, led by Wing Commander John Yonge. At the briefing it was stressed that the crews were not allowed to attack vessels under 1,500 tons unless they were escorted or showed hostility. Eighteen aircraft, nine each from 235 and 248 Squadrons took off into the gloom for an armed patrol near Gossen, hunting for targets seen by 333 Squadron's reconnaissance earlier in the morning. Yonge dodged up into the Leads and inside the islands to look for enemy shipping. In position 62.50N/06.40E, just west of Ålesund and in very poor visibility he spotted a vessel. Heeding the warning he passed the 700 ton vessel in Haro fjord. Kptlt.d.R. Ulm, commanding Vp. 6801 *Viking*, was towing a target buoy and heard the engine sounds of approaching enemy aircraft. He promptly fired on the rear of the formation. Yonge therefore decided to strike back. They circled out of the area to come in for attack, drop-tanks were jettisoned and he had just given the order 'Prepare for attack, target 9 o'clock, turning left' when his starboard engine failed owing to an air lock in the petrol system. Two MkVIs and one MkXVIII wheeled into attack, momentarily losing sight as the sea and sky combined. Flight Lieutenant Roy Orrock however, saw it. The anti-aircraft guns fired wildly again at the incoming aircraft, but were out of range and the red tracer arched back down into the sea. The attackers got through without any loss and the pilots concentrated on the target ahead, with their safety catches off. There was a deafening roar as cannon and machine-gun fire streamed out. Flying Officer 'Wally' Woodcock in the Tsetse pumped out 57mm shells and two punched holes into the funnel. Flying Officer James 'Jimmy' Ross in 'P' 235 struck the bows with his cannon. *Viking* was now ablaze aft and amidships. All three aircraft reported hits and rejoined the strike leader. Because of water leaks at the aft she was grounded at Hogstenen.

Fortunately Yonge had got the starboard engine going again, but he could not find the target. Nothing else appeared during their patrol so the Mosquitoes set course for

---

*Bjarte and Siri Skar, two Scandinavian divers, found the wreck of the *Mosel* Vp. 1605 in the summer of 2001 at a depth of 50 metres; the position is being kept secret to avoid looting.

home. As they crossed the North Sea flying conditions worsened by the minute and some aircraft became separated. They flew into thick low cloud in between heavy rainstorms. It was a dangerous moment with visibility down to one and half miles. Yonge's lead section began to climb; on either side the remaining sections opened out, trying to get over the front, but the storm persisted. They climbed cautiously but saw nothing except cloud and after an hour and a half with rain pelting against the windscreens and flying on instruments, Yonge received a message from a WAAF radio operator as they neared base that the weather was slightly clearer at Sumburgh. He switched on his radio telephone, 'All aircraft head for Sumburgh'. The airfield appeared to be deserted as the aircraft circled above. All landed safely. After they had refuelled and the crews had had an operational meal, they set off independently for Banff between 17.40 and 18.00 hours, landing in semi darkness having flown through the most appalling weather.

Those not on duty in mid afternoon had watched a football match take place between 333 Squadron and 8144 Service Echelon, with a crowd cheering on both sides. The final score was 9-4 respectively. In the evening Wing Commander McConnell brought Yonge a stiff drink and praised his airmanship. They were joined in the 'Strike' bar in the officers' mess by Flight Lieutenant Ward who had been posted back as adjutant to 248 Squadron. Overnight McConnell had his staff car stolen from outside the officers' mess. Yonge drove him around but could not locate it.

One hour before dawn on 19 October a convoy slipped out from Stadlandet, Norway, consisting of six escorts and 13 merchantmen with one trailing a barge, followed by another at Hellisøy that headed south. The crews drawn from the various squadrons at Banff were briefed at 09.30 hours. It was determined that if no shipping were sighted the formation would split into two then sweep north to south. The southern force was to be Mosquitoes the northern Beaufighters. Twenty-one Banff aircraft made up from 235, 248 and 333 Squadron flew out at 13.15 hours, on an armed Rover with 19 Beaufighters towards Askvoll anchorage. They crossed the enemy coast near Utvaer in order to attack vessels reported to be in Askvoll fjord. However, a low cloud base obscured the target area. Wing Commander Richard Atkinson instructed Squadron Leader Bob Schoales to turn north as previously agreed. The Mosquitoes swung south near Utvaer at 15.22 hours along the Norwegian coastline and flew over vessels at anchor, which sounded the alarm. A Very light burst below but the aircraft kept on track. At 15.27 hours four vessels were spotted line astern. Vp. 5111 was leading two miles ahead of *Süderpiep*, behind a tanker of 4,000 tons with another escort at the rear in Hjeltefjord. At 15.31 hours, after a briefing by the strike leader, the formation attacked from a height of between 50 to 200 feet, Mark IVs with cannon and machine-gun fire and the Tsetse with their 57mm cannon. Many hits were seen on all the vessels. The leading escort Vp. 5111 was raked by the machine guns, rounds peppering the bridge and amidships triggering a fire. In the first pass seven men were seriously wounded. On board crews battled to repair their vessel, while others put out the flames. It was a hard struggle to save her from sinking as boxes containing 88mm ammunition exploded for over an hour. With the vessel eventually water tight they made for Bergen at nightfall. One of the crew from Vp. 5111 said later that: 'We had been attacked by an aircraft carrying a big gun, emitting a long flame.' *Süderpiep* was then singled out by three Mosquitoes, their rounds ripping through the wooden deck sending sharp shards flying into the air, catching one of their attackers.

U-382 type VIIC sailed from La Pallice on 10 September, and together with U-673 set course for Norway, and both reached Bergen on 19 October. Owing to bomb damage and cramped conditions in Bergen, both U-boats set course for Stavanger. U-382, commanded by Oblt Hans-Dietrich Wilke, had surfaced near the *Süderpiep* as the

Mosquitoes swept in. His gunners returned fire, and tracer poured up hitting 'F' 235 flown by Warrant Officers Ian Martin DFC, and Ian Ramsay. Both men had flown one operational tour together and volunteered for an extension; this was their final combat operation. At 15.36 hours a message was heard by the Norwegian Petty Officer Mykkeltvedtt: 'I am hit, navigator to require escort'. A further message was received on VHF that both crew were hit and required escort.

The aircraft was shaking badly; they were in a hopeless position and the only option was to ditch. Martin managed to lose height steadily, trying to put it down as gently as possible. There was deceleration and their bodies were rammed forward. At 15.40 hours the aircraft broke in two; the nose sank rapidly and freezing cold water engulfed the cockpit. Ramsay groggily unclipped his Sutton harness and levered himself out of the top escape hatch, registering some pain in his legs as he shot straight through. Freezing water covered him but he reached the aircraft dinghy and hauled himself in. There was a heavy swell and the dinghy was buffeted along. Looking around, he could not see his pilot. Meanwhile Squadron Leader Maurice in 'M' 248 reported seeing one survivor waiting in the dinghy. Petty Officer Sjølie piloting HR279 and navigator Mykkeltvedtt noted the position 6053N/0448E and that a single survivor was seen in the dinghy waving and being approached by fishing vessels. As they all headed back it was thought to be Martin as it was his voice that everyone had last heard on the radio.

Warrant Officer Ian Ramsay said after the war in July 1945, when interviewed for the 235 Squadron magazine *Chocks Away*:

'I looked upwards from the cockpit and saw the surface of the sea above and the light of the evening sky above that. I was surprised when I bobbed up to the top like a cork. Despite both legs being broken I clambered into the dinghy which had also come up when the aircraft broke up.'

On the shore at Øygarden Island local fishermen saw a twin-engine aircraft in the water for a few seconds before it sank. The men did not waste time and jumped into rowing boats, altogether six made for the site of the sunken Mosquito. Ramsay began to drift then suddenly hands grabbed him and he could feel himself being lifted into a wooden boat. Safely ashore at the jetty the Norwegian fishermen explained to the airman that he needed proper treatment. They apologised to him, saying there was no alternative. The Germans came with a doctor and took him away on a stretcher. Once at Oslo hospital, surgeons removed some fingers because of frostbite. Ramsay remained in a hospital bed for some time while his wounds healed; it did not stop the airman attempting to escape, although he was recaptured twice.

Flying Officers Geoff Rouse and Ray Hall of 235 Squadron led this section. Ray Hall recalls:

'My pilot Geoff Rouse and I were leaders of the section, Martin and Ramsay were in 'F for Freddie'. There was very intense opposition from the two vessels and shore; a burst hit their aircraft and smoke appeared. Ian put out a distress call on the emergency channel and they then ditched; the camouflage blended in with the sea in the evening light as the aircraft disappeared in two halves. The Mosquito front half tended to go down, leaving the rear floating (a welcome advance on the Beaufighters, which went down in 90 seconds). We circled around to see what we could do, but when we left only one person was making his way to the dinghy.'

Vp. 5111 and *Süderpiep* were seen to be smoking as Mosquitoes departed the area although neither of the vessels actually sank. Warrant Officer Ian Martin DFC is presumed to have been unable to escape from his aircraft. The tide later washed ashore an undercarriage wheel from 'F' 235 near Hellisøy Lighthouse. After a three and a half hour flight both formations returned to Banff.

Away from operations that day Canadian personnel among the units had been voting for candidates to legislature in their home province in a polling booth set up in 404's education officer's hut. Some armament spares were running low on the base and a Beaufighter was dispatched to RAF Leuchars for them. Lieutenant Hoff began trade testing of airmen, elsewhere navigators from 235, 248 and 333 Squadrons attended a lecture on photography in the station cinema.

The weather curtailed any flying on 20 October. 18 Group headquarters and RAF Banff received a signal from Coastal Command Headquarters stating that 144 and 404 Squadrons would be moving to RAF Dallachy immediately. Despite some opposition towards this suggested redeployment when it was discussed at 18 Group and Northwood it went ahead. A letter was drafted on 16 October 1944. Wing Commander Ed Pierce DFC got in touch with Group Captain Max Aitken to see if the move could be 'scrubbed', however he could not influence these orders. Elsewhere on the aerodrome 235 Squadron aircrew scrambled onboard a liberty coach bound for Aberdeen, while their commanding officer held interviews for new aircrew, all being posted to 'A' Flight.

On 21 October Coastal Command ordered an immediate strike. Seventy-four crews were briefed by Squadron Leader Maurice for a strike in the Bergen neighbourhood at 09.00 hours. Taking off at 11.45 hours, there were four Mosquitoes and 15 Beaufighters in the first section which flew to Askvoll and a second section, which consisted of eight Mosquitoes, four Tsetses, and six Beaufighters. Landfall was made at Utvaer. Captain Erling Ullberg Johansen's Mosquito sped ahead of the main force. He was to radio back by saying one of three things; 'No Joy', 'Target' or 'I can't get in'. First he checked Askvoll for shipping, but nothing worthy of a strike was present. He radioed 'No Joy'. With no worthwhile objective the formation separated into two sections. Twenty-three aircraft turned northwards as far as Stadtlandet. From there six 404 Beaufighters returned to base. The second section headed south, with Maurice leading. A good landfall was made at Utsira and Captain Johansen flew ahead in Mosquito 'E' 333 down the main coastal shipping route carrying out a search of Haugesund harbour. Johansen tried to advise the strike leader that merchantmen were birthed within the harbour but his VHF did not function so they never heard him.

Maurice did the reconnoitring himself, complete with both sections which had combined again. Heavy flak opened up on them as they sped over a large collection of merchantmen. It was too formidable so the formation split again, as prearranged. On the southern excursion at 14.41 hours a vessel was sighted at anchor, estimated to be a 3,000 ton merchantman. Maurice announced: 'Ships in harbour. Target at 9 o'clock. Prepare to attack. Drop your tanks. Attack, attack, attack.' Further reports of other vessels came over the radio telephone and the aircraft dived in sections. Maurice lined up the small cargo vessel, *Taube*, in his sights and attacked from 150 feet with cannon and machine-gun fire, it was left smoking with one sailor falling into the water. Anchored at a wooden quay the 1,923 ton *Eckenheim* crewmen were unloading crates of Bergen sardines and a few passengers. People were stunned as the attack commenced. Civilians dived for any available cover as the place 'rocked with explosions', according to one eyewitness. Yonge got his cannon burst into the middle of the *Eckenheim*. His first entered a warehouse or the harbour master's office opposite. As Yonge broke over the mast the merchantman began to burn. In quick succession *Eckenheim* was hit by the rocket Beaufighters and the Tsetse Mosquitoes. 404 Squadron crews attacked from 3,000 to 100 feet, range 400 to 1,500 yards with cannon, and from 900 to 500 yards with rockets. Four claimed 18 dry and four underwater hits. Cannon fire hit the bridge and spread along the decks to amidships. The freighter's structure was holed by 22 rockets above and below the waterline, and was struck by 14 Tsetse 57mm shells. Onboard fire had taken hold amidships. Badly holed and taking in water with compartments flooded under the weight of such destructive firepower, she began to sink as smoke belched from the bows and amidships.

The Norwegian steamship *Vestra* of 1,422 tons was next to be targeted. Her crew were Norwegians but six German soldiers manned the anti-aircraft guns. With a cargo of limestone *Vestra* was laid at anchorage while on a journey from Nordmøre to Sauda. As the attack commenced the German soldiers were below deck on their coffee break, normally taken between 15.00 and 15.30 hours, and never got a chance to man the anti-aircraft guns. After several hits by cannon, machine guns and rockets the vessel sank bow first.

A Tsetse Mosquito turned for a second attack scoring at least two further hits on the *Eckenheim* which was now engulfed in thick black smoke, the superstructure ripped open by the Tsetse shells. Vp. 5310 and S. 11 suffered damage. The Mosquitoes and Beaufighters headed back out to sea in loose formation whilst Squadron Leader Maurice circled the area outside the harbour to observe their results. In Haugesund harbour, wreckage and bodies floated on the surface, it was a scene of carnage as two entire complements of crews perished. Remarkably, there were few casualties amongst the civilians during the attack, despite the fact that some had experienced some frightful near misses.*

During the strike return gunfire was accurate and 'M' 404, crewed by Squadron Leader W R Christison and Flight Lieutenant Toon returned with a large hole in the port tail-plane. 'T' 248 had a portion of its port wing badly damaged by flak and Squadron Leader 'Baby' Nunn had a hole smashed through the roundel of his starboard wing. Tsetse Mosquito 'I' 248 piloted by Flying Officer Robert Driscoll and navigator Tony Hannant, in PZ251, crashed into the sea three miles off shore, having been severely damaged by flak. Maurice last saw Driscoll at 15.45 hours off Haugesund harbour. The strike leader sighted a large patch of green fluorescent dye on the surface and wreckage in the water near the harbour as he circled overhead. A number of fishing boats in the vicinity were seen making towards the stain. Despite attempts by these fishing vessels to assist Driscoll and Hannant they both drowned near to where their aircraft went down. Mrs Driscoll received the unwelcome news. At her recent wedding the bride had worn a pair of gold RAF brooches on her dress, a present from the bridegroom.

Hours later in the darkness, Luftwaffe barge BP 31 searched the area, trawling back and forth, but never managed to locate the wreckage or bodies. The *Eckenheim* was so badly damaged after the attack that it took the Germans 60 days to repair aided by a pump steamer before it was sea worthy. Leading Aircraftman Ron Brooks, a radio operator serving with 'C' Flight 248 Squadron, saw Tsetse 'I' 248 off:

'I helped see this aircraft off on the operation and I was detailed to be there when it returned. Unfortunately 'I –Ink' did not come back and somebody shouted to me "Don't wait, he isn't coming." I have never forgotten Driscoll and Hannant.'

The remainder of the force made for Banff, landing safely between 16.00-16.45 hours. Visibility was poor on their return and the aerodrome was lit up, this unfortunately

---

*The Norwegian Government in exile made protests about this operation, complaining that a Norwegian fishing vessel of 75 tons had been wrongly identified as a merchantman off the south-western coast of Norway and targeted.

dimmed the lights elsewhere on the base as one of the generators needed to be repaired. Flying Officer J Symons, a young Canadian, landed safely after completing his first tour. His father, working for the Canadian Legion, was in attendance to see his son's return and later dined in the officers' mess. Out on the aerodrome in the darkness a pilot from 235 Squadron chose to ignore the signals from the airman guiding him in and taxied his Mosquito into a ditch, causing serious damage. His logbook was endorsed with 'Gross Carelessness'. As the intelligence was gathered a tot of rum was given to each member of air crew from a soda siphon.

During the afternoon some of those on the base had heard a running commentary from the German radio in Norway on the strike wing's movements along the coast. This was picked up by the wing signals section and translated by a Lieutenant of the Norwegian Navy. It read:

14.07 – 17 aircraft 90 kilometres north-west of Bergen, course north-east.
14.10 – 17 aircraft 60 kilometres north-west of Bergen, decreasing height, course south.
14.20 – 17 aircraft 90 kilometres north-west of Bergen.
14.25 – Passing west of Bergen.
14.26 – 20 aircraft 140 kilometres north of Bergen, course south.
14.40 – 6 Beaufighters/6 Mosquitoes 75 kilometres from Stavanger, course south.
14.50 – 6 Beaufighters/6 Mosquitoes 75 kilometres from Stavanger, course south.
15.05 – Enemy aircraft, set course for coast near Stavanger.

Yonge wrote: 'This was reasonably accurate. No mention was made of the attack though!'

Away from operations 235 and 248 aircrew had been training hard, practicing formation flying, low level bombing and shallow dive bombing. This was to be Wing Commander John Yonge's last operation of his tour. In the evening Group Captain Max Aitken told Yonge that he was wanted for operational duties at Northwood, London. Wing Commander John Yonge stood down as commanding officer of 235 Squadron, of which he had been in charge since April 1944. Aitken wanted youth at the helm. Yonge was 38-years-old and had been first commissioned in the RAF in December 1925. He had had a distinguished career, but had not been rewarded with any honours. His replacement was 'A' Flight's flight commander Squadron Leader Richard Atkinson DSO DFC, who had a fine record before joining the squadron. Originally from Emmavilla, New South Wales, Australia, he had a brief spell as a mining engineer, then brought a passage to England, joined the RAF prior to the war and was a flying officer at the outbreak. Seeing operational service with 205 Squadron Atkinson was posted to Australia, fighting in the Indian Ocean flying Catalinas and Sunderlands while on detachment, commanding Nos. 11 and 20 (RAAF) Squadrons. He joined 235 Squadron in August 1944 upon his return to England. 235 Squadron held a dance in the station cinema. Aitken and other distinguished guests attended. Flight Lieutenant Basil Quelch had organised 18 barrels of beer from Simonds Brewery, full NAFFI supplies and the station band; the place was well laid out and a good spirit existed. The evening was excellent fun with the WAAFs having to fend off amorous intentions by young airmen. Yonge had to make a speech as he was leaving and Atkinson followed. Afterwards Yonge, Butch Jacques and his girlfriend drove to the Crown in Banff.

Operational flying continued however on 22 October. Warrant Officer Andrews from Kilmarnock, Ayrshire who participated on his 34th operation on this day wrote:

'Recce in force Utsira to Kalsen anti-flak Beaus led by Squadron Leader

Duncanson. Main strike force R/P of 404 Squadron. Anti-flak and fighter cover from 235 and 248 Squadrons. Formation lost in cloud. Carried out patrol alone and returned to Dallachy with 404 Squadron due to bad weather at base.'

On the airfield a young airman LAC Owens of 235 Squadron suffered chest pains and reported to the station sick quarters. The medical officer, upon examination, found Owens to be suffering from 'chicken pox', he immediately telephoned 18 Group Headquarters. The reply was: 'Complete quarantine of the whole station, for a week, I'm afraid.'

The Miles Martinet was brought in for air to air gunnery practice with 235 Squadron but the drogue tower was called to Leuchars, so the aircrews were released for training on the base. Flight Lieutenant Thomas DFC returned from leave early because his wife, a WAAF, didn't love him anymore. He was going to divorce her. Another relationship ended when a WAAF came to say she had been jilted by one of Wing Commander Yonge's pilots; he passed this onto the new commanding officer.

Three hundred miles away German Intelligence in Oslo received coded messages of a planned raid by the Wing. Defence batteries between Nordfjord and Sognefjord went onto alert 'III' then increased to alert state 'I' on 23 October. In the aircrew canteen at 09.30 Yonge was joined by two Norwegians who had an operational breakfast whilst Yonge had a cup of tea, talk was of operations and losses. Both said their farewells and wished him luck in his new job. At 11.00 hours, a lone 333 Squadron aircraft headed eastwards on a patrol. Two hours later, while investigating the Leads and anchorages for targets between Utvær to Utsira the 333 Squadron crew Quartermaster Joannes Wollert Løken and Alf Mykkeltvedt observed a periscope, as a U-boat appeared to be just surfacing. The crew positioned themselves for an attack, Løken came in on his run from the starboard quarter, no depth charges were being carried and hits on the deck and conning tower were observed, two anti-aircraft guns returned fire, and the aircraft shuddered as a cannon shell caught them. This proved serious enough to abort their operation. The U-boat attacked was probably U-1061 a VIIF torpedo transporter boat commanded by Otto Hinriches, on a passage between Bergen and Trondheim later being heavily damaged by aircraft from 407 and 224 Squadrons during the night of 30 October. U-1061 later entered Malöy.

Mosquito 'E' 333 had taken hits whilst on a reconnaissance. After the long journey back once over the Scottish coast Flight Lieutenant Bob Golightly heard the voice of Captain Erling Ullberg Johansen saying 'I'll assist you.' Johansen had been doing local training. 'E' 333 approached the airfield, his navigator Flying Officer Frank Hawthorne fired a Very light, almost out of fuel, the hydraulics useless, the Mosquito belly-landing on the runway. On 23 October as the daily inspections were taking place, an unfortunate accident occurred. An airman of 333 Squadron raised the undercarriage instead of the flaps. At 11.45 hours Wing Commander Richard Atkinson led off 21 aircraft. They linked up and dropped down just to above sea level. They flew down their patrol route investigating the stretch from Marstein Light to Ålesund. No less than five merchantmen were seen, defended by two flakships in Hjeltefjord. A tug, Vp.5506 *Zick* of 220 tons, was on watch for the former torpedo boat *Trygg* of the Norwegian Navy, which was sunk in 1940 but later raised and repaired by the Germans and was now bristling with anti-aircraft guns. The flak streamed up from the flakships and Hjeltefjord shore batteries. Nevertheless everybody followed Atkinson's leadership. Navigator Warrant Officer Jimmy Hoyle together with his pilot Flight Lieutenant Aubrey 'Hilly' Hilliard were on their final trip on 23 October having started flying with 235 Squadron in 1942. Jim Hoyle recalls:

'We set off from Banff with a bunch of Mosquitoes and, while patrolling near

Hjeltefjord, we came across a large convoy of enemy ships which put up an impressive barrage of flak. We jockeyed into position, then came the order "Attack, Attack". For the last time I surveyed the scene of Mosquitoes streaking in from varying angles with cannon blazing while 'Hilly' pooped away with his Tsetse gun. There was a more than usual sense of relief when it was all over and we set off on the return trip to Banff. Although two aircraft had been damaged all the aircraft returned safely.'

The Tsetse were amongst the first to go in, they needed space, as they pumped out their 57mm shells. The MkVIs using 500lb bombs, cannon, and machine guns jockeyed for position. The pilots knew their business and opened fire at 1,000 yards. *Zick* bridge was the first to be hit, cannon fire spreading along her decks, Vp.5503 suffered the same treatment and casualties were heavy. Badly damaged *Zick* eventually sank. *Sheen* was also wrecked. Steam tugs *Aasenfiord*, *Vulcanus* and *Speer 14* now endured the force. All were damaged, two lightly, one seriously. Aboard the *Aasenfiord*, and *Vulcanus* the German seamen battled to plug holes and put out fires raging above and below decks. Their captains then sailed them slowly towards Bergen to render them watertight before continuing.

Wing Commander John Yonge, before departing borrowed a Hillman and drove to two farms near the camp. From the first he bought a goose and a duck and from the second one half dozen eggs. He then went around the base saying his farewells. At 15.00 he loaded all his belongings into 'A' 235 which had just had an engine change. Flight Lieutenant 'Royce' Turner would act as navigator and the flight south was marred by heavy industrial haze.

The following poem 'Extinction', was stuck on the Headquarters entrance door at Banff in late September 1944. The author, 22-year-old Flying Officer Ernest Davey of 404 RCAF Squadron, went back to his room one day and wrote this poem; he lost his life on 2 October.

Almighty and all-present power,
Short is the prayer I make to Thee;
I do not ask in battle hour,
For any shield to cover me.
The vast unalterable way,
From which the stars do not depart,
May not be turned aside to stay,
The bullet flying to my heart.
I ask no help to strike my foe;
I seek no petty victory here,
The enemy I hate, I know,
To Thee is dear.
But this I pray: be at my side,
When death is drawing through the sky;
Almighty God who also died,
Teach me the way that I should die.

A decrease in transport in the southern North Sea had led to a redeployment of the Scottish wing in mid-October. 144 and 404 Beaufighter Squadrons had departed on 22 October, coinciding with the arrival of 143 Squadron from North Coates Wing. Rapid production of de Havilland Mosquito MkVIs permitted another squadron to replace the two Beaufighter units and reinforce the Mosquito wing. Only 236 and 254 Squadrons remained at their original base of North Coates, where they continued to hunt in their Beaufighters along the Dutch, German and south-west Norwegian coasts for enemy shipping. A four-squadron Beaufighter wing was brought together by transferring 455 and 489 Squadrons from 16 Group in Langham, and a detachment of four aircraft of 524 Squadron to the RAF station at Dallachy, at the mouth of the Spey River. Here, on the north-east coast of Scotland, the airfield was exposed to the full force of the frequent gales which swept in from the North Sea. 455 Squadron left in three parties, by train, road and air. Most of the Beaufighters carried a third member, a mechanic, who spent the trip sitting on cannon boxes behind the pilot. An advance party flew up on 22 October, two days before the main body. Together with the Beaufighter units from Banff it made it a truly 'colonial' unit! At this time the head of Coastal Command, Air Chief Marshal Sholto Douglas, discussed new operations directives with the Admiralty. This resulted in the command's strike units operating during daylight hours and the Halifaxes of 58 and 502 Squadrons operating at night in the Kattegat, Skagerrak and north of Kristiansund.

For 404 'Buffalo' Squadron leaving Banff was to be their seventh move in five months and the Canadians were more than fed-up with being pushed around the countryside. Aitken was saddened to lose the Beaufighters though they soon became known as 'Dallachy Barracuda Wing' by those at Banff. Sholto Douglas wrote, 'This provided an ideal opportunity for the reorganisation of the strike forces.' Ultimately in October, Banff became an 'all Mosquitoes Wing' while the Beaufighters were at Dallachy. Blister hangars at Banff provided the only protection for the Mosquitoes against the weather. No such covering existed at Dallachy, though the Beaufighters where less vulnerable to the elements than the Mosquitoes. The additional advantages included ease of maintenance for the service echelons with similar aircraft at the same base. Until the move Dallachy had been used as a satellite by Banff. Consequently the parent station had robbed essential equipment from this base in order for theirs to function. 404 Squadron arrived at 09.00 in the morning and by 23.30 hours parties were still dashing around, with men searching the dispersed station collecting what blankets and 'biscuits' they could find. Two days later some semblance of order had been achieved, and by 26 October tables, chairs, bikes, telephone connections and motor transport began arriving.

Sergeant Jo Lewis, a WAAF working for the engineering officer at RAF Dallachy, recalls an incident shortly after the arrival of the Beaufighters from Banff:

'The Beaufighter cockpit was a very tight space to work in. One day a member of the ground crew preparing a 'kite' (Beaufighter), turned around in the small cockpit and sat on the firing button. My boss was somewhat relieved to hear that a crofter's cabbage patch had been the only damage!'

Earlier, on 21 October, a single 143 Squadron Beaufighter landed at Banff. Onboard were Flight Lieutenant Norman Carr DFC, his navigator Flying Officer Arthur Tilley and two passengers – Flight Lieutenant Bower and Corporal Best – as the advanced party to help arrange accommodation and other facilities. Arriving on 23 October were Wing Commander Sam McHardy DFC CdeG, leading 143 Squadron which converted immediately from Beaufighters to Mosquitoes using two Mk II trainers; familiarisation trips in MkVIs then took place. Flight Lieutenant Norman Carr recorded in his logbook flights lasting 45 minutes over the local countryside and over the sea.

Over Askvoll on 21 October, Warrant Office Llewellyn Compton from Pangbourne, Berkshire in 'B' 248 led a section of his squadron when they were bounced by Fw190s but all escaped unscathed. Owing to the shortage of serviceable aircraft on 281

Squadron at Banff and Wick on 23 October two Hudsons of 279 Squadron had been brought up to the aerodrome. They departed at 13.58 hours searching for a ditched Mosquito. Both aircraft ran into rain and sleet and in the search area the showers became so heavy it was impossible to find a dinghy. It was considered the sea was too rough to allow any chance of survival. Both returned, landing away at Wick before returning to Banff.

Earlier in the month Luftwaffe 12./ZG 26 Me110 aircraft had transferred from Ørlandet to Fliegerhorst Herdla, and had begun intercepting Coastal Command long-range shipping patrols. To meet this problem 18 Group instructed Banff on 24 October to mount a Rover off the west coast of Norway to patrol Marstein to Stadlandet. Two 235 Squadron Mosquitoes departed from the base. Four enemy aircraft were then intercepted, the first seen by 235 Squadron since 9 August 1944. Warrant Officer 'Coggie' Cogswell in 'M' 235 sighted the four at 60.30N-04.45E in a line astern formation. He flicked up his intercom switch and shouted: 'Enemy aircraft ahead'. Flight Lieutenant 'Butch' Jacques in 'K' 235 closed in rapidly to 600 yards and fired a burst. At the same time, a German gunner fired a long burst, the Me110 banking off to port. As Jacques followed it down the enemy aircraft took more evasive action trying to save its skin. Jacques pressed the trigger, pulling back gently, and his cannon and machine-gun rounds quickly penetrated the fuselage with a large flash and explosion on the starboard side. There was no return fire. Another well-aimed burst hit the stern quarters and the pilot struggled to keep the aircraft under control, but there was nothing he could do, it hit the sea burning furiously. Meanwhile, Cogswell had closed in, like a cat ready to pounce, proceeding cautiously within range of Me110G-2 (Wr.5414) without attracting the rear gunner's attention. He opened fire from dead astern, firing two 3-second bursts and two 4-second bursts at 450 yards, and trailing black smoke the Messerschmitt hit the water. He then pursued the second Me110G-2 (Wr.6188) and fired at 150 metres, hitting the port engine. Flight Lieutenant Jacques completed the kill, shooting down the third Me110G-2 (Wr.120110). He watched it catch fire and the aircraft was burning brightly as it fell before him. With two Me110G-2s credited to Jacques and a Me110G-2 to Cogswell the dogfight had only lasted three minutes. One of those shot down in the mêlée was the staffelkapitän of the Me110 Staffel at Fliegerhorst Herdla who had been credited with a 'four-engined flying boat' belonging to 330 Squadron on 4 October.

Warrant Office Cogswell later recalled the event:

'After the dogfight, Butch Jacques and I joined up, finished our patrol and returned to base. When we got back our gun cameras were taken away quickly. Our victories were confirmed by the boys. That was the first squadron victory since August and the first time the Jerries had shown up since our move north.'

On October 25, the newly formed Dallachy Strike Wing's first offensive patrol took place. Twenty-two Beaufighters, with Squadron Leader Don Rogers leading the force in 'R' 144, were airborne between 12.57 and 13.05 hours. After six minutes they set course, linking up with two Mosquitoes from 235 Squadron; Flight Lieutenant Noel Russell DFC led in 'Y' 235 with Flying Officer Donald Douglas (RCAF) in 'P' 235 taking off at 13.07 hours, and a single Warwick was airborne minutes earlier. At 14.40 the three had linked up with the Beaufighters flying at 100 feet and they turned to starboard and flew a southerly course to patrol between Eigerøy to Kristiansand. After a further seven minutes and with the weather deteriorating Rogers called 'Return to base' and they turned back. The sea was very calm on the way back and several whales and seals were sighted. The Mosquitoes flew ahead, landing at 15.55, the Beaufighters landing at Dallachy at 16.29 hours.

281 Squadron, flying Vickers Warwicks, was moved to Banff from Dallachy to provide further air sea rescue cover with aircraft and personnel arriving throughout the day, joining the detachment already on the station.

Air Chief Marshal Sholto Douglas needed to increase the range of his Banff Mosquitoes, a matter which was raised at a conference held at headquarters and subsequently taken up with de Havilland, the manufacturers. He also made a request for an increase in the numbers of Mk XVIII Tsetse Mosquitoes for 248 Squadron, but was rebuffed by the Air Ministry because the rocket projectile installation was beginning to get underway, following the successful trials on 28 September and in mid-October of test flights at Hatfield with rocket rails installed under the wings, using HX918 against targets on Ashley Range in the New Forest. Sholto Douglas changed his mind and suggested the Air Ministry should immediately abandon the MkXVIII project and called for all his Mosquito squadrons to be quickly equipped with rockets. Marshal of the RAF Charles Portal, Chief of the Air Staff, agreed to these proposals.

The three Mosquito squadrons therefore underwent intensive rocket projectile (R/P) training at a range near RAF Tain on the Moray Firth coast between Invergordon and Dornoch, an RAF launch anchored target markers off Macduff, while arrow markers were placed on the ground. Making their first operational sortie on 26 October with this new weapon, developed for its present purpose of attacking vessels by Group Captain John D'Arcy Baker-Carr, 235 and 248 Mosquitoes took off at midday, searching between the Naze and Hombersund. At 13.56 hours the strike leader saw a merchantman but continued to Hombersund. At 14.10 hours the formation of 23 returned to the vessel near Lista in position 58.08N/08.17E. Despite severe opposition from shore batteries they turned to attack. Flight Lieutenant George Lord took the attack down low. He said, 'I dived on the trawler, firing cannon and dropped the two 500lb bombs; one hit the stern.' This attack left the cargo of poison gas onboard *Biri* of 940 tons burning. The vessel was already half sunk after a navigation error on 22 October, which holed the vessel. It was abandoned quickly. Two aircraft were hit; one had its port engine feathered and was the last to return to base at 16.39 hours.

With the rocket projectile, the Mosquito squadrons acquired much needed potency. Effective when aimed with skill and precision, the aerial torpedo was a costly weapon, though not without imperfections. Sometimes there were hang-ups on the rails. If this happened, crews were told to bail out because if they tried to land the rockets were liable to explode! However, this was not always the case as aircrews of the Banff wing can testify. The installation of four racks under each wing, capable of carrying four 60lb rockets, with an ideal diving angle of 20° meant that the Mosquitoes could deliver the equivalent of a broadside from a light cruiser. A semi-armour-piercing rocket could rip as many as three plates out of a ship's hull and the 60lb high explosive heads were the equivalent to a 6in shell. They could then repeat the dose a few hours later on receipt of updated intelligence. The rails had to be set so that they were parallel with the airflow at correct diving speed, otherwise the rockets would weather-cock, and then either under or overshoot the target; and similarly if the pilot dived at the wrong airspeed. At first, the aircraft were armed with 60lb semi-AP (armour-piercing) heads of the type used in the desert for tank busting. However, these did not penetrate the vessels and caused little structural damage and they were soon replaced with 25lb solid armour-piercing warheads.

The advantages of the 25lb solid heads were that they caused flooding and for this it was not necessary for the projectile to strike the ship directly, owing to its penetration power and underwater performance, as the R/P head entered the vessel below the waterline. In the confined spaces of the Norwegian fjords, pilots often only had one chance, so they usually fired all eight at once. After entering the vessel's hull each would punch an 18-inch hole at the far side of the hull for the water to flood in, while the remains of the motor burned inside to ignite the cargo. Incessant assaults now began by Coastal Command's rocket-equipped de Havilland Mosquito anti-shipping strike wing.

Squadron Leader Bill Clayton-Graham DFC briefly tells how the wing attacked using rocket projectiles:

'Normally when making an attack on shipping, the dive at 45° was started at 2,000 feet, opening up with machine guns as sighters at about 1,500 to 1,000 feet. Hopefully the cannons were to knock out the enemy's guns, bridge and so forth, and we then fired the rocket projectiles (four under each wing) at about 500 feet. These were set to form a pattern spread on impact, so that if aimed correctly about half hit the target above the waterline, the other four under shooting slightly to hit below the waterline. The main danger in this sort of strike was the possibility of flying into your target. Being in a dive with a closing speed of 300 mph, you had to pull out very smartly.'

The air gunners on 'S' 281 got some gunnery practice in while covering Dallachy Beaufighters on 25 October. At 16.19 hours they sighted a ship's raft to port and investigated. After clearance from control at 16.47 the water erupted as 5,000 rounds were unleashed, unfortunately it remained afloat! Afterwards Warrant Officer Reynolds set course for base, touching down at 18.09 hours. Reynolds wrote: 'We left it and toddled home, seeing nothing on the way but a few fishing boats.' The following day 18 Group and 13 Group Headquarters were alerted that an unidentified aircraft was approaching the coast. Thirty miles east of Aberdeen a Junkers 52 of II/Transport Group force-landed in the North Sea after signalling that it wanted to surrender. The two crewmen were taken onboard the *Eric Stroud*, an Aberdeen-based fishing boat, and brought ashore. The Germans sent out a Junkers 88 to destroy the aircraft and kill the crew, but despite doing an extensive search they sighted nothing and returned to Norway.

On 27 October, 455 (RAAF) Squadron and 489 (RNZAF) Squadron notified 18 Group that both were ready for operations. Ten from each squadron flew out during the afternoon after a briefing to patrol from Helliso Light to Stadtlandet but with poor visibility the patrol was abandoned and Flight Lieutenant Brandon led the formation back to Dallachy.

A fatal accident occurred on 28 October at Banff. Mosquito HR298 had just become airborne when it hit another, HR136, piloted by Flying Officers James Ross DFC, and navigator Frank Walker, which had for some inexplicable reason during a dusk take-off unfortunately taxied around the perimeter the wrong way across the end of the runway. Leading Aircraftman John Hill, a flight mechanic with 235 Squadron, explained:

'Outside at the dispersal the two crew had walked around their Mosquito completing an external check, with the pilot and navigator secured in the aircraft and alert for the signal to start engines. The calm was broken by hesitant splutters as the propellers began to turn, followed by the roar of engines. This was the last I saw of them. Ross, waving to us ground crew, released the brakes, and moved away from the dispersal and taxied along the track. Minutes later they would be dead. It was thought at the time that perhaps they had misheard the watch tower's instructions or their radio had suddenly gone unserviceable.'

Both crew were killed instantly, the canopy shattering as propellers tore through the perspex leaving a bloody mess within the cockpit area. Rescue personnel arrived at the scene and were confronted with headless torsos. The bodies were hastily taken away to the station morgue. While the aircraft was towed away afterwards two junior airmen hosed out the cockpit. Both men had begun their second tour on 235 Squadron after Wing Commander John Yonge called for volunteers. This was their first second-tour operation and sadly their last. Out of six crews who volunteered from 235 Squadron only one crew would survive to the end of the Second World War. Ross's usual navigator had decided not to volunteer and he spent the next few weeks trying to drink the officers' mess dry. Sometimes he woke up on a slow train bound for Aberdeen after fellow officers had pushed him on, only to return so that the performance could be repeated.

In the second aircraft HR298, the pilot, Flying Officer Harold Powell, a New Zealander, maintained control despite the damage and turned to safely belly land on the grass. The crew managed to get out through the escape hatch, shocked and bruised; the tail section had come away on impact. Powell and his navigator Flying Officer Norman Redford (RNZAF) would see their fate sealed only days later.

Written by LAC Eddie Mackin (RCAF) a Canadian poet in peacetime, serving with 235 Squadron, the following poem appeared in 235 Squadron's magazine *Chocks Away* and is dedicated to the crew of 'P' – Peter, who were killed in the flying accident:

These we have known;
They clove the heights, at one with sun and stars
And like the seagull poised on graceful wing,
Were wholly of the air, a perfect thing.
A clean-cut jewel from the crown of Mars...
Now hurtling in to kill, now out, with scars.
So fond of life and all that life could bring
Yet laughed at death and chased him, carolling
Across the skies, and broke his sacred laws
A thousand times, and mocked him to his face.
Oh! Irony of ironies to meet
Him here on earth and not in boundless space...
Knights of the sky be their winding sheet
And let the stars invest their sightless gaze
Who took their 'oriflamme' by arduous waves.

Another loss occurred on 28 October in the early hours. A young Canadian, Flight Lieutenant Edwin Ashbury from Toronto with his experienced crew from 521 Squadron were flying a Hudson, taking off at 00.01 hours. They were tasked to fly a special THUM (temperature and humidity) sortie near Stavanger, with a general weather reconnaissance along the Norwegian coast. The object of Ashbury's operation was to confirm if the weather was suitable for a Beaufighter or Mosquito strike on a convoy expected in the area at dawn. The weather conditions were very poor and the report, which should have been transmitted at 03.00 hours, was never received. Nothing more was heard of the aircraft. This was 521 Squadron's first loss in over a year.

Strike aircraft from both wings were airborne on 30 October. First off were 12 aircraft from 144 and 12 from 404 Squadron on a search, with 235 Squadron providing the anti-flak support together with a Norwegian outrider patrolling from Ålesund and Utvaer. An armed reconnaissance of 18 Beaufighters made up from 455 and 489 Squadrons took off from Dallachy at 08.16 hours to fly a Rover patrol between

Stavanger and Utvaer Light, after an earlier sighting of a U-boat in the area. Once in the air they set course for Banff at 08.29 hours to join the two Mosquitoes 'T' 235 and 'U' 235 providing fighter escort; a Warwick participated in an air sea rescue role. Squadron Leader D Hammond DSO, DFC & Bar led them away at 08.33 hours. By 09.58 hours the force had begun their watch, sighting a dozen whales and seals. A single Mosquito kept to the starboard side and checked the Leads, sighting a small stationary coaster east of Leirvik. Flight Lieutenant Jackson-Smith in 'U' 235 investigated other anchorages and radioed 'Negative'. Nineteen minutes later two small convoys of neutral vessels were seen some distance away. Warwick 'N' 281 swept the withdrawal area for this force. Occasionally these trips were boringly monotonous for the Warwick airmen for much of the flying was at 100 feet above the waves. They identified an empty dinghy adrift in the North Sea as the type in service with the Luftwaffe. The pilot brought the aircraft in low at 50 feet, sweeping over it and making sure no survivors were clinging onto the sides in the icy water. After this first pass the pilot radioed the mid-upper gunner to fire a short burst of machine-gun rounds to sink it, thus ensuring no other allied aircraft would waste operational time investigating it.

The wireless operator Warrant Officer Don Mabey heard a distress call on the emergency channel at 10.41 hours; a 455 Beaufighter had got into difficulty after the port engine failed. The pilot called up and asked for an escort home. 'K' 455 called up saying, 'It's all right, I'm with him.' Warwick 'N' 281, together with 'K' 455 shadowed it while the navigator onboard the Warwick plotted a direct course to Sumburgh. Fellow Australians in 'K' 455 guided the Beaufighter, now low on fuel, into Sumburgh, landing at 10.45 hours. The Warwick skimmed low over the airfield, touching down at Banff after an operational flight lasting five hours and fifty minutes. Nothing else was spotted on this Rover and in loose formation the Beaufighters made for home.

Five Banff aircraft then participated in offensive patrols probing along the southern coast and the Leads searching for enemy shipping. The crew of 'R' 235 reported: 'Three merchant vessels sighted proved neutral.' Dangerously low cloud prevented further sightings in the fjords between Ytterøyane and Utvaer. Four Mosquitoes of 235 Squadron led by Wing Commander Richard Atkinson with two from 248 and another from 235 patrolled Marstein Light to Utvaer light, and a lone Junkers 88 (D7+UH) was intercepted north-west of Holmengrå at 15.54 hours while firing Very cartridges. In the fight that followed 'O' 248 fired five rounds of 57mm shells, Flight Lieutenant Jacques, with his navigator Flying Officer Eric Saree, DFC in 'E' 235 straddled the starboard side; the Junkers' starboard engine caught fire and its pilot struggled to retain control, now flying virtually at zero feet. 'O' 248 struck again from 500 yards, firing two 57mm shells. Atkinson chased it down in 'Y' 235, and made a pass, coinciding with 'T1' 248 attacking from astern. At 15.57 the Junkers exploded less than 50 feet above the sea. The entire crew died but records for this date show only four on board. Two bodies, Ass Werner Hast and Ogfr Walter Haase were found by a Norwegian fishing boat. Fw Josef Riedmeier and Uffz Karl E Mazur disappeared along with the Junkers. Returning from this encounter the four Mosquitoes swept over the Scottish coast with fleeting glimpses of those in Banffshire engaged in agriculture, for which the month of October had seen one of the most miserable harvests for many years with heavy rain on at least 24 days of the month.

On October 31 1944, 279 Squadron arrived at Banff, having flown up from RAF Thornaby. It was scheduled to convert to Warwicks but made a temporary diversion to Banff and flew out, still with its Hudsons, to assist in the search for a Bomber Command Mosquito crew.

The next day RAF Peterhead, 28 miles from Aberdeen, saw 315 'Deblin' Squadron with its Mustang MkIIIBs arrive to provide escort for both strike wings for a period of three months, although, on occasions 315 were diverted to non-maritime roles, so in effect only half a squadron was made available for operations with the strike wings. On 31 October, eight Mustang IIIs escorted 25 Bomber Command Mosquitoes of 21, 464 and 487 Squadrons taking part on the daring low level attack on Aarhus University, Denmark, which housed the Gestapo Headquarters for the whole of Jutland. Shortly after their debriefing it was announced to the crews that they would be moving north to act as escorts for two shipping strike wings – no whoops of joy here!

Dan Nowosielski recalls:

'I was young, twenty-one, but already a veteran on 315 (Deblin) Squadron, as I had served continuously since July 1943. A posting to Peterhead in the north of Scotland scared me, even with a Merlin-Packard 1650. Most of my colleagues thought the same but we had a job to do. 315 flew escort for both strike wings during our longish stint at Peterhead from 1 November to 14 January. We really admired those Mosquito and Beaufighter boys who had done these strikes, we took our hats off to them!'

During October Banff aircrews had completed five operations and a number as anti-flak escort for Dallachy. Aircrew also did numerous training flights and practiced bombing at various heights on targets moored off Portsoy, with the average flight being 45 minutes. On the domestic side of station life five airmen's dances were held to which locals were invited and an ENSA concert was staged in the cinema complex. Bill Knight of 143 Squadron recalls: 'An ENSA repertory company performing a Chekhov play were invited back to the officers' mess – the ladies took one look and fled outside.' The WAAF hockey team at Banff played two matches on one of the sports fields against RAF Dallachy WAAFs who won 3-2, followed by another defeat against the Banff ladies team on the 21st, 6-0. The station cinema presented *And the Angels Sing* and a double feature of *Johnny Vagabond* and *Flying with Music*. This was followed by *Road to Singapore*. 235 Squadron was busy doing auditions and castings for a station show with Corporals Wilkes, Les Dollimore and Sergeant Kidney as directors.

The local village of Banff lay just over two miles from the airfield entrance. It did not take very long for the airmen and women to get to know the place. Bicycles were the usual way of getting around and parking spaces were almost always full outside every pub and club in Banff and the surrounding villages. On average ten bicycles were reported lost a week and those found were transported back by police lorry and dumped outside the guardroom for collection. The Sheriff Court at Banff was kept busy dealing with airmen and women who were picked up nightly by the Banff police and fined ten shillings (50 pence). They had been riding their bicycles without lights and a column of names appeared in the local newspaper every week. During these two months the Carlton Cafe and the Crown Hotel became a favourite with all the men and women stationed at Banff, as did the Deveron Fish and Chip Restaurant in Bridge Street. Another meeting place frequented by personnel was Rose's Temperance Hotel, which served afternoon cream teas. One pilot, Warrant Officer Bill Parfitt of 248 Squadron remembers: 'After an operation we'd telephone Rose's Temperance Hotel in Banff then jump in the squadron Hillman if transport was available and drive down for afternoon tea with some WAAFs from the airfield.' A young lady called Sybil recalled: 'Banffshire was soon filled with young RAF officers and airmen. You just couldn't get away from them. You kept getting your heart broken. I met one chap at a dance in Whitehills and thought he was my ideal. He was as smitten as I was. He said; "See you at Rose's Temperance Hotel, seven o'clock next Saturday." Of course I went, but he never came. His friend came instead. He'd been killed.'

CHAPTER 5

NOVEMBER 1944

October passed into November with little let-up, and with constant searches by the two wings between heavy rainstorms and low cloud between Obrestad, Egeroy and Skudesnes. It was an early start for the Dallachy Wing and the aircrew of a single Warwick at Banff on 1 November 1944. Australian Wing Commander Colin Milson DFC led 22 Beaufighters in LZ409, departing from the airfield at 05.27 hours; it was his first operation from Dallachy as the 455 Australian Squadron commanding officer. They were to patrol from Obrestad Light near the southern tip of Norway and east round to Kristiansand. Milson lead the force away from the Scottish coast at 300 feet. At 07.01 hours 'S' 489 on the outer edge of the formation saw four clusters of bright lights from a single vessel below as they raced past. Seven minutes later the Drem flares dropped by the Warwick some 30 miles off the Obrestad Light were sighted.

Twenty-two pilots circled the flame floats waiting for the signal to set course. Then suddenly two aircraft collided while circling at 300 feet. The starboard Beaufighter from 489 Squadron did a stalling turn and dived into the sea and the other, flown by Flying Officer George Hammond of 455 Squadron, disappeared into the darkness with smoke trailing and was not seen again. Two bright orange flashes were spotted from Hammond's aircraft thought to be two of his rockets going off. A number of others saw the collision and 'F' 489 called the strike leader and was told to circle the spot; 'F' 489 switched IFF to distress and tried to call the Warwick on VHF but failed. Milson had already called up the Warwick, but no trace was found of either aircraft. Several Beaufighters could see the Warwick still searching for survivors as they departed, setting course to patrol from Obrestad Light to Egersund. The force was further reduced in size when three 489 Torbeaus failed to find the rendezvous. At 07.33 hours the weather was poor, but it improved near Kristiansand to give visibility of nearly 25 miles. At 8.13 hours at the end of their patrol area, they set course for base having sighted nothing. Intelligence reported that while lying in Billefjord, Norwegian trawler *Stortind* of 160 tons carrying a cargo of benzene self-ignited and sank.

At Banff, the following day Lieutenant Robertsen of 333 Squadron attended the funeral of Second Lieutenant Cato Vermeli of 330 Squadron who had been killed in a road traffic accident in Lerwick. On 3 November Group Captain Aitken flew a reconnaissance patrol between Egersund relaying a sighting and weather report at 11.25, subsequently landing at 13.00 hours. Aitken wrote in his book: 'Heavy Flak, No Fighters'. A senior officer from 18 Group was on the telephone upon hearing of the station commander's 'jolly' saying that he should not participate in any more operations off the Scandinavian coast. Max Aitken's reply was a blunt 'Fuck you'. Beaufighter 'Y' 489 paid a quick visit to Banff, piloted by Flying Officer Edwin Burrows DFC, departing with Flying Officer Bill Carson and Bill Kelly.

On 4 November Wing Commander Sise was again the wing leader for a sweep. Sixteen aircraft streamed into the air at 11.29 hours and set course for their patrol area – Bremanger to Utvaer. An hour later Warrant Officer G A Macaskill landed back with engine trouble. Arriving over the Norwegian coast the force began their search for targets. Near the island of Kinn, 12 miles west-south-west of Florö, two merchant vessels of 2,000 tons were sighted alongside the quay with a single escort. At 13.25 hours Sise ordered an immediate assault. At 13.30 hours flak defences opened up; tracers of light flak hosed up into which the Mosquitoes had to fly following their intrepid leader. 248 Squadron concentrated on Vp. 5106, whose captain had manoeuvred his flak ship into open water for a better firing position. *Raketen Geschuss'* parachute mines were also fired at the incoming aircraft. Flight Lieutenant A McLeod DFC in 'X' 248 was opening up on the shipping with cannon and machine guns when his port engine was hit. With coolant streaming out of the radiator McLeod continued his attack to good effect and broke away over Florö. Others picked their targets and cannon shells and rockets hit both vessels, while 235 Squadron aircraft, carrying 500lb bombs were prevented from releasing them, due to low cloud and the proximity of the village. All attacked with cannon and machine guns to good effect from 500 feet to deck height from ranges of 500 to 1,000 yards, all scoring strikes. HR127 was one of them: cannon and machine-gun fire slammed into the merchant vessel, and simultaneously the sky was littered with explosions when the flak hit Flight Lieutenant George Lord's aircraft. He quickly checked for damage, finding plenty of holes in the tail and port main plane, and banked to get out of harm's way. Defensive fire from Vp. 5106 was successful in hitting Sise's aircraft; a 37mm shell burst near one of the engines, and orange flame billowed out. He managed to carry on his attack as he extinguished the fire.

The shore batteries gave others a rough time, and another casualty from the intense anti-aircraft barrage was HP967 flown by Flying Officers Harold Powell (RNZAF) and his navigator Norman Redford (RAAF); although hit, they pressed home their strike, paying with their lives. Mosquito 'L' 235 was seen to crash into a bog at Storøya, a few miles east of Kinn. A debriefing reported reads: 'We had not seen Powell's aircraft on fire before it crashed, but it caught fire when hitting the ground. There were no survivors.'

Their bodies were recovered from the crash site by locals and buried at Florö, but were later reinterred in a joint grave within Stavne cemetery in Trondheim. At 28-years-old the young New Zealander Harold Powell was lost on his third operation with 235 Squadron. He had already completed an operational tour with 179 Squadron which was equipped with the two-engine Warwick.

The merchant vessel that had been attacked was smoking heavily. There was a violent explosion onboard Vp. 5106 and debris flew into the air, a Tsetse 57mm shell having found its mark. One of the towers with anti-aircraft guns on deck also took hits. When the attack had finished three men lay dead and 12 were wounded, whilst four other men were unaccounted for. The force turned out to sea with four 248 Squadron aircraft suffering battle damage. McLeod had feathered his damaged engine, and once out of the area asked for assistance. Two Mosquitoes formatted either side, and gave encouragement. Sise nursed his crippled aircraft, 'J' 248, back on one engine with Flight Lieutenant George Lord acting as escort, shepherding Sise to Sumburgh, before returning to Banff. A further two made emergency landings at Sumburgh and the third, 'X' 248, crashed outside the airfield when the remaining engine suddenly stopped. Both crewmen escaped unhurt. On the aerodrome at Banff, a senior intelligence officer from CIU Medmenham briefed the station commander on the latest information from Norway over a glass of wine and an exceptional meal.

On 5 November, accompanied by a single Mosquito from 333 Squadron, Flight Lieutenant Kimpton in 'K' 455 led six Beaufighters on an anti-U-boat sweep in the afternoon to Obrestad Light. At a height of 1,200 feet over rough seas they picked up a second Mosquito, 'H' 333, when their patrol commenced. Nine minutes later 'K' 455 heard a 'Negative' from Mosquito 'N' 333 and they completed their patrol, landing at

Dallachy at 17.02 hours. On the 6th Group Captain Max Aitken took off for Sumburgh to bring back two flying crew who had crashed. Making his way through snow and ice he successfully landed and with Flight Lieutenant McLeod and Wheeley strapped in, he took off at full boost, touching down at the station after a 50-minute flight. On the 7th the newly converted 143 Squadron flew its initial sortie in HR141 and PZ419 accompanied by their New Zealand born Wing Commander 'Sam' McHardy DSO DFC in 'D' 143. They were looking for Luftwaffe activity between Obrestad and Lindesnes but the results were negative. Hourly searches at intervals the following day by 235 Squadron had little success.

On 8 November training sorties took place at Peterhead over the local countryside. Sadly during one of these Warrant Officer Adolf Richter, flying Mustang HB882 crashed into the ground at high speed near Maud during a practice dogfight for reasons unknown. Halifax DT803 was seen to crash in the same area. Richter's body was buried at Longside Cemetery in Aberdeen. Further along the coast 25 Dallachy Beaufighters and two Mosquitoes of 333 Squadron flew out on a Rover patrol briefed to search between Utvaer and Bremanger. Wing Commander Tony Gadd from 144 Squadron led the Beaufighters off from Dallachy at 9.11 hours, picking up 'P' 333 at 09.25 over Banff, and set course for Norway. 'N' 333 had already departed.

Two hours later the force made landfall at 11.12 hours, flying north along the coast to Bremanger. The Mosquitoes flew ahead separately, making landfall near Utvaer Light, opposite the entrance to Sognefjord. They flew inside the small islands that wrapped up the Norwegian coastline from Utvaer to Sognefjord and Stavfjord, but found nothing. Proceeding along the coast a little further north, on the northern side of Midtgulenfjord the pair investigated anchorage for vessels. Above the mountain ridges one of them saw two merchantmen sheltering at anchor on the northern side of Midtgulen. Lieutenant Ole Tobias Mehn-Anderson in 'P' 333 estimated they were two boat lengths apart, his navigator then spotted further along the fjord two more coasters and at the entrance a merchantman steaming on a northerly coarse. 'P' 333 called up Wing Commander Tony Gadd in 'D' 144 about the first two sightings, while at the same time Lieutenant Eriksen, flying 'N' 333, radioed at 11.41 hours saying five coasters were stationary in the fjord. These first two merchantmen sighted by Mehn-Anderson were those seen by 'P' 333 and were bound for Ålesund. The convoy had taken cover in Midtgulen on the northern side to await further escort and the dark before they could continue their journey north. The smaller of the two was D/S *Helga Ferdinand* of 2,566 tons carrying coal, with D/S *Aquila* of 3,495 tons, whose cargo is unknown. They were lying at right angles to the shore and a short distance from it. They had old-fashioned stacks and carried Norwegian markings and flags.*

The strike leader signalled, 'Better attack larger force'. Mehn-Anderson led them up Loch Froy and turned starboard before nearing the flak battery at Berle on the island of Bremanger, leading the Beaufighters up into the mountains, towards Aalfot Glacier, then turning to port over steep mountain ridges above the fjord where white snow lay, to attack down the fjord from the south-east. The Norwegian informed the Beaufighter crews of the targets and how to attack and the best way to escape.

Suddenly, rising out over the mountain they were looking down on the vessels 2,000 feet below. The gun crews were taken completely by surprise and the aircraft attacked unmolested at 11.50 hours. As the gun crews recovered aboard the merchantmen, together with their escort Vp. 5114 and Vp. 5115 they put up an intense box barrage.

---

*Today the wreck of the *Aquila* rests at a depth of 45 to 60 metres listing towards port side. The stern is broken down and the propeller is more or less destroyed, apart from which the wreck is intact.

Australian Flying Officer Tom Higgins' aircraft 'C' 455 was hit by 40mm cannon in the starboard tank, starboard engine and in the nose camera. Flak shells were bursting on the lips of the glacier far behind the aircraft but this flak became spasmodic as the attack developed. In total 17 Beaufighters hit the *Helga Ferdinand* in quick succession. 144 Squadron attacked with cannon and made numerous strikes on the bridge and superstructure. Momentarily flak found their range and three were caught by the vessel's anti-aircraft guns. 'B' 144 was one of those blasted and suffered damage along the underside of the fuselage and starboard mainplane. 404 and 455, armed with 25lb rockets, were the next wave. Claiming 14 dry hits and 12 possible dry hits, all turned in again to strafe with cannon, opening up at 1,200 yards to 50 yards. *Helga Ferdinand* caught fire and began to burn, belching a mass of black smoke which rose to 500 feet. An explosion then occurred onboard which hit Pilot Officer Payne flying in 'S' 455, buckling the canopy and the bottom cannon plate. Cannon, machine-gun and rocket fire raked the *Aquila* amidships and smoke appeared. 40mm anti-aircraft fire came up from Midtgulen as Beaufighters caught Vp. 5114 and Vp. 5115 with all their weaponry, severely damaging them both.

Seventeen minutes before the strike had commenced, at 11.43 hours in position 61.42N/04.58E, the Norwegian passenger packet *Famnaeses* had also been spotted by the force. The civilian vessel of 307 tons, was now steaming through the fjord on her regular run. The vessel was passing the anchored convoy carrying some 60 to 70 passengers, dry cargo, mail and some livestock and became caught up in the attack. The steamboat's amidships caught fire and the hull was badly damaged after several hits from rockets. The captain steered into shallower water aided by a pump. The crew worked desperately against time, eventually successfully beaching the vessel. Two crewmen were killed; Chief Engineer Adolf Kristian Hendriksen and Able Seaman Kristoffer Vangen, together with six passengers. Many were wounded and two more later died in hospital.

Five Beaufighters were damaged. A 489 Squadron Beaufighter pilot reported, 'A shell hit the cowling of one of my engines and blew it off. It kept going and got us home safely.' Others got back too. Two Canadians were awarded DFCs from 404 Squadron after leading and inflicting damage, and sinking two large merchantmen in Midtgulen. Lieutenant Mehn-Anderson received a letter of thanks from the station commander for the admirable assistance received on the day.

Flying Officer Jack Cox DFC of 455 Squadron said:

'As with most rocket attacks damage could not be assessed but a PR Mosquito flew over the next morning and revealed the outline of the ships on the bed of the fjord and discoloration around them. 25 Beaufighters had sunk four ships without a single aircraft being lost.'

Frequent snow and hail was a feature of operations flown from Banff during the morning and afternoon of 8 November. Mosquitoes on a Rover patrol between Lister and Stravanger strafed the Norwegian vessel *Austri* and when looking for targets off Ytterøyane, Marstein, and Askvoll the Mosquitoes made a night landing in a snowstorm with winds of 25 mph. In the darkness a lone Warwick departed Banff at 18.00 hours detailed to search for a missing FAA Swordfish in conjunction with a HSL from Fraserburgh. Six hundred miles away in London Air Marshal Aubrey Ellwood gave an outline of Coastal Command's war entitled *From Defensive to Offensive* at the Royal United Services Institute. He spoke at length about the anti-shipping campaign being waged by the Beaufighter and Mosquito aircraft in the North of Scotland. The lecturer ended with a tribute to the courage and skill of these aircrew and maintenance men and women working under harsh conditions.

On 9 November the weather interfered again: Flight Lieutenant George Lord and his navigator Flying Officer Douglas Turner set off with 12 others in a hail storm on an armed patrol in HR918. Mechanical problems forced four aircraft from 248 Squadron to return early. The remaining nine looked for enemy ships in anchorages from Ytterøyane to Askvoll, all they found was low cloud and fog obscuring the fjords and leads. Lord recorded in his logbook that he flew through frequent snow and hail, then landed crosswind in a gale.

On 11 November, at Peterhead, two Mustangs rendezvoused with seven Coastal Command Liberators, who were to act as escort. At 15.00 hours the formation was flying on a southerly course at 1,000 feet when Flight Sergeant Antoni Ciundziewski in FB391 on the port side spotted something on the surface below. Banking away to investigate and levelling out just above the waves, he found a tug towing a barge. Ciundziewski attacked with machine guns across the tug. Suddenly he was up against heavy flak from camouflaged land positions, and shortly afterwards intense light flak was experienced from Marstein Light. Against his section leader's orders, this naval shore battery was strafed and a few minutes later he reported being hit. His section leader yelled, 'Bail out' over the radio telephone. The Mustang was on fire and slowly losing height and it gave the battery great satisfaction to see the single-engined fighter plough into the sea at 15.49 hours (German time). Antoni Ciundziewski did not escape and no parachute or dinghy was seen.

Station security was tight at Banff on 11 November as the Commander-in-Chief of Coastal Command arrived with Air Vice-Marshal Aubrey Ellwood and senior naval officer Captain D V Peyton-Ward RN and other staff from 18 Group Headquarters. During the day, the airmen and women had been getting the station ready. Sholto Douglas then presided over a conference on the policy to be adopted by both the Banff and Dallachy strike wings; Aitken and commanding officers from both strike wings were present. The mess cooks had organised sufficient ingredients to prepare a buffet equal to the occasion. This coincided with the Banff Ball held during the evening to which many local personalities were invited, although even with the women folk swelling the ranks there was a distinct shortage of female company! The Coastal Command band provided the dance music. Not surprisingly 18 Group cancelled all operations until the following day. Aitken, after this gathering of senior officers, impressed everyone with his state of well being at breakfast and laughed off the idea that flying might not be on. He proceeded to execute a beautiful low roll in his Mosquito in front of the gathering. WAAF Corporal Joyce Trovey recounts:

'The officers' mess bar at Banff was reputedly the longest in the Air Force. I still have the memory of Max Aitken going around the bar during the base's first Banff Ball especially when the WAAF officers were present, with a soda siphon pushed down his trousers. The spout was pushed through his button flies and he offered to top up anyone's glass.'

For some months the Coastal Command strike crews had been tracking the movements of the German battleship *Tirpitz* since the first attack on 15 September 1944 by Bomber Command Lancasters from 9 and 617 Squadrons. Badly damaged but repaired, *Tirpitz* had been moved to Tromsø. On 12 November, 32 Bomber Command Lancasters from 9 Squadron and 617 (Dambuster) Squadron flying from the snowbound RAF Lossiemouth, attacked again. They were accompanied by a single Lancaster from 463 Squadron to film the attack, known as operation 'Catechism'. Led by Wing Commander Tait they struck, capsizing the battleship, and immuring most of her ship's company. Returning with their escort from 315 Squadron the Lancasters were dispersed around 18 Group's airfields at Dallachy, Banff and Sumburgh as Lossiemouth ran out of space. The airfield control officer at Banff had known for some time that a unit of Bomber Command Lancasters were undergoing training at Lossiemouth. On this drizzly day in the afternoon the control room officer received word that a couple of Lancasters were in the circuit, and they landed at Banff one after the other. A fault or mechanical defect had prevented one of the 'Tallboys' (a 12,000lb bomb developed by Barnes Wallis) being dropped and it was brought back. This highly explosive load was still hung up owing to the weather conditions during the flight. The crew got safely down; upon switching off the Merlin 24s the 'Tallboy' came away, and the crew without debate made a hasty and undignified exit in front of the control tower. Happily it did not explode otherwise it would have taken half the station away! Everyone beat a quick retreat while a bomb disposal team was called, and the base was out of bounds for two days while they made the 12,000lb bomb safe. The following day the offending crew had a photograph taken for the squadron scrapbook sitting on the defused Tallboy. Although no official record exists of this incident many of those stationed at Banff can recall it well. Ron Brooks gives an account of this dramatic occasion:

'The Tallboy dropped fairly close to where I was standing while on the 248 dispersal. As it fell I thought it was a piece of the aircraft that had been damaged by flak. The loudspeaker nearby roared into life and the voice requested us to immediately evacuate the aerodrome as it was a 12,000lb bomb. We all stopped what we were doing. An engine fitter on my dispersal, a Corporal Bird, jumped from the ladder he was using and we moved like lighting to safety!'

Flight Lieutenant George Lord said:

'Those of us out on a Rover had to be diverted to a nearby airfield. One of the Lancaster's bombs came away landing near Flying Control, armed airmen were dispersed, aircraft diverted and the place was evacuated for the next 24 hours until the local bomb disposal team had de-fused the bomb.'

On Sunday evening, November 12 1944, at 23.00 hours, two of the Royal Navy's cruisers *Bellona* and *Kent* and destroyers *Myngs*, *Verulam*, *Zambezi* and *Algonquin* went into southern Norwegian coastal waters under the command of Rear-Admiral McGrigor and found a German convoy of 11 mixed craft off Lister. Hours earlier convoy number Ks-357-St had moved through the darkness from Kristiansand to Stavanger, consisting of the merchant vessels *Cornouaille*, *Greif*, *Palermo* and *Rosenberg I*, escorted by M 427, M 416, M 446, UJ.1221, UJ.1223 and UJ.1713. The convoy commander was the commanding officer of 30.M-flotilla, Korvettenkapitän der Reserve Köhler, who was on board M 427 (he survived). Gunnery Officer Henry Brooke planned and executed this night attack at 23.59 hours. From close inshore the cruisers and destroyers stalked the German convoy independently, avoiding the shallows. Brooke fired off a star shell to illuminate the enemy and then brought their firepower to bear, switching from one target to the next until nine of the craft were sunk off Lister Fjord near Egersund. The task force was observed by UJ.1221 and UJ.1223, both had just been commissioned and were being transfered to their flotilla. Although inexperienced they fought courageously but ultimately they had no chance. *Cornouaille*, loaded with various munitions, blew up. The convoy was put out of action very quickly. The *Palermo*, *Rosenberg I* and M 446 survived, while all the others were sunk. The experienced UJ.1713 survived the fierce fighting, but returned to the scene to rescue survivors. Then she was attacked and sunk by the destroyers during the rescue work. Total losses are given as 161 casualties (civilians and soldiers); among those that died were German, Norwegian, Ukrainian, and Dutch sailors. Several hours later, all useable minor vessels were ordered out to search for survivors. M 427 was beached near Rekefjord lighthouse, where she later capsized and was a total loss. The wreck was pounded by the heavy waves, but it is still sited there at a depth of 4 metres. The crew scrambled ashore and refused to be taken off by the rescue vessels, as they wanted them to continue conducting sweeps for survivors offshore first. These vessels were still sweeping the area as dawn broke the following day. During the engagement two men lost their lives on *Kent* and three were wounded. Brooke received the DSC for this action.

Five hours later rescued survivors and crewmen were to experience a further attack, this time from the air. On 13 November Beaufighters from 144 and 489 Squadron were assigned to fly a Rover patrol. 489 were led by Flight Lieutenant Osment DFC and took off. There were six Torbeaus armed with MkXV torpedoes set for 10 feet contact, and cannon-armed Beaufighters, together with 18 Mosquitoes armed with cannon and machine guns. They were briefed merely that a convoy had recently been softened up by the Royal Navy and they were ordered to attack the three remaining vessels. Setting course at 8.30 hours the weather was typical of the North Sea in winter. Low grey cloud and the surface of the sea blended into one. Flying at about 1,000 feet the formation was spread out loosely. Flight Lieutenant Geoff Rouse of 235 Squadron was the leading aircraft, and his navigator was steering the combined wing. Hunting down the coast at 10.02 hours the formation flew out into clear air, and suddenly Rouse saw the convoy just west of Rekefjord, outside Egersund, in position 5823N/0558E. They counted six vessels in total; the *Palermno*, *Rosenberg I* and the four escorts. Two were in line astern, a short distance away from the remaining vessels. One was still burning from the previous encounter.

Owing to the size of them, the Torbeaus did not join in the strike. The force climbed to 1,500 feet and selected their targets. At 10.18 hours the attack commenced. Mosquitoes and Beaufighters were swooping in at heights of 500 feet to zero feet. Rouse selected the nearest vessel R-32 as his own target. Making his attack with cannon, racing towards R-32 before striking the structure, Rouse banked away. The remaining six 235 aircraft went in, swooping across, their cannon and machine guns devastatingly effective, tearing into the wooden superstructure and causing extensive damage. R-32 was not sunk, but damaged. Increasing the speed its captain turned for the shore and being strafed by 'A' 144 it eventually foundered and sank. In addition UJ.1754 and the tug *Lom* were damaged too. Having survived the first attack the day before, an explosion occurred on *Rosenberg I* of 1,964 tons, as it was hit in quick succession by two strike aircraft and serious destruction was caused. Although badly damaged the vessel remained afloat. Air sea rescue craft Fl.B.529 of 597 tons had been struck by 'K' 235, 'D' 248 and 'R' 248 and was in flames and sank under the force of repeated hits. During this attack two of the submarine chasers were still afloat. One, after being hit, was down at the stern. Suddenly an explosion aft of the funnel sealed its fate. In all, seven seamen were killed, and three were lightly and one badly wounded.

The strike aircraft now turned towards Scotland, some hit by anti-aircraft fire being coaxed along by fellow aircrew. As they neared the Banffshire coast, a WAAF radio operator gave instructions for the Beaufighters to land at Banff because of poor visibility at Dallachy, the last touching down at 12.00 hours. Flight Lieutenant Osment led the aircraft back to base at 13.20 hours. A Tsetse pilot from 248 Squadron's 'C' Flight landed skilfully in spite of a 57mm shell stuck in the breech, the barrel of which protruded 2 feet from under the nose. Armourers were assessing why the weapon had malfunctioned when suddenly there was tremendous recoil as a 57mm-calibre shell was fired, the blast injuring seven airmen. An ambulance hastened to the scene from the nearby control tower. The airmen had unfortunately sustained burns to their faces, hair and hands with severe cuts to their heads and face together with deafness.

In Norway the loss of this German convoy to the Royal Navy and Coastal Command aircraft strengthened German suspicions of an impending Allied descent on Norway or Denmark and led them to move E-boats (fast motor torpedo boats which were capable of making between 35 and 40 knots, so their operations were purely offensive) into the area for the first time. Moves were also made to reinforce their fighter strength.

In the mid-afternoon of 14 November, 17 Mosquitoes led by Wing Commander Atkinson in 'B' 235, were on patrol, approaching Sognefjord looking for potential victims. The passenger steamer *Gula* of 264 tons was proceeding northwards from Bergen at 14.00 hours. Nineteen minutes later, the aircraft spotted two vessels, one of which was the *Gula* in Sognefjord. Aircraft from 143, 235 and 248 Squadrons attacked the vessels which disappeared under spray and thick smoke. On board *Gula* most of the crew were injured, and the trawler *Sardinen* of 177 tons sank with one crewman dying; its remaining crew survived. The Norwegian Naval Attaché in London, Captain Jacobsen, asked if 18 Group's aircraft would refrain from attacking its lifeboats and steamers which could be identified by their two white striped markings down the port and starboard side. Flight Lieutenant Richardson recalled:

'A tug and a launch were near the minesweeper, and as we approached, the launch raced for the shore. We went after it, as we thought there might be someone important aboard.'

The Admiralty informed Coastal Command's 18 Group that they had received from signals intelligence earlier in November that the battleships *Admiral Scheer* and *Lutzow*, heavy cruisers *Hipper*, *Emden* and *Prinz Eugen*, and cruisers *Köln*, *Leipzig*, *Nuremberg* and *Emden* were in the Baltic ports and all were believed to be battle worthy and ready to put to sea. The proposed operation, codenamed 'Kidson' and 'Dormore' would be put into force on 14 November 1944. The American Eighth Air Force with their Flying Fortresses would attack first with a second force to follow up, drawn from the Royal Air Force Coastal Command strike wings at Banff, Dallachy, and North Coates. Fighter Command's 11 Group would provide a fighter wing to reinforce 13 Group's Mustang Squadron at Peterhead. This operation was never put into practice. Possibly because of the potentially high casualty rate, as most of the ships had automatic self loading guns.

On 15 November the Beaufighters were put on readiness at Dallachy for a shipping strike, elsewhere patrols off the Norwegian coast continued. A Liberator VI of 206 Squadron on a U-boat search was mauled by three Bf110s from 12./ZG 26. The three enemy aircraft came in from sea level making nine separate attacks in an aerial duel lasting 40 minutes, reducing the Liberator's speed to 150 knots and killing Sergeant K D Conway in the port beam gunner's position. In the final attack the mid-upper gunner New Zealander, Flight Sergeant Mervin Gollan hit one of the Bf110s with machine-gun fire. All three Bf110s were now low on ammunition and broke off. Flying Officer M J 'Jack' Frost set a course for Sumburgh in the badly damaged Liberator; the crew manually jettisoned the depth charges as the aircraft's hydraulics had been ruptured in the first attack. Now extremely low on fuel and sighting Sumburgh they called up the tower but were refused permission to approach, as the Dallachy Beaufighters were due to land on the runway; the control officer suggested the 206 Squadron aircraft should ditch in West Voe. Flying Officer Jack Frost was already on his approach, so he shut down his remaining engines and crash-landed on the runway, the Liberator finally coming to rest on the grass. Frost was awarded the DFC, and DFMs went to the two New Zealanders, Flight Sergeant Gollan and Flight Sergeant J A Nicholson.

On 16 November, hazards were not confined to operational flying. At 07.00 hours with impending sorties, ground crews were hard at work on the exposed dispersal areas. At one of these areas a Mosquito was having its electrical equipment connected for firing rockets when suddenly two were fired off, scattering personnel, who dived for cover. Two airmen, Walter and Ames, were both treated for minor burns in the station hospital. Shortly after take-off on a search 'M' 248 was forced to land as the pilot became sick on the outward trip, the rest ploughed on making landfall at 08.05 hours. An hour later no targets had been sighted in the harbours or Leads, so at 09.45 hours the strike leader spoke on VHF: 'Operations completed, return to base, no attack'. During the evening an ENSA performance of *Nine Till Six* took place at 19.45 hours in the concert hall. Further action on 17 November saw a host of aircraft sweeping the Norwegian coast. A pilot wrote: 'Not a single ship worth attacking was seen, not even in a harbour! One Warwick ditched.'

'Q' 281 piloted by Flying Officer Jenner and his crew was on an operation with the Dallachy Wing. When over the Shetland Isles Jenner's aircraft BV520 developed trouble with the port engine failing and was forced to ditch in West Voe, near Sumburgh airfield, at 13.02 hours. The weather report was 'very high winds'. 'H' 281 piloted by Warrant Officer Bolton was scrambled at 13.15 and upon arrival immediately dropped a lifeboat to the survivors but the parachutes did not release and the boat blew away downwind at an alarming rate, finally striking the rocky shoreline. The whole episode had been observed from the shore and small boats put out, picking up five of the aircrew alive and recovering one body, that of the 24-year-old Warrant Officer Eric Roberts, the crew's wireless operator/air gunner, who was later buried at Lerwick New Cemetery.

An experienced Canadian officer Flight Lieutenant 'Slippery Syd' Shulemson arrived on the base, having joined 404 RCAF Squadron in March 1943. He flew his final operational sortie with the squadron on 17 November 1944, and was then appointed rocket projectile officer for the Banff strike wing. Shulemson was recognised as the top expert in the business, able to devise the best tactics. He flew many harmonisation trails, working out such things as ideal dive angle and speed. Many rockets had been falling short of the target, and Shulemson was able to prove that this was caused by minor warping in the wooden wings of the Mosquito as it dived. With this determined, rocket rail angles were appropriately adjusted. His duties included training the aircrews in marksmanship on rocket projectiles; he devised his own system of firing practice to train the new formation, and had to adapt his methods to the Mosquito with the improved RPJ type head. A new 25lb AP streamlined design had replaced the old RP model and now gave the rocket better underwater travel, allowing extra firing range to the pilots. He would later be rewarded with the DFC for his perseverance in turning the Banff Wing into a deadly anti-shipping strike force.

Two Hudsons arrived in the circuit from Thornaby on 17 November, on detachment from 279 Squadron. They landed and were marshalled into an empty dispersal to be refuelled ready for operations. Upon arrival one became unserviceable, the remaining aircraft, 'W' 279 flown by Flying Officer Elliott, was then immediately tasked to search for a missing Liberator between Rattray Head and Sumburgh Head. This first sortie of the detachment was unsuccessful.

On 18 November a search off the Norwegian coast found three vessels of 3,000 tons and several in Egersund anchorage. Further east at Porgsunn a merchantman and a U-boat were sighted but heavy interference by the German radio location stations jammed the communications during this patrol and prevented a strike. Further flights between Utvaer and Mandal were mounted. As Flight Lieutenant George Lord was on his way home, the port Merlin coughed 35 miles from the coast and Lord hit the feathering button. On making his landing approach he shouted into the R/T: 'Coming in on one engine' a young voice said 'Repeat please'. Seconds after this HP918 landed. A mechanic on 'B' Flight found that the plugs where u/s.

From time to time the Mosquitoes began to operate in increasingly larger formations. Planning started on 18 November for a strike using 100 aircraft in an attack on Ålesund. Group Captain Max Aitken flew in the station Airspeed Oxford RL456 to Donnybristle together with Squadron Leader Thompson to meet with Wing Commander Jack Davenport and Air Vice-Marshal A B Ellwood. Intelligence was gathered, making good use of agents with information on composition of convoys and strength of flakships as well as daily reconnaissance. On 21 November the opportunity to use it arrived. A Rover was flown in 'P' 333 to Ålesund before first light, which discovered some craft in the outer harbour at 09.28 hours, landing back at 10.30 hours.

A deafening roar of Hercules engines woke many from their sleep, while those preparing the Mosquitoes for the forthcoming operation raised their heads skywards as Beaufighters, which had made the 15 minute flight east to Banff, joined the circuit and landed. Airmen and women guided them to a subsidiary runway. All the newcomers could do was wait for a full briefing with the Mosquito crews. Flight Lieutenant Des Curtis of 248 Squadron remembers:

'Briefing was fairly extensive with very detailed plans of the targets within the harbour. We were assigned to silence an anti-aircraft battery within the harbour to clear the way for the R/P aircraft. One of the Norwegian pilots from 333 'B' Flight came over with a photograph taken at low level. He pointed to a house close by the gun site and asked if we could be careful as the house belonged to his parents. He didn't say if his parents were living there at the time.'

As the briefing got underway, the service echelons worked relentlessly but were still suffering from a lack of petrol bowsers, as the Beaufighters' fuel tanks had been topped up for the big strike. Six minutes after midday Bill Sise jointly led with Tony Gadd, the largest strike so far against shipping in the vicinity of Ålesund. There were 73 aircraft from both wings, made up of 32 Mosquitoes, 35 Beaufighters armed with cannon and AP R/P with the J-type heads, and six Beaufighters of 489 Squadron armed with torpedoes. Flying Officer Ken Gainsburgh fired off a green Very cartridge from the watch office. They swarmed into the air until 12.30 hours. Pilot Officer 'Eddie' Edwards, waiting for the petrol bowser to finish refuelling, brought up the rear. The strike leaders did a wide sweep before the final pass above the watch office as Edwards started his engines and taxied rapidly to the runway. As soon as his wheels were up he began a tight turn at 300 feet with some flap down and fortunately he slotted into position on the left side. All were soon cruising in poor weather, skimming low over the North Sea at 2,000 feet, strung out behind the lead aircraft for some miles. 315 Squadron provided 12 long-range Mustangs as escort.

Ten minutes after setting course two Beaufighters left the formation, NT954 with airframe trouble and NE682 with engine problems, both landing safely at Dallachy. Delayed by some 40 minutes due to engine trouble a Warwick of 279 Squadron finally flew out to cover the strike wing, the first operational sortie in this type. This unforeseen delay was boldly overcome by increasing speed and sacrificing precious fuel in order to save time. At 13.02 hours 'E' 144 signalled 'Starboard engine being shut down, setting course for base.' When asked if they required assistance they declined. Before gaining height the pilot jettisoned the torpedo for their passage home. Group Captain Max Aitken flew 'MA' 01 leading 235 Squadron. The Poles flew on the port side of the strike force, in the standard 'finger four' formation. Somewhere in the middle of the North Sea the leader of the fighter escort received a message that a Halifax needed urgent assistance. Warrant Officer Bronislaw Skladzien from 315 Squadron detached himself from the composition and set off in pursuit. The Mustangs adjusted. Shortly before reaching the coast a group of whales were sighted. The force made land fall at Stadtlandet at 14.15 hours and swept along the Norwegian coast northwards. Flying ahead of the main force the Norwegian crew in 'N' 333 were investigating the Leads and anchorages, with only small vessels being seen. The main force waited, ready to pounce on word from the Norwegians but still had no communication at 14.48 hours. Beaufighter 'E' 455 flew outside the leading aircraft searching the Leads and inside as they slowly seeped towards Ålesund. 'N' 333 pilot Lieutenant Leith called the force leader at 14.52 but found the radio had malfunctioned but he saw the force going in towards Ålesund. Three 235 Squadron aircraft attacked two anti-aircraft positions lying close to the shore at Vigro from 500 feet using cannon and machine guns, silencing both. Rejoining and formatting on Aitken, he was heard to say 'Good show'. Nothing else was seen by 'E' 455 except a small white Norwegian passenger packet seen stationary, south-west of Flemso. Unfortunately poor visibility along this stretch forced Sise at 15.19 hours to abort and return to base.

One Mosquito landed at Wick, another at Sumburgh, which, along with Beaufighter 'R' 489, had flown all the way back on one engine. At Banff a fast heavy landing occurred. After a quite fast approach for the second runway, a Mosquito veered resulting in the port undercarriage collapsing. Snow showers were falling as the 315 Mustangs landed at Peterhead. During the night Bomber Command's 6 Group had 13 Halifaxes airborne from 424, 427, 429 and 433 Squadrons on mining operations in the Kattegat, dropping 44 1,500lb mines at 500 and 15,000 feet. On the way out on this early morning operation the navigational aids of aircraft NR257, piloted by Flying Officer W Britton from 427 Squadron, stopped working. After attempting to drop mines visually for some considerable time, the weather intervened. Britton diverted, landing at Banff while the people in the surrounding villages were just waking. In the control tower Control Officer Ken Gainsburgh, chalked up the landing time at 08.21 hours. Twenty minutes earlier another pilot had called flying control with the station call-sign and, after identifying his aircraft as 'Z-Zebra' asked for permission to land. Gainsburgh or one of the WAAF radio operators replied, giving directions to Flying Officer D Gillis to bring his Halifax III NR157 safely down at 08.00 hours. Others were diverted to Dallachy and Kinloss, unfortunately Halifax MZ304 crashed 100 yards off shore at Kingston, Morayshire, with the loss of all crew.

Two Hudsons carried out an uneventful search for a Mosquito on 23 November. Nothing was sighted and the 279 Squadron aircraft aborted the sortie due to adverse weather conditions, diverting to Skitten. Proctor P6262 landed at Dyce, crewed by Wing Commander John Yonge making a visit to the Photo Reconnaissance; he saw some 'strike wing types' in the bar whilst staying at the George Hotel, Aberdeen, where bed and breakfast cost 11/6.

On 25 November the weather in Scotland was holding and the wings had three clear days in a row! Rover patrols began early with six Mosquitoes, two from each of 143, 235, and 248 Squadrons, airborne at 07.40 hours. 'Q' 235 in a search reported vessels in Haugesund, famous for its herring, and this was the next target. Both strike wings joined forces putting up 80 aircraft; 42 Beaufighters and 38 Mosquitoes. Two 143 Squadron Mosquitoes were damaged en route from the hard standing to the perimeter track. The Beaufighters from Dallachy flew to Banff to join the Mosquitoes. Twelve

Mustangs provided escort, together with a Mosquito from 138 Wing, DZ592, flown by Flight Lieutenant William Jones and his navigator/cameraman Flying Officer A J Newell who hoped to obtain photographic evidence. Before the war Newell was a cameraman at Pinewood Studios. Three Warwicks brought up the rear. They departed in force at 12.35 hours and made the Norwegian coast at Karmøy, south-west of Haugesund harbour, and wheeled north up the coast when the weather again interfered. Australian Flight Lieutenant Ted Watson wrote in his diary: 'Flew through most continuous rain ever. Clouds did not break until we were right on top of the coast and it was impossible to form up in time to attack.' A few miles from Haugesund the force encountered heavy flak from shore batteries. The area was shrouded in rain showers and the cloud base, down to 1,500 feet, prevented a good view.

This time Wing Commander Atkinson had no alternative but to turn back. He radioed that the target they had been looking for, a troopship, had moved and he ordered 'Abandon! Abandon!' They swung around. In one of the 455 Beaufighter sections Flying Officer Steve Sykes DFC in 'U' 455, started to bear away to starboard. Slightly above him in formation was Flying Officer Jack Cox. His navigator Warrant Officer Allan Ibbotson saw Sykes' aircraft come up towards them and he called out to Cox 'pull up!' But the aircraft kept coming up and over Cox and the propellers smashed Ibbotson's cupola. He was ducking, and Sykes' propeller grazed him on his helmet. Warrant Officer Ibbotson owes his life to that helmet. The propeller sliced the piece of leather covering his helmet as he ducked and Ibbotson saw the machine gun knocked from its mounting, cutting through the fuselage. The tips of Sykes' propeller blades were bent back and damaged. Ibbotson recovered to plot a course home for Cox and for Sykes. Both remained airborne and eventually in the rain and heavy cloud the Beaufighter force-landed back at Dallachy.

The only exception was 'X' 143, their intercom went dead and they could not communicate with other strike aircraft when they sighted a single merchantman and a minesweeper. They attacked the 1,500-ton merchantman with rockets, which undershot. The aircraft's cannon and machine guns then malfunctioned, stopping abruptly. Flak was intense from both vessels, injuring the pilot when plywood fragments penetrated the cockpit from the portside after being caught by anti-aircraft fire. His navigator applied a bandage to the open wound that was streaming blood. Fortunately they brought 'X' 143 all the way across the North Sea landing at 15.43 hours, with 'L' 279 shadowing them. The Canadians in Bomber Command's 429 Squadron were again required for 'Gardening' during the night of 25 November. They flew to the vicinity undetected, dispensing with their cargo on the return journey. The weather conditions deteriorated and crews were advised to land at Kinloss or Banff.

On November 26 both Banff and Dallachy aircraft took part in separate armed Rover patrols along the southern Norway convoy route with no sightings. Beaufighters from 489 found U-877, a type IXC40, on the surface with an escort. It had sailed from Kristiansund to relieve another weather boat, U-870. Eberhard Findeisen, commanding U-877, crash-dived as two Beaufighters swept into attack; during the dive the retractable antenna of the Hohentwiel radar was ruined. Crippled with equipment failures the U-boat was scuttled on 27 December after the Canadian corvette St. Thomas was credited with the kill. Together with another corvette, Edston, they rescued all 55 Germans and took them to England.

After sweeps by both wings during 27 November a convoy consisting of Fidelitas, a former Italian merchantman, together with Hersberg and four escort vessels were about to enter Ålesund but as it reached Sula near Storholmen natural harbour 404 and 489 Beaufighters dived across the vessels with rockets and cannon firing; torpedoes were dropped by 489 but none struck. The Fidelitas was heavily damaged, riddled by rocket strikes and later disappeared below; 48 crew perished. *Hersberg* and one escort vessel were left almost stationery and ablaze. Three Beaufighters were claimed as damaged by the gunners onboard the flakships. In 1997 the ship's bell from *Fidelitas* was salvaged by the Norwegian naval vessel KNM *Tyr*.

A series of photographs were taken for *Illustrated* and *Flight* magazines during 28 November with Group Captain Max Aitken leading 235 Squadron. There was also an anti-shipping strike demonstration against buoys off shore near the base, with 100 Mosquitoes taking part for the distinguished journalists, and senior air and naval staff. Six Mosquitoes came close to sinking the wing's first U-boat on 29 November when they mounted an anti-U-boat patrol west of Lista. At 100 feet above the waves, they visually sighted a conning tower and a wake at 1,000 yards at dusk. MkVIs made an attack run, opening fire from 5,000 yards, and at 100 feet in height, with cannon and machine guns, and then dropped MkXI depth charges from 50 feet. Flying Officer Wallace Woodcock in a Tsetse fired off eight 57mm shells, scoring two hits. Aircraft 'J' and 'W' 143 took evasive action as the second Tsetse attacked across their path. Unfortunately the U-boat then dived and contact was lost. Flight Lieutenant Geoff Rouse in 'T' 235 carried out a search off Haugesund to see if the vessel spotted on 25 November had sailed four days later. No sighting was made but a fair amount of flak was experienced. Another U-boat patrol on 30 November found no target. November closed; frequent gales had reduced operations from this exposed aerodrome, nevertheless the Banff and Dallachy wings had made five formation attacks with the operational hours for Banff being 1,128 hours. Lectures were given in the cinema on the air war in the Middle East, U-boat warfare, escape and evasion and aerodrome security while dinghy training took place in an inflatable pool. Meanwhile WAAFs received talks on knitting, sewing, and personal hygiene.

On occasions men and women from the base had time to relax and perhaps let their hair down a bit. They might rush off to the little dance hall in Whitehills, which was much frequented in the evenings partly because of the fact it was easy to get to and the entrance price sixpence (2$\frac{1}{2}$p). Portsoy had a dance hall where a dance was held a couple of times a week but unfortunately the airmen and women had to wait until the whist drive finished, so one was lucky to get to bed by about 2.00am. Drinking at local hostelries was boisterous. On the last night of November the station padre made a trip into Banff and Macduff to chase airmen and women back to the airfield! For those that wished to go further afield a railway line ran near two of the RAF airfield's entrance picket posts. The Great North of Scotland Railway had a platform made from railway sleepers near Ordens Farm, known as Ordens Platform and another called Ladysbridge. From both halts one could, if in the mood, get a direct (though never quick) train to Aberdeen for a weekend.

One of those who received postings was Flying Officer Harry Hollinson DFC of 235 Squadron. Earlier in June 1944 he began the unit's *Chocks Away* magazine with the help of Corporals 'Freddie' Wilkes, Les Dollimore, Les Taylor, and Tom Wilkinson, using a flatbed duplicator. His departure saw Flight Lieutenant Geoff Mayhew DFC take over the editorial until the end of July 1945. Group Captain Max Aitken got the squadron commanders to organise a football competition and the rivalry was fierce during November. 235 Squadron was in first place with their own Warrant Officer Coggie Cogswell the leading goal scorer. 235 and 248 Squadron combined against 143 Squadron in a rugby match on 1 December, only to draw six points each. The highlight for the crowd was seeing the Australian Ken Beruldsen pick up the ball, brush off his attackers and score a try under his own posts! The winning teams from both competitions were taken down to the Seafield Arms in a five-ton truck for an all-ranks booze-up.

CHAPTER 6

DECEMBER 1944

The strike wings were now causing considerable damage to the German convoy system. The commander-in-chief of the German Navy, Karl Doenitz, had been an officer in the German Navy since 1913, seeing service during the First World War in the Mediterranean before being transferred to submarines in 1916. In 1935 Doenitz was put in charge of the new U-boats being developed, but by 1939 he only had 57. In an address to German Naval staff on taking command he said: 'The entire German Navy will henceforth be put into service of inexorable fight to the finish.' Between 1940 and 1943 the U-boat wolf packs invented by Doenitz had taken a heavy toll of Allied merchantmen, but they were now feeling the same pressure. At the Führer's conference on 1 December 1944, Doenitz told Hitler that because of 'constant heavy attacks... off the Norwegian coast, the time is not far off when all shipping movements in this region will come to a complete standstill.'

December opened in Scotland with adverse weather conditions and four days of operations were cancelled. The only people to venture out were those taking part in the station cross-country run. The Commander-in-Chief prompted the Air Ministry about making modifications to 235 and 248 Squadron aircraft. After a conference at Coastal Command's headquarters at Northwood, London, it was decreed that the Mosquito should be adopted as the main strike aircraft. The rocket had finally surpassed the torpedo as the most important element in the strike wing's armoury. Operations began as usual. 333 Squadron's Norwegian aircrews were kept busy with searches. Fenrik Løken and Quartermaster Nils Skjelanger in 'H' 333 caught sight of a convoy through the murk in Ålesund, and then west of Kristiansund they encountered a Junkers 88. During an 11-minute air battle they expended all their ammunition. The Junkers slipped away with smoke coming from the starboard engine. It plunged into the water at 12.59 hours off Ålesund. Mosquito HP864 returned at 15.04 with a bullet hole in the port airscrew boss.

Strikes commenced on 5 December with 34 Mosquitoes. There were 14 of 248, ten of 143, nine of 235 and a MkIV of 138 Wing recording the action. Most were armed with 25lb J-type head and the formation included four Tsetse Mosquitoes. Half an hour before the operation commenced a Miles Martinet made an emergency landing on the 1,400 yard runway and was promptly towed out of the way. Taking off just before midday Wing Commander Bill Sise led this armed patrol in 'A' 248, as earlier craft had been discovered in the fjords; the largest vessel was a transport seen in Voldafjord. At 13.45 hours Nordgulen fjord, a broad stretch of water flowing inland near Florö, came into view. Four merchantmen were spotted moored at the tip, protected by a cluster of flakships and two tugs. Sise looked at these unexpected targets but he had been ordered to search the neighbouring fjords. Over the radio-telephone he gave a quick command, dispatching two Tsetse Mosquitoes to give Jerry a couple of squirts. Flying Officer Wallace Woodcock fired off fifteen 57mm shells whilst Flying Officer William Cosman DFC, fired another six. Both reported hits on the superstructure on one of the moored merchantmen, then rejoined the formation. The vessels in Nordgulen fjord formed part of two convoys, one heading north the other south, which had arrived coincidentally at the same daytime anchorage point near the village of Svelgen. The northbound convoy Be-1075-A1 consisted of three vessels, the *Tucuman* of 4,621 tons, *Magdalena* of 3,283 tons and the *Helene Russ* of 995 tons. Though the latter of the vessels was the smallest, she was perhaps the most important for her loaded cargo was ammunition, supplies for the German garrisons. Protecting them were four flak ships Vp.5102, Vp.5111, Vp.5305 and Vp.5306 of the 51st and 53rd Vorpostenflotte. At the same time there was a southbound convoy with the damaged *Ostland* of 5,273 tons in tow by *Aasenfjord* and *Fairplay*, two armed tugs, with an escort of Vp.5109, Vp.5308, and Vp.5310. The sight of reconnaissance aircraft had alerted the Kriegsmarine officers earlier in the day and they had manoeuvred their flak ships closer to the steep cliffs. The merchantmen had also moved closer to the sides of the fjord but the moorings for the larger merchantmen were inadequate and they where positioned further out in the waters. The vessels put up a barrage of fire, thinking they had driven the Mosquitoes off. In fact they had not.

Sise was still heading for the primary target, leading the wing north-east and finding a coaster of 1,500 tons in a nearby fjord. He found the main target in Voldafjord, a vessel of 6,000 tons, together with a coaster, but these were in an anchorage sheltered by the steep mountains at the narrow end of the fjord. It was impossible to attack through the low cloud that hung over these mountains. So Sise ordered the formation to swing round and head back to Nordgulen. On the short return flight, the strike leader addressed each section of Mosquitoes over the radio-telephone detailing the sequence of attack. Twenty-five minutes after the first token attack by Woodcock and Cowman's aircraft, Sise gave the order and led the first wave in on his portside. Minutes afterwards the starboard section followed them down for it was impossible for them all to attack at once in the confined space. A German gunner, Karl Werner, serving on an armed merchantman in Norway during the winter of 1944, describes one such attack:

'We heard the distant sound of aircraft engines again, assuming them to be British Moskito (Mosquito) aircraft; the engine noise increased as they neared our vessels. Looking through the field glasses, I could see them closing in fast, and shouted "Attack Alarm", at the same time pressing the alarm button on the exposed watch platform. The gunners ran to their gun platform, some trying to put their lifejackets on or helmets. Orders were shouted giving range and height as the 20mm and 37mm cannon streaked from all quarters of our vessel's guns, wild at first. With vessels (and shore batteries) joining in, tracer headed towards the mass of diving aircraft, with flashes of light coming from their noses. I joined a crew at a gun platform. We didn't see the first rocket strike, but suddenly there was a great shaking and a column of water, which went up to about 600 metres. As aircraft came in, I ordered "Fetch more ammunition" while yelling instructions at the corporal on his 37mm cannon, shouting "Lower, lower". Together we directed a stream of explosive and armour-piercing shells into a Mosquito. An orange flame erupted from the starboard wing. Our vessel rocked with impact from more rockets and cannon. Four colleages were thrown from the gun platform into the sea. With hands covered in oil and uniform drenched in sweat, I threw one a line, only to see him disappear into a bloody mess hit by cannon or machine-gun fire from another of our attackers. When I assessed the damage afterwards, I found cannon and machine-gun fire had hit the deck, funnel and bridge area while rockets had reduced the engine and radio rooms to a shambles; we were lucky to be afloat. During this attack, six were killed, and 14 wounded on the vessels we protected. The attacks usually lasted minutes but it seemed like hours.'*

Mosquitoes went down the snow-covered fjord; flak burst in the sky from the northern shore batteries, which were positioned several feet up on the mountainside. Accurate intense anti-aircraft fire was also experienced from the whole eastern end of the anchorage. Flying his 44th operational sortie, the 21-year-old Warrant Officer Bill Parfitt dived from 1,200 feet, his airspeed indicator showing 360mph. He felt Mosquito 'V' 248 jolt as it flew through a barrage of heavier 88mm and 37mm flak thrown up from the ships and the shore, but he kept his sights on the *Magdalena*, the most westerly vessel in the fjord. The Mosquito juddered as he opened fire with his cannon, with splashes straddling the target. Then he released his salvo of eight rockets, flew over the target and broke away to port, heading westwards out to sea. *Helene Russ*'s defensive fire dwindled as the rest of the aircraft came in. On Parfitt's port a Mosquito was on fire losing height and German anti-aircraft fire had claimed another. Flight Lieutenant Leslie Collins and navigator Flying Officer Robert Hurn both skilfully pressed home their attack on a heavily armed ocean-going tug despite their aircraft 'G' 248 being on fire. With starboard engine ablaze and a trail of thick black smoke behind, it crashed into the sea at 14.15 hours with no sign of survivors. As the aircraft swept down the fjord, weaving to avoid anti-aircraft fire, 'C' 143, on sighting the wake of an E-boat, blasted it with their remaining ammunition. The E-boat's engines were hit and after about a mile, they seized up. Geoff Mayhew DFC describes the strike:

'The first wave vanished over the edge of the mountain as I watched and a few seconds later I went over in 'E' 235, as part of the second wave, switching on the camera in the nose that recorded rocket shots. The fjord was full of shell bursts and my target apparent to me, I lined up on the *Helene Russ* and the camera was taking pictures steadily. Afterwards photographs showed rocket and cannon hits. Like the rest I exited towards the sea down the fjord, whose high sides rose beyond each wing. My navigator Flying Officer Stanley Farrow and I found to our discomfort that the enemy had placed anti-aircraft guns on either side and we dived below a stream of tracer from one position.'

After the attack the Germans began to assess the damage and count the casualties. It was a shambles, with vessels on fire and ammunition exploding. *Magdalena*, *Ostland* and *Tucuman* were reported damaged but because of their closeness to the shore, some craft were prevented from sinking. On board the *Helene Russ*, the cargo of anti-aircraft ammunition exploded as men on board battled to douse the flames until extinguished, plugging the rocket holes so that it would remain afloat until the vessel could be towed to shallower water. The *Ostland* was thought to be damaged but was not, all her armaments were fired which caused large amounts of smoke to hang over the vessel. Most of this was due to her firing parachute-assisted cable rockets. She was reported as hit as photographs taken during the attack showed smoke coming from her fore and aft decks. German seamen reported three Mosquitoes shot down during the attack and three that left the scene on fire. The harbour master at Florö said that three Mosquitoes had crashed in the sea after the attack. As usual, these statements were somewhat inaccurate: eight aircraft sustained flak damage with a further three flying on one engine and five landing away at other bases. Shortly after this attack, the Dallachy aircraft set off for Nordgulen.

---

*Unfortunately Karl Werner died in 1995, and in his translated letter he did not state the name of the merchantman he served on, or the date of the attack to which he refers. However it is useful to illustrate the feelings of a crew under attack.

Squadron Leader John Pilcher led 16 Beaufighters away from Dallachy and set course for Norway together with a single Mosquito from 333 Squadron and 12 Mustangs of 315 Squadron. They made landfall 90 minutes later, just two miles south of Ytterøyane Light, and there they parted. Pilcher took the main force north-east towards Nordfjord. He continued north and some 14 minutes later crossed Nordgulen fjord, the site of the Mosquito Wing's gritty strike less than half an hour earlier. Beaufighter crews saw one of the smaller vessels well alight and a column of black smoke rising over the fjord. The German defences laid a heavy barrage over their position. Pilcher flew over Nordgulen a second time to Nordfjord, sighting five vessels which he thought were unsuitably positioned for attack, then on to Ørstafjord where he found three merchantmen. The convoy Be-1073-Al had arrived earlier in the morning and cast anchor. On the south side were the merchantmen *Radbod* of 4,354 tons, which was sailing southwards for repairs after an accident outside Bodø four months earlier, and *Albert Janus* of 2,275 tons with a cargo onboard of 3,100 tons of munitions and the third merchantman, *Dockenhund*, was at the eastern end close to the village of Ørsta. Guarding them was Vp.6805, which kept watch circling on the north side opposite Selervik. Inside the fjord the water was quite calm, especially at the eastern end and the sky was cloudless.

The Beaufighters were in two sections. At 14.28 hours Pilcher made his attack with two other crews up the fjord to strafe the merchantmen anchored near Ørsta. He attacked with cannon, which fell short into the water at first, but then moved up striking the superstructure, forecastle and amidships and over the water to the foreshore. As he pulled out of his attack and banked hard to port the second aircraft came in and they continued in a sweep over Ørsta then turned back down the fjord to hit the other two vessels. These Beaufighters from 455 Squadron hit *Radbod* with their rockets and seriously holed it. With the engine room flooding the crew could not stem the tide and the ship sank. The sailors made for *Dockenhund* and all survived. In the second section Flying Officer James Austin Hakewell and his navigator Fred Sides were flying 'V' 455 on the port side of Flying Officer Bill Herbert. Suddenly there was Vp.6805 ahead steaming towards the fast approaching Beaufighters, which were flying as low as possible and weaving about as tracer from ground positions bounced off the sides of the fjord. This minesweeper with an 88mm on its bow was firing at the attackers. Hakewell in NV438, flying 100 yards on the port side, received a direct hit by rounds from *Albert Janus*, his starboard wing disintegrating as he returned fire. His aircraft dived in flames, exploding just in front of the minesweeper and with debris hitting the bridge of Vp.6805.* On board Vp.6805 they saw the Beaufighter remains and petrol burning on the water, while five comrades lay dead. Pilcher in 'D' 455 watched Flying Officer Neil Smith, leading the second wave, make another attack with cannon on two vessels near the shore and under steam. Two men from Bordflakabt 5 Kiel were killed in this pass: Helmut Hille and Gerhard Schlar.

After this attack Pilcher's force made for the coast, climbed to 3,000 feet and set course for Scotland 400 miles away. Shortly after leaving the Norwegian coast a distress call was heard from 'M' 455, which was answered by 'R' 455 at 15.00 hours, ably assisted by 'X' 455. As Flight Sergeant Dunn in 'X' 455 reduced height to 1,000 feet he noticed zero oil pressure on his starboard engine. Soon afterwards the engine

---

*In 1947 the parents of Fred Sides travelled to Ørstafjord to visit the spot where their son had died. The Beaufighter had been retrieved from the waters; all that remained was tangled wreckage. On that spot they held a memorial service and dropped wreaths in commemoration. A memorial stone was unveiled. The inscription reads: 'Our beloved boy Frederick Gordon Sides Australian Air Force lost in Ørstafjord 5 December 1944. Erected by his sorrowed parents and sister on their visit from Australia June 1947.' Today the *Radbod* rests at a depth of 25 to 70 metres, 200 metres from the shore. Unfortunately in 2001, foreign divers looted the wreck.

failed and Dunn set coarse for Sumburgh. Warrant Officer John Ayliffe accompanied 'M' 455 flown by Pilot Officer Arthur Winter. They headed straight for the Shetland Islands, but as they came within reach of the base at Sumburgh they were forced to ditch. Both crewmen climbed into the dinghy then half a minute later Beaufighter NT914 sank. Markers were dropped over their position and Ayliffe circled until a Warwick arrived. Flying Officer R Garven piloting 'H' 279 dropped marine markers to illuminate the dinghy. Garven's wireless operator unsuccessfully tried to make contact with the orbiting Beaufighter. Its pilot Ayliffe departed at 16.45 hours. A further investigation of the area 6038N/0021W found no sign of the dinghy. The Warwick crew were further frustrated when the interior lights fused, amongst other failures. Their spirits were lifted when the mid-upper saw red Very lights coming up from the surface. At 17.55 hours Garven messaged, 'Live bodies in water' and the wireless operator sent a signal to base. Shortly afterwards an RAF launch was observed approaching which duly plucked the aircrew from the sea. 'H' 279 left the area heading for base but was ordered to land at Banff. They joined the circuit, touching down at 19.50 hours.

In the afternoon of 5 December 1944, Sumburgh airfield received the casualties from both strikes. One of the first to arrive was a Photographic Reconnaissance Mosquito MkXVI from Dyce on a sortie to cover various anchorages along the Norwegian coast including Ålesund and Molde. They had just completed their run over Ålesund at 27,000 feet when the navigator Flight Lieutenant Frank Baylis noticed droplets of black liquid coming from the starboard engine, which soon went into overspin and caught fire. Piloted by Flight Lieutenant 'Danny' Daniels, a gritty Canadian from Windsor, Ontario, he pressed the extinguisher which put the fire out, but his attempts to feather the propeller were unsuccessful and it started to wind mill – the liquid had been hydraulic fluid. Turning for the Shetlands they started to lose height due to the excessive drag caused by the wind-milling propeller. Baylis sent out an emergency radio call and one of the Warwick Air Sea Rescue aircraft that had been covering both strike wings vectored towards the PR Mosquito. They lost height steadily, levelling out at 800 feet. With both feet on the same rudder pedal, Daniels persuaded the Mosquito to fly along for a further 150 miles before the Shetlands came into sight. They came in on one engine, landed and rolled off the end of the runway. Hardly had Daniels and his navigator Flight Lieutenant Frank Baylis arrived in debriefing when a Dallachy Beaufighter 'X' 455 slammed into the runway with wheels up and slid in a shower of sparks onto the grass; the navigator shot out of the cupola with feet running before they hit the ground. Hours later when the engine cowling was removed from the Dyce-based PR Mosquito, most of the Merlin engine fell out!

Another of those flying on a single engine was Mosquito PZ418 with Flying Officer Bob 'Baldy' Gilchrist and navigator Flying Officer Bill Knight. The port engine had stopped soon after their attack at Nordgulen fjord and Gilchrist feathered the propeller. His navigator gave him a course for the Shetland Isles and the flight over the North Sea was uneventful although Sumburgh Flying Control fired off Very cartridges because of the hazy conditions, so that they could find the airfield. As they prepared to land, it was clear that the Mosquito had no hydraulics and Gilchrist was unable to use the flaps or wheels, which left Knight little time to retrieve the emergency hand pump stowed on the cockpit door; it would take four minutes to lower the undercarriage. The approach onto this runway at Sumburgh is quite difficult even when carrying out a left hand circuit, but the angle of glide has to be particularly steep when landing off a right hand circuit due to the high ground. Gilchrist was forced by the hill to make a right hand circuit, rather than against a dead engine, attempting to belly land. Flight Lieutenant 'Taffy' Crocker and Ron Simmons in 'Y' 143 had diverted to Sumburgh themselves after both engines began to overheat. Having reported in at the control tower they both watched their friends coming in high and at speed. It was 15.35 hours. Gilchrist landed PZ418 too fast, badly overshooting. The undercarriage was retracted in a vain attempt to slow down, finally coming to rest when it crashed into a brick wall at the end of the runway overshoot area. The 22-year-old sustained a fractured skull caused by the radio and radar equipment situated behind him being thrown forward when hitting the wall. The canopy shattered, and Knight was showered with hundreds of perspex fragments, sustaining cuts to his forehead. He was surrounded by debris and the instep of his right foot was caught by one of the metal parts of the fuselage. As the noise subsided Knight saw the head of an Italian prisoner of war appear above the offending wall. He had been tending the station's garden beyond. The starboard engine was smoking and the navigator beckoned him to come and release him, but the Italian's courage failed him!

Within minutes, the rescuers had arrived. Gilchrist was unconscious and his navigator advised them to get him out first. There was a large amount of blood on Knight which he took to be from his pilot but was in fact from his head wound. The blood wagon returned eventually to lift him out, and they laid him on someone's sheepskin jacket. He spent one night in the station's sick quarters, then he was transferred to Lerwick Military Hospital. The next morning Bill heard the unfortunate news that his pilot had died of his injuries. The young flying officer's body was flown back to Lanarkshire to be buried in his home village of Crawford. Gilchrist now lies next to the graves of his parents.

After being discharged from the hospital and still wearing his torn battledress trousers Flying Officer Knight went to Sumburgh airfield clothing store for a new pair, ready to return to his squadron in mid-December. He recalled: 'I was amused when the warrant officer in charge would not release a pair saying – You're not on the strength sir!'

A second member of the strike force headed into Sumburgh. Flying Officer 'Alfie' Lloyd on his first operational strike with 235 Squadron recollects:

'They put up accurate heavy flak into the middle of the formation and aircraft went wheeling all over the sky to evade it. While attacking our target I was busy taking photographs with an F24 camera when suddenly the aircraft was stopped in its tracks, then plunged forward. Banking over the target, we weaved madly down the fjord out into the open sea. The port rev counter dropped rapidly and my pilot feathered the port engine and I put out a distress call. Our Mosquito limped along at 140mph during which the Warwick 'G-George' nursed us along and upon reaching Sumburgh they departed back to Banff. We could not go in for an approach because another Mosquito had just crash-landed, with the pilot Gilchrist killed. We eventually ran in and touched down, but the tail would not get down owing to having no brake pressure. We went whizzing along and ground looped rather viciously towards the sea and eventually came to rest.'

During the evening of 5 December 'D' 248 returned to base having landed at Wick after the operation, while five Torbeaus from 489 Squadron flew out on a Moon Rover searching between Stad and Kristiansund. Meanwhile Sholto Douglas was applying pressure on Portal at the Air Ministry for another long-range fighter squadron to be made available as escort for the coastal wings. At Peterhead, 315 Squadron's first few trips had been uneventful. Their next flight was on 6 December, as a convoy sailed towards Ålesund. A mixed force flew out at 11.18 hours, with 'M' 235 joining from Banff, on a Rover near Bremanger, with an escort of 315 Squadron Mustangs flying above at 4,000 feet. Seconds after take-off one of 'H' 489's petrol tanks started leaking, Flying Officer Bill Carson landed and quickly had the problem fixed then took to the air. Wing Commander Ed Pierce of 404 Squadron led the force in 'J' 404. Shortly before reaching the Norwegian coast Flying Officer Bill Kelly brought 'H' 489 to the port of the Beaufighter force and took up their position. At 13.22 they were joined by a second Mosquito 'U' 235 whose crew had scouted ahead sweeping along the coast between Følo to Vaagsoy. Probable targets had been seen in Vaagsoy. The force proceeded out to sea across Bremanger after experiencing heavy flak in the Vaagsoy area. They ploughed on to attack from the north, the strike leader calling, 'Over the ridge and straight down on our target.' Over the ridge they went amid light and heavy flak. At 13.35 hours 'H' 489 independently left the formation and Flying Officer Bill Carson attacked anti-aircraft batteries in Kråkenhes with cannon and machine guns. The aircraft became the focus of concentrated 27mm flak and shortly after rejoining the force the starboard engine began to smoke. Despite attempts to extinguish the fire 'H' 489 ditched in 62.03N/05.12E. The Beaufighter slammed into the water with the tail unit breaking off.

After spending approximately 10 minutes in the water Flying Officer Bill Kelly could not see his pilot. He then heard Carson calling, his foot had got caught and been pulled down forty feet before it came free, leaving one boot behind. His Mae West had brought him straight to the surface. As the cold began to grip them they started swimming towards the dinghy which was 100 yards away, after 20 minutes they reached it. Exhausted they held onto the knotted rope, but their hands were so cold that they had no grip or feeling. Eventually Kelly got Carson into the dinghy and Carson reciprocated and pulled Kelly in. Both lay exhausted for a little while, taking stock of their injuries; Carson had hit the gun sight and had an inch cut on his forehead and a small cut on his chin, Kelly had cuts on his head, seven of his fingers and legs. They got the paddles out and started for shore, but the effort proved too much, progress was slow and eventually both stopped. Kelly began to massage Carson's feet, which were both dead white with no feeling. Kelly rubbed them with his bloody hands which he couldn't feel either. From the air a rowing boat could be seen putting out from a nearby island, 'Z' 144 signalled that the boat was 50 yards away before leaving the area.

Once Carson and Kelly saw the rowing boat approaching they both collapsed and waited for it to pick them up. They were pulled aboard; Carson in the stern, Kelly on the floor. Suddenly the Germans started shelling the small rowing boat, but their Norwegian rescuers rowed harder around an island until they reached the shore. The two Norwegians conversed then started rowing further around the island where another Norwegian waited on the shore together with four or five others scattered on various vantage points keeping watch. One got out and disappeared with the watchers, while the one that was left began to row. Kelly said 'Germans' and the Norwegian nodded. Minutes later a German R boat which had been taking provisions to the local anti-aircraft battery arrived and both were lifted bodily aboard and helped below, where they were stripped and given dry clothes. One and a half hours later both were helped ashore, had preliminary interviews and were told a doctor would see them in two hours. Both were handed over to Luftwaffe officers and changed for a third time into boots (no socks), trousers and great coat all of which were old, shabby and smelly. They were made to walk to the doctor in agony through ice and snow for about half a mile, both making several stops, clinging onto a guard on either side. Kelly was given an injection but nothing further, and they were told they would be leaving for Oslo that night. A truck took them to the railway station. With stops and hold ups they got to Oslo on 9 December. Carson was placed in jail at Oslo aerodrome. Kelly was taken to a nearby hospital for treatment. After ten days in Oslo they were put on a ferry which took them to Fredrikshaven in Denmark from where they made their way through Germany with four guards to the Interrogation Centre near Frankfurt-am-Main. It was now 21

December. They remained POWs until 2 May 1945.

At 13.40 hours three merchantmen, one of 3,000 tons and two of 1,500 tons, were at anchor off Molde. Severe gunfire together with the narrowness of the fjord prevented the force attacking as they could not be reached. One aircraft of the Mustang escort, flying at 2,000 feet, piloted by Pilot Officer Jan Borowczyk, was flipped upside down from the power of the blast of a German shell, but he managed to regain control. The formation broke out to sea and reformed. 'C' 489 breaking over land attacked with cannon firing 200 rounds at a 2,000 ton merchantman at anchor on the east side of Sorpol fjord, but no results were observed. Pierce signalled to formation, setting course for base at 13.58 hours. At 15.08 hours on the return journey one of the escorting Mustangs HB833 got into difficulty 40 miles from Sumburgh. Flying Officer Harrison in 'W' 144 saw a Mustang circling and went to investigate. Visibility was poor through heavy rain and Harrison strained to sight and fix either a wreckage or a dinghy, but he did locate an oil slick on the surface at 59.30N/00.20E. Flight Lieutenant Jerzy Schmidt presumably waited too long before selecting another tank and some air got into the system; the engine stopped and he tried to ditch. Fellow Pole, Borowczyk watched HB833 go down; it touched the water and rode the waves smoothly for 200 yards then twisted to port, the nose of the aircraft plunging vertically into the water. Borowczyk remarked later: 'His aircraft twisted suddenly, the white nose plunged vertically into the water, both pilot and aircraft vanished.' Landing at 15.50 hours at Peterhead, crews were rather depressed at the loss of yet another experienced pilot and the lack of Germans to shot down. Dan Nowosielski commented: 'He did not get out of his aircraft! We were rather depressed, another good friend ended in the drink.'

The vessel *Tucuman*, attacked on 5 December, was seen entering Ålesund harbour by a Photographic Reconnaissance Mosquito the same day a further sortie from Dyce covered Gossen airfield but found no aircraft.

Over the past three months enemy air opposition had been absent against the wing but the Germans were now not content with sending out single or mixed small groups of fighters to attack the Mosquitoes and Beaufighters. On 7 December JG 5 Staffels moved to southern Norway. The Banff and Dallachy wing would from this point on be met by up to 40 German fighters at a time. These principal Luftwaffe fighters defending Norway had some 30 Fw190As and 50 Bf109Gs at various bases.

The first large-scale counter attack occurred when 42 Beaufighters and 21 Mosquitoes with Mustang escort took off on Thursday 7 December at midday (the 5 torpedo Beaufighters from 489 Squadron were not armed with torpedoes, but would act as anti-flak aircraft). Two crews woke at 04.30 hours; after a briefing two Mosquitoes from 235 Squadron took off at 06.41 hours, circled to 1,000 feet and headed towards the Shetland Islands. 'X' 235 flew into bad weather and landed at 10.10 hours, while 'M' 235 passed over Ålesund to find five merchantmen flanked by two escorts, with further reports of vessels in Nordfjord and Vaagso. During this time all the remaining aircrew had been woken by the various squadron duty officers and, after a meal of three eggs and bacon in the airmen's mess, they waited for the briefing. The crew landed at 11.16 hours and were quickly interrogated by an intelligence officer. The information was then passed onto 18 Group. Air Vice-Marshal Ellwood decided a force should attack the convoy holed up in Ålesund, or any suitable targets midway between Bergen and Trondheim. A third aircraft from 235 Squadron flew out at 10.42 hours; Flight Lieutenant Basil Quelch of 235 Squadron in 'U' 235 made for the Norwegian coast passing many islands. Quelch flew over Ålesund where he found two stationary merchantmen, his navigator sent a report of their discoveries by VHF. The Beaufighters were airborne from Dallachy between 11.18 and 11.30 hours and set course for Banff at 11.50 hours to join the Mosquitoes taking off from their bases at

11.35 and 12.00 hours, together with three Banff-based Warwicks of 279 Squadron and one from Wick.

The formation was jointly commanded by Squadron Leader Barnes of 235 Squadron who led the force in 'J' 235, and Squadron Leader W R Christison who led the Beaufighters in 'Y' 404. The Air Sea Rescue Warwick's leader was Squadron Leader R B Simpson. The force swept across the Scottish countryside to rendezvous with 12 Mustangs of 315 Squadron, whose leader was Wing Commander Kazimierz Rutkowski.

The mixed Coastal force was led away from Banff at 11.48 hours while aircraft were still taking off. Mosquito PZ466 was the last aircraft in this great armada to get airborne, Lieutenant Alexandre (USAAF) retracted the undercarriage, as his navigator jotted down the exact time as 12.00 hours. Warrant Officer Llewellyn Compton in 'A' 248 had radioed that he had suffered an engine failure and landed at 11.45 hours, thus delaying Alexandre's departure. Squadron Leader David Pritchard, flying 'B' 143 PZ451 suffered a radio malfunction at 12.03 and with hand signals he gestured to Flying Officer Howley that he was returning to base, touching down at 12.15 hours. Within the Beaufighter force 'N' 404 signalled to 'M' 404 by Aldis that his radio had packed up and they dropped out of formation and headed for Dallachy, landing at 12.43 hours.

At 12.04 Barnes lost height and brought the combined force down, almost to sea level, below the German radar. One minute later as a result of a loud screeching noise on Channel D a visual signal was sent by Clayton to 'V' 235: 'Is your radio ok?' the reply was 'Channel D unusable'. Two more aircraft confirmed this. Clayton then passed visual messages to the same two aircraft: 'Change to Channel A – pass this on by Aldis'. Mosquito 'E' 235 at 12.30 hours in position 59.33N/00.10E heard, 'Rest of message lost in interference on set' at the same moment Flying Officer Howley in 'J' 143 heard 'Switch off transmitter' using collective call sign, which was acknowledged. Unfortunately for some inexplicable reason 'J' 143 had no Aldis lamp and therefore could not pass this important message on to the remaining formation. This break down in communication would have dire consequences for those who didn't get the change to Channel 'A'.

At 13.21 hours the strike leader could see coast to starboard. The force was further weakened when Flight Lieutenant A McLead DFC and Warrant Officer N Wheeley in 'Y' 248 experienced engine problems and turned back with 'F' 248 piloted by Warrant Officer G A Macaskill and Warrant Officer W J Jeffers in 'M' 248 acting as close escort, together with two Mustangs. The Mosquitoes landed at Fraserburgh at 15.15 and 15.50 hours. A second crew with engine problems also landed at Fraserburgh, Flight Lieutenant Johnny Lown's aircraft had problems with the petrol feeder in the port inner tank. He had flown in via Sumburgh, touching down at 16.05 hours.

Meanwhile the Mustangs wove protectively in a 'finger four' formation at 100 feet on the port side. There was a misty horizon but the weather was good, except for the frequent showers encountered on the way across. At 13.30 hours the strike leader's navigator heard on VHF from 'U' 235 'Good target, Ålesund outer harbour four merchantmen'. Flight Lieutenant Basil Quelch DFC and his navigator Flying Officer Burkett Barber immediately sent an updated sighting report from 'U' 235 at 14.00 hours. This read: 'Four vessels still at anchor. Good target in Ålesund outer harbour,' signing off with a message of 'Good luck' on the VHF. The strike wing's ASR cover was diminished when the Wick-based aircraft 'C' 279's port engine developed an oil leak at 14.10 and returned to Wick, landing at 15.15 hours. Simpson adjusted the remaining three to a 'Vic' formation. Flying Officer 'Paddy' O'Reilly flying 'N' 279 sighted the Swedish merchant vessel *Dagmar Saleu* but his flight was interrupted at 15.14 hours when his starboard engine started to cough. O' Reilly was given a course immediately for Wick by navigator Flight Lieutenant 'Johnny' Drinkwater. Informing the strike leader that the two remaining Warwicks would be needed to accompany 'N' 279 the three turned away and headed for home. The journey across the North Sea was uneventful apart from the odd whale being seen, but it was too soon to relax as there were ample opportunities to dive into the drink. Once the Scottish coast was in sight O' Reilly called Wick Flying Control and asked for permission to land. With the engine feathered a left hand circuit was made, landing at 16.30 hours. Simpson in 'G' 279 and Pilot Officer 'Phil' Horsburgh flying 'L' 279 diverted to Fraserburgh on instructions from control.

As the strike force neared the coast the weather improved and the aircraft began to climb to 4,000 feet about 15 miles off the shore. Making landfall 15 miles west of Ålesund, near Harøy Island, it was spot on thanks to the lead navigator, Flying Officer Clayton. Regrettably his pilot and strike leader, Squadron Leader Barnes DFC in 'J' 235 ignored his navigator and led the formation in a west-south-west direction towards Gossen, a Luftwaffe fighter base 65 miles further up the coast, Barnes then intended flying down to Ålesund. With the Mustangs now flying on the starboard side some were experiencing very bad radio interference.

Gossen Group III Staffel Kommander Von Dörr was on leave and Oberleutnant Glöckner was standing in for him; in his absence Glöckner had divided them into two units, 10 and 11 Staffel. A few hours after their arrival at Gossen on 7 December, these pilots would engage the enemy strike force. The alarm sounded when the Mosquitoes and Beaufighters were 15 miles west-south-west of Gossen, and seconds later Focke-Wulfs and Messerschmitts were in the air, flying at 500 feet as they headed east. Von Podewils recorded 'Take off in Alarm start, Gossen 14.05 hours.' The strike force arrived over Gossen at 14.12 hours and gradually lost height as sections on the outer fringe of the armada had already started to encounter enemy aircraft.

It was too late for the strike force to avoid the German attack. Some R/P rails were quickly being jettisoned, falling away into the icy grey waters below. By 14.10 hours the first sighting of bandits was being reported as 'Z1' 248 PZ252 pilot Flight Lieutenant Brian Beattie was engaging three Bf109s at 2,500 feet, five miles west of Gossen. The dogfight broke up when another Mosquito joined the mêlée. 'Z1' 248 then went down to sea level, watching an enemy aircraft crash into the sea at 14.12 hours. At the same time, 'T1' 248 PZ301 piloted by Flying Officer 'Wally' Woodcock made a ground attack run on Gossen airfield using the 57mm cannon and machine guns to good effect, turning away on the starboard quarter. An enemy aircraft at 1,000 feet fired a burst at 'T1' 248 which was at 100 feet. No damage could be seen and the aircraft handled normally. Three Bf109s were seen and Woodcock hurled his aircraft earthwards to 60 feet in an effort to shake off his pursuers, their rounds churning up the ground ahead of the Tsetse as they tried to get the twisting aircraft in their sights. After a few very anxious minutes Woodcock evaded them. Almost immediately a Norwegian outrider in the leading section called out 'Bandits at 12 o'clock' followed by Barnes with 'Bandits ahead'. Flight Lieutenant Konrad Stembrowicz and other pilots in Blue section saw them but were unable to shout a warning because of interference on Channel D – the Brummer radio system was active at Gossen. One section of enemy fighters went through 315 Squadron flying at 4,000 feet and Mustang HB857 'C' 315, flown by Flying Officer Andrzej Czerwinski crashed into the sea between Flatflesa Lighthouse and Krabben and became the first casualty. Rutkowski thought there was a mixed enemy force of about 15, as he saw one comrade go down in flames. A Polish pilot, Flight Sergeant Jakob Bargielowski, looked in his mirror to see one of the Mustangs was going down. The victor of this hit did not have time to relish his success as Bargielowski immediately went after him and shot him down. The Bf109G broke up in mid-air, and the remains fell to the ground a mile south-west of Gossen, this was Bargielowski's fifth victory and he became the youngest Polish ace. Another Bf109G closed in on Bargielowski's Mustang but the leader of Yellow section, Flight Lieutenant Franek Wiza fired a burst, and fragments were seen to fall off the enemy aircraft which immediately broke away turning for Harøy Island. The German aircraft crashed into the ground at Harøy, but the pilot escaped unscathed and managed to walk to the radar site at this location. Wiza claimed another Bf109 shot down during this combat. Fellow pilot Oblt Walter Smejkal went down in flames. Seconds later Wiza saw rounds flash by and pushed the column sharply to avoid them. At the time Czerwinski was hit Wing Commander Kazimierz Rutkowski turned the remainder of the force 180° to face the approaching enemy, singling out an aircraft he recognised as a Focke-Wulf. Soon heavy smoke came from its cowling after rounds found their mark, and Rutkowski lost it from his field of vision. He claimed one Fw190 probably destroyed. While Rutkowski was engaged in the dogfight his wingman Warrant Officer Ryszard Idrian saw two Fw190s racing along the deck towards Gossen. He gave chase and the enemy fighters collided while taking evasive action against the fast approaching Mustang; their remains fell on the west tip of Gossen. Without firing a shot Idrian claimed them both. Seventeen strike aircraft turned and set course for base as the air battle began. Ten miles out Squadron Leader Don Rogers in 'B' 144 signalled on VHF to the Beaufighters: 'Formation check petrol and divert if necessary.' Barnes was then heard to say to the sections: 'Turn out to sea, seek cloud cover, and engage if in a position to do so, but continue to withdraw.' Six enemy fighters, most probably led by Oblt Rudi Glöckner of 11 Staffel, were flying a course of 200° and in line abreast made for the Torbeaus flying at 40 feet. The slower Beaufighters increased their speed to 200mph, but could not keep up with the Mosquitoes. It was now the turn of the Mosquitoes to receive the attention of the German fighters. They swept through the middle of the Mosquito formation, which broke for the encounter. Mosquito 'J' 143 HR436 was jumped by five 190s, three miles west of Gossen at 14.12 hours. Dispensing with his R/Ps Howley was engaged on the starboard quarter at 1,500 feet, banking tightly and counter-attacking with cannon and machine-gun fire. Later two enemy fighters approached from the port and starboard quarters, but were just out of shooting range. Howley headed for Scotland after this run in, just managing to reach Sumburgh and landing safely at 15.50 hours. Gefreiter Dieter Baasch of 10 Staffel became separated from his comrades and then paired up with 'Gelbe 12' flown by Glöckner. After about 12 minutes flying time they both pursued three Torbeaus five miles from Gossen and Glöckner engaged two of them. One crashed and the other turned westwards. One Beaufighter 'S' 144 NE423 was flown by Warrant Officer R McAfee and Flight Sergeant F Rhodes, who survived three attacks after corkscrewing down to 200 feet. The first was from 300 yards astern, the second from 250 yards and the final encounter from 400 yards. During the evasion McAfee jettisoned his torpedo but Glöckner's cannon fire had racked the port engine and tailplane. Rhodes wrote the time down as 14.12 hours. Glöckner claimed this aircraft as his 32nd victory. Baasch was to become a successful pilot as, like Glöckner, he had the courage to close right up to his target. He attacked the third aircraft from behind in a heavy dual with Flight Sergeant Max Graham, and as Glöckner broke away to port at 200 feet Graham lifted the nose and from 800 yards, fired. At the same moment Baasch's rounds struck their port engine. A light coloured flag appeared from the Beaufighter minutes afterwards and the burning Beaufighter tried to ditch. Baasch saw and heard the impact of the crippled aircraft hitting the water about ten miles north-east of Almestad.

As aircraft fought across the sky at 14.45 hours allied aircrew saw a white Red Cross vessel on the horizon. At 15.00 hours Warrant Officer Ian 'Nobby' Clark saw Beaufighter 'X' 144 appear and flashed the message 'Stay with me – port engine packing up.' They were flying at a height of 50 feet, and a few minutes later jettisoned the torpedo. Straight away Graham pressed the button to feather the propeller on the port engine but it wouldn't work, a rare occurrence on a Beaufighter. Feathering would have increased the speed by 15 to 20mph, however because of the drag the airspeed was down to 140mph (the minimum recommended) and Graham decided that as he risked stalling and spinning in, he would ditch while he still had some height left. It was a hopeless position. He shouted 'Get ready hatch, we are going in!' Clark jettisoned his cupola by pulling the release lever on the port side of the fuselage then strapped himself in the seat. There was quite a swell so landing would be rough. Graham lined the aircraft up and tightened his own safety harness straps. At 15.15 hours LZ448 skimmed along the surface and gradually slowed, it then hit a big wave, and abruptly stopped. The water began to pour over and into the aircraft as they went down, into a world of darkness, then the aircraft rose to the surface and daylight. Clark was out in seconds and along the wing to secure the dinghy which had popped out. He pushed it down off the wing on to the water and climbed aboard. In the cockpit Graham released his straps but found his parachute buckle hard to release, it wasted precious seconds in his climbing out. Once unbuckled the parachute dropped away and he climbed out on to the wing where he observed Clark tugging on the rope which held the dinghy, suddenly the rope broke and the dinghy started to drift away. Graham dived in, swimming furiously and as his navigator was helping him on board, LZ488 sank. Beaufighter 'X' 144 flew over and dropped markers and the navigator Warrant Officer Bates got a Gee Fix position and dropped a marker. 'U' 143 also got a fix on the dinghy of 60.25N/00.20E at 14:30 hours. Baasch had claimed his first success.

At 14.15 hours Leutnant Heinrich Freiherr von Podewils attacked a Beaufighter at 250 yards from the rear below him, firing a burst into the right engine, which caught fire. The aircraft subsequently span into the sea a few miles from Gossen. Lt Rudi Linz witnessed this downing by Podewils.*

At the same time Blue section of 315 Squadron was in a series of dogfights and the section leader watched as a Bf109 he had engaged went down in smoke. However Stembrowicz was unable to finish him as his wingman put some accurate bursts of cannon fire into the Mustang's starboard wing. He was forced to disengage not knowing how serious the damage was. Warrant Officer Czerwinski was trying to help his section leader, but he himself was attacked by four Bf109s. He shot one down but dived away at full throttle being chased by the remaining three.

In the increasing confusion Flying Officer William Cosman and Flying Officer L M Freedman in 'O' 248 NT225 and Flying Officer K C Wing and Flight Sergeant V R Shield flying PZ346 were shot down with the loss of both crews. One of them is likely to have been one of the Tsetse Mosquitoes that Lt von Podewils engaged at 14.15 hours. 'X' 248 pilot Flight Lieutenant Lewis Bacon reported a Mosquito going straight in at 100 feet into the sea, by Maavær off Harøy, after being chased by a Bf109. The enemy fighters broke off when attacked by 235 Squadron Mosquitoes. 'K' 235, flown by Warrant Officer Coggie Cogswell singled out a lone Messerschmitt at 14.16 hours, and attacked from the starboard quarter at 200 yards with cannon and machine guns, but could not see the effects. Later Cogswell wrote 'estimate nil damage' in his logbook. Flight Sergeant McCall of 143 Squadron reported a Mosquito with one engine on fire, flying at sea level just north of Gossen, however it was not seen to

---

*Von Podewils flew a Messerschmitt 109G with the symbol 'Gelbe 12' but because a 'Gelbe 12' already existed a letter 'A' was painted after the '12' to identify his aircraft in an air battle. He had a total of 18 victories by the end of the war.

crash. A couple of Mosquitoes were observed to attack a merchantman by Beaufighter crews but time and position were not noted.

Other Beaufighters were also being attacked. Rounds flashed by the confined cockpit of Flying Officer Flynn in 'S' 404. It was too late to take evasive action and his navigator Pilot Officer Michael received minor wounds when a cannon shell shredded its metal skin and exploded inside the navigator's compartment as they were attacked from 250 yards from the underside. The Bf109G broke off to starboard when a Mustang got on its tail. Two Beaufighters then escorted Flying Officer Flynn and his wounded navigator to Sumburgh.

The air battle end suddenly; Squadron Leader Barnes climbed to 5,000 feet and gave the instructions to 'reform out to sea' as he tried to rally his crews around him. Then came another message at 14.17 from the strike leader, 'Check petrol and divert if necessary', followed later at 14.23 by 'Proceed to base individually'. With the fuel almost exhausted owing to combat, the force was now strung out flying individually or in pairs bound for the Scottish coast, but on approach they were asked to divert to either Sumburgh or Fraserburgh. Just under a dozen Beaufighters and Mosquitoes landed at Sumburgh, between 15.35 and 15.57 hours. Flight Lieutenant 'Wally' Webster, piloting HR130, wrote in his note book while at Sumburgh: 'Attack Ålesund harbour – shambles – attacked by 109s, bad weather front passing through Banff, landed in Shetlands.' Most aircraft touched down by 16.30 hours with less than 10 gallons in their tanks.

The fighting was over, but exhausted crews on both sides now had to give their intelligence officers details of the operation and combat. Beaufighter crews reported seeing one enemy aircraft go down at 62.51N/06.42E and two shot down. One of the enemy fighters went down in flames from 4,000 feet at 62.43N/06.32E, and this account was also reported by 'Z1' 248, being downed at 14.12 hours. The crew of 'R' 235 reported: 'We saw an explosion in the water followed by oil marks and wreckage at 62.25N/06.04E which could not be identified with many dog-fights seen in the area.' Several crews on this operation reported seeing a lone Junkers 88 in the vicinity; it is not known why it was in the combat area.

Meanwhile in Norway, pilots of the Eismeerjäger had successfully prevented the attack on the merchantman, the German pilots claimed 13 twin-engined and two single-engined aircraft as shot down, but this was grossly exaggerated. The strike force actually lost one Mustang 'C' 315, two Mosquitoes ('O' flown by Flying Officers William N Cosman DFC (RCAF)* and his navigator Flying Officer L M Freedman and 'Z' PZ346 from 248 Squadron with Flying Officer K C Wing and navigator Pilot Officer V R Shield) and Beaufighter 'R' 489. There was jubilation from pilots of 315 Squadron who claimed four Bf109s shot down, one probable, and three Fw190s as probable. German documents confirm four losses. Later came the news after the battle at Gossen that two German pilots were missing from III/JG5, and both had perished: Offizier Harry Bernhardt of 10 JG5, flying 'Schwarz 11' (Wr. 410818) who was seen to come down in the sea by one of his comrades while attempting to crash land and Offizier Raimund Bruscagin from 11 JG5 in 'Glebe 11' (Wr. 410816) who had gone down into the water near Gossen. The RAF and Commonwealth aircrews had fought their way through with the Poles and now the tension was over, they all talked at

*Cosman had already completed one tour of duty before joining 248 Squadron at Portreath in June 1944. The Distinguished Flying Cross was awarded to him on 17 November 1944. The award was sent by registered airmail to Yarmouth, Nova Scotia, to his next of kin. The citation reads: 'This officer, now on his second tour, has unfailingly pressed home his attacks with outstanding courage and determination. He has taken part in attacks on U-boats, a destroyer and mine sweepers. Flying Officer Cosman has displayed great skill and his devotion to duty has been of the highest order.'

once in a flood of chatter in the messes. Weeks later on 29 January 1945, 315 Squadron's intelligence officer received confirmation from Fighter Command that four had been shot down during this dogfight. More of this story unfolded 12 days later when in the Caledonian Hotel Flight Lieutenant Richardson saw the familiar face of Wing Commander John Yonge. While awaiting for the weather to lift at Dyce he had caught the bus into Aberdeen to do some Christmas shopping. Richardson told him about the fiasco on 7 December: 'Cosman, Wing, and Shield were shot down when a strike force led by Squadron Leader Barnes was set upon by about 20 190s and 109s. This was the result of making a bad landfall. The formation was broken up completely, Cogswell was the only one who seemed to get in a decent attack from 235. Barnes was immediately sent on an administration course the following day.'

315 Squadron pilot Dan Nowosielski was flying a Mustang IIIB as escort on the day:

'Nearing the coast my leader Flight Lieutenant Konrad Stembrowicz pointed out a Mosquito returning on one engine, I thought he wanted me to escort that kite back, so cursing him I swung round with my wingman. 15 minutes later the interference cleared, we heard our friends shouting in combat. We did not turnabout; it would have been too late. We touched down at Peterhead after a trip of four hours. Thus, we missed the fight with the enemy in which the squadron shot down six [*sic*] confirmed and Stembrowicz got a probable. However, it was not without loss: Flight Lieutenant Andy Czerwinski was shot down. "Job well done" said the brass hats at 13 Group. The squadron's return to base was the worst part. Andy Czerwinski was due a month's leave and his very heavily pregnant wife was awaiting his safe return in the mess. She came out with others to watch the Mustangs landing. Flight Lieutenant J Polal and his wife who had also arrived to collect her husband took care of the widow and drove her home to Blackpool.'

One crew were quickly briefed and dispatched from RAF Banff. 'Plumpbird 12' was tasked with doing a square search in the area for the ditched 489 Squadron Beaufighter crew; it proved negative. For the two New Zealanders they were searching for things were getting worse. Their dinghy had a rip across the bottom so they were sprawled in a rubber ring of water. It was almost mid-winter; a breeze was blowing and darkness would descend on them within the hour. The first night they saw lights on the horizon but couldn't attract them. They did have rations and the emergency Very pistol with cartridges. The next day, 8 December, nothing was sighted. Coastal Command aircraft were searching for them in heavy driving rain, HR130 spent an hour and 40 minutes searching 60 miles east of the Shetlands. Two Hudsons from Thornaby were airborne at 07.39 hours, nothing was sighted and the two landed at Sumburgh at 12.25 hours. A Wick-based Warwick continued the search. Flight Lieutenant Murray's crew scoured the expanse of water but didn't sight the dinghy and returned low on fuel to Sumburgh. For Graham and Clark time dragged, wet and cold, until daylight on the third day of their ordeal.

At 11.55 hours on 9 December the American, Flight Lieutenant Shanks (USAAF) in 'G' 279 Warwick joined the pursuit while covering the Banff wing, together with Squadron Leader R B Simpson flying 'F' 279 waiting to intercept them on their return journey. In mid-afternoon Graham spotted the Warwick, Clark fired the Very pistol to attract their attention but the cartridge didn't go off. The Warwick flew right over them. By the time he'd reloaded with a fresh cartridge they could only watch as it turned out of sight. After another agonizing half an hour it suddenly appeared again a few miles away. Clark fired a Very light in its direction and their prayers were answered. Forty-five miles east of Fetlar in the Shetlands the crew onboard 'G' 279 observed a red light in the water at 15.00 hours. Shanks immediately turned towards it and was thrilled to find the ditched crew. The two flight sergeants in their aircraft dinghy waved frantically as the aircraft flew over them. The Warwick then began to circle them. Twelve minutes later 'F' 279 arrived and Simpson sighted the American circling the 'M' type dinghy. Shanks immediately prepared to drop the airborne lifeboat, dropping marker flares to give some light in the growing darkness. At 15.44 hours, 100-150 yards downwind of the dinghy the parachutes blossomed as they splashed down and the rockets fired off lines deploying 175 yards of buoyant rope over each side of the airborne lifeboat. Graham and Clark paddled like demons and successfully clambered aboard it at 16.00 hours. There were survival suits in the boat which were similar to inner flying suits but waterproofed and with feet and hood attachments. Graham had been saturated since his unplanned swim and wriggled into the warm dry gear, Clark's body was dry but he had soaking legs and feet. They drank some water from the rations, and got the motor started by the light given off from a second drop of illuminating flares. The two men then set off on a compass course after being advised on a note by the Warwick crew to steer 270°.

Flight Lieutenant Hanson-Lester in Hudson 'N' 279, who had previously flown on 8 December, rejoined the search from Sumburgh, dropping flame floats all around the area. After two hours the Warwick left them. Shanks now looked for further aid in the immediate area, this came in the form of a fishing trawler called *Molde* which the American pilot skilfully led on an intercepting course. A second Hudson 'K' 279 relieved 'G' 279 at 16.57 hours, orbiting over the markers. Pilot Officer E Hill saw a white light coming from the fishing trawler; the aircraft's navigator Pilot Officer W Fenton used the Aldis to signal them. At 20.12 several flares were fired into the air from the HMNS *Molde*; the crew had finally located the two New Zealanders. The crew of the fishing trawler gently lifted them on to the deck at 20.50 hours and a few minutes later handed the pair a mug of steaming hot tea. Using a handheld torch the words 'crew safe' were flashed in Morse code, Fenton wrote this down and showed it to his captain. 'K' 279 turned on a heading for Sumburgh but was forced to divert to Wick, landing at 21.30 hours. Graham and Clark soon partook of a hot meal, followed by more tea laced with rum. A cabin was provided for sleep and rest but sleep wouldn't come. As their feet heated up they began to burn as if on fire. This was due to their immersion in cold salt water for such a long period of time and it was to plague them for the rest of their lives. On arrival at Lerwick on 10 December, the HMNS *Molde* put Graham and Clark ashore at 03.45 and they were taken to Lerwick Military Hospital. After a week Flight Sergeant Ian 'Nobby' Clark was well enough to return to Dallachy.

Two days later the Dallachy Beaufighters patrolled the Norwegian coast, escorted by 315 Mustangs and a Banff-based Warwick 'F' 279. A single Mosquito flew ahead as the 144, 404, and 455 aircraft approached the coast, where the outrider reported a target sighting to the strike leader, Squadron Leader Duncanson from 144 Squadron. Making landfall at Utvaer Light, they turned north over Utvaer and flew past Sandøy Light to the recognizable shape of Ytterøyane Light. Here the force swung out to sea, climbed and turned south again meeting up with the outrider, which led the main force to the target. A few of the aircrew recalled that at the briefing before the strike they had been told by 18 Group intelligence that the Norwegian *Havda*, which was classified as a merchantman and had a funnel displaying a black Swastika in an orange circle, might be carrying high-ranking Nazi officials and German officers, so it deserved special attention. The target sighted by the Mosquito was indeed the unescorted steamship, *Havda* of 678 tons, built in 1881, which was travelling south near Vilnesfjord on a journey from Måløy to Bergen. It had earlier had only 12 passengers on board but the pilot had berthed at Måløy and now it steamed towards Bergen with its complement swelled to 20. Half an hour after she departed from Florø without opposition and on her regular route, six 455 Squadron Beaufighters launched cannon and rocket attacks across the beam, one by one like a procession the Beaufighters swept in, with several circling to make a second run using cannon and machine guns. During the line astern attack the pilot, an able seaman and a female crewmember were killed from machine-gun fire. *Havda* caught fire, ablaze from bridge to stern, and two explosions were observed from the air.

Miscalculating badly, a crew from 404 Squadron, on only their second strike, took their Beaufighter down so near to the vessel that it hit the mast. The port wing fell off, the aircraft turned over onto its back and fell into the water exploding in front of the coaster. Flying Officer Cooper and his navigator were killed. Flight Lieutenant David Whishaw riddled the vessel with cannon as the Beaufighter crashed and exploded on his starboard. Flying Officer Steve Sykes DFC obtained cannon hits across the centre of the ship and Flying Officer Clive Thompson shot up the bow. Of those who were on board six died. Smoke several hundred feet high formed over the steamship, with only the front section now visible.

Three aircraft circled to make a second strafing run. Overall, nearly 60 hits were scored with rockets as the Beaufighters set off for base. *Havda* was left ablaze, while her remaining crew tried turning towards land. The 17 survivors managed to scramble to a small island until a rescue vessel could pick them up. A reconnaissance aircraft 30 minutes later reported the vessel beached and still burning fiercely. When put ashore the injured were sent to a nearby hospital while the crew and passengers were taken to Askvoll. The same reconnaissance aircraft sighted more shipping further south in Flekkefjord. Dan Nowosielski flew as escort with his comrades: 'The sky was clear over Norway. For me it was an uncomfortable flight of four hours and ten minutes, as I had to sit on a very badly packed dinghy pack with the air bottle sticking up my backside. On landing I invited the mechanics and WAAF packer to get it changed.'

On 9 December the Director of Operations (Maritime) told the Commander-in-Chief Sholto Douglas to allow 235 and 248 Squadrons to begin modifications to their rocket heads and the chief armaments officer had five weeks to complete. On 10 December Coastal Command received intelligence through SIS and photographic evidence that a vessel was stationary in Flekkefjord and if sunk it would seal off the fjord. Squadron Leader Butch Jacques DFC was to lead the attack. Once briefed and the aircraft airborne they passed over a fishing fleet out in the North Sea. When they arrived in the area their mission proved fruitless, as the vessel had already sailed. Three vessels were spotted travelling west-south-west in Strandfjord in the afternoon; D/S *Gudrun* of 1,485 tons carrying a cargo of cement and ammunition and being escorted by the anti-submarine vessels UJ.1706 and UJ.1767 were sailing for Flekkefjord. The subsequent attack by ten aircraft lasted 12 minutes. During the run in a Mosquito suffered damage from expending shell cases from 'V' 235 which embedded themselves in one of the wings. *Gudrun* caught fire and began burning amidships, cargo began to explode. Rockets had also penetrated the lower hull in several places and it slowly started to flood. When things had calmed down one of the escort vessels towed her into the shallows near Abelnes. Kriegsmarine crewmen began the long job of stabilising the fragile ammunition and six men worked through the night until daybreak repairing the damage.

On 12 December 20 Mosquitoes led by Wing Commander Bill Sise in 'M' 248 with 'N' 333 acting as an outrider, took off from Banff at 12.30 hours. They made landfall at 14.19 hours and began searching Ytteroerne and the Leads without success, reaching Eidsfjord towards dusk. At 14.30 hours Flight Lieutenant Bob Golightly in 'N' 333 sent the strike leader a sighting report on VHF, five minutes later the strike got underway. A convoy consisting of *Wartheland* of 3,678 tons accompanied by the Norwegian steamer *Tore Elisa* and the Bergen-registered *Molla* of 815 tons was protected by two flakships, Vp.5101 and Vp.5303. The attack left the Germans in disarray. The captain aboard *Wartheland*, realising the situation was hopeless as the fire on board was out of control, ran aground. Eventually the vessel sank and all that remained on the surface was her funnel. The two steamers also received damage during the attack.

Kaz, a young Polish airman serving with 315 (Polish) Squadron from Fighter Command's 13 Group base at RAF Peterhead, remembers the routine when flying as escort to the Coastal Command anti-shipping strike squadrons:

'I found escorting Mosquitoes a bit more pleasant than escorting the Beaufighters simply because the Mosquitoes flew faster, around 240mph instead of the Beau's 180, making the Mustang's controls much firmer. Secondly, that blasted awful trip took less time, although I am surprised when looking at my logbook on 13 December 1944, to find that a trip to Mölde with the Mosquitoes took only ten minutes less. I have an idea that we loitered in the target areas with the Mosquitoes who were looking for additional things to hit. The Dallachy crews were just in and out on the one pass. If the weather was good, which was rare, we used to like to hang around a bit and make sure the Beaufighters got away safely and we would try to find something German to shoot at. We could just about double their speed and so could afford to let them get away from us. With the Mosquitoes, we did not have such a great speed advantage and so we couldn't let them get too far away. At the target we tended to sit high over the coast and watch for fighters while they did their business on the flakships and merchantmen. More often, the weather was pretty poor and so we just stuck like glue to either the Banff or Dallachy aircraft so we wouldn't get lost.

'We were all on the deck under the radar and we headed to our primary target via Sumburgh Island. We always hung behind and out to the sides of our charges, just out of their prop washes. These were long, stressful yet boring and usually quite cold flights. I was quite thankful that the manufacturers of the Mustangs had included heaters, which I put to good use. Even more useful was the ashtray, which the Americans had so thoughtfully provided, although you had to supply your own lighter and cigars. At the beginning of every flight we were issued with ten Woodbines which came in very handy. Flying along at around 200mph was like walking for us, so a smoke was a nice diversion. We were also given a small packet of sardine sandwiches for every flight. On the long flights, those sandwiches kept the wolves in our stomachs at bay and gave us something to do. Unfortunately, the Germans never invited us down for a drink to cap off the afternoon.

'I only once had the need to use the piss funnel also fitted by those thoughtful North American designers but that was on a Beau raid. Using it in flight was quite a feat in its own right. I remember I was bursting and couldn't hold on any longer, so I pulled away to port, still at 50 feet and unbuckled all my harnesses. Then with the stick between my knees I undid my fly and with one hand dug around inside my pants till I found my own little hose and exposed it to the passing seagulls. I pulled the funnel over into my lap and let loose. What a blessed relief! Being that low there was plenty of moisture around so the side of the plane got a wash before our mechanics had to work on it. Then it was the whole process in reverse with the trickiest bit being buckling my harness back on. That was a two-handed job with the stick back between my knees.

'The trips to Norway with the Mosquitoes and the Beaufighters were always staged through Sumburgh as we need to ensure that our tanks were topped up in case of our having to fight an engagement over the target and then make it back home to Peterhead. Sumburgh was a wretched little windswept island out in the middle of an inhospitable grey sea. The landing strip was just that. A strip. Depending on wind direction we would land either on the long strip or with the normal wind direction on the short strip across the width of the island. There were no taxiways and we would let our charges land first. With two squadrons of Beaufighters or Mosquitoes packed at the far end, our squadron would land and hope our brakes would work. Then the Mustangs would turn about and taxi along the strip to dispersals where we would be followed by the Mosquitoes or Beaufighters. We'd jump out and the resident ground crews would refuel us and give our aircraft the once over. We'd step into the canteen if it was close to eating time and have a bite to eat and attend to internal pressures. Then it was back into the cockpit, strap in, start up and wait for the attack aircraft to get into the air and we'd follow, set course and settle down for the run to target.

'Once they found the target, we'd pop up a few thousand feet, weather permitting, and keep our eyes peeled for trouble coming out from land. My logbook doesn't note any interference from the Luftwaffe on the two Mosquito flights I was on, fortunately for them. They must have been warned that I was flying that day. Possibly they thought that either I was a fearsome warrior, not to be trifled with or that it was simply too dangerous for anyone to be in the same airspace as me as my flying was so erratic. I don't ever remember meeting the Mosquito guys face to face as we moved fairly often and were very busy, although even now I can still remember their helmeted heads under their canopies.

'On one of these trips we were just tootling along when my engine coughed and died. At 50 feet and 180mph in a Mustang, that's a dire situation. I glanced at my wing tanks and noted one had just dropped off. With some consternation, I flicked the fuel switch over to the main tank and hit the booster pump. With prayers to the god of ground crews, I thanked them all sincerely as the motor responded and I could pull away from the cold sea. Afterwards my friends told me that they saw the wash from my prop on the sea as I recovered. I count myself as fortunate that ever since I had been flying I had rehearsed such a situation in my head and was subconsciously ready for it. Only a couple of weeks later, the same thing happened to a flight lieutenant but he went in and was killed.

'Anyway, I mentioned this to my mechanics who looked gravely at me and said that it would be fixed. I think that they were a bit disappointed that something had gone wrong with the aircraft they had loaned me. Anyway I had no more problems with a tank dropping off. In January 1945 we were moved back south and were escorting B-17 Flying Fortresses into Germany.'

On 13 December 18 Group called for a special strike. Eighteen Mosquitoes made up from 235, 248 and 143 Squadrons, escorted by six Mustangs of 315 Squadron and a Warwick returned to Eidsfjord, because of the importance of the targets. The 30-year-old Australian, Wing Commander Atkinson, who a few days earlier had been awarded a bar to his DFC, led the force. At 12.21 they began to take off. They were due to be accompanied by three Norwegians but this number was unexpectedly reduced when HP864's port engine lost power at 100 feet, just as it got off the ground. The pilot managed to swiftly make an emergency landing. Just after 14.00 hours the rest of the force made landfall near Utvaer Light, a tall red tower protruding from the rocks. While the outriders searched along the inner Leads the remaining aircraft flew outside the

Leads. Norwegian Lieutenant Stensrud sent the radio message 'Target in Eidsfjord' at 15.07 hours. Mosquitoes swept in towards the daunting mountain terrain, gaining height and turning towards Eidsfjord, guided by 'N' 333 all the way to the target. Below D/S *Falkenfels* was the only merchantman in convoy Al-1097 together with two escorts; Vp.5503 and Vp.5110 on watch.

A hot reception awaited them. The force prepared to attack, and the 18 Mosquitoes went down in sections with Atkinson leading. Behind him others were queuing up to hit the vessels. Projectiles of all calibre were streaming towards them from the flakships and shore batteries. Shells exploded in a swarm. Inside the cockpit of Atkinson's aircraft 'R' 235 was his navigator Flying Officer Val Upton. As they thundered towards the target the gun crews at the German fortress at Furuneset lined the aircraft up in their sights and began firing rounds. Suddenly Flying Officer Harold Corbin of 248 Squadron saw an explosion in front of him and knew that Atkinson's aircraft had received a hit. The starboard wing was ripped off and below the gun crew shouted with joy as they watched the doomed Mosquito spiral out of control into the fjord a few feet from the vessel; no survivors were seen. Lieutenant Dymek (USAAF) and Flight Sergeant Harvey in their respective aircraft hit these anti-aircraft positions with rockets, machine guns and cannon fire causing many fatalities. Flying Officer Harold Corbin recalls:

'I followed "Dickie" down, directly behind him slightly to starboard. Tracer passed us and kept coming. Suddenly there was a burst and it ripped off his starboard wing, fragments embedded themselves into our aircraft as I continued looking through the sights, our Mosquito juddered from the blast. Atkinson's aircraft just spiralled in.'

Lieutenant Stensrud wrote: 'Circled to take photographs but owing to increased intensity of flak unable to.' D/S *Falkenfels* was left smoking.

It was not only anti-aircraft fire that caused damage to the Mosquito aircraft. Flying Officer Angus McIntosh of 248 Squadron encountered a mallard duck as he pressed home his attack, which damaged the port mainplane. As the Mosquitoes set course back to Banff, led by Wing Commander Maurice, one of Vp.5303's crew noticed bits of the debris from 'R' 235 and human remains floating on the surface. Vp. 5303 edged nearer and retrieved some documents and Upton's navigation map. The additional information was quickly taken ashore and dispatched to Måløy for interpretation. The remaining Mosquitoes landed at 16.46 hours with the last one touching down at 16.53 hours in a numbed state having lost another two good men: one a much decorated and highly skilled pilot, who had shown himself in every way to be a first class leader. A small group of personnel waited outside the WAAF canteen for a scheduled dress rehearsal for a forthcoming play by the RAF Banff concert party. A navigator in 235 Squadron, Warrant Officer Ron 'Ginger' Burton remembered: 'A passer-by told those of us waiting for Val Upton that he wouldn't be coming to open-up as he had not returned from the operation.'

The following day the station commander appointed Flight Commander Squadron Leader Norman 'Jacko' Jackson-Smith DFC, to take charge of the unit. Wing Commander 'Junior' Simmonds was then posted as the squadron commander; this 27-year-old was a veteran having flown constantly throughout the war.

On 15 December the night was very dark as a German convoy, Be-1102-Al, crossed the Sognefjord heading for a narrow sound in the inner Leads, the Krakhellesund. On board the leading vessel S/S *Ferndale*, formally Scandinavian, and now under a German flag, Captain Karl Wagner looked for the dim light from the *Klaus-Feuer*, as the Germans call it, a small lighthouse which would show the tiny entrance to Krakhellesund. Suddenly out of nowhere it was in front of the vessel. He ordered a new course, north by north-east in order not to run aground on the Seglstenen, the rock in the middle of the narrow Lead. However, the current was very strong at the time and the Seglstenen loomed out of the darkness all too fast, tearing the S/S *Ferndale*'s metal hull and grounding it at 05.15 hours. The other vessels in the convoy, the S/S *Wihelms* and tug *Fairplay X* narrowly passed the disabled vessel. Captain Karl Wagner radioed 5. KSV in Bergen, and S/S *Wilhelms* was ordered to sail on, along with two escorts to Ålesund. The third escort, the Vp.5303 Jäger, a former Norwegian whaler *Hval VI*, received orders to stay by the *Ferndale* as did the *Fairplay X*. The Kriegsmarine officers asked for more assistance. Inspection of the *Ferndale* revealed they would need divers to repair the badly damaged hull. During the day they needed more assistance and a special salvage vessel *Parat* was ordered to the site. Work began but by the 16th *Ferndale* was still steadfast on the rock, with *Parat* at her starboard side and *Fairplay X* aft.

Captain Wagner then observed a single unidentified aircraft pass over them high up in the sky. They all knew what this meant, and the alarm sounded onboard every vessel. Vp. 5305 moved into the shadows of the steep cliff, just south-west of *Ferndale* thus affording it some protection and making it difficult for it to be observed from above. It was well camouflaged and almost invisible against the cliffs. *Fairplay X* was a short distance away. In a few minutes all the guns on board all the vessels were manned as well as all the RAG on board Vp. 5305 *Jäger*.

Between 09.46-09.52 hours, Wing Commander Maurice led 22 aircraft from 143, 235 and 248 Squadron, on a Rover patrol. Within minutes of being airborne 'L' 248's starboard engine lost power, the propeller came to a halt and the undercarriage unit failed to retract. Flying Officer 'Wally' Woodcock tried to restart by pressing the feathering buttons but was unsuccessful. This navigator, Vacher radioed base and fired off a Very cartridge, it was clear that the airfield could be reached, but height could barely be maintained. Woodcock turned in for the approach, lowering the flaps, feathering the remaining engine and switching off everything to avoid a fire for an emergency landing. Both tightened their harnesses ready for the impact; with a jolt MM425 slammed into the ground ripping off the undercarriage leg, and causing extensive damage to the underside as it slid along. After finally stopping both crew scrambled clear through the escape hatch. It was later found that the constant speed unit had failed.

Above in heavy wintery showers with 10/10ths cloud the aircraft formed-up and finally set course at 10.10 hours away from Banff skirting Sumburgh. Warwick 'F-Freddie' provided the ASR cover for this operation. They made landfall at Utvaer Lighthouse, at the western entrance of the Sognefiord at 11.40 hours and began searching along the coast while a single 333 (Norwegian) Squadron crew flew ahead. Nine aircraft broke off and flew north along the inner Leads. The wing had received information in advance that a large vessel was aground at Krakhellesund, and this was confirmed at 11.40. By 11.44 hours Maurice had heard from the 333 Squadron crew that the disabled *Ferndale* had been sighted. The force prepared to attack. German gunners on board began firing and defending themselves, various calibres ranging from 88mm, 37mm and 20mm streaked into the sky, but failed to prevent a line astern attack which was made down the fjord because there was so little space for the Mosquitoes to manoeuvre. (The escort, which was hiding between rocks with overhangs on either side, was sighted by aircrew.)

The sound of 40 Rolls-Royce Merlins at full power was deafening as the 22 Mosquitoes went down low through the narrow sound, attacking from the south. At 11.48 hours, 248 Squadron anti-flak section were first in, their task to clear the decks with machine-gun and cannon fire. Next came the Tsetse and R/P Mosquitoes. The attack lasted two minutes but the damage to the vessels was heavy. S/S *Ferndale* was engulfed in smoke with eight crewmembers killed, one seriously wounded, and four slightly wounded from her complement. *Parat* was burning fiercely, but the flak from Vp.5305 had been effective. The anti-flak section had taken heavy fire from all quarters. In Mosquito 'W' 248 Flying Officer Gilbert 'Geep' Peckover sat beside his pilot, Flight Lieutenant 'Alec' Gunnis a Scotsman from Clackmannanshire. During their run in accurate anti-aircraft fire had badly damaged the fuselage and wings and the windscreen had shattered. Gunnis pulled out low over the fjord. Virtually unable to see through the perspex he headed out to sea with another Mosquito guiding them. Accurate 27mm flak found its mark on Mosquito 'R' 248 as pilot Flight Lieutenant John Kennedy made his run in. Somehow he pressed home his attack with guns blazing, despite the port engine being hit. Kennedy reported being hit and his navigator Flying Officer Frank Rolls fired off red Very cartridges. The distress call was heard at 11.53 by the two Norwegian outriders and answered by 'Z1' 248. Attempts were made to contact 'R-Robert' on VHF but Rolls' replies were very faint. 'R' 248 turned slowly out to sea, burning and losing height rapidly. Both crew prepared to ditch. Flying Officer 'Johnny' Hayton circled in 'Z1'248, reducing height as he followed them down, while the strike leader's navigator, Flight Lieutenant Cochrane, radioed 'Plainsong' reporting a Mosquito in trouble. At 12.03 hours the aircraft ditched successfully at 60.59N/04.09E; both crewmen got out. 'P' 333 and 'E' 333 circled the dinghy. Sweeping low they were able to see one man in the dinghy and one in the water alongside. For several minutes their aircraft remained afloat before being swallowed by the sea. They were also kept company by 'U' 248 and 'F' 143, all four circled overhead for a few moments but then left the area low on fuel. Another Mosquito took their place over the dinghy. In the drifting dinghy both men, whilst being tossed up and down, watched eagerly as the 279 Squadron ASR Warwick 'F1' 279 flew overhead guided in by 'P' 333. One of Warwick 'F1' 279's crewmen, Flight Sergeant 'Goldie' Goldstone, sighted the dinghy in position 61.00N/04.00E at 12.06 hours. Flying Officer 'Paddy' O'Reilly dropped his airborne lifeboat, unfortunately although the parachutes blossomed they parted company in mid-air from their charge and the lifeboat partially sank on striking the water; a Lindholme was then sent down at 12.23 as closely as they dared, but still there was no positive response, Kennedy and Rolls apparently too weak to attempt to reach it. Both were drenched and freezing cold, clinging to the handling rope on the rim of their dinghy. Minutes later one survivor with immense effort entered the Lindholme, at 12.28 hours. A second Lindholme was dropped for the remaining survivor but it evaded him. The person afloat in the dinghy instead paddled away towards the wreck of the airborne lifeboat and attached a rope to it. O'Reilly flew over at 100 feet then continued to orbit, dropping markers until nearly out of fuel. Wireless operator/air gunner Don Mabey radioed for a relief aircraft. The second Warwick located them, at 15.05 hours and began circling as 'F1' 279 left the area. Wick-based 'P' 279 pilot Warrant Officer Boulton sighted the survivor still clinging onto the wrecked lifeboat. An airborne lifeboat was dispatched at 15.12 hours but the parachutes failed to release and it capsized, being dragged for approximately one mile. Momentarily they lost sight of it then saw the up-turned lifeboat again. It was now some considerable distance away from the survivor. Attempts were made to drop the Lindholme but this was aborted because of rough sea. Meanwhile both the young men from 248 Squadron were sitting up in their respective craft, the second Warwick stayed with them for hours, finally dropping marine markers before leaving.

At 15.52 Flight Lieutenant Bob Golightly in HR116 was diverted from Utvaer, and over flew the dinghy with five marine markers nearby. The darkness had by now completely enveloped Kennedy and Rolls apart from the small lights intermittently flashing on their Mae West. A third Warwick arrived on the scene having taken off at 18.20 hours. Flying Officer Garven and his crew located them, circled and descended to 500 feet. From this height more markers were dropped but as 'U' 279 came in on a second run the mid-upper gunner Warrant Officer Stewart shouted a warning: 'Skipper unidentified aircraft fast approaching to the east' and evasive action was taken immediately as it came within 700 yards. A bright light shone from the unidentified aircraft, which was quickly extinguished as it approached, it is highly probable that this was the relief Liberator. Garven lost the other aircraft then resumed his search and more markers were dropped with a delayed timer. With nothing sighted in the search area, 'U' 279 set course for Sumburgh, landing at 23.33 hours. Shortly before midnight the Coastal Command Liberator orbited their position dropping illuminating cartridges in an attempt to see the survivors, as they experienced a perilous night being buffeted by the elements in the darkness 20 miles off the Norwegian coast. Next morning a Warwick relieved the Liberator which, with little fuel remaining, headed for the nearest base. At 12.00 hours the following day Warwick 'E' 279 together with a single Mosquito from 235 Squadron for fighter protection flew out from Banff, with a second Warwick 'C' 279 joining the search from Wick. The Mosquito flew ahead and found a dinghy in position 61.05N/03.53E and also spotted the second Lindholme. A yellow dinghy bobbing in the swell with its drogue strung out behind was flown over at zero feet with an occupant sitting upright, apparently dead. It is not known whether this was Flight Lieutenant John Kennedy or Flying Officer Frank W Rolls. The 235 Squadron pilot radioed 'Am over dinghy with one aircrew dead', nothing further was sighted, an international broadcast was made requesting the Germans to rescue them. Both were exceptional men.

Flying Officer Frank W Rolls came from the Parish of St. John's Church in Reading, Berkshire and like many others had trained at Mount Hope, Canada. His name appears on the 1939-1945 War Memorial in the church. Don Mabey of 279 Squadron remembers returning to base:

'It was a welcome sight as it was one of the few flat strips of land on Shetland. Having spent seven hours in the air willing the ditched crew to attempt to reach the Lindholme we had to leave the area nearing the end of our endurance. We stayed overnight for a hot meal and after refuelling at Sumburgh we took off for Banff. The whole crew had the narrowest of escapes, accelerating down the runway and just reaching take-off speed when a vehicle crossed right in front of our path – a Hillman Pickup obviously being driven by someone half asleep! By some superhuman effort Paddy O'Reilly, our pilot, practically hauled the Warwick into the air, jumped over the Hillman and bounced back onto the runway and somehow took off by banking steeply – we got away with it. The relief and the language afterward! We never did find out if the bod in the Hillman ever got charged...'

As the rescue of the 248 Squadron crew began, fellow strike crews returned to their Scottish base. One Mosquito had its windscreen shot away; a lot of others were damaged. On board the *Ferndale* and *Parat* the crews tried to control and put out the fires – but this was made difficult by exploding ammunition. This was the situation for about an hour when the Germans once again heard the engine sound of fast approaching enemy aircraft, a second wave of six aircraft hunting for a reported U-boat with escort north of Bergen. No U-boat was observed, but as they passed Hellisoy Lighthouse they saw billowing smoke at 12.22 hours just south of Krakhellesund, and

Wing Commander Bill Sise decided to finish off the vessels in there. Entering from the south they took a turn over the sound and attacked from the north – going down at mast height into the sound like a string of pearls. Gun crews on board Vp.5305 *Jäger* had lined up on 'S' 235 flown by a 22-year-old Australian Flight Lieutenant Ken Beruldsen (RAAF), and the aircraft received a direct hit. Lieutenant zur See Otto and his crew on board *Jäger* witnessed the Mosquito hit the mountain of Losna, directly opposite the burning *Ferndale* and *Parat*. In a nearby village a resident, Mr Johannes Kraakhellen watched the aircraft come down and informed the local police. Mr Olav Boe, the district police officer, was put in charge of recovery operations at the crash site, and in his search for survivors found Beruldsen's body and that of his navigator Rabbitts. Both were recovered. Between them they had flown 50 operations together and had continued into their second tour of operations. Beruldsen's surname indicates he had Norwegian origins: his father, Einar Bjorn Beruldsen, had left Norway for Scotland as a young man, where he met and married a Scottish girl. In 1923 the Beruldsen family emigrated to Australia. Like so many fellow Australians Ken Beruldsen volunteered for the RAAF in 1941 and began his pilot training. In 1943 he was posted to 235 Squadron and together with his navigator participated in 35 strikes off the French coast, and 20 along the Norwegian. After having completed 50 operations both could have chosen another type of duty but instead continued into their second tour. Beruldsen was promoted to flight lieutenant when only 22-years-old. Both servicemen were buried at Eivindvik cemetery after a short service attended by 80 local people, and some years later the bodies were transferred to Sola churchyard in Stavanger. It was a quirk of fate that Beruldsen crashed in Norway where his ancestors can be traced back to 1585.

A third aircraft taking part in the attack also received hits. With the port engine streaming out glycol its pilot, Squadron Leader Robinson, now faced a climb over the mountainous ridges around the dead-end fjord, but the one good Merlin engine got them back to base safely. Robinson found the undercarriage did not operate so a wheels-up landing was considered. Flight Lieutenant Taylor, his navigator, tried the emergency hand pump and managed to get the wheels down and locked, but owing to the loss of hydraulic pressure, the flaps would not operate. As the aircraft came into approach, it drifted slightly, landing on rough ground; it lost the undercarriage in a ditch, while the tailplane came away from the main fuselage on a fence. The aircraft finally came to a halt when it hit a building on the far side of the airfield. The starboard engine caught fire but the crew escaped by way of the hatch in the roof; the airfield's crash tender and blood wagon had followed their progress to the Mosquito's final resting-place. Fire crews set about extinguishing the flames but only a small amount of foam trickled out of their hoses. Another tender was called for, which rapidly appeared, though instead of putting the flames out it caught fire itself and both blazed away merrily in the darkness all night. Those relaxing in the station's officers' mess or raising a glass to the two aircrew who did not return listened to the radio as it announced that the US 9th Army had captured Aachen, the first major city in Germany to fall to the Allies. The next morning all that remained of Robinson's Mosquito was wood ash, engines, cannon and machine guns and armoured plate.

On 16 December those in the north-east of Scotland listened attentively again to the radio announcing that Hitler's Ardennes military offensive had begun. The operation 'Wacht am Rhein' (Watch on the Rhine), eventually to become known as the Battle of the Bulge, had the objective of splitting the American and British ground forces, in a gamble to drive west which momentarily threatened to reach Antwerp. On 19 December, Group Captain Max Aitken returned from 14 days leave and was briefed by senior officers. After hearing about the operation on 16 December the station commander wrote to Sholto Douglas asking for the squadrons to have 'Walter' installed in their dinghies, a VHF transmitter, mounted on a short mast, which acted as a homing beacon which would permit the Warwick crews to maintain contact throughout the night and thus save valuable and experienced strike aircrew.

At Banff, Dallachy, Fraserburgh and Peterhead personnel were going on leave for Christmas. Many were to be found awaiting transport south in Aberdeen. Polish 315 Squadron pilot Dan Nowosielski was about to embark on catching the stream-train south to London for a ten-day leave, when Squadron Leader Tadeusz Andersz detailed him to take 'W' 315 to Croydon for repairs since he was going that way on leave. The Mustang gun ports were blocked off and the gun spaces were taken by parachute bags containing a turkey, a goose, butter and eggs from a friendly Peterhead farmer. Nowosielski flew out for southern England but on the way the weather began closing in and a WAAF diverted him to Biggin Hill. He landed just as a real pea souper covered the 'Bump', after a flight of two hours and thirty minutes because of the detours. The mechanics were rather puzzled when he fished around in the gun bays and pulled out the parachute bags. It took a further four hours to reach his home in Harold Wood, Essex. The extra rations were very warmly received by his parents especially so near to Christmas time. While on leave Nowosielski heard that he had been promoted to flight lieutenant.

On 21 December, with operations postponed, there was a further loss when Mosquito HR284 from 248 Squadron spun into the sea on the edge of Halliman Skerries, Lossiemouth. While on an air test the pilot Flight Sergeant William Livock was carrying out some practice dives on a rock. The approach was too close, making the pilot climb away steeply which forced HR284 into a high speed stall. The 20-year-old pilot tried to regain control, but at low altitude, it flicked over onto its back killing him and his navigator Flight Sergeant Godfrey L West. At 11.25 hours the coastguard saw the Mosquito crash in the sea two or three miles north-west of Lossiemouth. The RNLI auxiliary rescue-boat was out at sea fishing. Six men put out in the motorboat *Dayspring*, and reached the position at 12.50pm. They found wreckage floating on the surface but no survivors. Later the crew picked up an empty dinghy and a Mae West. Their reward was £4 10s plus 10 shillings for the fuel. The men returned the money as a donation to the Institution. A Thornaby-based Warwick, two Dallachy Beaufighters and a Mosquito also participated in the search but sighted nothing of interest. The scattered wreckage was discovered in 1988 by a team of divers from RAF Lossiemouth's Sub Aqua Club. It still rests on the sea bed in 30 metres of water on the edge of Lossiemouth's treacherous Halliman Skerries, a quarter of a mile from Lossiemouth harbour. The site is littered with live rounds from the cannon and machine guns.

22 December saw the arrival of 235 Squadron's new commanding officer Wing Commander Arthur 'Junior' Simmonds who had previously flown operations with 254 Squadron as a 'B' Flight commander before taking up his new appointment. Simmonds was a skilled officer having first started flying in November 1936 and had managed to stay with Coastal Command throughout the war.

On 23 December, 19 Beaufighters led by Squadron Leader Schoales, together with a single 333 Squadron Mosquito, flew out at 07.15 hours to rendezvous with Warwick 'E' 279. The Warwick laid down the Drem system at 16.10N/03.00E. At 08.32 hours, whilst circling the flame floats at 500 feet, the tail gunner Warrant Officer N J Bird sighted a Mosquito at 100 feet investigating the floats. Seven minutes later the colours of the day were fired off, it then raced off in an easterly direction. Fifteen minutes afterwards some Beaufighters appeared. Bad weather prevented the strike crews from locating the Drem; independent searches were flown and the Mosquito Norwegian outrider crew advised Schoales there was nothing to attack. The crew flying HR116,

2nd Lieutenant Loken and Petty Officer Skjelanger, had a narrow escape flying back though. Seeing a formation of 11 Mustangs flying at 800 feet, the pilot called the Mustang leader over the radio-telephone. Receiving no reply they edged nearer, the Mustangs jettisoned their long-range tanks, turned sharply and began attacking on both starboard and port quarters. The astonished crew immediately took avoiding action, Loken screamed into the radio that he was a Mosquito outrider to Dallachy Beaufighters, while Skjelanger hurriedly fired off the recognition colours of the day, after which the Mustang leader called out 'Cease fire, cease fire'. A conversation followed in Polish, which Skjelanger partly understood: 'A Mustang was in distress with a rough engine. The whole formation was apparently escorting it to Sumburgh.' Flying Officer Haynes, the navigator on board 'E' 279, picked up the distress call at 10.30 hours from a Polish pilot: 'Comrade requires urgent assistance', he then informed control and his pilot Flight Lieutenant Carmichael. At 10.35 hours Pilot Officer Tadeusz Lubicz-Lisowski's glycol system had malfunctioned and the Mayday signal sent out on VHF was picked up by a Warwick aircraft and one of the Fraserburgh-based RAF high speed launches which was returning from covering the anti-shipping strike. Twenty-five miles east of the Outer Skerries Lubicz-Lisowski bailed out too early, over the rough sea. A second Warwick 'D' 281 joined the search at 10.42 hours from Sumburgh. At 12.58 hours flying at less than 50 feet in poor visibility 'D' 281 collided with an unidentified object which severed six feet three inches off the port wing. The wing dropped rapidly, followed by the nose. Height was lost as Warrant Officer 'Johnny' Stephenson instantly began the recovery, retrimming the aircraft, jettisoning the airborne lifeboat and setting course for the nearest haven.

Warwick 'P' 279 left Sumburgh at 11.04 hours. Twenty minutes later it came across two Mustangs circling a K-type dinghy but the crew could not see an occupant. Markers were dropped at 11.29 hours but were extinguished in the swell and the dinghy was not seen again. A Sunderland flying boat and HSL also swept the area without success. Unfortunately Lubicz-Lisowski had drowned before anyone could reach him. He was the youngest pilot on the squadron, having joined them at the beginning of the month, he was an accomplished writer and when colleagues collected his belongings together they found one story describing in detail how he would die on 23 December.

Meanwhile a force of 40 Mosquitoes from Banff took part in an armed sweep from Stadtlandet to Egersund during the day with Max Aitken leading in 'MA-01', though no shipping was attacked or fighter opposition met. Flight Lieutenant Noel Russell DFC, with his navigator Pilot Officer Harry Hosier who had also been awarded the DFC, led another 12 aircraft on a search from Karmoy to the Naze, the formation making landfall at Geitungen Lighthouse. Bad weather intervened and the 12 returned to base while Russell stayed to check other Leads. It was with some difficulty that they landed and at snail's pace they taxied their way back to dispersals. A 235 Squadron Mosquito was being taxied back too fast on the icy runway, and as the pilot attempted to turn the aircraft skidded sideways and the undercarriage collapsed with the crew slightly shaken by their misfortune. Russell made a sweep on his own inland but with failing visibility set course for Scotland, landing at 17.58 hours.

During this time many men and women in the RAF or Commonwealth Air Forces were posted either in or out of the base. The base commander, Max Aitken had some influence and assembled some of the most experienced personnel to lead this strike wing and that of Dallachy. One of the personalities on the station at this time was Flying Officer 'Buster' A J Mottram, who was born in Coventry, Warwickshire. Pre-war he was a tennis-player of some repute, joining the RAF in July 1940, and had served with 489 RNZAF Squadron flying Hampden torpedo bombers in 1942. The station intelligence officer was Squadron Leader George Bellew. When not helping to brief or debrief aircrew, he indulged them using his artistic talent to the full having been appointed Portcullis Pursuivant of Arms at the College of Arms in 1922. Bellew painted the various squadron crests, their history and awards on large oak boards then placed them in the entrance to the station headquarters. He also depicted all the wing's tallies on the walls of the operations block (which can still be seen today although the ravages of time have taken their toll on the artwork). George Bellew later helped to organise the Queen's coronation in 1953. WAAF code and cypher officer Joy Hickey remembers what it was like to be in this unit:

'We were part of a closely-knit and enormous clan at Banff; most WAAFs were bent on making Christmas 1944 as merry as any previous or future one. There were dances every night in one mess or another, and what was better, with a choice of partners, the men out numbering the girls three to one. The cigarette smoke was dense, the laughter loud, and the jokes raucous, a lot of banter and merriment with exaggerated courtesies on both sides, with the aircrew living for the moment.'

CHAPTER 7

MOSQUITOES HIT LEIRVIK ON BOXING DAY

The winter of 1944/45 was especially harsh. Christmas 1944 was one of the coldest recorded for 50 years with temperatures down to -10°C. As the buzz bomb rockets rained down on London, Allied troops were pushing their advance deep into the continent after the German Wehrmacht's last glimmer of resistance in the Ardennes forest in Belgium was nearly over on 15 December after 31 days. Field Marshal Montgomery in his Christmas broadcast on BBC radio said, 'This is the Lord's doing, everyone should rejoice'. Christmas Day was the only day in the calendar when no airborne operations within the RAF fighter, bomber and coastal command groups were ever launched and this brought some relaxation in the tempo of work. However, at Dallachy 455 Squadron was notified that a strike had been called for, though it was later cancelled. For those personnel staying on the camp at Banff, there was an early morning carol service and special Christmas dinner. Officers served NCOs in the officers' mess; while senior officers served the other ranks dinner in the airmen's mess, in keeping with RAF tradition. Many had already started to celebrate and their 'waiting' was not necessarily of the highest quality, since it was often accompanied by the splash of spilling soup and the noise of breaking dishes. On the menu for Christmas 1944 there was cream of tomato soup, followed by roast turkey, Cambridge sausage, roast pork, apple sauce, stuffing and roast or creamed potatoes, brussel sprouts, green peas and braised celery. For dessert there was Christmas pudding with brandy sauce or sherry trifle and Dundee or Christmas cake, followed by coffee, cheese and biscuits and beer and cigarettes. All ranks joined in the singing of traditional songs and then officers and NCOs did the washing up. The sergeants' mess held a staff party in the afternoon with whisky on tap until the following day when the stock ran out, which many lived to regret.

Back in the airmen and WAAFs Nissen huts after dinner, some of them warmed themselves up by mulling beer or a punch with the aid of a red-hot poker heated in the stove. A few just put on as much clothing as possible and went back to bed, but other airmen and women went to local homes to take part in their festivities or went to a dance in Keith. Mustangs from 315 Squadron overflew the airfield while on their way to Dallachy for Christmas drinks. The Poles took their presents with them in the cockpits to the Beaufighter wing, and a wild party ensued.

Early in the morning of 26 December, a mixed strike force from Banff and Dallachy carried out a patrol off the Norwegian coast. The operation had been prepared following a sighting by 'N' 333, one of three searching for targets in the early hours. At 09.48 Lieutenant Andvig sighted stationary vessels in Leirvik. Even before the aircraft landed, the planning had begun since the two vessels were an obvious target. Both D/S *Tenerife* and D/S *Cygnus* had sailed into Leirvik in the early morning shortly before the reconnaissance. *Tenerife* with its cargo of pyrite had navigated from Sagvåg and now laid at anchor in Leirvik waiting for an escort to carry on the journey to Kõningber.

At 06.00 hours groans and complaints about hangovers could be heard from inside the Nissen huts spread out amongst the fields and woods at Banff. Those on readiness for the forthcoming operation in the afternoon went to their respective messes for a meal of roast beef, Yorkshire pudding, roast potatoes, brussel sprouts, green peas and horseradish sauce, all topped off with a dessert of sherry trifle. Each also received a ration of chocolate and boiled sweets for comfort on the flight. The crews were expansively briefed about routes to be taken to and from the target, fuel loads to be carried, take-off times, which runway to use and the recognition colours (known as 'colours of the day') for emergencies. The intelligence officer reported on likely enemy opposition, either in the form of enemy fighters or coastal anti-aircraft positions. Shortly after this briefing, Group Captain Max Aitken wished them good luck. A formation of ten MkIVs and two Tsetse Mosquitoes began taking off at midday, each carrying an assortment of rockets, or cannon and machine guns. Led by the veteran Squadron Leader Jacko Jackson-Smith, the journey to the enemy target had begun and they picked up their Air Sea Rescue support at 12.30 hours from Wick. Flying Officer Ken 'Ginger' Webster, serving with 235 Squadron, takes up the story: 'Take-off for us was just six minutes after 12.00 hours; we formed up and set course at low level in loose formation Vics of three. The weather was not bad; there were rainsqualls here and there, but visibility was reasonably good. Everything was going according to plan.'

At 13.00 hours the outriders flew ahead, and at 13.33 they made the Norwegian coast at Helliso Light. Both investigated the Leads and anchorages, searching for other targets. Landfall by the main strike force was at 13.34 hours.

The outriders were over Leirvik at 13.48 hours, their Mosquitoes skimmed low over an island, turning south at 13.57 hours. The sighting reports were sent by the navigator in 'F' 333: 'Two merchantmen stationary in position east side of Leirvik harbour.' As the message came through the headset, Jackson-Smith's navigator Flight Sergeant Griffith Hodgson from Newcastle, quickly worked out a slight alteration of course, checked the wind speed direction and headed eventually to join the outrider over Bømlo, west of Leirvik. At 13.58 hours the Norwegian crew skilfully led the main force into position by firing off red and green Very cartridges. 'E' 333 fired the last of the green flares over the target then called: 'Weaver 2 to leader position indicated by greens.' Four minutes later Jackson-Smith led the attack, feeling his Mosquito jolt as it flew through heavy flak thrown up from both sides of the shore. The rocket-firing and the Tsetse Mosquitoes opened fire quickly, releasing their salvoes towards D/S *Cygnus* and D/S *Tenerife*. Surrounded by the brightly coloured wooden buildings, camouflaged 37mm guns on the shore began opening up. The steamer *Cygnus* caught fire easily, with its cargo of timber and artificial manure/fertilizer. One of the casualties was machinist Oddmar Jens Klepp who was working onboard. D/S *Tenerife* was left smoking, with the first engineer wounded by cannon fire. The Mosquitoes from 143, 235 and 248 Squadron passed out low over the heavily defended harbour, and various calibres of munitions streamed up towards them from the local army artillery unit assigned to coastal defence (*Heers Kusten Batterie* –HKB 61/977 Leirvik), making it a dangerous place to be!

Both outriders orbited the area, keeping a watchful eye out for enemy fighters. Flight Sergeant Griffith Hodgson said: 'We all dived on the ships in our sections and as we were coming out we saw German fighters waiting for us. We'd used up most of our ammunition on the ships.'

One of the radar stations near Leirvik had sounded the alarm as the Mosquitoes crossed the Norwegian coast and the Luftwaffe 16 Staffel grey-blue painted fighter aircraft with drop-tanks had taken off to intercept at 13.50 hours. Leaving the target individual aircraft ran into crossfire from mobile flak batteries. At 14.12 hours, the strike crews encountered 12 Fw190s circling the narrow entrance to Bømlo fjord, while at the same time a mixed force of about 12 Bf109G-14s and Fw190s approached

Bømlo from the south. 16 Staffel would have their first success. The Banff aircraft were in loose formation as the force headed out to sea, and individual aircraft engaged enemy fighters as they passed through the area. Flight Lieutenant Bill Clayton-Graham's aircraft was flying on one engine; the port engine having been hit by a shell. He flew around the headland to go down the fjord and out to sea climbing to 1,000 feet. Flak stabbed the sky all around, and enemy fighters appeared in line astern 1,000 feet above on the starboard quarter. Messerschmitts dived to attack, jettisoning their sixty-six gallon Rüstsatz R3 drop-tanks. Tsetse Mosquito 'Z1' 248 fired one 57mm shell from 200 yards at the enemy formation. Clayton-Graham hauled his Mosquito 'N' 235 around on the single engine which was being pushed through the gate (full throttle) and into the midst of the enemy aircraft firing with machine guns, as all the cannon was spent. These bursts forced the oncoming 12 Bf109G-14s to pass through the line of fire, which was effective for it hit one enemy aircraft and winged a few others. However, Clayton-Graham was a sitting duck for the attacking fighters; he dived for the wave tops with the good engine at full throttle, waiting for the second attack.

The fate of a second 235 Squadron crew hung in the balance. A red Very cartridge burst into the air: Flight Lieutenant Ernest Fletcher and Flying Officer Alfred Watson, in aircraft 'G' 235, were caught by flak over Leirvik, they requested assistance at 14.07 hours: 'Being attacked by Bandits.' Before anyone could respond, however, they became easy prey for Feldwebel Heinz Halstrick in his Bf109 G-14 Blau 8 named 'Kølle Alaaf'. Fletcher made a valiant but vain effort to shake off his pursuer, but as Halstrick fired his cannon and machine guns at short range the Mosquito crumpled under the impact of exploding shells and plunged into the water. Halstrick, a very experienced pilot from the Eismeerfront flying with 16 Staffel had claimed another victim, his 13th. Halstrick landed at 14.48 hours and wrote: '13. Abschuss, eine Mosquito'.

The battle continued. Mosquito 'Z' 143, being flown by Flying Officer Smith and Flight Sergeant MacBean attacked a pair of Bf109s and was in turn attacked by another brace of Bf109Gs. Smith turned steeply to starboard and aimed a three-second burst at one with cannon and machine-gun fire, and the Bf109G quickly disengaged. Smith headed out to sea. The other Bf109G followed and thus began an aerial duel lasting for ten minutes, the Luftwaffe pilot expending all of his ammunition. Finally the Mosquito pilot managed to do a high-speed turn and return fire, flames and smoke emitting from the damaged DB 605 power plant of the BF109G which was seen to crash into the sea in flames by 'Z' 143. Smith claimed one enemy aircraft destroyed. RS509 piloted by 'Wally' Webster took violent evasive action at full throttle as six Fw190s made persistent attacks, shredding the port wing, the bandits finally broke off five to ten miles out to sea. Mosquito 'L' 143 saw another enemy fighter, the leader of seven Fw109s being escorted away by the other six after having suffered some battle damage. At 14.30 Flying Officer 'Ginger' Webster sent a distress message but was unable to give their exact position.

Squadron Leader Jackson-Smith told Clayton-Graham over the radio-telephone to fire a Very light after having seen his predicament, as he had lost sight of the aircraft. Clayton-Graham replied 'Not bloody likely, they'll see me too!' and pressed on. Twenty miles out to sea Clayton-Graham's navigator called up the Warwick again, but it had already received a message from the strike leader, and at 14.58 hours in position 58.55N/01.36E located this aircraft with its port engine feathered. Flight Lieutenant Murray in 'E' 279 shepherded them back to Banff. Although they were minus an engine the flying qualities of the Mosquito were not affected, Clayton-Graham making a perfect landing. Later inspection revealed that a piece of shrapnel had cut the coolant pipe in the port engine. The ground crew who serviced Clayton-Graham's aircraft described him as 'the antithesis of the Hollywood-style leader.' A change of underpants and several pints of beer were the only repairs needed. Flying Officer Ginger Webster says that this operation 'proved to be one of the more interesting ops.' He describes what happened:

'A 190 got onto our tail. Bill was taking the most violent evasive action to shake off the fighter, frequently seeing streams of bullets churning up the sea but not hitting the aircraft, when I noticed the port wing was about to dip into the sea. I shrieked into the intercom and he corrected just in time. Heading well out to sea the Focke-Wulf flew off. I contacted the Warwick by radio-telephone (R/T) being safely 20 miles out from enemy fighters, and fired off all the Very pistol cartridges I could find – red, green, yellow any colour you name. Eventually the Warwick located us and escorted us back to base. I remember Bill thinking it was a huge joke when he asked the pilot of the Warwick if we were flying too fast for him. I can't recall the reply but I don't think it was particularly polite.'

Ted Russell was flying in the Warwick and briefly recalls: 'We followed a Mosquito back home to base with its port engine u/s on 26 December. All went OK and we landed after four hours and 30 minutes.'

A third Mosquito had been hit by flak, 'N' 248 which had a damaged engine, causing a loss of glycol coolant. Warrant Office Harold Corbin CGM seeing German fighters waiting for them, gave the engines full throttle, got down on the deck and hoped that the damaged engine would last until they were out of danger and no enemy fighters could pick them off. Corbin and his navigator Flight Sergeant Maurice Webb DFM finally got out of the area, but the damaged engine gave up, having done what was necessary. He feathered the propeller and once again headed home on a single Merlin engine. Having got safely back to Banff Corbin misjudged the approach and realised that 'N' 248 was going to touch down in a field some 100 yards short of the aerodrome boundary and main runway. The crew were not unduly worried until just after touch down when a stone wall appeared. Warrant Officer Harold Corbin continues:

'Well, dear old "N" hit the wall just as I switched off to avoid possible fire and selected "wheels-up" on the undercarriage to allow the wheels to be knocked back up by the wall. I felt we might somersault otherwise and end upside-down. Both the props and wheels were torn off but otherwise we were on an even keel. Maurice and I were trapped in the wreckage but within seconds, Max Aitken had raced around the perimeter track in his station wagon and dragged us out, he then took us to the station hospital. The "Doc" looked us over, we were only slightly injured and soon recovered, but 248 Squadron's CO, Bill Sise, came to see us and said: "I'm giving you a rest. No more operations, but I want you to stay with the squadron to help the newcomers." We then went off to the aircrew officer's course at Hereford. After a month we returned to find the Squadron had suffered many casualties during our absence. Many good friends had gone including our beloved Frenchman Maurice Geudj who had been lost to Focke-Wulfs.'

Once each Mosquito landed its time was chalked up on the blackboard. Too often, however, time went by and still one of the aircraft did not radio in. The word 'missing' was chalked up on the board for Fletcher and Watson next to 'G- George'.

The force had left *Cygnus* on fire. It burned for two hours after the strike, and was kept under control by her dedicated crew and was eventually extinguished. Sixty-three holes were found in the hull. The *Tenerife* had only slight damage through cannon and machine-gun fire, and managed to sail to Stavanger for repairs where the workforce counted 99 holes in the hull. The vessel was seaworthy again by 28 December 1944. Of the 24 enemy fighters engaged, one was claimed as destroyed. The Norwegian underground later confirmed this, but official records state none were lost.

Several houses were hit around the harbour area, but no people were hurt. A Norwegian eyewitness at Espevaer recalled:

'I shall never forget this day, as the force came out being attacked by the Germans, one aeroplane chasing another they were so low that they flew between two houses!'

This attack was used as propaganda: a notice appeared in the locally controlled newspaper *Sunnhordland*. It gives the impression that the Mosquitoes were firing at houses for 'fun' and said nothing about the attack on vessels. The translation reads:

'In the afternoon of the day after Christmas German fighters shot down four Mosquitoes off the west coast at Leirvik. The planes belonged to a fast enemy fighter unit. The German planes had no losses. On this day the people of Leirvik experienced for the first time what it means to be in a war zone. The alarm warning sounded just before two o'clock and thereafter a message was heard warning that a small force of British Mosquitoes were heading for the coast. Soon they heard the sounds of engines and shooting, and we all witnessed that the German fighters attacked in a duel of life and death and as the military message said it ended with four shot down British Mosquitoes off the coast. Some of the planes set their course directly over the centre of Leirvik, and the bullets from the machine guns rained over a populated area, a wonder nobody was hurt in Leirvik. Damage was done to the Museum, a Gym Hall and six to eight houses.'

Another eyewitness of this raid said: 'One of the gun positions manned by German soldiers was abandoned when the crew leapt over the side in terror, it was an unpopular job and demoralised them.'*

During this month having been awarded the DSO, and promoted to wing commander on 6 December, Maurice succeeded Wing Commander Sam McHardy as the next commanding officer of 143 Squadron. McHardy was rested from operations. Maurice had a reputation for being one of the leading strike pilots, and his appointment confirmed his popularity within the Banff Wing. Flight Lieutenant Charles Corder had completed 72 operations with Maurice while serving with 248 Squadron and described him as: 'An excellent pilot, and a born leader.' While commands changed, fresh aircraft headed in from various ATA Pools between 25 December 1944 and 18 January 1945 and were dispersed between 235 and 248 Squadrons. Ground crews were dispatched from both units making their way by road along the A98 to Fraserburgh. After accommodation had been arranged and a much needed meal eaten, the teams began the process of fitting rocket projectile rails and electrical wiring. On average the procedure was taking two and a half days. As a teenager Geoff Cooke was formerly in the Air Training Corps during the war and describes the delivery of one such aircraft destined for the strike wing:

---

*The Boxing Day attack made by the Coastal Command Mosquito wing was reported in *The Aeroplane Spotter* issue of 28 December which stated simply: 'Rocket-firing Mosquito fighters of Coastal Command attacked shipping off the Norwegian coast.'

'Joan Nayler of the Air Transport Auxiliary (ATA) was issued with a priority chit for Mosquito MkVI RF602 from Anstey to Fraserburgh on January 8 1945. I was her pilot's assistant and was dubious about being asked to go as bad weather was forecast. But Joan cheerfully said "all right" and we set off to Ansty in an Anson MkI. I flew RF602 for 30 minutes to near Marston Moor, but then handed over to Joan as the weather suddenly deteriorated with heavy snow. She tried three times to go through, but after 90 minutes in the air we were forced to return and land at Church Fenton for a weather forecast. The Met. Officer said conditions were slightly better on the west coast, so Joan decided to try for it. We took off and headed north-west at 9,000 feet, eventually seeing Kirkbridge through a gap in the clouds. We came down to 1,000 feet past Prestwick, overflew Glasgow, headed north-east to Perth and then around the coast through heavy rain and low cloud to our destination, landing at 16.30 hours in a gale, after two hours in the air. The other six ferry pilots with similar priority Mossies had been unable to get through, while Trevor Hunter and Opal Anderson landed at East Fortune. Over night, it was very stormy, but blew itself out. The morning turned out cold, but bright and sunny. I spent the night in a rather damp and depressing Nissen hut, and was rather glad when an Argus from the ferry pool at Lossiemouth arrived to take us out. Unfortunately they had nothing going south, and so we spent the night at the Gordon Arms in Elgin. I passed the time by going to the local flicks, returning to the hotel to find that I had been given a king-sized double bed in a very large room with two old fashioned metal hot-water bottles. The following day Lossiemouth had one ferry Anson, MkI LV145, going south, and First Officer Thomas took Joan, myself and three other ATA pilots (including Opal, who had since arrived) to Prestwick.'

On 27 December the Air Sea Rescue Warwick detachments from 279 and 281 Squadrons relocated from Banff to Fraserburgh a few miles away. Training began for individuals on 235 Squadron, which lasted until the end of the month with aircrews practicing firing rocket-projectiles. Flying was constant. Flight Lieutenant George Lord piloted HR434, rocket-diving and rocket-firing with four 25lb APs at Tain, HP918 rocket-sighting, HR434 rocket-firing at a towed target in Spey Bay, and HR434 firing at ground targets at the Tain range.

Over the past two months 18 Group intelligence had learnt that the German fighter defences in southern Norway were now stronger than they had been since 1940. Recent flights by the PR units at Wick and Dyce found there were 35 twin-engine night fighters on the Danish coast at Grove. These were to react strongly to 18 Group's Halifax aircraft on shipping and U-boat operations in the Kattegat. Intelligence had also been gathered by the Norwegians that streams of German transports had been plying between Norway, Denmark and Germany carrying reinforcements. The Wehrmacht were now hurriedly moving whole divisions south for the defence of their homeland. For most part these troops were transported by rail to Oslo then across the Kattegat by sea – despite the poor weather in the area throughout December 1944. This was more shipping than Sholto Douglas had expected. The Kattegat was well within range of the Halifax and Liberator squadrons deployed by 18 Group and despite the unfortunate weather conditions in the area throughout December the two Halifax squadrons 58 and 502 kept up their attacks. With these squadrons being active through the night Coastal Command hoped it would cause them to sail convoys through the Kattegat by day, though at present it was not within range from Banff without the 100-gallon drop-tanks.

In Whitehall, London, Sholto Douglas applied considerable pressure stressing the urgency to those within the Air Ministry for a modification to allow the stowage of tiered rockets, and for the 100-gallon drop-tanks to be fitted. In the meantime Air Vice-Marshal Aubrey Ellwood had passed orders to the Banff wing for the inner rails to be removed as a temporary measure thus reducing the firepower to only four rockets when long-range tanks were used. They also accepted a reduction in strikes over Norway's fjords and coastal waters if the probable Kattegat operations went ahead. Modification started in mid-January, in preparation for these extended operations. Unfortunately, soon after this, the new drop-tank and rocket-projectiles stowage showed many shortcomings in practice, which required a complete redesign by the Ministry of Aircraft Production. From time to time Sholto Douglas and Aubrey Ellwood protested about the costly delays during January and February 1945, and it was not until March 1945 that the Mosquitoes were satisfactorily modified. Sholto Douglas had written to the Air Ministry asking for the transfer of two Beaufighter squadrons from the Middle East but this was not approved because of the likely German retreat through the Balkans and Douglas had to make do with what he had.

At 13.15 on 28 December, 12 Mustangs took off from Peterhead to cover two coastal patrols. Six Mustangs led by Squadron Leader Tadeusz Andersz in 'A' 315 rendezvoused with the 12 Mosquitoes off Rattray Head before setting course for Norway. On the way across the vast expanse of the North Sea the force came under fire from four E-boats in line astern travelling at 8 knots. The route taken was to make the landfall at Utvaer Light but Wing Commander Roy Orrock (who had taken command of 248 Squadron) flying in 'D' 248 wheeled them south, but found nothing. Then, at 15.00 hours a little further south near Haugesund through the heavy snow showers, they found a target. It was the Norwegian-owned *La France* of 647 tons used in the herring trade in the North Sea and Baltic. The vessel had been laid up in Skudeneshavn awaiting maintenance; some repairs were carried out but due to the Christmas celebrations the work had been abandoned. The command to attack came from the leader. Several aircraft struck from the starboard side as the Mosquitoes were converging on the target, flying dangerously close to each other so that PZ451 was crowded out. Flying Officer Brown put eight rockets into a warehouse. Then one Mosquito came in from the portside and finally two swept in aft. *La France* sank and capsized after 20 minutes. On shore the owner and master arrived just as the vessel sunk in shallow water. *La France* was salvaged later in 1946 and returned to merchant trading in 1949. While proving air cover over Skudesnes 315 Squadron saw a Bf109 dive into the sea.

In the deteriorating visibility as the 12 Mosquitoes and fighter escort turned towards the sea and set course for Banff with 'U' 235 flying on one engine, the Mustangs saw 14 Messerschmitts from 16 Staffel JG5 flying in from astern. Orrock heard over the VHF radio, 'Bandits at six o'clock'. The six Mustangs broke to intercept them but did not engage the enemy because of the terrible weather. They then broke away and made for base and, battling through several snow showers, Peterhead was reached at 17.00 hours. Landing at night in a snowstorm it took the controllers 50 minutes to bring all the aircraft down. Pilot Officer Jan Borowczyk landed after three approaches. He remembers: 'As we finished debriefing after our mission, we came out to see a brilliant full moon sailing through a now cloudless sky.' Although one 16 Staffel pilot Unteroffizier Schmejkal claimed and was credited with a Mustang, Allied documents for this day state that no single-engine fighters were lost. During the day two Mosquitoes flew with the Dallachy Beaufighters and found a merchantman but the weather was still poor, and it became hazardous to attack so Squadron Leader Duncanson wheeled them round away from the coast and ordered the force to return to base. Warwick 'R' 279 had been covering this strike without incident from Fraserburgh but on the return journey it was found that the undercarriage and flaps would not lower owing to hydraulic failure at 18.37 hours. The crew spent an agonizing hour in the air over Fraserburgh when they received a 'Land at Banff' signal. At the diverted aerodrome Flight Lieutenant D Carmichael made a low pass over the flying control tower. Carmichael notified the crew and tower that he was going to try the hand pump again. Selecting the lever marked 'Emergency' on the hand pump located to the right of his seat, and with help from two members of the crew it finally worked. The undercarriage was pumped down successfully after some 20 minutes and after making a faster than normal landing, the wheels screeched onto the concrete runway and they were finally down. During the evening five Lancasters from 49 Squadron Bomber Command were among 55 aircraft from 5 Group that bombed the battle cruiser *Köln* which was berthed near Oslofjord. Although low cloud obliterated the target, the raid was assumed to have been successful. In trying to discover the extent of the damage, the Norwegian underground confirmed that the end of the fjord was still being used as a U-boat base.

On New Year's Eve 1944 a crew from the Norwegian 333 Squadron took their Mosquito down close to Flekkefjord ahead of the main force, and a report was sent back of three merchantmen. A strike was on, 20 Mosquitoes were dispatched taking off at 13.00 hours led by Wing Commander Bill Sise. One of the vessels targeted was *Palermo* which had been severely damaged earlier in the year on 12 November. It had sailed from Hamburg to Tromsö and was the 'Seasonal Christmas Vessel' for the garrison at Narvik. Her crew were now unloading some of her cargo to the *Achilles* which was on a return voyage to Germany with ore and 100 tons of ammunition loaded from *Palermo*.

The force wheeled round and found the three merchantmen; the attack left one badly damaged, two sunk. *Palermo* of 1,461 tons and the *Achilles* of 998 tons were sent to the bottom. *Wally Faulbaum* of 1,675 tons was heavily damaged but remained afloat with her cargo of straw. Mosquito 'U' 248 was hit by return fire and, with coolant pouring from the engine, the pilot, 24-year-old Flight Lieutenant Johnny Lown, attempted to return to base on one engine. An IFF distress call was made by Sise and received by 'B' 279 at 15.42 hours. Rendezvousing with the four escorting Mosquitoes the battle-scarred aircraft was seen losing height steadily and with the sudden failure of the live engine which developed a leak the crew were forced to ditch. Plunging into the water 'U' 248 broke up immediately 100 miles off Stavanger. With water up to his waist Flight Lieutenant Lown managed to clamber through the escape hatch and jumped into the freezing water. Lown couldn't see Johnny Daynton. Shouts of 'swimmer in the water' were heard over VHF. Sise recognised Lown making for the dinghy, he managed to haul himself up by the handling rope and got his feet inside, but his vision became impaired from the aviation fuel which had been on the surface of the water.

The wind was gusting very strongly and the crew inside the Warwick had to keep a sharp eye on his position. Lown was sighted amid the wave crests at 15.58 waving and apparently uninjured. Sise was heard to call 'Circling Mosquito, one man in dinghy'. An airborne lifeboat was dropped at 16.16 hours, 200 yards from the dinghy, though the rockets, which were supposed to fire out lifelines, failed to fire and the boat was dragged half a mile, too far away to be of any use. At 16.08 a second Warwick appeared on the scene to assist, a most welcome arrival. Pilot Officer D Duthie in 'G' 279 dropped an airborne lifeboat at 16.27 hours using the light given off by flares. The lifeboat splashed into the water 50 yards away from the survivor. Again the parachutes failed to release and carried the boat further downwind, although all the rockets functioned. A signal was heard saying 'We will try and shoot them away' from the Mosquito strike leader. Despite gunfire from a Mosquito and the gunners from 'G' 279 they were unsuccessful in shooting the parachutes away and one remained billowing open. Soon afterwards the dinghy overtook the lifeboat and although it passed within

30 feet of the survivor with the floating lines reachable no attempt was made to grab them. At 16.44 hours the survivor in the dinghy seemed to be nearing the lifeboat. Both aircraft types continued circling until shortage of fuel forced them to leave the scene.

The glow of markers dropped by 'G' 279 guided another Warwick, 'T' 279 into position. A dinghy was sighted at 17.25 with the occupant flashing a torch as it was buffeted by a 35mph gale. Instructions were given by control to drop the airborne lifeboat but suddenly the dinghy was lost and could not be relocated. Catalina JU993 of 333 Squadron 'A' Flight left Sullom Voe at 19.30 hours to help locate the ditched airman. Reaching the area at 21.46 the pilot Lieutenant Garstad flew low over the flame floats dropped by a Warwick, which they were unable to contact by radio-telephone. Using a handheld flashlight to send 'Relieved' seconds later the Warwick left the area. An hour later 57.52E/0305E began dropping fresh markers, awaiting the arrival of RAF HSL. Garstad noted '15 hours fuel left'. Pilot Officer D Duthie 279 Squadron Fraserburgh said:

'I sadly recall that no effort was made to grasp the floating lines or to board the boat. I formed the opinion he was injured, which with the extreme cold rendered him either unconscious or completely helpless.'

It is presumed that Flying Officer Johnny Daynton went down with the wreckage. Flight Lieutenant D Robinson and his navigator crash-landed after returning from this operation and, having crossed the North Sea on one engine with a large proportion of the port wing missing, they escaped uninjured.

In the evening various messes on the base were in a sombre mood as people presumed that Johnny Lown had died. Men and women immersed themselves deeper in alcohol as the night progressed into wild singing, ending as dawn broke. 315 Squadron pilots ended up in Montrose but none could recall how they got there or back on New Year's Day. December was a disastrous month for 235, 248 and 143 Squadrons who between them lost nine crews on operations, and one non-operationally – this was an exceptionally high 40% loss rate. The casualties among the Coastal Command aircrews caused a great deal of concern at Northwood. For those who survived it was impossible to ignore the risks to each and every operation and impossible to forget the fate of colleagues who had succumbed to those risks. Despite the losses of men and machines in the three months from September to December 1944, the Mosquitoes sank 17 vessels of 23,589 tons, shared in the sinking of two others, and damaged eight ships of just over 10,000 tons. Figures also showed that during the whole of 1944, aircraft controlled by Coastal Command were credited with sinking 170 vessels totalling 183,192 tons, and damaging 39. Most of these were sunk off the Norwegian coast. In total 165 aircraft had been lost.

Fortunately newly experienced aircrew arrived at the station. One of them was Flight Lieutenant Richard Young, posted to 248 Squadron. He had previously flown with 143 Squadron in early 1944. Young wrote of his arrival on 30 December 1944 in a letter home wishing them a Happy New Year:

'Having arrived safely after a rather poor journey I am now trying to settle down under somewhat rough conditions. Arriving at Aberdeen at 1.20pm my pal – who was on the train when it reached Dundee – and I went to have something to eat before catching the northbound train at 3.20pm. The lunch was quite good. Now, where we had had a carriage to ourselves from Dundee to Aberdeen when it came to going on the next one we found we had to stand in a crowded corridor from 3.20pm until 6.15pm when we arrived at Portsoy railway station, the one nearest to our airfield. Once at the railway station, I telephoned the mess for the orderly officer and transport was sent to fetch us and our luggage. While waiting for the van we went to a church canteen in the village hall and had a very nice of tea. We finished just as the transport arrived and before long we were at the aerodrome. At present it's a bit early to say what the verdict should be about the place but I believe in about a week's time I shall be quite at home and probably enjoying the life. As there is little activity going on outside I do not expect to have a busy time – the rest may do me good.'

CHAPTER 8

JANUARY 1945

Despite the seemingly never-ending losses suffered over recent months, the strike wing started the new year in good spirits. Their contribution to the war would escalate in 1945.

Coastal Command units continued to search for Lown. In rain and drizzle on Monday 1 January, the crew of Catalina JU933, which had been on station overnight, hoped that the sea would be calm enough to pick Lown up but unfortunately the sea state remained very rough. An RAF HSL finally arrived at 02.08 hours and began searching, 40 minutes later neither had sighted the dinghy. The Catalina crew found the dinghy at 08.58 hours then temporarily lost sight. Two Thornaby Warwicks relieved the Catalina at 10.35 hours; half an hour afterwards one of the mid-uppers sighted a person kneeling in a dinghy in position 5754N/0321E. One began circling the survivor but during a circuit at a height of 70 feet in the appalling conditions could not relocate the airman or his dinghy. They then commenced a square search but both continued in vain. With fuel being consumed at an alarming rate, they finally aborted the search for their own safety. A relief Hudson continued until first light on Tuesday 2 January. At 15.55 hours, the Lindholme dinghy, which displayed the number '7', was found in position 5755N/0350E apparently empty. A Gee fix was then passed on to another Mosquito, which orbited it. A light, which might have been a flare, was then observed some 200 yards from the boat. A 235 Squadron crew also spotted it but contact was lost by both aircraft orbiting in adverse conditions. Station commander Group Captain Max Aiken also led a search in his personalised aircraft HR366 with its distinctive burgundy coloured spinners. The next day a crew momentarily sighted the lifeboat and gave an approximate position around which subsequent searches were made and then abandoned. The last image remaining of Flight Lieutenant Johnny Lown is of him alive sitting in his dinghy waving. A WAAF serving at Banff's Signal Section recalls the sadness of sending the telegrams to the next of kin:

'Immediately I set foot in the Signals Section I was always given the bloody awful job of sending telegrams to next-of-kin: "We deeply regret to inform you, etc". Sometimes we received a telephone call saying that a single aircraft from this station had safely landed at Sumburgh. But more often than not at Banff it was "We deeply regret", many of my friends consoled one another when one of the boys had bought it.'

Reconnaissance continued on 3 January between rain and snow showers. Severe weather curtailed operational flying for the next couple of days. However, Group Captain Max Aitken ordered 333 Squadron to remain operational at all cost and the Norwegians managed four sweeps. On Saturday 6 January, Lieutenant Finn Andvig with Sergeant Lefdahl as navigator search from Holmengrå, Alden, Askerøya, Florø, and Kallevåg but found nothing of special interest.

A barge, MW151, operated by the Speerflotte, a former Seeadler (a type of barge used in the Rhinehessen area) from Mannheim was spotted sailing from Bergen bound for Fedje under her own engine, carrying military stores and vehicles. Onboard were 20 Russian POWs. MW151 together with a tug boat reached Fedjefjord. 455 Squadron were given their first anti-shipping patrol of the new year. Twelve Dallachy aircraft, led by Wing Commander Colin Milson and a 315 Squadron Mustang provided escort, it took 20 minutes to get ready over Dallachy before setting course at 1,000 feet for Norway at 13.42 hours. ASR cover came to an abrupt end when an electrical fire started under the wireless position. Not long into the journey 'B' 404 returned to base with mechanical trouble. At 15.14 the force crossed the Norwegian coast near Helliso Light. One of the outriders radioed the formation leader with his position and fired green cartridges at the target location. Nearby they found the self-propelled oil-burning barge MW151. Three 455 Squadron Beaufighters went into attack at 16.00 hours, piloted by three Australians, Payne, Cox and Farr. They struck the barge together with rockets from 1,000 metres then cannon from 600 metres. 'E' 404 made a second run in with cannon. Three from 404 Squadron made a simultaneous strike on the target. Four 20mm anti-aircraft guns located on Maro Island gave moderate defensive fire but the barge was left damaged and adrift on an easterly heading. After the air attack the crew beached MW151, but in the heavy swells she sank, with the loss of three German soldiers and 14 POWs wounded. Milson led the rest of the formation on a sweep further along the fjord. There they found a merchantman close inshore and circled ready to strike, but a heavy snowstorm broke and Milson had no alterative but to call off the effort.

Adverse weather conditions were making flying extremely hard on 7 January, but at 14.20 hours Banff, Fraserburgh and Peterhead were requested to have one aircraft standing by to give assistance to 'Sugar 519', which was in difficulty. In the heavy wintery showers a Polish Mustang took off with poor visibility to intercept 'Sugar 519', a Hudson on a Rhombus flight from Bircham Newton. The pilot located and guided the Hudson back to Peterhead, landing at 16.00 hours.

During the night a convoy of four moved silently along the west coast of Norway at 04.30 hours (local time), travelling unmolested in the twilight. All that could be seen was the dim glow from their navigation lights and the sound of their engines. It was 8 January and a convoy consisting of the *Sevre*, *Claus Rickmers*, *Bjergfinn*, and the escort vessel Vp.5304 *Seehund* was bound for Bergen. On the bridge of *Claus Rickmers*, the conscripted Norwegian pilot Waage stood beside Captain Stengel. The convoy edged into Bømlafjord, with its underwater rocks making it difficult to negotiate. A command was given which the helmsman misunderstood, he altered course and within seconds the bow ground on to a rock known locally as Bloksene between Haugesund and Leirvik. Captain Stengel ordered 'Stop' and the vessel came to a standstill. Water poured into the forward hold and flooded it. The crew worked tirelessly and managed to get the vessel to reverse using her own power. Within an hour it needed to be set ashore at Leirvik harbour in order not to sink.

The cargo onboard was particularly important to the Germans, for it was carrying 7,002 tons of marinecoke crucial to the Kriegsmarine. In the hold was 175 tons of military supplies. Knowing that the RAF visited the area daily, Admiral Otto von Schrader at once ordered the local coastal batteries to be on Alert State 1. Reinforcements of flak units from Bergen and Haugesund arrived the following day. The 120 tons of mines and depth charges which made up part of the vessel's cargo were hastily off loaded and secured while the Wehrmacht military equipment remained. Flakships Vp.5304 *Seehund* and Vp.5308 *OB Rouge* were ordered to provide further protection from within the harbour, together with R63. All were extremely heavily armed and manned by experienced gunners.

Meanwhile Coastal Command activities were just beginning in Scotland. Four

Beaufighters had been airborne since 08.50 hours searching for targets from Utsira to Bremanger, landing back at Dallachy at 14.15 hours. Twelve Banff aircrews were briefed on providing fighter cover for 14 Dallachy Beaufighters, 12 armed with R/P drawn from 455 and 404 Squadrons, and two acting as outriders led by Flight Lieutenant Noel Russell DFC of 235 Squadron. Flight Lieutenant Bob McColl led the force. 'D' 144, piloted by Flying Officer Andrews, made landfall at Utsira at 14.18 hours, tasked to search through the Leads. Looking into Leirvik his navigator thought he saw a merchantman of about 1,500/2,000 tons lying at the north end of the bay. This was not investigated because 'D' 144 was doing reconnaissance of Leirvik. Andrews then flew north. On the way across the North Sea at 13.55 hours, 'O' 404 hit a bird, smashing the front and side windows and making intercom impossible; he set course for base. 'E' 404 had taken evasive action five miles from landfall at 14.20 hours and then lost the rest of the force in cloud. At 14.24 hours the main formation swept north beyond Roversholm Light, near Haugesund, led by Squadron Leader Christison in 'H' 404. They darted into Bommel fjord, up the Inner Leads and then around Stord Island, drawing light flak from a fort on Leirvik (as they passed near the harbour) and heavy 88mm flak from Hauge. At 14.32 hours Christison heard one word 'M/Vs' on VHF then suddenly communication was lost completely. Andrews' navigator heard the full message: '4 M/Vs in position from which flak is coming' from an unidentified aircraft. Christison led a search around Bjørne fjord and saw four vessels in another convoy, one described as a 2,000 ton merchantman, which was near a rocky outcrop. 'D' 144's pilot called the strike leader asking 'Have you got a target? If not I have one, one merchantman.' The reply was not understood. He then flew over the main force which was heading west, and said, 'Target at 3 o'clock behind island'. Before the formation turned to starboard and attacked these at 14.46 hours, one was already firing. Christison was in the lead section as the Beaufighters streamed in, hitting the *Trygg* and a barge nearby with cannon and rockets from a height of 450-200 feet. The merchantmen, together with Vp.5116 *Unitas* were simultaneously hit. On the day of the attack Vp.5116 had been waiting at the Korsfjord outlet together with the tug *Hjeltenfjord* for a damaged vessel arriving from Marstein in order to take it to Bergen. Now ensnared, both defended themselves, laying a barrage of light flak. A nearby German fort opened fire as well. It is possible that the Beaufighter crews believed all the vessels were firing upon them, although the next vessel to be targeted was in fact unarmed.

The *Fusa* was a 70-year-old Swedish-built passenger/cargo vessel of 172 tons and therefore under the 500 ton limit – it should not have been attacked. Although the passenger vessel was clearly marked, this operation was carried out without the usual Norwegian outrider. The vessel had departed from Bergen on the regular scheduled service to Sævareid terminal at 12.30 (local time); on board were 31 passengers and 11 crew and a cargo consisting of fertilizer, flour, bales of straw, empty milk churns from the local dairy and general supplies for the local community, as well as local mail. The conditions were clear on this winter's day with excellent visibility as they approached Nordstrøno, their next scheduled stop. Some of the crew observed the fast looming grey shapes of 12 aircraft, while high above them the Mosquitoes kept watch. The aircrews spotted the increased activity in Leirvik harbour and the disabled *Claus Rickmers*. Able Seaman Hauge counted 18 aircraft altogether.

Suddenly as four of them attacked Vp. 5116, Captain Nils Størnen in the wheelhouse of the *Fusa*, ordered: 'Stop the machine and blow the alarm on the horn.' As he stood at the helm, a 0.303 round sliced through a finger and the ship's wheel. It was 14.45 hours (local time). In a maritime declaration Størnen stated that all the attacks came from the starboard side. One of those attacking the *Fusa* was McColl, who took the target to his right, which was making dark smoke from the funnel. He strafed across the merchantman, his cannon shells exploding on its decks and hull. Only the bow could be seen because of thick heavy smoke as others followed him in. As McColl's attack finished cannon and machine-gun rounds had set the straw bales alight. First Mate Stein Anderson Hagevik, in the corridor at the starboard side, went over to the port side to take shelter there and met one of the passengers, the 23-year-old Henrik Henriksen Søfteland. Both came from the same parish. While talking Søfteland was hit by a cannon shell in the face and crumpled to the floor, causing panic among the passengers. After a third aircraft struck, the Dallachy Beaufighters banked hard to port, searching for other targets.

On board the *Fusa* several passengers were dead and among the wounded were four crew members; one, Stoker Fridtjof Urdal later died in hospital. Hit above and below the waterline, with two large holes in the starboard bow hull, the vessel's lifeboats and rafts were in bad condition having received cannon and machine-gun rounds. Captain Nils Størnen, ordered 'Full steam ahead' in an attempt to beach her, but the hull hit the bottom before reaching the shore. First Mate Stein Hagevik lowered the port lifeboat but found it leaking so together with four passengers he tried to go back onto the vessel to find something for bailing. It began to sink, however, so he and another person began building a raft out of a consignment of timber from the cargo. Twenty minutes later the *Fusa* sank by the bow, capsizing to starboard. A fishing boat rescued Hagevik and the passenger from their makeshift raft half an hour later. A local restaurant owner, Mrs Hilma Zahl, was seen on deck but returned to her cabin to rescue some documents and money and is presumed to have perished. Survivors were brought ashore at Korsnes assisted by German troops, before being sent onto Bergen for medical treatment. Two brothers, Otto and Jonn Strønen, began rescuing survivors. Otto says:

'At Korsnes an angry German officer came on board. He had seen us pass the German guard vessel Vp.5116 and it was illegal to pass a ship in distress. We steered south of Korsnes when he suddenly pulled a gun into Jonn's ribs. Jonn was at the rudder and grabbed the barrel not realizing what it was and moved it away. The German officer thought this funny and began to laugh. Shortly afterward we began helping the crew of Vp.5116; they brought aboard a wounded soldier, and we asked him if we should sail for a coastal hospital. But he said he did not want that because there was 'kein wein und kein fraulein' (no wine and no women) in Norwegian hospitals. He was then transferred onto a Norwegian rescue vessel.'

The tug boat *Trygg* drifted ashore and was tied up at Langøysundet, she was later moored at Korsnes, until she sank. The captain and two crewmen of the tugboat landed at Skåtøy in a lifeboat. Henrik Henriksen Søfteland, the passenger who had died on *Fusa*, was a member of a SOE-supported Milorg unit. Earlier on 26 September 1944, an RAF Bomber Command aircraft had crash-landed, and its Canadian crew were helped by Søfteland, who smuggled them to Britain on the Norwegian sub chaser *Vigra*, operating from Scalloway. He had been staying in Strandvik since November 1944, and gone under cover after a rather careless SIS agent had been arrested; on board *Fusa* he was carrying false identification papers in order to contact SOE Milorg connections to get supplies for himself and 20 hiding in the area. These supplies had been hidden amongst the cargo on board *Fusa* with the help of the crew.

The German forces in Norway used this attack on the *Fusa* as propaganda, and this incident raised objections in Britain from the Norwegian government in exile. After assurances were given by Coastal Command that the aircrews involved thought that they were attacking a 2,000-ton merchantman, however, the matter was dropped by the Norwegians.

The night saw a snow flurry, but the morning was clear and fresh and both wings were active on Tuesday 9 January. Searches in the area of Haugesund-Bergen by 11 Mosquitoes were recorded by the Germans between 14.21 and 14.46 hours (local time) on 9 January. 18 Group received intelligence from debriefing notes of the 8 January strike that there was a promising target at Leirvik, just north of Haugesund. A strike wing was despatched, with its primary target the disabled merchantman *Claus Rickmers*. A mixed force of 20 Mosquitoes, including three Tsetse types, was airborne at 09.45 hours, led by Wing Commander Maurice. At 09.00 hours 12 Mustangs from 315 Squadron provided cover. 'N' 235 was forced to turn back early because of an engine failure, landing at 09.51 hours. Closing up, the formation made landfall at Utsira Light at 10.45 hours, and the main force turned north along the coast while one Norwegian outrider left, heading up past the many islands, up the Inner Leads, as far as Leirvik. No shipping was sighted. Below in the vicinity of Leirvik the local alarm was the first warning *Claus Rickmers* received of fast approaching enemy aircraft. Lieutenant Thor Stensrud identified merchant ships in the harbour, at 11.10 reporting 'Target is Leirvik!' a minute later followed by 'Have one large merchantman and seven others visible'. The leader then flew in that direction and 'Plumbird 1' was asked to fire off greens over the position once the force was insight. The second outrider then led the force skilfully over the extraordinary scenery of snowcapped mountains to the target, approaching from the north-west. The Mustang's escort orbited Stord Island and a message was transmitted on VHF at 11.00 hours that one had engine trouble. It left the formation with one as escort. Maurice requested 'O' 333 to contact the Mustang and escort it home. Permission was obtained from the strike leader for the Warwick on ASR duty to follow. Through wintry showers they headed back, where the Mustang landed without mishap at Peterhead, with the Warwick crew touching down at 12.50 hours.

Once greens were fired, outriders watched the force form up for attack. The strike was on. At 11.15 eight aircraft with 25lb rockets and cannon, one Tsetse, and three Mosquitoes firing cannon struck from the landward side and were engaged by the flak gunners from the vessels in the harbour and from the shore. Hits were secured on the vessels with rockets, cannon, and machine guns. *Claus Rickmers* of 5,165 tons received 40 hits from rockets (26 dry, and 16 wet) and one Tsetse 57mm, all of which mainly penetrated the forward structure due to the protection given to the aft part of the ship by the quayside fish factory. The vessel began to burn. Flying Officer Wallace Woodcock, flying a Tsetse, described the attack in *The Isle of Wight County Press*: 'I saw a six-pounder shell hit the stern, then right in front of us, a shore flak position opened up, and we let it have about half a dozen six-pounder shells. It did not fire again.'

Stray rounds during the strike struck a house in the centre of Leirvik and fragments injured a father and daughter; both were treated in hospital. On board the moored *Claus Rickmers* six or seven underwater hits by rockets had penetrated Numbers 1 and 2 holds. Hold 1 was already flooded with water ballast but the hits on hold 2 resulted in the flooding of both this and hold 3 as there was no bulkhead between the two. Fire broke out on the forecastle and bridge. Kriegsmarine personnel battled against the blistering heat to save their deadly cargo of small arms ammunition and coal from catching alight. As the Mosquitoes left smoke was rising to 150 feet. Eventually after an hour, they had managed to put it out. The large merchantman, limp already, was resting on the bottom on her bows with two to three feet of clearance aft. She settled quickly and on an even keel. At the quayside, ambulance personnel took away the dead body of one her gunners and two wounded. Local intelligence reported, 'One ship sunk at moorings, four others severely damaged.'

A German document states: 'At 10.40 hours (local time) a formation of 25 Mosquitoes and Beaufighters was sighted near Utsira heading towards Bergen. A formation, of 18 Beaufighters made a strike at 11.23 hours (local time) in the harbour of Leirvik with rockets. The accommodation quarters were set ablaze with heavy black smoke. Vp.5304 was damaged with two crew members injured.' Unfortunately in some cases, identification between the two types of aircraft was not always correct. The Germans report three Mosquitoes shot down and several others damaged and flying away in flames. This was wishful thinking as all returned to base though some had flak damage. The German admiral had requested fighter support but none appeared, simply because there were none at the nearest airfield, Herdla, outside Bergen. The next day, 10 January, the 9 Staffel of JG5 Eismeerjäger (polar sea hunters) flew in from Trondheim with Fw190s. Its orders were 'Küstensicherung' (coastal defence).

All the Mosquitoes returning landed at 12.56 hours, 'J' 235 with slight flak damage. The pilots and navigators were debriefed on return, but to those on the flight line engaged in servicing the aircraft, described at Banff as 'a taxi rank', it was no different from any other day. The serviceability state was discussed by overworked ground crews, who often missed meals to get the Mosquitoes ready, as each squadron on the airfield tried to top 18 Group's statistics for aircraft serviceability. Air tests were started by aircrew. From 235's dispersal hut Flight Lieutenant Donald Douglas (RCAF) walked out to Mosquito HR159 and the 32-year-old mechanic LAC Gerard Robbins asked for a trip, Douglas duly obliged. It was miserably cold as they climbed through the hatch on the starboard side of the Mosquito; after the pre-flight checks the aircraft taxied carefully around the perimeter track.

Just after 15.20 hours, HR159 accelerated after the brakes were released, the tail lifted, then when airborne the two men relaxed a little, though nervous until single engine safety speed, 130 mph, was attained. Engine failure before this could be trouble. The aircraft turned to port and headed out over the firing ranges to sea; minutes later HR159 having dived, swept in low over the airfield at roughly 1,000 feet whereupon Douglas went into a slow barrel roll apparently unintentionally – perhaps to impress the airman. The speed dropped quickly as did the nose during the second half of the roll, and the aircraft stalled and spun into Hopeton farmhouse four miles west-south-west of the airfield, at 15.30 hours. The farmhouse was occupied by Mrs Bremner and her semi-invalid mother. On impact HR159 burned; both crew died instantly and thick smoke rose to 700 feet. The alarm raised both Banff and Portsoy fire tenders who were on the scene within minutes.

Their task was hopeless however, as although water was pumped into the totally burnt-out farmhouse it could not extinguish the flames. Both occupants were unhurt miraculously, although Mrs Bremner's mother went to Chalmers Hospital in Banff, suffering from shock and was kept in overnight under observation. The charred remains of the two airmen were taken to the station mortuary. Flight Lieutenant Donald Douglas (RCAF) from Belleville, Ontario, was buried with full military honours at Banff Cemetery at 15.00 hours on 12 January with fitting last tributes from members of the squadron, while LAC Gerard Robbins was laid to rest a few days later in Dundee. Condolences were sent to his wife, Pauline Robbins. In claiming damages, the Bremners were confronted by the fact that the aircraft was not taking off on operations, but was only on a test flight, which raised many difficulties. It is unclear whether their claim was finally settled. An extract from the *Banffshire Journal* reads:

'Mrs Bremner sat on the edge of the bed chatting to her mother. Then like a bolt from the blue came a fearful roar and crash that shattered the house to its foundations. The aircraft, crashing to earth out of control, collided with the gable end of the house, demolishing the wall and instantly burst into flames, petrol at once engulfed the house. Mrs Bremner realised they were trapped.

'With presence of mind, she dragged her dazed mother to the bedroom window. She climbed through it and with great strength pulled her mother up and out of the window; two men arrived and helped them away from the scene. The Portsoy and Banff units of the NFS battled for several hours, with darkness falling before the fire was extinguished.'

Meanwhile Squadron Leader John Pilcher in 'R' 455 had led the Dallachy Beaufighters away from their base at 09.46 hours on a separate strike to Norway. Two Warwicks from 279 Squadron joined them. Flying to Helliso Light at 11.38 hours, the strike leader heard on VHF '4 small ships visible on westerly course, mouth of Sogue Loch, size uncertain.' A further message came in from Flight Lieutenant McGaughran in 'E' 144 who had passed it on to 'R' 489 who then radioed 'Rakit' leader. 'E' 144 then left the target and resumed the search flying over Dals fjord and Vevring fjord. 'R' 489 proceeded to position, indicated by 'E' 144 6104N/0548E. Pilcher took his force north-east edging near Sognefjord in excellent conditions. McGaughran then heard the force was going to the target found by him, a merchantman moored in Fuglsaet fjord, near the entrance to Sognefjord, on the southern side. Pilcher entered from the south, flying fast and low down Fuglsaet towards Sogne. 'R' 489 sighted the target and fired off green cartridges at 12.05 hours. The merchantman *Sirius* of 938 tons was awaiting nightfall, anchored close to the eastern shore of the fjord, near the town of Hoga. The aircraft went in over Hoga and hills covered with heavy snow in line astern on a northerly course on the ship's port beam; at 12.10 hours, rockets crashed into the *Sirius*, whose name was clearly visible on the portside of the vessel and eventually she rested on the bottom, just feet from the shoreline. On the way out navigators reported seeing a chimney radar installation in the course of being constructed, with the base heavily camouflaged on Fedje.

On Wednesday 10 January, a morning reconnaissance had found merchantmen north of Ålesund near Storholm Light. 18 Group requested RAF Banff to provide two Norwegian outriders for an early sortie with Dallachy Beaufighters. Two of those on standby at Dallachy were Pilot Officer Arthur Winter and his navigator Cliff Dunshea, who had ditched off the Shetland Islands on 5 December and were now totally recovered. The men had been playing a traditional pub game 'shove ha'penny' when they were called to the operations building. At 11.50 hours Squadron Leader Christison led the force of 22 Beaufighters away from Dallachy which comprised 18 with R/P, and 4 with torpedoes using the 18 inch Mark XV with a lengthened warhead. They set course for Banff at 12.06 hours, picking up 12 Mustangs as fighter escort from 315 Squadron and two Warwicks. The journey across the North Sea was in clear conditions, the sea calm. At the briefing the crews had been asked to pay special attention to their altitude, but Flight Sergeant Peter Ilbery's wave top indicator (radio altimeter) was consistently reading in the red at thirty feet! 'L' 144 and 'G' 404 returned to base at 13.20 and 14.20 respectively owing to mechanical failures. At an estimated 45 miles away from the Norwegian coast, the two Mosquitoes detached themselves from the formation and flew ahead to have a look for targets. Lieutenant R Leithe in 'Q' 333 crossed the coast at Skopen at 13.45 while Major E Johansen crossed over at Storholm an hour later in 'P' 333. Landfall by the main force was made at Lepsø Island, north of Ålesund, at 14.26 Johansen received a message of target and position. Leithe radioed 'Target steaming south between Lepsø and Haramso' to Squadron Leader Christison at

14.35 hours as Johansen led the force into attack.

The Beaufighters flew within sight of the target, climbing to 1,500 ft and dived back down. On the way in minesweeper M.322 was seen heading for a jetty at Haram on the southern tip of Haramso Island. It was a long approach and the Vics picked their target. Thirteen Beaufighters attacked M.322. One of those was Christison, hitting the target with rockets and cannon. On breaking away he strafed the M-class minesweeper. At 14.42 hours Lieutenant Herbert von der Hoff, captain on M.322 had watched the bridge disintegrate and the ship was on fire. The attention now swung to the M.5610 sailing at 4 knots in position 62.39N/06.12E. 'F' 144 soon fell victim to flak and crashed on shore with the loss of Warrant Officer Charles Foster and Flight Sergeant Roland Cunningham. One vic of three Beaufighters piloted by Ilbery, Winter and Proctor, chose the M-class M.5610. Seven 25lb armour-piercing rockets were observed passing forward of the bridge and cannon shells were sighted all over the target. Ilbery in 'T' 455 was one of those who followed a quarter of a mile behind. Bursts of flak from shore batteries appeared into which Winters' Beaufighter 'M' 455 RD141 disappeared. Suddenly 37mm shells smacked into the port engine, setting the whole wing alight. 'M' 455 soared to starboard, but Winter gained enough height to fly over a small hill on Haramso upon breaking away. However, when 'T' 455 flew over the hill 'M' 455 had disappeared. With the port engine on fire, 'M' 455 rolled over onto its back and crashed into the icy waters on the north-east side of Haramso at 62.39N/06.15E and began to burn on the water less than 200 metres from the shore at 14.45 hours. No survivors were seen.

The remaining sections hosed the vessel with cannon hitting M.5610 at 600 yards. The rockets were fired, a number set the former fishing boat ablaze and a pall of smoke rose to 700 feet. It exploded killing seventeen German sailors, only one survived, he was picked up from the water an hour and a half later. Below debris floated to the surface and the leader broke off the attack. The formation followed him, leaving both vessels crippled. Lieutenant von der Hoff on M.322 was able to beach the minesweeper, with six crew seriously injured, and eleven with minor injuries. They succeeded in repairing M.322 and she was refloated the same afternoon and sailed to Ålesund and returned into service. The Beaufighters set course for Dallachy at 14.47 hours. 'T' 455 low on fuel, landed away at Sumburgh, the rest between 16.57 /17.13 hours at Dallachy. Pilot Officer Arthur Winter and Cliff Dunshea were posted as missing, they had been with 455 Squadron since 19 July 1944, and it was their twenty-first sortie. Dunshea's body was recovered from the shore at Haramso, and later buried in Trondheim. Winters' next of kin requested that his bicycle be forwarded to Miss Maureen Geddes of Port Gordon, Banffshire. During the afternoon a reconnaissance of Leirvik by a Dyce reconnaissance aircraft found the *Claus Rickmers* down and aground by the bows.

The Royal Navy Home Fleet had been conducting sweeps along the Norwegian coast since October 1944; one of its vessels was a Dutch submarine named *Dolfijn* part of the 9th British Submarine Flotilla based at Dundee. *Dolfijn* had undergone major repairs since June 1944 and begun training patrols at the beginning of January 1945, setting sail again at 10.00 hours on the 10th, on its second patrol. At 12.45 hours 14 Mosquitoes, including a Tsetse 'E1' 248 were out on a Rover patrol between Bergen and Haugesund, guided by Flight Lieutenant Lewis Bacon in 'X' 248, searching the broad wastes of the sea, while the two Norwegian aircraft flew ahead to check the Inner Leads. By chance 'O' 143 flown by Pilot Officer Symons (RCAF), sighted what appeared to be sun shinning on the hull of a U-boat travelling at about eight knots on the surface in position 6003N-0027E. The time was 15.42 hours.

A Mosquito approached the vessel, undetected on its radar because of their approach – fifty feet from the beam. On the conning tower was the first officer who, for some inexplicable reason, did not fire flares when challenged. The submarine men on watch saw the twin-engine aircraft gain height and dive. Bacon shouted into the radio he was going down. Aboard the submarine the alarm sounded, hatches quickly closed as it crash-dived. When the attacking Mosquitoes came across at approximately 200 feet the submarine had not fully gone below the waves. Volleys of machine-gun and cannon fire struck the boat from 'X' 248, followed by three 143 Squadron aircraft with rockets. Sergeant/observer Van Oosten describes the scene: 'It was like handfuls of pebbles were strewn onto the boat.'

Having been under water for ten minutes its commander J B M J Maas went to periscope-depth. However, the periscope did not function anymore. On investigation, further battle damage was found, including to the aerial, which was unserviceable. Maas maintained course. The attack was over in three minutes at 15.47, the aircrew being unable to see the effect as the Mosquitoes now turned for home. Unfortunately, days later the crews from this patrol were told by Group Captain Aitken in his office the U-boat they attacked was in fact the allied Dutch naval submarine *Dolfijn*.

Out at sea the submarine emptied its tanks at 16.39 hours, surfacing to inspect the damage. Having installed an emergency aerial it submerged and went deep; a signal arrived from its homeport to which the *Dolfijn* indicated her position, and a reply was sent immediately. The *Dolfijn* was recalled by the Admiralty. On the 11th, it safely entered the harbour at Leirvik at 14.00 hours. Maas later remarked in his report: 'I would have liked to inform the crews of the aircraft involved how well executed the attack was, and with excellent marksmanship.'

Thursday the 11th began with an early morning reconnaissance over Norway by five Norwegian Mosquito Mark VIs which had taken off from a snow bound airfield, for both Banff and Dallachy were under a covering of snow. Lieutenant Plyn piloted 'F' 333. He made landfall at Bremanger and headed north-east, covering the Leads and fjords up to Ålesund. He strafed a merchantman which returned fire, splintering the port propeller blade and damaging the nacelle and drop-tank. At 10.45 hours he flew over the North Sea, and as he turned west, towards Scotland, he feathered the port engine. At 11.00 hours another maximum effort by 18 Group was called for. The two wings combined to attack three vessels reported in Flekkefjord by reconnaissance aircraft. With still only one Mustang squadron available some of the Mosquito crews were assigned as escort. Fifteen Mosquitoes were airborne between 12.15 and 12.34 hours to rendezvous with 21 Beaufighters at 12.41 hours, two Beaufighters returned early before meeting up with the Banff wing. At 12.48 hours the armada finally set course from Banff with Flight Lieutenant Bob McColl leading the force in 'M' 455. As they flew at 500 feet on the way to the target interference was twice picked up for three seconds but sounded different to the usual RDF. Five minutes later four white Swedish fishing vessels were seen heading north but no sea gulls or fishing nets were observed. Immediately afterwards the strike leader sighted a Warwick with the two 333 Squadron outriders in 5813N/0500E.

Landfall was made at 14.35 in 5812N/0638E. The following conversation then took place between the two outriders and the leader: Weaver 1 to Weaver 2 – 'Target as indicated, 90° across Flekkefjord.' Weaver 2 to leader – 'Indicate position to come to by greens.' Seconds later McColl sighted three aircraft ahead of the force and going to port followed by two Mosquitoes. He then called on the formation to stay together and called Weaver 1, 'Being attacked by Bandits and abandoning target'. Weaver 1 responded asking for the position of the formation and the leader replied, 'Heading west from Lista.'

Lista was home to fighter group 14/JG 5. The German air defence had already reacted to their presence. Below at 1,000 feet, the German fighters were waiting, there seemed to be seven Messerschmitts Bf109s and several Focke-Wulf 190s with further aircraft taking off under a cluster of anti-aircraft fire at 14.36 hours as the force approached Lista at a height of 1,500 feet. At the same time Focke-Wulf and Messerschmitt fighters engaged from the north, diving out of cloud cover. The Beaufighter leader ordered his aircraft to take evasive action when fired upon while the more manoeuvrable Mosquitoes went into individual dogfights in order to cover the Dallachy wing's withdrawal. Beaufighter 'R' 489 on the edge of the formation opened fire on a Focke-Wulf at 14.36 but no results were observed. At 14.40 hours, as the remaining Beaufighters tightened up their formation and turned out to sea on a reciprocal track, McColl sent a radio message, 'Attacked by fighters – target not attacked'.

Duels were taking place over the vast expanse of water between Lista and Flekkefjord. A section of Bf109G-14s attempted to engage the Beaufighters at speed, one got caught; Flying Officer Kaufman in 'F' 143 saw a Bf109 on the tail of Beaufighter 'C' 144, the enemy tracer rounds were seen hitting the Beaufighter at 300 yards. No evasive action or return fire was seen from the Beaufighter and after another burst of fire from the Bf109 the Beaufighter was seen crashing into the sea on fire. 'D' 144 also saw this enemy aircraft make a tail attack on 'C' 144. Flying Officer Don Clause in 'X' 143 chased the Bf109 and while taking evasive action this victorious Luftwaffe pilot hit the water. There was no sign of a survivor.

At this moment some of McColl's crews saw Mosquito 'R' 235, flown by Flight Lieutenant Noel Russell DFC, in a dogfight with Offizier Clemens Köhler flying a Bf 109G-14. 'R' 235 hit the aircraft dead astern with cannon rounds which caught fire and exploded on impact. Russell then turned his attention to two more 190s; this second engagement was over quickly. Offizier Werner Nieft's aircraft went into a gentle dive, hit the water and burnt until swamped. These two enemy aircraft were seen to crash into the sea by navigators who also reported seeing a Mosquito crash. 'C' 235 made four repeated attacks on a single Fw190, and cannon shells exploded on the fuselage and wings. Another aircraft, 'H' 235, was receiving attention from two Fw190s. This Mosquito was piloted by Flight Sergeant Frankie Chew and reacted to a warning from his navigator (Flight Sergeant 'Jock' Couttie) by taking evasive action, then saw another Fw190 disappearing under his port wing before losing both Focke-Wulfs. In the ensuing battle a Tsetse Mosquito, 'Z' 248, fired off four 57mm shells at a Focke-Wulf; it then homed in on a distress call. Suddenly at 14.41 hours the Lista-based fighters broke off into cloud. A call then went out by the strike leader Flight Lieutenant McColl to return to base. Bordeaux leader called the formation leader and asked whether the formation required further escort. The leader replied in the negative.

The RAF claimed four of the enemy fighters but only Köhler and Nieft were reported as lost. The wing suffered casualties too: Flight Sergeant Pierre Smoolenaers, a 20-year-old Belgian flying with 143 Squadron in 'M' 143, was under fire from a pursuer. Smoolenaers had seconds to react. Sweeping low over the seascape and trying to evade, he ploughed on at speed; someone managed to call out faintly 'Urgent assistance required' on VHF while the IFF was switched on, before the ferocious enemy fire forced the Mosquito down impacting into the water. The hunter Leutnant Vollet of IV JG 5 listed the 'M' 143 as shot down and destroyed.

Onboard 'B' 279 Flight Officer George Gallway the wireless operator, passed the position to his captain, Flight Lieutenant John Moreton. With the air battle still raging overhead the Warwick's skipper headed for the location of the ditched aircraft at 500 feet. From the wreckage one crew member was seen managing to reach the inflated L type dinghy. At 14.37 hours the crew sighted the dinghy in the choppy sea. The Warwick flew over the top and immediately climbed before making a dummy run. At

14.46 a Beaufighter orbited the area. At 14.47 in position 58.13N-06.30E (approximately) the Beaufighter crew saw 'B' 279 Warwick HG209, piloted by Flight Lieutenant John Moreton, with a Bf109G-14 from IV JG 5 in close pursuit. Moreton was seen attempting to drop a lifeboat in the proximity of the ditched Mosquito while his two air gunners tried desperately to shoot down their hunter which carried out a series of attacks, severely damaging the aircraft's hydraulic system and both engines.

HG209 went down. All six crew perished, Flight Lieutenant John Moreton, Pilot Officer Frederick Bentley (RCAF), Flying Officer George Gallway, Warrant Officers Andrew Goodall and George Mansfield and Flight Sergeant William Bryan. There was also a seventh member onboard, an Australian Warrant Officer William Sandercock from South Australia, a 29-year-old who, it seemed, had gone along to see the homeland of the composer Grieg. As the Messerschmitt left the scene the bulk of the Warwick had broken into three parts and sank within 10 seconds. An inflated dinghy marked the spot. Another Beaufighter sighted some wreckage from the Warwick about 20 miles off the Norwegian coast, but the rescuers of 11 January were beyond aid as all had perished.

Three minutes later the Mosquitoes reported the last enemy fighter seen departing the area. Flight Lieutenant Wainman in 'M' 404 backed this up at 15.00 hours with 'Negative, enemy fighters'. As the allied aircraft flew back four white fishing boats were seen on a north easterly course. 'D' 455's navigator noted 'Same vessels as seen on the way out.' At 15.35 McCall repeated the message sent earlier, 'Attacked by fighters, target not attacked.' The Beaufighters landed at their respective bases between 16.10 and 16.27 hours. One, 'H' 489, had been hit by friendly fire in the starboard wing. Warrant Officer Michael Day and Flight Sergeant John Roddis from 'C' 144 were posted as missing. All the Mosquitoes landed safely back at 16.12 hours except Flight Sergeant Pierre Smoolenaers and his navigator W Harris (RAAF) who were both reported missing. Further wreckage from HG209 was sighted 54 miles west of Kristiansund by another RAF aircraft. At Fraserburgh that evening Flight Lieutenant Carmichael was sent out in 'F' 279 to search for Moreton and his crew but no trace was found. On 12 January Second Lieutenant Noreland, on a reconnaissance between Lindesnes and Marstein, dispatched a Junkers 52 from Transportstaffel 3/TGr 20 piloted by Ofw. Kurt Näth into the sea. On their return journey they sighted empty dinghies near Obrestad.

CHAPTER 9

WING LOSES FIVE MOSQUITOES
IN ONE OPERATION

On 6 January 9 and 12 Staffel JG 5 had arrived at Herdla aerodrome direct from Vaernes, equipped with Fw190A aircraft. There was a mixture of pilots, from those with vast experience of fighting on the eastern front, to many straight from fighter training schools in Germany. With little or no sources of fuel, what they had was reserved for alarmstarts (scrambles) which the new pilots had to learn during operational sorties against the allies. Sadly on 12 January Offizier Ludwig Kirchner and Fw George Lieber were lost in two separate accidents; it was a bitter pill to swallow for the newly arrived 9 Staffel. Admiral Otto Shrader's instructions to the pilots were that they should be on full alert; everyone in the area was prepared for a new attack.

With new aerial intelligence gathered from PR Mosquitoes at Dyce, the RAF interpretation unit based in Oxfordshire calculated that the *Claus Rickmers* was still loaded. Coastal Command Headquarters at Northwood ordered 18 Group to assign the Banff wing to destroy it. For two consecutive days while carrying out their sweeps over Norway, sightings were made of *Claus Rickmers* together with three flakships by 333 Squadron. The information was then assessed by a Norwegian naval officer on the station. Group Captain Aitken told one of the Norwegians, Thor Stensrud: 'You'll have to destroy this damned vessel whatever the cost, as the cargo is very, very important for the Germans'* Thor reminded Aitken that there were at least three large coastal batteries in addition to various flak positions; there were three forts located at Tittelsnes, Naeheim and Bjelland, next to Leirvik. Therefore, the merchantman now represented an extremely dangerous target for aircrews. Nevertheless, orders were given. The strike would go ahead weather permitting on 15 January.

By this time in the war, Coastal Command had had a great deal of experience with shipping strikes, having perfected them during three intense years of operations. A navigator with 235 Squadron 'Syd' Gordon explains:

'In these types of strikes the aircraft could break seaward on completion of the attack and get a good start for the journey home. It would usually be completed with a minimum amount of time being spent over enemy territory, therefore there was a good chance you would be on your way home before enemy fighters could reach the target area.'

On Monday 15 January, Norway was to have the second largest air battle over its country during the war. An early morning flight had sent a sighting report back before the aircraft had landed; the planning stage of the attack had begun. The crews were awakened early at 05.00 hours, and briefed to fly to Leirvik for a strike against *Claus Rickmers* which had been previously attacked on 9 January and known to be in the same position. The experienced Norwegian Thor Stensrund would lead 18 heavily

---

*What Aitken said led to rumours amongst the Norwegian, Commonwealth and RAF crews that the cargo was 'heavy water' for the German atomic bomb.

armed Mosquitoes, while Wing Commander Maurice would command the whole force. After a meal in the aircrew canteen, the briefing took place. At 09.00 hours Maurice headed up the briefing saying 'Any Luftwaffe fighter interception will come from the south, therefore after the attack turn north – break starboard.' Photographs together with a model were used to inform the crews during the meeting in which Group Captain Max Aitken momentarily participated stating 'Blast that bloody ship to smithereens.' The Met Officer forecast snowstorms over the North Sea and the Norwegian coast and this prediction proved correct. Sixteen Mosquitoes took off in continuous rain from Banff at 09.30 hours. 143 Squadron had six aircraft in two Vics; in the leading one was Maurice on his 150th operation, his No. 2 was Squadron Leader Fitch, and his No.3 was Flight Sergeant Morton-Moncrieff. The second Vic was led by the American Lieutenant Alexandre (USAAF), his No.2 was Flight Lieutenant Don Clause, and his No.3 Fight Lieutenant Tony Hawkey. The remaining aircraft, two from 235 and two from 248 were led by Wing Commander Junior Simmonds, in 'W' 235 RS579. Warwick 'G-George' accompanied the Mosquitoes having taken off from Wick at 10.34 hours in atrocious weather which enveloped the aircraft.

The wake formed in the sea by the propellers of the aircraft stretched back towards Cairnbulg Point near Inverallochy. Snow bespattered windscreens and the crews peered out into the murk; from time to time the sea and the snow merged into an opaque moving wall through which they carved their way anxiously towards the Norwegian coast using the altimeter to stay low. The Mosquitoes make landfall at Geitungen Light at 11.10 hours. The main force then banked northwards while the two 333 Squadron outriders flew two miles ahead searching along the Inner Leads but nothing was seen; battling through rough weather Thor Stensrud on approaching the coast between the numerous islands in 'G' 333 realised that they had been seen by enemy radar as a humming began in his earphones. Closing in on Leirvik Thor, he and his navigator Erik Friis realised that a hot reception awaited the force. The 'Attack Alarm' was sounded at 11.18 at about the same time Herdla was informed and at 11.20 nine Fw190s streaked into the sky and headed south for Leirvik harbour.

A barrage of flak rose up ahead of the Norwegians. Stensrud registered a blinding flash to their starboard side – Gausland and Sjolie in 'R' 333 had taken a direct hit from one of the 88mm coastal batteries and exploded in mid-air. A ball of fire fell earthwards with a smoke trail. Maurice in 'K' 143 received negative sighting reports from two locations (Skudeneshaven and Havgesund) but shortly afterwards at 11.24 Stensrud reported 'Target in Leirvik' and the main force turned to starboard over Stord Island. Maurice broke radio silence with 'Target sighted' in his distinctive French accent, and five minutes later the attack began. Stensrud identified two merchantmen and a TTA. *Claus Rickmers* was seen lying near the wharf, south-east of the steamship quay. Below in Leirvik the little harbour looked like an armed fortress, with gun barrels pointing skywards towards the approaching Mosquitoes. The attackers were unaware that the *Claus Rickmers'* flak guns which had been masked by the quayside buildings during the attack on 9 January had been taken off and set up in clear ground at the head of the inlet. At 11.29 hours, Maurice led them in shouting into the radio-telephone 'Bordeaux leader, attack, attack, attack.' The decision to move the ship's gunners proved profitable as the Mosquitoes approached directly over the flak positions. Flying through the intense opposition, they nevertheless hit the merchantman. First in were the anti-flak aircraft which smothered the flak positions with cannon and machine-gun fire, then the remaining sections ran in with armed R/Ps. Mushrooms of smoke appeared after salvoes of rockets rained in above and below the waterline. Squadron Leader Fitch, flying 'U' 143, recorded two possible dry hits and numerous cannon strikes on *Claus Rickmers*. A Tsetse Mosquito 'Z1' 248 fired off 12 57mm shells at her. Nine dry and one wet hit was estimated by the Tsetse crew. Vp.5304 *Seehund* jolted as a salvo of eight rockets hit the bridge and funnel, fired from 'S' 235. She was holed as more rockets penetrated the hull and, engulfed with water, *Seehund* sank. Survivors were rescued, with only one crew member killed and 12 wounded. Some Mosquitoes came in for a second run, hitting Vp.5308 and R63 which were left slightly damaged. A 143 Squadron pilot (who wishes to remain anonymous) took part in this strike flying in the second Vic, and remembers the events of 'Black Monday'. He wrote in his diary on 15 January 1945:

'We made the approach from the north-west. There was lots of snow and everything looked bleak. I watched Maurice go down to attack and Freddie [Lt. Alexandre] kept our section well to the left, leaving me to have a clear run in on a TTA [Vp.5304]. The leading sections had fixed the main target well. I saw Tony Hawkey's rockets go and there was a considerable explosion on the TTA as the boiler room blew up. I released my rockets too early and would only score underwater hits... then I turned my cannons on to a horrible 'M' Class Vp.5308 that was pumping up all forms of flak at us. I remember one red lump bursting just a few yards above and in front of us. There was no way out except to go between an island and the shore, both were firing at us. Consequently, we passed over the 'M' Class Vp.5308 at mast height. I just kept pressing the gun firing button all the time; we could see our rounds knocking pieces off his bridge and super-structure; anyway, it made them keep their heads down! Clear of the ship, I broke to port and lost the remaining few feet of height down onto the water, weaving as hard as I could. Maurice's orders after his "Attack, Attack, Attack" was to break to port. This I did and found myself all alone flying up a fjord in a northerly direction with high mountains on either side. I saw a gap between two of the mountains on the left, and realised if we continued up the fjord, we would find ourselves in Bergen. I climbed at full throttle just managing to go through the gap and dived down the other side. While climbing through the mountains I heard a 235 aircraft call up and say he was on one motor; and this was followed by Freddie saying, "All right I will keep with you." We crossed out over the coast just south of Marstein Light, and went straight into a huge snow cloud, groping our way through the maze of flakes. As I cleared the snow-storm and continued westwards the voice of Maurice came up: "Bandits, get together everyone." Just ahead I saw another Mosquito; he formed up as my No. 2 and then another one joined us making a section. I decided that this dogfight would develop just about where we had crossed out, (i.e. on the northern side of the snowstorm). Hence, I took my section back to the coast looking for trouble. On the way Maurice's voice came over very cool, calm and deep: "Help, help, help I am being heavily attacked." We again found the coast and I circled with the section formating on me, but saw no signs of any other aircraft. We were truly mystified. Then over the air came Fitch's voice, "I'm badly hit and need escort and assistance. Please protect my tail somebody." My navigator Tom suggested a south-westerly course from the coast where we had been waiting, this skirted us around the snow and in the rough direction of home. On the way out, we saw a large fishing fleet, and my No. 3 Wally Woodcock went over and photographed it to check for "squealers" [radio masts]. After 15 minutes or so away from the coast I called up Fitch and said, "Now you are clear, fire a cartridge to see if we can locate you." This he did and at about 2,000 feet and a couple of miles ahead I saw him and the starburst. We climbed up and formatted, then reassured him he had an escort of four other Mosquitoes. A Norwegian then joined us, one of the outriders. I then chatted to Fitch about his damaged ailerons and tails telling him what course to steer... We all got home all right, landing in 2,500-yard visibility.'

The *Claus Rickmers* gunners stationed at the head of the inlet were jubilant, claiming to have hit three enemy aircraft. 'F' 143 flown by Hawkey and Milloy passed over Vp.5308 and an explosion flung debris up all around the aircraft, embedding itself in the wooden structure. The attack lasted three minutes. Many had been mauled by the heavy anti-aircraft fire protecting the vessels and bits of the 'Wooden Wonder' fell over Leirvik during the attack. Out into clear skies after leaving the target area and over the islands some of the formation broke to port and they were split up; a number followed Maurice to starboard, heading north towards Langenuen. Some went west for Selbjørnsfjord while others crossed out over Stord Island. Behind them smoke rose up from the already crippled merchantman. One of the Mosquitoes hit by anti-aircraft fire, 'A' 235, had flames and black smoke pouring from one engine. Flight Sergeant 'Frank' Chew pressed the extinguisher button; the propeller milled to a stop and while they were trying to regain control they headed out toward Stord Island. Seated on his right Flight Sergeant Jock Couttie, unable to help his friend, gazed out at the still blazing wing, flames licking the sea-grey-green camouflage. The aircraft was losing height and trailing thick black smoke. As Chew tried to steer the aircraft towards a small passage between the mountains, heading north-east, Couttie called for assistance. On the ground a Norwegian, Bjarne Agdestein, was at work at Lundeseter Electrical Power Station and had heard the commotion down at Leirvik. His wife and child who lived close by appeared, and once safe inside Bjarne could not resist a look outside. He recalls briefly what he saw:

'It was almost shot to pieces; the aircraft "A-Apple" thundered low through Tysekaret, belching black smoke and flames and so low I thought it would crash. [I saw] the red, white and blue roundels and code, [and] it then disappeared out of sight. Only the smell of smoke and fire lingered.'

Seconds later 'F' 143 and 'V' 143 flew over Stord following the trail of smoke, one on either side of the damaged Mosquito. Upon reaching Selbjørnsfjord Lieutenant Thore Stensrud did a tight turn and swept back over Stord searching for stragglers, and then returned to the main force. This was still spread over a large area, some with battle damage and all low on ammunition.

Flying time from Herdla to Selbjørnsfjord is 13 minutes. On this fateful day 9 Staffel had nine Focke-Wulfs on readiness. The grey and blue painted fighters had white identification numbers painted on their fuselage sides, white signifying 9 Staffel; the nose rings were also painted in the appropriate Staffel colour. Their mission was the interception of the large enemy force in Leirvik, and they were led by Staffelkapitän Werner Gayko, a very experienced combat pilot credited with 12 victories, flying a Fw190A-8 Weisse 1 (Wr. 931 862). Almost immediately the German pilots heard his voice over the radio-telephone: 'Achtung, achtung – mehrere Tommies vor Stord!' The Fw190s split into three flights of three aircraft apiece and dived into attack.

At 11.32 hours Stensrud in 'G' 333 recognised the black dots above as Fw190s. At the same moment off the northern tip of Stord Tsetse 'Z1' 248's navigator sighted three Fw190s, and a call came: 'Bandits'. An aerial duel developed.

Over the radio-telephone Stensrud could hear the 32-year-old Maurice call in a calm manner, 'All aircraft to keep together'. Squadron Leader Fitch was flying number two to Maurice in a tight pair with three Fw190s closing at speed dead astern. Fitch was down to 450 feet, already weaving to port, and he tightened his turn on Flying Officer Les Parker's instructions. The Fw190, exhibiting its manoeuvrability, quickly turned and fired a stream of rounds from under 600 yards, hitting 'U' 143 with the 20mm cannon shells and machine-gun fire, disintegrating the starboard tailplane and striking the port outer petrol tank, port wing tip, and port aileron. The all-wood structure of the wing held together. With the flying controls damaged 'U'143 executed two flick rolls in succession owing to the damage to the port aileron. Fitch needed Parker's assistance to regain control and straighten out. His navigator then saw a Focke-Wulf dead astern at 500 yards. Pulling the stick hard to port at the same time he saw Maurice and Langley in 'K'143 taking hits from astern by two Fw190s; the Mosquito was in a steep turn with the enemy aircraft. Flying Officer Les Parker recalled:

'We had been briefed that after the attack we should go out the quickest way possible, which we were told was the more dangerous. Most of the crews ignored this and had no trouble. Wing Commander Maurice, Freddie Alexandre, my pilot Squadron Leader Fitch and two others followed the briefing instructions and went out the way we had come in. After a few seconds I heard Freddie calling "Bandits". I turned around and saw a Focke-Wulf on our tail. He was firing and rounds found their mark, blowing large chunks out of our tailplane. A minute later he was right behind us again after we threw the aircraft about the sky at about 400 feet and below. We were a sitting duck – but he never fired! It was a black day for 143 Squadron and the Wing. Despite the damage to our plane Squadron Leader Fitch, who was a superb pilot, got us home safely.'

The strike leader was heard calling for urgent assistance over the radio-telephone. Stensrud had heard his call but was unable to assist as he was forced to take evasive action when a 190 attacked from the port side. Eventually he managed to lose his adversary in a snow cloud. One of the FW190s in a turn appeared dead ahead of Fitch who managed to fire a two and a half second burst at one of those attacking 'K' 143 from 100 yards. Fitch and Parker watched the blue-grey aircraft pass them on their portside. This heroic effort was in vain, for seconds later the sky was empty; there was no sign of the third 190 or trace of 'K' 143 – with the port engine on fire the Mosquito was seen to crash into the fjord by other crews at 11.36 hours.

Suddenly below the starboard wing of 'U' 143 cannon flashed past from an enemy aircraft astern at a range of 400 yards. Fitch and Parker were now at 50 feet, but the Fw190 broke off the attack, giving the RAF crew the impression that its pilot had run out of ammunition. They then saw two 190s heading inland. With milling aircraft twisting and turning in the sky Chew and Couttie were still struggling desperately to keep their aircraft in the air at a height of 50 to 30 feet. At 11.35 hours Fitch in 'U' 143 heard the American voice of Freddie Alexandre piloting 'V' 143 report: 'Lookout Bandits'. The two crews were searching the sky when three Fw190s in line astern were seen, but they passed over the three Mosquitoes. They peeled off to come into attack from astern, and approaching from 3 o'clock and at between 300 and 1,000 feet, two attacked. 'F' 143, piloted by Hawkey, broke quickly to starboard to drive the enemy away from Chew and Couttie. Less fortunate, however, was Lieutenant Alexandre who also broke to starboard as he tried to ward them off 'A' 235. A brief dogfight ensued, the plywood began to splinter as machine-gun and cannon fire from two Focke-Wulfs astern tore into the structure. Shaking them off he turned to starboard to attack the third Fw190, and this was the last sighting of the young American. Colleagues made frequent attempts to raise 'V' 143 over the radio-telephone but nothing further was heard. Both enemy fighters then trailed Hawkey for one mile; a single Fw190 came into attack at 7 o'clock at a range of 800 yards, but did not open fire; 'F' 143 managed to slip into the cover of a snow shower and lost contact with the enemy. Hawkey later reported seeing a plume of smoke near Mogster, and three enemy aircraft were circling and firing into the sea at something in position 59.55N/04.50E. Flight Lieutenant Williams in 'J' 235 opened up at 500 yards, firing a couple of bursts at these aircraft which were attacking a single Mosquito from three sides and which now broke off and climbed to port. Their prey can be assumed to have been 'K' 143. Williams then pulled up at a height of 50 feet and raced off to select another target.

In the air battle taking place further north several events occurred simultaneously. The first concerned Flying Officer Peacock with his navigator Flying Officer Field in one of the Tsetses who singled out a Fw190A-3 on the tail of another Mosquito. They fired the Molins gun and three 57mm shells streaked away; the Fw190A-3 broke off its attack, turned towards land with its smoking BMW 801 engine coughing and disappeared out of sight. Two Norwegians, Ingebrikt Melingen and Nils Olav Hufthammer recall the German loss:

'It was a cold day, thick ice lay on the lakes, and suddenly engine noises could be heard. We ran up a hill and saw many twin-engined aircraft, spotting also smaller ones coming fast with a different engine note. These began firing and colour streaked across the sky; dogfights started. There were some four to five bigger bangs like shells being fired, and then we heard a plane in trouble flying low and sluggishly over us at Austevoll (north of Stord). His canopy came off with a bang, and the German single-engine fighter began circling looking for a place to land. Suddenly it fell out of the sky, narrowly missed crashing into some houses and hit the ground yards away. We ran to its resting place, reaching the cockpit area (the hood had come off). The pilot was struggling to get out of his harness, we had to cut it to free him, while 7.92 ammunition exploded around us. The plane was in flames as we pulled him clear of the wreck. His skull was crushed over the right eye, he had probably knocked his forehead on the Revi 16B gunsight on impact; he was making gestures but became unconscious. A crew from a German guard vessel (flak-ship) lying nearby intervened and took him away to be treated. Later we were told that he had died in hospital.'

The vibrating aircraft 'A' 235 hit the water shedding fragments into the air at Slåtterøy. As those that were left from this encounter turned away from the Norwegian coast in the fading light a single crew member from it bobbed up and down in the yellow dinghy. Flight Sergeant Jock Couttie had managed to escape after the ditching; braving the icy cold water he had scrambled into the emergency dinghy. Couttie was in RAF battle dress (though sometimes he wore only shirt sleeves) and flying boots, the normal clothing worn by Mosquito strike wing crews, and soon began to feel the chill and the pain from his broken ankle. He noticed pillars of black smoke drifting over the water from a burning aircraft near Mogster. The dinghy began to drift but there was no sign of Chew. On a mountain named Sata overlooking Selbjørnsfjord where the air battle took place there was an observation post on the highest spot which was manned by the Kriegsmarine and gave them excellent views up and down the coast. A Norwegian Harald Kvarven remembers what happened next:

'I was 21-years-old and lived with my family in Brandasund, located on the northern tip of Bømlo, east of and near Slåtterøy lighthouse at the entrance to Selbjørnsfjord. My father Torkel and I were preparing our fishing vessel Sjofuglen (7 feet long with a 7hp engine) and getting ready to go out, as fishing was our livelihood. Suddenly a party of Kriegsmarines from the observation post came running up to our vessel and demanded in very bad Norwegian the use of it and our service. We understood that many aircraft had been shot down in an air battle that we did not witness. Three Germans boarded the vessel and in a short time we were scouring the water in Selbjørnsfjord. I noticed something yellow out there, closing upon it there was the body of an airman lying on his back in a very small rubber dinghy. He appeared lifeless, but we got him on board quickly and enveloped him in blankets; the Germans thought he was dead but they did not complain. There was a pulse, and his eyes opened – he was alive! Very weak, frozen and bleeding from his hands, otherwise he seemed unhurt. One of the Kriegsmarine with us began questioning him – what unit was he with, what operation – but he shut up when my father told him to let him be. They then ordered us to make for Slåtterøy lighthouse, where they had some guard huts. We came alongside the jetty and the airman was put ashore, laid on a stretcher and moved into one of the houses. From that moment on we did not see the flyer and the Kriegsmarine did not tell us what happened to him. As we left the lighthouse, it had become dark and we lit our lanterns and made our way home.'

In 1997, Harald Kvarven recalled those events on 15 January 1945 saying it was indeed a pleasure for him to learn that the airman Couttie survived, 'as we doubted it!' During January in Norway darkness falls at about 15.30 to 16.30 hours even on a bright day, the force had been engaged at 11.32 hours. Flight Sergeant Couttie, therefore, may well have been floating around in the water for up to four hours. Couttie then spent four months as a prisoner of war.

The dogfights lasted for at least 12 minutes, spread over a wide area. Stensrud asked his navigator to note the time as they turned for the North Sea. It was 11.47 hours and the surviving Banff crews battled through the weather, all landing back at base utterly exhausted between 12.53 and 13.14 hours. Three landed away; 'S' 235 at Fraserburgh at 12.57 and two Tsetses at Dallachy, logged at 13.06 and 13.12 hours. They began their debrief. During interrogation the remaining aircrews reported the ship on fire, with explosions and smoke rising to 800 feet. The photographic section of the ground checking party at Banff were quickly at work processing the gun camera footage and handheld camera stills. They found that unfortunately there were no photographs of the *Claus Rickmers* under attack and those taken by aircraft attacking other vessels in the harbour during this strike did not show the quayside or the main vessel. An in-depth discussion led by Max Aitken took place in the operations room, with telephone calls being made to 18 Group Headquarters and Fraserburgh regarding whether a search and rescue could be mounted. Unfortunately no search for survivors was possible due to the weather conditions. In total five Mosquitoes were lost on this single operation, three from 143 Squadron; Maurice alias Max Guedj, and Flight Lieutenant John Langley were the first to be shot down; Flight Sergeant George Morton-Moncrieff and his navigator Flight Sergeant C Cash crashed near Fjell in 'D' 143 and Lieutenant Freddie Alexandre (USAAF), with Flight Sergeant J A McMullin never returned. All were experienced crews. Only two bodies of allied crew members were ever found: Flight Sergeant Cash was found on the shore and Flight Sergeant Chew's body was eventually recovered and buried on 25 January 1945 at Mollendal Cemetery in Bergen. These two 235 Squadron members (Chew and Couttie) had had their Mosquito badly damaged by flak over the Gironde and had been captured on 12 August 1944. Badly beaten by their captors in Royan, both then escaped, fought with the Maquis and finally got back to England via Spain and Gibraltar on 3 September. Three days later they were back at Portreath. 333 Squadron lost Lieutenant I S Gausland and K Sjolie. It was a bitter blow to this tight knit wing.

The wing's adversaries suffered casualties too. Three German pilots failed to return to base after the encounter; the first two being Offizier Waldow Zeuner (Weisse 4-

737410), and Offizier Richard Lehnert (Weisse 16-350183). Lehnert is buried at Solheim. Both men flew Fw190A-8s, and it is most likely that both were engaged in battle with 'V' 143 and 'D' 143 and shot each other down. None could tell afterwards. The third Luftwaffe pilot was Feldwebel Oskar Helbing flying an A-3, (Weisse 14-0132172) who is also buried at Solheim. Helbing was the only one flying this particular mark. Only one Mosquito was in position to shoot down 'Weisse 14' during the air-battle; Flying Officer Peacock in the Tsetse, although no claims were made by the Mosquito crew upon their return.

After the second attack the *Claus Rickmers* crew of 34 began pumping out holds 1, 2, and 3. She was patched up temporarily and made watertight and on 24 January proceeded to Bergen under her own power with a tug in attendance for repairs. Shortly after the end of the war a survey of damaged ships was made by the British Bombing Survey Unit, a team examined her when lying near Bergen. They found that all the damage was restricted to the bridge and forward of it, except for a small amount of cannon damage on the stern from the second attack. Several rockets had struck forward in Nos. 1 and 2 holds but No. 1 hold was still full of water from the damage due to running aground. Thirty rockets had entered above the water-line on the port side slightly forward of abeam. The forecastle had been burnt out, as had the greater part of the bridge.

Claus Rickmers sailed for many years before being scrapped in Spain, in 1964. One of the 'M' Class flakships defending the *Claus Rickmers*, Vp.5304, was raised in 1951, overhauled and sailed as a whaler until 1971, when it sunk off the South African coast. The Staffelkapitän Werner Gayko died in 1996, and his flying book records a total flying time of 51 minutes with JG 5 on this day.

The sudden rise in losses of aircrew from Banff and Dallachy since December 1944 was now causing a great deal of concern. 18 Group commented in a report: 'This group of 190s displayed a fighting spirit reminiscent of 1940.' 315 Squadron with its long-range Mustangs departed for 11 Group Fighter Command on 14 January, its pilots had done sterling work during their short stay, but lost a number of good experienced aircrew. They were replaced by 65 (East India) Squadron who arrived at Peterhead on 16 January. Prompted by these losses the Commander-in-Chief of Coastal Command asked the Air Ministry on 11 and 15 January for a second Mustang fighter squadron, and with unusual speed, the Air Ministry permitted the appeal. The additional Mustang squadron would move to north-east Scotland in mid-February. 143 Squadron was now without a leader and Group Captain Max Aitken appointed Squadron Leader David Pritchard as acting commanding officer of 143 Squadron. The position was short lived as Wing Commander Christopher Foxley-Norris DSO DFC became the new commanding officer a few weeks later. The aircrew union on the station thought that Pritchard deserved the promotion.

248 Squadron relinquished five of their Tsetse Mosquitoes (NT225, PZ252, PZ300, PZ301 and PZ468) after the 15 January strike and moved to 254 Squadron at North Coates during March, commanded by Flight Lieutenant Wally Woodcock. There they received new identification letters before operations commenced.The son of Rev. D Findlay Clark of Banff, now Dr David Findlay Clark was a boy at the time and recalls:

'One late afternoon, when the aircraft had come in widely scattered, usually a bad sign, and many badly damaged, I watched a Mosquito pilot, so low that I could clearly see the cockpit canopy had been largely shot away and that the navigator was slumped, perhaps wounded or dead, in the right seat. To my horror one of his rockets had "hung-up", worse still, one of his undercarriage legs seemed to be waggling about, unlocked down and not rigid at all. As he touched down it collapsed and I watched the aircraft skid and slide sideways along the runway, licks of flame appearing under it as it careered off the concrete on to the grass. There was a huge explosion and when the smoke and flame died down not much of the aircraft was left.'

The conditions in the north of Scotland were bad for the remainder of January with heavy snowfall. The *Daily Mail* for 24 January 1945 reads: 'Snow which held up trains and buses for hours isolated Scottish villages. WAAFs at an RAF Coastal Command station in the north-east of Scotland saved the aerodrome from becoming isolated in a five day battle during 50mph gales.'

An icy runway did not prevent 16 Mosquitoes from flying out from Banff on 25 January. Led by Squadron Leader Alec Gunnis of 248 Squadron in 'Y' 248, they were to search for convoys or vessels at anchor in Eidfjord and Askvøll. A stationary convoy consisting of three vessels accompanied by a flak ship was sighted. There were in reality two convoys consisting of five merchantmen and five escorts. Be-156-Al comprised *Ilse Fritzen* and *Bjergfinn* with Vp.5111, Vp.5115 and Vp.5310 while the other, Al-134-Be, included the Norwegian *Lovass*, *Tor Hund* and the German *Radue* with escorts Vp.5105 and Vp.5305. Gunnis led the force through a wall of flak, strafed with cannon and then let his rockets go to hit two merchantmen. The other Mosquitoes followed close behind. The German *Ilse Fritzen* of 5,088 tons (formally the French-registered *St.Octave*) had 30 rockets hit her superstructure, above and below the waterline, and sank without reaching her destination, Tromsö, with a cargo of coal and mines. The unarmed Norwegian *Bjergfinn* of 696 tons then came under attack. Formally known as *Svanholm* the vessel had been sunk in Nordmøre in 1940 by German aircraft and later raised and put back into service. Caught in Eidsfjord near Florøy *Bjergfinn* was on a voyage from Bergen-Harstad with a cargo of 15,000 sacks of flour from Stavanger. The captain, Gunnar Færevaag, was killed whilst on the bridge and two men were badly injured. Smoke was seen rising up to 150 feet as the force departed, but although one Mosquito was hit by return fire, all returned home.

Approaching the airfield the returning formation tightened up and flew low over the aerodrome. It climbed and started to break up in the normal half rate left hand break away but No. 2 of the leading section did not wait for Gunnis to break. Tragedy struck, no order had been given to break away and for some unaccountable reason, as the No. 2 was an exceptional pilot, he flew straight underneath and cut off his tail. 'F' 248, flown by the 32-year-old Flight Lieutenant Darel Crimp, hit SZ959 piloted by Alec Gunnis and Bert Mudd. Crimp's aircraft was seen to turn over onto its back gliding into Roughilly woods and killing both aircrew, including his navigator Flying Officer John Bird. Gunnis managed to regain control with 'Y' 248 flying one wing low, and landed safely. Flying Officer John Bird's body was brought back to Barnsley and buried in the cemetery.

Alex Rix served as an LAC on (8)235 Service Echelon and recalls:

'My first memory of Banff was on my arrival at the railway halt in the cutting nearby, this consisted of a wooden platform of sleepers, perhaps made by those on the station. Before you boarded the train at Aberdeen you informed the driver and guard to stop at RAF Banff Halt. The struggle up the embankment to the station guardroom was quite arduous due to the deep snow in January 1945. While I was lugging my kit through the snow, Mosquitoes were in the air and before reaching the guardroom I was shocked to observe a mid-air collision between two returning aircraft. No doubt this was a common occurrence during these times but to happen on the return of a successful operation was looked upon as a great sadness by all personnel. This was my first posting to an operational unit and I was assigned to 235 Squadron.'

Weather continued to hamper operations in northern Scotland, and squadrons were stood down for seven days. A U-boat sortie led by Squadron Leader Roy Orrock returned after encountering heavy snow showers. The aircraft attempted landing in sleet and snow with zero visibility making it extremely hazardous for the crews concerned; HP911 was lost, while another swung, broad siding into a snow bank at the side of the runway which caused the undercarriage to collapse. The pilot was rendered unconscious, but managed to release himself from the aircraft. Although conditions were difficult at the time six other aircraft landed without incident and the pilot was reprimanded by the station commander. Two days later, snow again fell during the evening, it was 12° below freezing. The Norwegians got out their skis and enjoyed some skiing, using flares to see in the darkness. At first light in the morning two lorries from the motor transport section with a special snowplough attachment were put to use clearing the perimeter track and runway 30/12. These efforts were hampered by a very strong northerly wind. All available personnel on the station were called to shovel thick snow from the dispersal areas assisted by cars or lorries when they could be spared. The runway was eventually cleared completely, sanded and gritted, but a further heavy snowfall overnight covered this up!

The Commander-in-Chief Sholto Douglas was told by correspondence from the Air Ministry that Banff had been over working their Gee-fitted Mosquitoes and that should any be lost there was likely to be a production shortage the following month! The weather was, it seems, on the Ministry's side with the thermometer dropping back below freezing point which curtailed operations once more in northern Scotland. Dispersed Mosquitoes were carefully muffled on the exposed dispersals. The perimeter track took on a treacherous guise and riding a bicycle to any of the units' dispersals over the surface of snow and ice required some daring and an exquisite sense of balance. Group Captain Max Aitken requested that ground crew should be given naval rum after servicing aircraft on their dispersals. WAAF Corporal Joyce Trovey remembers the cold and conditions:

'The WAAF site was some way from the main aerodrome. We slept in Nissen huts – 20 to a hut including one NCO; there was an iron stove in the centre which stood on a stone plinth – very useful as when coal was unavailable we burnt the toilet seats! Three fire buckets stood at the end of the hut and through the winter were permanently frozen solid. Their purpose seemed mysterious to me seeing as there was nothing to burn. A toilet was situated at the other end, and this too was frozen in winter. Efforts were made once or twice to supply the WAAFs stationed at Banff with protection against the weather. Fisherman's hats and coats were issued at one point but proved useless. The thick black oilskin did not allow us to bend our arms. The sou'westers reached our chests and the coats scraped the floor – a cause for much hilarity! We had wellingtons, sea-boots, socks, and pyjama legs under our battle dress. Very welcome were the patchwork quilts sent by Americans and Canadians. The camp cinema was attended dressed in pyjamas under our uniforms, together with two blankets and a hot water bottle!'

The strike wings were about to get a boost. The Commander-in-Chief received a letter from Portal: 'The Air Ministry agree and now recognise the employment of Mosquitoes as fighter escort to Beaufighters as uneconomical.' A new fighter unit duly arrived at the base with the weather still hindering operations in northern Scotland on 23 January. It was not until 12 days later that the pilots of 65 (East India) Squadron got airborne. Led by 27-year-old Squadron Leader Ian Strachan, who had just been appointed as commanding officer on New Year's day. A detachment of 13 Mustang IIIBs flew to Banff from Peterhead, Strachan in 'N' 65 FB356. Ground crew with spare equipment made this journey by an unusual mode of transport – fishing trawlers, which had been hastily requisitioned, and their crews had sailed through the icy waters from Peterhead to Banff harbour on 28 January. Three seven-ton lorries from the MT section waited on the quayside and transported them to their temporary base. After a hot meal in the airmen's canteen and having been reacquainted with their charges they were made ready. That night there was a big party in the mess and the Canadian Legion Show, *Follow the Drum*, played in the concert hall. After waiting all morning a show finally came off. The fighter crews were briefed to act as fighter escort to 27 Dallachy Beaufighters. At 13.30 hours, as the force assembled in the skies above, a Mustang crashed while on take-off. Two others returned early to Banff, one with compass trouble and one as escort. Now they had only ten fighters, and the formation flew directly into a blinding snowstorm at sea level a few miles from the Norwegian coast.

The strike leader ordered the force to turn back. Squadron Leader Ian Strachan told the pilots to make a 180° turn. He was last seen banking steeply less than 100 feet above the icy water before becoming separated in the storm; in pairs the pilots managed to reform despite the missing Strachan. Nothing was heard and it is possible he flew into the sea. With no aerodrome open in the north of Scotland, the whole force diverted to the Orkneys landing at 17.10 hours.

For a total of 14 days, operational flying was nil. Practically the whole area was at a standstill; the motor transport section at Banff carried on its work clearing 50,000 tons of snow from the runways and various roads around the camp. One of the station's vans returning from RAF Fraserburgh found the road blocked by a tanker. The WAAF driver reversed in spite of the snowdrifts, making her way back towards Fraserburgh, she found the road blocked and then made her way by foot to the nearest farmhouse, where she remained isolated for nine days. On the station all the pipes burst and the snow blew under the eaves of the Nissen huts, which froze solid. When the thaw started on 27 January bedding, blankets and bedsteads were all equally sodden and the following days found several living quarters flooded to a depth of four feet or more. WAAF Joyce Trovey from station headquarters said:

'We had to cross a field to have a bath always assuming there would be some hot water available. One would set out in a blizzard complete with light bulb, bath plug, etc., one officer put it very neatly when he said RAF Banff is a place where a bath ceases to be a luxury and becomes a painful necessity.'

In the face of the appalling weather the strike wings at Banff and Dallachy made only seven attacks along the Norwegian coast. Earlier in the month Flight Lieutenant Noel Russell had received an immediate bar to his DFC for his outstanding leadership when bounced by enemy fighters. His description and summing up of the dogfight in which he destroyed two 109s was heard on the BBC war report. It was his second decoration received on this, his second tour.

An article appeared in *Illustrated* magazine on 27 January featuring many Banff wing personalities, causing the local post office to sell out. Flight Lieutenant David Pitkeathly joined 235 Squadron on his second tour in February 1945: 'There was a nice Salvation Army canteen in Portsoy in the church where you could get a reasonable snack, and it was cosy and warm there. Warmth was always a constant consideration at Banff in the winter when you were often cold and miserable.'

The final sortie on 29 January was flown without incident but marred by the crash landing of the Air Sea Rescue Warwick on its return to Wick.

CHAPTER 10

FEBRUARY 1945

February too opened with operations curtailed, with continuing bad weather. Attacks were bitter and bloody with the main weapons now cannon and the 25lb rocket warhead. It was a grim struggle but the balance was beginning to shift in the strike wing's favour. The Germans were forced to improve their defensive measures and merchantmen began sheltering deeper into the fjords, where steep cliffs hung over the narrow approaches. Mobile 37mm light defensive positions were being built on the cliff faces using Russian and Polish prisoners as labour, to intensify the barrage fired by the defensive gun crew. Yet, the wing continued to attack.

On 3 February 17 Mosquitoes with a Mustang escort on a Rover patrol between Utvaer and Bremanger, south-east of Ålesund, spotted enemy fighters. Messerschmitts with a top cover of Focke-Wulfs were observed. Bf109s of 10/JG5 went straight for the Mosquitoes, and 65 Squadron Mustangs directly intercepted these while the Mosquitoes headed for base, all returning without loss. Three enemy fighters were claimed as destroyed and one probable without loss to themselves. For some inexplicable reason the Fw190s did not intervene. No German losses are documented, however.

During the night of 3 February Coastal Command dispatched 14 Liberators of 206 and 547 Squadron from Leuchars. With heavy snow falling in the darkness they set out for the Skagerrak. One had an engine fire upon take-off, landing away at Wick and a second ran low on fuel and was forced to take evasive action for almost three hours against enemy aircraft before it returned to base. The depleted force began attacks on an assortment of merchantmen and U-boats. Two Liberators' ('C' 206 and 'E' 206) radar operators received contacts of six U-boats with a destroyer escort an estimated ten miles away. 'C' 206 managed two sweeps with no effect but in 'E' 206 Flight Lieutenant Beaty DFC switched on his Leigh Light (a 22-million candlepower, 24-inch searchlight) and came under a hail of fire which damaged two engines and put another out of action. A damage report on the Liberator revealed 20mm and 37mm cannon in the mainplanes, a holed rudder, severed rudder trim cables, the bomb bay door-closing mechanism hit, and a large hole near the beam gunner's position as a result of the flak. With the crew throwing all heavy equipment out, Beaty managed to reach 4,000 feet and set course for Sweden, known as 'Brighton' to all Allied aircrew. After checking the total damage he decided to make the return trip to Scotland. As dawn broke somewhere over the North Sea the exhausted crew hoped their luck would hold out. At 09.30 hours 'E' 206 touched down at Banff where a crowd gathered to view the battle damage. The crew were taken to be debriefed over a steaming mug of coffee laced with rum, then to the messes for bacon and eggs. The duty officer at Leuchars was informed that 'E' 206 had diverted to Banff, and that the crew was safe.

On the wintry airfield during the beginning of February were the renowned aviation photographer Charles E Brown and fellow journalist R Montgomery. Brown was working as chief photographer for *Aeronautics* and Montgomery accompanied him to write an article on the Coastal Command Banff wing for the editor Oliver Stewart. Clad in an RAF battledress top for warmth, Brown and his faithful Palmos camera, accompanied by Group Captain Max Aitken in 'MA-01', took colour and black and white photographs of the rocket-firing Mosquitoes in action on the practice range near Macduff, and on the ground at the airfield's own range. 281 Squadron supplied a Warwick piloted by Flying Officer 'Paddy' O'Reilly in which Brown took many aerial photographs of Squadron Leader David Pritchard DFC, flying RS625 and RS627, both on 143 Squadron's strength and the Standard Motors-built HR632, which joined 248 Squadron at Banff in January 1945. 143 Squadron dispersal areas were used for ground shots, with aircraft being loaded with 25lb rockets. Brown took many pictures for *Aeronautics* during his period on the base and the May 1945 issue was lavishly illustrated with his photographs, some of which were in colour in the article entitled 'Coastal Attack' written by Montgomery.*

On 4 February, the squadrons were busy doing rocket-projectile exercises and a 248 Squadron crew on training duties had a lucky escape when severe vibration occurred while flying at 2,500 feet. The pilot throttled back the engines in turn, and found the port engine to be at fault, it was then feathered and immediately followed by the loss of power in the starboard engine. A straight ahead forced landing was executed and RS629 slammed into a pole at Birkenbog Fordyce near Banff. Flying was then curtailed again because of the weather.

On Monday operations began again with Dallachy busy carrying out reconnaissance between Helliso and Stadtlandet from 08.31 to 15.00 hours. Norwegian Lieutenant Noreland searched as far as Utsira, having sightings in Leirvik and Karmsund. The same area came under scrutiny again the next day with one sighting near Marstein Lighthouse. Visibility was poor around the Leads and fjords reducing to zero with the cloud base below 400 feet; it was impossible to fly up the shipping lanes, so aircraft kept on a northerly course before turning about, landing just after midday.

The Met Officer was summoned to see the station commander and asked when there would be clear skies, his conclusion was Friday. With the weather unfit all were released until 23.59 hours. With operations cancelled Australian Flight Lieutenants Harry Parkinson and Ken Jackson of 235 Squadron practiced on the rocket range and afterwards flew over Inverness and along Loch Ness for a look around.

The following day a Rhombus flight from Bircham Newton sent a negative weather report, but at 08.20 hours Mosquitoes set out from Banff targeting Lista to Kristiansand South. Six miles from Lindesnes they encountered rain and a low cloud base. Signalling 'Washout' the force set course for base. The Beaufighter operations were cancelled and the wing were again released for training until 23.59 hours.

On Friday 9 February, Z-33, one of the famous Narvik-class destroyers, was one of the few remaining Kriegsmarine warships seeking refuge from the ever-increasing allied bombing raids on the naval bases in Germany. On 7 February Z-33 had grounded whilst enroute to Bergen from Trondheim, but managed to reach the capital of western Norway. The next day it was decided to return the vessel to Trondheim and during the night, together with its escort, it lay at anchor in Vevringefjord. Early next morning, 9 February, Z-33 entered Fordefjord and took up residence between Mula and Heilevang.

Early morning reconnaissance flights began from Banff and Dallachy. Two New Zealand crews, those of Flight Sergeant Ross 'Snow' Priest in 'K' 489 and Warrant Officer Brightwell in 'H' 489, flew out from Dallachy at 08.30 hours and made landfall south of Utvaer Lighthouse, at 10.30 hours. At the entrance they turned north-east and sighted an R-boat and a tug towing two buoys. They flew up to Songefjord and saw a merchantman. Continuing northwards, in the narrow Fordefjord, on the south side of

---

*Brown's Banff photographs are part of his entire collection which is housed at the Royal Air Force Museum at Hendon. Charles E Brown died in the RAF home at Storrington on 9 October 1982.

Vevringefjord, they saw a Narvik class destroyer of 2,300 tons, with escort, and encountering flak they continued across the fjord from north to south. With both crews frequently conferring on VHF they flew back down the northern side. Further north in Nordgulen, they spotted five vessels ranging from 5,000 tons to 2,000 tons, a very attractive target. Spotting three smaller vessels further along their route, the two turned west at 11.20 hours towards Dallachy while both navigators sent reports of their sightings. They landed at 13.21 and 13.24 hours. At Dallachy, the staff studied the reports; both wings were on stand by, waiting to pursue vessels because of the short daylight hours. There were two targets: the five merchantmen in Nordgulen were in a fairly good position for a wing attack; the Narvik class destroyer was in an awkward spot and heavily defended, but had to be the main target. The Admiralty had given orders of target priority; destroyers were top of the list, while merchantman came further down.

Operations were planned for both wings to commence in the afternoon, 18 Group's Air Vice-Marshal S Simpson deciding that an attack on the naval target was first priority. During the debrief Priest reported that the destroyer and merchantman could not be attacked by more than two or three aircraft at a time. A strike was on. Thirty-two Beaufighters (23 R/P, eight A/F and one outrider) set out at 14.05 hours to carry out a patrol to position 61.27N/05.39E. Twelve 65 Squadron Mustangs were acting as fighter escort. Two Warwicks from Fraserburgh, bringing up the rear, were briefed to patrol 61.30N/03.20E. At the neighbouring airfield 36 Mosquito aircrew were briefed to fly a Rover patrol from Ytterøyane to Stord. Group Captain Max Aitken directed the pilots and navigators to pay close attention to Nordgulen. Led by Squadron Leader 'Robbie' Reid, in 'R' 235, they set course for Maloy, just a few miles north of Nordgulen. Alerted by the sight of the two 489 Beaufighter aircraft earlier in the morning the five merchantmen and one flakship had anchored closer to the steep sides, and were in Vindspollen, the southern arm of Midtgulen. The configuration of the land made a rocket attack impossible. 'Weaver' leader ordered the force to return to base. Group Captain Max Aitken led a search between Molde and Bremanger and himself encountered three Fw190s from Herdla. He raced inland, losing them in snow showers. Later two Norwegian outriders overflew Nordgulen at dusk, noting five vessels still at anchor, with one at around 8,000 tons evidently full of ballast, and an M-class minesweeper and two small rowing boats nearby.

Unfortunately the Beaufighters suffered heavy losses; nine out of 32 failed to return from the strike. The Luftwaffe lost four aircraft and two pilots were killed. One of the Germans that died was Lt Rudi Linz, 28-years-old, flying Weisse 1 (Wr. 931 862). He was one of the most successful German pilots in Norway at this time, having been credited with 70 victories, most of them against Russians. 'Damage to a destroyer and two armed trawlers was hardly worth this loss of 14 young lives;' wrote a Canadian in a letter home. At Banff they heard the news about Dallachy. In the middle of the mess the adjutant was relaying a report to those assembled around him and the report just spread. There wasn't any official announcement, just 'talk' that the 'Beau-ee boys copped it'.

This expensive attack by the Dallachy wing led Air Officer Commander-in-Chief Sholto Douglas to invite the Admiralty to revise their target priorities. Meanwhile Air Staff Officer Air Vice-Marshal Ellwood wrote to Air Vice-Marshal Simpson at 18 Group concerning the 'recent rather expensive Beaufighter strike against the destroyer.' But whatever the priority, 'Black Friday', as it became known, was the last operation in which Coastal Command aircraft were sent in against well-defended destroyers of the Kriegsmarine. A month later Ellwood remarked that 'Simpson gave priority to the enemy destroyer' and suggested that tankers were more important. Surprisingly they acceded, dropping destroyers to the bottom of the list. Even with the addition of 65 Squadron, the strike force was still not sufficiently powerful, and Douglas asked for an additional Mustang squadron to be released for escort duty, since a great number of enemy fighters were now being thrown against Coastal Command's operations around Norway.

Rear Admiral E D B McCarthy from the Admiralty duly supplied the revised target list on 26 February 1945. A copy was issued to all groups connected with the anti-shipping campaign, stressing it was only a guide:

Surface U-boats
Pocket battleships
Tankers (laden)
Troopships
Merchantmen
Escort Vessels
Other Naval Vessels

The Allies wanted to force the German transport away from the Inner Leads at selected points and into more open water, making them accessible to air and naval attacks. The Admiralty did not possess moored mines that were capable of being laid by aircraft, but the enemy did not know this. Coastal Command headquarters recommended that moored minelaying could be replicated by dropping 500lb bombs from low altitudes at selected points in deep water channels. Special missions were flown from Banff using these tactics, dropping 500lb unfused and delayed-action fused bombs in the harbour mouths. The fuses on these bombs were set to give the impression of premature mine explosion. It was thought that the splashes linked with dropping mines might be reported and authenticated by some subsequent detonations, which would result in serious delays to departure schedules while the German minesweepers swept the waterways used by merchantmen.

On Saturday 10 February at 10.27 hours the remaining serviceable Beaufighters took off to carry out an air sea rescue patrol for the missing aircraft from 'Black Friday'. Two aircraft from Fraserburgh brought up the rear. Wing Commander Ed Pierce led them in line abreast formation. They flew at an average height of 400 feet through a frontal system for the entire trip, except the last ten miles. Twenty minutes after midday 'P' 144 saw what appeared to be part of an aircraft wing or tailplane floating. Aircraft circled but could not relocate it. After further searches at 12.38 hours the leader radioed 'Break for Sumburgh'. After a brief stop over at Sumburgh all aircraft landed at Dallachy between 14.40 and 14.59 hours.

On 11 February the station duty officer, Flight Lieutenant Ken Jackson, woke at 05.30 hours in the operations room to call the reconnaissance crew. Squadron Leader Robbie Reid, the newly appointed 'B' Flight commander and his navigator flew out and had a most successful sortie, downing a Junkers 188 during their coastal search. A force of nine Mosquitoes hit a convoy comprising of four merchantmen and three escorts in Vindspollen. Lieutenant Mehn-Anderson observed no results. On their journey back they shot up and destroyed Ytterøyane Lighthouse with cannon and machine-gun fire.

Mosquitoes crossed the Norwegian coast flying through snow flurries for a strike against the targets sighted near Åndalsnes, comprising one cargo passenger liner and two large vessels. 'R' 333 led the 21 Mosquitoes with a Mustang escort. The Mosquitoes used delayed action bombs which were dropped in a narrow fjord off Midtgulen to roll down the 3,000 feet cliff to explode among the vessels in the harbour below. A day later 11 Mosquitoes took off under the leadership of Squadron Leader

Junior Simmonds at 14.25 hours. Major Erling Ulleberg Johansen acted as outrider, flying ahead at 14.58 hours. Johansen searched Alden and reported vessels in shallow water near Fladøy. Minutes later Simmonds ordered 235 and 143 to deploy for action; all were carrying rockets. The merchantman *Sivas*, previously hit on 9 January and listing to port at 45°, received another salvo of rockets. A powerful explosion was observed and wreckage was thrown into the air. Some light flak met the Mosquitoes from a battery but this ceased. On their return from this sortie they encountered Fw190s but these turned back when attacked by Mosquito fighter cover. Back at base one 'A' Flight aircraft, RS620 from 235 Squadron, was found to have been hit quite severely in the port elevator by one of their own.

Experienced replacement aircrews were now hard to find for anti-shipping warfare, but a person at the Air Ministry made a clerical error with one squadron returning from abroad. 603 (City of Edinburgh) Squadron spent the final days of November 1944 packing up, following news of the squadron's intended return to Britain after a tour in the Middle East flying Beaufighters on shipping strikes off the Dodecanese and Aegean islands. On 26 December 1944, the squadron set sail from Port Said, landing in Liverpool on 6 January. They proceeded to RAF Coltishall still wearing their Middle Eastern issued shorts. The plan was for all to be given the statutory disembarkation leave and then reunite to fly as a squadron. The former commanding officer of 603 (City of Edinburgh) Squadron, Wing Commander Christopher Foxley-Norris (now an Air Chief Marshal), recalled during an interview in 1997:

'By lunchtime the needs of the men had all been arranged and Arthur Donaldson (one of the legendary Donaldson family of three brothers) and I adjourned to the mess bar, where my aircrew officers were already obviously enjoying themselves – especially the company of some very attractive WAAF officers, something we had not encountered for a long while. Over drinks, Arthur and I sorted a few more matters of detail (I was off on leave afterwards). He said, "Oh what are your squadron's identifying letters? We will get them painted on your Spitfires so that you can start operating as soon as you come back." I choked on my beer. . I said now please look around carefully at my officers – does anything strike you as unusual about them? "No, I do not think so... There seems to be rather a lot of them. . .and, good God, half of them are wearing observer's wings!" That's right, Sir. We are a Beaufighter anti-shipping squadron. I did some frenzied telephoning. I then remembered that our old boss and mentor, Max Aitken, was now commanding the anti-shipping wing at Banff in Scotland. I reached once more for the telephone. Could he use 23 experienced anti-shipping crews? He certainly could, as they had been experiencing the usual heavy losses. Max, who had unusual channels of communication and areas of influence, duly fixed the whole thing. I took command early of 143 Squadron, whom I been with eighteen months back, after I received a telephone call from Max whilst on leave at my parents, saying the Frenchman Maurice had bought it, and he wanted me to take over command.'

The air crews found out about the move when a young officer yelled through the door of a Nissen hut, 'You've all been posted to Banff' the reply was 'What are they posting us to bloody Canada for?' After breakfast they were formally told of their posting to the Mosquito wing and informed that the ground crews were to be retained and put on the strength of 229 Squadron, which was thereupon renumbered as 603. The young pilots and navigators with their bags caught a train north to Aberdeen. Unfortunately no trains ran to Banff on Sunday, since it was a day of rest, and the airmen found quarters at The

Aberdeen Hotel until Monday morning. Later in the hotel bar a few seasoned 'strike wing types' lectured them on the finer points in flying operations off Norway! Within three weeks, they were detailed into the three squadrons, the majority going to 235 Squadron. Max Aitken rated them well above average, and they began making their weight felt in the respective squadrons. Training on rockets, Gee, and fighter affiliation continued at a furious pace between operations over the next few weeks. Fighter affiliation training was with the 65 Squadron Mustangs from Peterhead, and Squadron Leader Jacko Jackson-Smith, noted: 'This was rather good fun. We broke the rules by diving down to zero feet to elude them. The Peterhead pilots were good types and enjoyed the exercise.'

No operations took place at Banff on 13 February but 12 Mustangs from 19 Squadron landed at Peterhead in readiness to carry out fighter escort duties. Searches between Sandøy light and Utsira in appalling weather on 14 February forced the Mosquitoes to return with their rockets still on the rails. On Thursday 15 February the station commander Group Captain Max Aitken celebrated his birthday, receiving three hundred telegrams, one from each of the aircrews. Drinks were held in the officers' mess from 18.00 hours and the session was boisterous with many raised voices singing RAF songs and dancing with WAAFs who had been invited for supper. At 04.00 hours the last officer reached his bed. The following day both wings combined, with an escort of 12 Mustangs from 65 Squadron. Lieutenant Nodeland and Captain Wenger send separate reports of vessels seen in Vindspollen, Ålesund and Norangsfjord. Wenger in 'F' 333 dropped two 500lbs bombs on a bridge outside Aandalsnes after experiencing light and heavy flak. After reports had been collated four Norwegians went on a strike with eight from 143, 235 and 248 Squadrons to Norangsfjord. They swept in, claiming one sunk but results not observed; intelligence later confirmed one vessel was heavily damaged. Lieutenant Mehn-Andersen in 'Q' 333 led 12 Beaufighters on this operation to Norangsfjord but these were prevented from participation as low cloud and rain now obscured the area. 'Q' 333 called up the leader stating 'Weather unfit' and set course for base. Coming down out of the clouds Flight Lieutenant Harry Parkinson and his navigator Flight Lieutenant Ken Jackson found themselves going the wrong way up a fjord, sighting one of their Norwegian colleagues heading the other way. Parkinson turned tightly to follow him out of the fjord and safely out to sea.

As they crossed out at 14.55 hours, 30 Fw190s were seen, but these continued on their respective course. A second force of 14 Bf109s of 10 Staffel from Gossen then came in from the south, hitting some Mustangs out of the sun. As other sections went for the Mosquitoes their pilots quickly jettison their bombs or rockets into the North Sea and increased speed. Although none were shot down a few had sustained damage when hit by enemy fighters. 65 Squadron broke to engage and a series of dogfights developed. The entire force landed safely; one 235 Squadron aircraft had a hang up on a 500lb bomb causing a panic when they landed. Flight Lieutenant Ken Parkinson wrote, 'The whole show was a shambles in my opinion – but all returned safely.' Three enemy aircraft were claimed as destroyed, one probable. Flying Officer Peter Banks serving with 65 Squadron was flying on this operation as a section leader and recalls the meeting with JG 5:

'We met 20 Bf109s and 30 Fw190s. I was flying 'Yellow 3' my number two 'Yellow 4' should have stayed with me and I was attacked first by five Bf109s looping around each firing in turn, then two Fw190s and finally five Bf109s whose shells ripped into the aircraft. In trying to out-turn them I turned too tightly spinning down towards a fjord some 5,000 feet below. I lost the Bf109s by flying up the fjord instead of out to sea where I, along with my aircraft, would have been a sitting duck in a shooting gallery. Climbing gradually in circles, the sides of the fjord were getting very close, my final turn at the top began so tight I thought that she would hit the side of the fjord. However all was well and I gained altitude to 11,000 feet and looked to see what damage had been done. My tailplane on both sides was in tatters and the rest of the aircraft had been hit a number of times by cannon shells – how many it was impossible to tell – she still responded. Minutes passed. I spotted six Bf109s well below me and thought about diving at speed through them giving them a squirt – a taste of their own medicine. Sense prevailed, and with my aircraft in such poor condition I spent a very lonely and anxious two hours nursing the Mustang (using low engine revs and high boost to conserve fuel though this caused the plugs to carbon up. The policy was to open up the engine every 15 minutes or so). My chances of survival were small if the Merlin packed up over the freezing northern waters before I landed at Peterhead. I could at least speak to the squadron who were well ahead of me on the radio-telephone – but the real relief was when I could talk to the Control Tower at Peterhead.'

On 17 February, 19 Squadron Mustangs took off at intervals to do local reconnaissance to familiarise themselves with the area. There was a hurried recall from the tower at 16.15 hours and the pilots returned to find that scotch mist was over the airfield. It took several attempts to get everyone down on the ground. On 20 February, the Mustangs were in the air again, flying from Peterhead to Dallachy for tea and a talk with the Beaufighter crews, but unfortunately as the squadron was landing an aircraft FB199 flown by Flight Lieutenant Hussey DFC DFM, spun in on approach and Hussey was killed.

CHAPTER 11

AUSTRI

Orders were received from 18 Group for a force to carry out a Rover patrol off the Norwegian coast on 20 February. Wing Commander Junior Simmonds was detailed to carry out this Rover using 14 aircraft from his unit, 235 Squadron, which was between 59.48N and 05.06E to Helliso lighthouse, when the operation was postponed owing to inclement weather. It was instead arranged for first light the next day, Wednesday 21 February. With the operation postponed crews dispersed. Five members of 235 Squadron set off on a country walk to Whitehills and then caught the bus to Banff where they had tea (egg, bacon and sausage). Afterwards they went to the Crown Hotel for a quiet 'session' followed by supper at the Deveron fish & chip shop, finally taking the 10 o'clock bus back to camp.

The crews from 235 Squadron who were on operations woke at 05.00 hours, although some had had little sleep. Briefing was carried out at 06.30 by Group Captain Max Aitken who explained the route and possible targets, tactics against enemy fighters and the positions of the Mustang escort, friendly and neutral vessels. The crews listened attentively, for a few of them this was their first strike off the Norwegian coast, and there were no questions. Take-off was at 08.00 hours, just as it was getting light. The force formed up over the aerodrome and set course for Peterhead at 08.14 with Simmonds leading 15 Mosquitoes, without the usual 333 Squadron outrider; they picked up the Mustangs of 65 Squadron at 08.23 hours, and the combined force then set course for the patrol area. They continued across the expanse of the North Sea in drizzle and poor visibility, towards an unsuspecting and innocent target. This was civil coaster *Austri* built in 1910, sold to the Stavangerske Dampskibselskap in 1912 and which had undergone modernisation some time in the mid-1920s. The vessel was operating her regular route between Stavanger and Bergen, filling up with all kinds of cargo and passengers. During these winter months, the Germans forbade all vessels to travel at night and these moored at Haugesund.

Captain Adolf Christiansen guided *Austri* out of Haugesund for Leirvik at 07.00 hours with about 130 passengers. While in Haugesund some 'unwanted cargo' boarded, 50 German soldiers, along with 16 Polish and Russian prisoners. The Germans occupied the first class saloons and most of the cabins for themselves. The Polish and Russian women, some with babies, were locked in the ladies cabin – they were being transported from Sauda to a camp near Åsane. Forty-two Norwegians with travel permits were also onboard. The Norwegians, who did not have cabins, were in the corridors and on the stairs; baggage was lying along the walkways, making it difficult to move about. Around 09.30 *Austri*, of 491 tons, was closing in at Leirvik, just passing a shipyard called Stod Verft. At this yard there were three vessels undergoing repair, the *Ibis* of 1,367 tons, which had been lying damaged in this position for several months as a result of an attack in Åalesund in August 1942, the *Gula*, of 264 tons, which had received rocket damage on 14 November 1944 in the mouth of Songefjord, and nearby the seal-catcher *Søndmøringen*.

At approximately 09.30 hours the strike force was one minute from ETA and its first turning point. Simmonds radioed the crews to climb above the rain showers; by now they were over the coast. The Mustangs were persuaded to follow by the strike leader, although their leader wanted to turn back. The veteran Flight Lieutenant Bill Knowles DFC, leading White Section, then set about getting the force back into attack formation as the Mosquitoes had became somewhat spread out during the climb. Flying along the top of this cloud until 09.34 hours Simmonds sighted a vessel through a gap in the clouds, thought to be travelling at 6 knots, and in position 59.44N/05.30E. It was followed by a merchantman and a smaller vessel close by at 59.45N/05.25E. The force passed very low over the mountain of Siggio near Bømlo, when suddenly at 09.32 hours it saw another vessel heading for Leirvik. Because of their speed Simmonds now only had seconds to judge whether or not they should hit it. The order of attack was given. At 09.34 the pilot Anton Rebnor spotted the aircraft passing on the *Austri*'s port side; her captain shouted a warning to the men in the engine room before signalling 'Stop'. At the same moment two sections of three aircraft which nobody on board had seen dived into attack, and hit the *Austri* with rockets, six below the waterline and six above, while 20mm cannon and machine guns also caused a lot of damage. Afterwards the two squadrons rejoined the formation. As well as considerable damage to the vessel they had caused a lot of human injuries. The lights had gone out and hot steam gushed out from the engine room through holes made by the cannon and machine-gun rounds, making it difficult for the passengers to see what was happening in the chaos of strewn luggage and injured or dying people.

Otto Horneland and Bjorne Kannelønning were standing amidships when the first rockets hit. 'They came in, the whole boat rocked. We took cover and lay still until it was all over. Dusting ourselves down we looked at the damage. Outside the ladies cabin lay a Russian women, badly wounded, screaming in great pain and losing blood. I [Bjorne Kannelønning] took off my overcoat and lay it over her to keep her warm.'

Just before the first attack the strike leader had spotted the vessels under repair in the A/S Stord Verft Shipping Yard, the *Ibis* and the seal catcher *Søndmøringen*. The *Gula* was also berthed nearby but hidden by these two and was not seen at first by the attackers.

At 09.35 the remaining sections were addressed over the radio. One minute later nine aircraft struck the vessels. Captain Olav Helland was onboard the *Ibis* with a stoker and some workers from the yard. The stoker, Isak Nordvik, was in hold three at the time and climbed quickly up on deck; he saw the attackers and managed to get himself to safety on the port side. Neither he nor the captain were hurt, but a few yard workers did receive minor injuries. While this was taking place the chef on the *Gula* looked out of the galley to see what the noise was but quickly dived back inside when the knife he was holding was shot out of his hand. All three ships were now burning fiercely and about to sink following numerous wet (17) and dry (19) hits with rockets. The nine aircraft were then led in by Simmonds on another attack on *Austri*, using cannon and machine guns and breaking to starboard as they crossed her. This had a devastating effect on the passengers, with terrible scenes ensuing. Junior Simmonds gave an account:

'I immediately gave orders for Green and White Sections to attack the starboard vessel which I estimated to be about 1,500/2,000 tons. Red, Yellow and Blue Sections were to attack the main target, which was the stationary merchantman and smaller vessel, which I estimated to be at about 4,000/5,000 tons. I carried out the attack on the main target with rockets and cannon and I then climbed up to 500 feet, did a rapid turn to starboard and attacked the secondary target, which was by now obscured by smoke and flames.'

The *Austri* was ablaze, with several fires taking hold, and had begun listing to starboard. One of the Norwegian passengers on board was Olav Larse who takes up the story:

'I was sitting in the corridor outside the second class saloon cabins, when the vessel suddenly 'jumped' as if it had run aground. As rounds and rockets found their mark, along with other passengers I was thrown forward landing in a heap on the floor with the baggage. The sound was deafening as more rounds hit the *Austri*. The lights went out and the corridor was thrown into total darkness. Panic broke out in the blackness. The passengers went forward towards the stairs, which could be made out from the light of the fires. I was scared but tried to remain calm, making my way back along the corridor, thinking it would be easier to get to the deck. I felt my way along the panelling until I came to a large hole through which I could see the sea! A rocket must have gone through to the engine room; the corridor was full of smoke and hot steam blowing through. I ventured onto deck as the aircraft attacked again, I flung myself down on to the deck and lay there until the attack was over, fortunately I had not been hit. I rose to my feet, all around me lay the dead and wounded. The bridge had taken hits, and both Captain and First Mate were amongst the dead. The stricken vessel began to sink; some of the surviving crew and passengers were getting lifeboats and rafts out, which proved useless as they had been damaged. The first began to fill with water, and the second; it was hopeless trying to bail them out. We then jumped overboard into the water and swam for land. All this happened in seconds, but it seemed like hours.'

As lifeboats were being lowered by her crew on the second pass, the lifeboat falls were cut by machine-gun and cannon fire and one boat fell into the sea. One of the aircrew remarked that he had seen one of the boats with its load of desperate people crashing into the freezing cold water. During this third attack several pilots were able to see the name *Austri* on the side of the boat and the following was noted in a report: 'As a result of these attacks M/V (a) was seen to be burning fiercely and listing to starboard and the crews reported the name as *Austri*, the former Norge passenger packet now under German control.'

Otto and Bjorne survived the third attack, hiding behind some steel plates in the foreship, together with a dog which had also sought refuge there. On the other side of the fjord another passenger vessel, *Akrafjord*, had just departed from the jetty at Tittelsnes and the crew witnessed the attacks. The last of them was over in less than a minute and as soon as the Mosquitoes headed out of the fjord *Akrafjord* approached the *Austri* at full speed to help with the rescue. Other vessels in various shapes and sizes including those in the shipyard were manned and sailed towards the stricken *Austri*. The Norwegians Otto and Bjorne caught sight of the *Akrafjord* but decided to wait before jumping into the cold water. Somebody, perhaps a member of the crew, threw lifebelts down from the bridge and they grabbed one each. They then spotted a woman, a Polish prisoner, just sitting quietly, staring straight in front of her. Her shoulder had been torn away and her chest had received wounds from machine-gun rounds. Otto offered her his jacket, but she just looked at him, shaking her head.

The *Akrafjord*, under the captain's direction, came as close as she could to the sinking *Austri* and several surviving passengers, including Otto and Bjorne, lowered themselves into the sea along a wire and swam towards the lifeboats from *Akrafjord* which managed to pick up 50 from the water. The *Akrafjord* went as near as she could to the survivors in the water; her crew threw out lifebelts and a scramble net was thrown over the side. Many in the water were exhausted, trying to cling to anything that would float, bodies were everywhere and screams and moaning could be heard from the suffering people. They could not stay afloat. *Austri* was now moments from sinking. An account from the *Akrafjord* reads:

'En route from Tittelsnes to Leirvik when the *Austri* was attacked. I counted seven aircraft that attacked twice. There was 15 minutes sailing time between the two ships, I could not see any others about and asked the engine room to give me full speed ahead, making for the *Austri* which was now enveloped in flames and beginning to sink. Ten minutes after the third attack, she had disappeared and gone down.'

Patrolling out at sea, the Warwick wireless operator intercepted a message on VHF that the strike had been made, and at 09.55 the pilot set course along the track of the Mosquitoes.

On shore, the Civil Defence and Red Cross were mobilised. Two members of the Stord Red Cross Rescue Services, Trygve Oma and Thomas Jansen, were told to report to the quay at Leirvik immediately. They were taken onboard the German *Fjord 20* and, together with the German complement of two, headed towards the *Austri* at full speed. By the time they arrived the vessel had sunk and they faced a scene of dead and injured floating in the icy water, entangled with debris. Trygve saw several people clinging to some chairs, perhaps part of the cargo, while a German soldier frantically tried to hold onto a barrel of wheat beer, but it kept on rolling around, eventually he had to let go and drowned. The four on the *Fjord 20* immediately started pulling people of all nationalities to safety; those who could walk were placed in the salon aft, while those with multiple wounds and the dead where sited on deck. There was no first aid equipment onboard *Fjord 20* but they did what they could for the injured. One of the Germans, Wallinger, impressed Trygve because he did an excellent job regardless of nationality. On arrival back at Leirvik the quay was bustling with people, and the injured were taken off to either the hospital or the jail, where the Red Cross had its base. A nearby barn was used as a morgue.

Akrafjord signalled their arrival at the Tittelsnes quay with several short blasts of the horn, and there were people on the quay ready to take the wounded off. After the *Akrafjord* a German flakship and several smaller boats arrived with more injured. A terrible sight greeted Halvdan Hystad. There were people with missing limbs, burnt flesh, and survivors brought ashore with or without clothes. Doctor Emil Moe was also seeing to the wounded, and the seriously injured were ferried away by German ambulances. Those Norwegians not injured were provided with hot soup and dry clothes. The uninjured German soldiers were driven to the flak battery at Bjelland. Doctors, nurses and volunteers worked desperately to save as many as they could in Leirvik; a sterilized saw was used for urgent amputations done on site. By 19.00 hours (local time) 76 people had received medical treatment. Those still alive and wishing to travel resumed their journey by a freighter to Bergen.

All Banff aircraft returned safely, landing at 11.35 hours without any damage, though two flown by Flying Officer G Parkinson and Flight Lieutenant Harry Parkinson each had one rocket hung up. The escorting Mustangs could not induce the Luftwaffe up on this occasion – they reported afterwards: 'A really good show by the Mossies.' Flight Lieutenant Bill Knowles' description of this mission at debrief reads:

'I received the order for the section to attack a vessel ahead and slightly to starboard. We peeled off from the main formation and went straight in to attack.

We opened fire at 1,000 yards and I concentrated on the attack, through the ring sight. I broke away after the initial attack heading away in the direction of the opening of the fjord, and having swung around, carried out a second attack. No flak was observed during the first but it was beginning to open up during the second.'

Flight Lieutenant Ken Jackson wrote: 'My first real strike and I returned with somewhat mixed feelings – it brought the destruction of war home to me with a shock.' As a result of this attack all three vessels; the *Ibis*, *Søndmøringen* and the *Gula* were sunk. It was subsequently found that the *Gula* received four hits by 25lb J-type rockets; one had penetrated almost from end to end of the 264 tons vessel, this was undoubtedly from rockets fired at the *Ibis* as the *Gula* was not reported by the air crews so no claims were made.

Information from SIS agents in Leirvik to London indicated that the vessels had sunk on 21 February 1945. After this disastrous incident Major Ulleberg Johansen together with the remainder of 'B' Flight, 333 Squadron aircrew and ground crew talked about going on strike but they knew this was impossible. The German-controlled press used this attack as propaganda against the Allies – claiming that passengers killed on board the *Austri* numbered 300. Today it is reasonable to assume that 30 passengers perished.

On 22 February the newspaper *Aftenposten* wrote:

'25 British aircraft were over the *Austri* but the formation split up; while ten attacked the *Austri* the rest of 'The English Bandits' attacked and badly damaged three other Norwegian ships near the herring factory at Leirvik.'

Another article appeared the following day in *Sunnhordland*, which had an announcement about two of the dead from the *Austri*.

'Two Russian women who lost their lives after the attack on *Austri* will be buried at Stord Church on the 24th February 1945 at 14.00 hours. Wreath orders will be taken by Vågens Flower Shop. All that wish to follow can do so.'

On Saturday at Stord Church, 150 local people attended to listen to the sermon given by Pastor Alksel Mjøs. The locals then followed the coffins of the two young girls to their final resting-place. The two Russian women where named as Olga Rusack and Olga Zecoth. Consequently the Norwegian Naval Attaché raised the question with the Air Officer Commanding 18 Group, as to why in a single operation on 21 February Coastal Mosquitoes attacked four Norwegian vessels, sinking one, an unarmed civilian steamship, and damaging three more. Dissatisfied with the answers they demanded a full enquiry. Air Vice-Marshal Simpson ordered one to take place at Banff on 2 March and the conclusion reached was that bad weather had caused difficulty in identifying the vessels. 235 Squadron's commanding officer wrote in his logbook: 'Leader on attack against 2,000 ton MV and 500 ton passenger packet. Purely a squadron outing.'

Twelve Mosquitoes made up of three from 333 Squadron and nine others from 143 and 248 Squadrons flew the same day on an anti-shipping patrol between Ytterøyane and Sandøy, with Flight Lieutenant Bob Golightly leading in 'P' 333, however, bad weather prevented flying inland and they were forced to abort. At 10.41 hours the Warwick covering the force intercepted a message from 'Polestar Outrider' (Golightly) to the effect that the weather was unfit, consequently the Warwick set course along the homeward track of the Mosquito force. Later a further mission codenamed 'Ashfield' was carried out in conjunction with 524 Wellingtons in a 'Drem' rendezvous. In total four of these operations were flown, without positive results. On the 22nd two Norwegian crewmen were involved in an unfortunate accident near the airfield. Thor Stensrud and Erik Friis were testing a new camera in 'F' 333 and an accident occurred when they dived on a fishing vessel. Friis who was leaning over Stensrud was thrown forward in the dive and struck the pilot's arms, and Stensrud momentarily lost concentration. Flying fast and low at 50 feet towards the stationary vessel they collided with its mast and crashed into a hillside near Buckie. Thor recalls:

'That damned vessel had had the tops of her masts painted black so I did not see them until they almost chopped my wings off – on one engine partly running we hopped over the shore, then a small hill emerged in front of us. Erik was crying out over the intercom "Don't hit that one too". Next thing I remember was sitting on the ground outside the cockpit, strapped to my seat, looking at a big hole in the fuselage where I had been thrown clear. Erik was injured too, and the blood wagon transported us to a small hospital near Buckie, where the nurses were beautiful. With no bar I had to steal my uniform back one night and leave and return through a window to get me a beer!'

Squadron Leader 'Alec' Gunnis DFC left for Norway in fading light at 16.37 hours leading six Mosquitoes. They began checking the Leads, flying south and north, but with the weather closing in by 18.30 hours, Gunnis detailed the two sections to make for base as it was getting very hard to distinguish between rocks and vessels. They set course and having observed nothing touched down at 20.36 hours.

An experienced 'ship-buster' was sadly to lose his life two days later. It was Saturday 24 February and five crews were airborne to give a demonstration of a new type of tactics which the Banff wing was developing. Crews were briefed by Wing Commander Roy Orrock who led one section. Flight Lieutenant Lewis Bacon was his No. 2, and he took off in RF603 with Flight Lieutenant Richard Young flying as No. 3. They were to carry out a high level rocket-firing practice on anchored coloured buoys on the R/P range near Tarlair, just outside Macduff a mile or two to the east of the airfield. Senior officers Group Captain Max Aitken, Air Commodore T Warne-Brown and Air Vice-Marshal Aubrey Ellwood from 18 Group watched the targets which were 4,000 feet from the shore in the shape of a cross, red for the centre white for the outer, from the relative safety of the cliff edge. A mobile ground unit from the station tried to maintain radio contact, but this was aborted after the equipment malfunctioned. The practice consisted of two attacks with aircraft in line astern diving from 6,000 feet, down to 3,800 feet. At an angle of 25° one pair of rockets were fired on the first attack, followed by three pairs on the second. Both these attacks were carried out without incident at speeds of 300-330mph. Whilst carrying out the third Orrock pulled out in a climbing turn to port, coming down to 2,000 feet at 330 knots. He noticed that all his section had fired and one aircraft was following in a climbing turn. Orrock wrote: 'My navigator then informed me that only one aircraft was rejoining the formation and looking around I saw a fire widespread on the headland near the golf links. This proved to be Bacon's aircraft that had crashed.'

Having released the rockets Bacon had pulled out at the end of the dive and came back round behind the range, following Orrock who was flying at 1,000 feet. Bacon pushed the control column forward and levelled out. After reaching the centre of Macduff the pilot turned and flew along the coastline at 150 feet. At 11.50 hours, RF603 sped past the onlookers watching from the seaward side of the road, near the red flag at the firing point. After travelling one and a half miles Bacon eased the stick back when instantaneously the aircraft's port wing came off in an upwards direction. The fuselage and the remaining wing were propelled forward for a split second before it rolled to port crashing upside down, and commenced to break up, catching fire as it rolled the two occupants. Flight Lieutenant Lewis Bacon and his navigator Flying Officer William Miller DFC were killed instantly as the cockpit was completely smashed upon impact. The wreckage was spread over an area approximately 500 x 250 yards. A 12-year-old girl walking nearby entered in her diary: 'An aeroplane turned in the air and then spun down and down. There was a thud and black smoke rising up. Bells could be heard soon afterwards.'

Young wrote:

'Unfortunately one of the machines ahead of me got into some trouble and crashed. I have had to take his place as deputy flight commander. This of course is not a promotion nor do I get more pay. If anything it just means that I have more work to do – and less thanks for doing it.'

Thick black smoke rose from the crash site as local people rushed to the scene together with emergency personnel. Another local recalled: 'Two RAF personnel in their light blue shirts walked past carrying a stretcher, a brown blanket covered a body, as it got level with me a burnt, blackened arm slipped out falling limp at the side with skin hanging off.'

Operations were abruptly halted. At Banff the squadron service echelons carried out immediate inspections on all their aircraft, including Group Captain Aitken's plus a Mosquito from Sumburgh. A number of similar incidents were traced after checks with other air force units operating Mosquitoes. A senior staff officer, Wing Commander Woods, led an investigation team, who subsequently found a major component failure of the front and rear spars at ribs 4 and 8 respectively, poor workmanship on the flaps, and the control column showing that the top castings housing the aileron top socket had not been recessed (by machining) on the starboard side. The result was that the handgrip made contact before the bottom stop came into action. Full aileron control had been achieved by filing the casting at the point where it should have been machined. With Standard Motor Company and police help they established that an inspector had links with the Irish Republican Army (IRA) working at one of the shadow factories. Consequently the person was arrested and shot for sabotage.

Both these two experienced members of 248 Squadron were laid to rest, Bacon in the grounds of Banff churchyard after a short service while the body of Miller was returned to Bangor, County Down. Bacon had begun operational flying in March 1943 with 235 Squadron before being transferred to 248 Squadron in April 1944. He had 190 hours on the Mosquito Mark VI. His flying book contained three 'Above Average' assessments of his ability as a pilot, the last being in July 1944 when flying Mosquito aircraft. David Findlay Clark witnessed the crash:

'We were watching it practice at a target anchored in the sea near the shore. The crew had no chance to bail out at such low level and high speed. It crashed on the golf course, off we cycled to see whether we could salvage some cannon shells or perhaps a compass or radio set. As it happened the Macduff police and an RAF salvage team arrived there first, and it was days before we could pick about the little wreckage left. The RAF team had tidied everything recognisable or usable away. Two more families were left to grieve.'

No operations were carried out on Sunday 25 February, after a Hudson on a Rhombus flight found visibility deteriorating badly 15 miles from the Norwegian coast and had set course for Banff, landing in slight rain. Before the inspection could be carried out on HR366 Aitken flew a practice-bombing test with Flying Officer Barrett, taking off in driving rain with the cloud base at 2,000 feet and visibility down to two miles. They reached 6,000 feet and dived to 3,000 feet. As they commenced a fast dive at 380 knots unfortunately the bomb doors tore off 'MA-01'. Regaining control at 1,500 feet from the violent yaw to port by slapping the starboard Merlin right back, Aitken reduced speed and managed to crawl back to base, finally coming to rest with the aircraft's back broken. During inspection another Mosquito serving with 248 Squadron, which had recently arrived from Bircham Newton preparation pool, was found with damage. A bolt inboard of the port mainplane rear spar was forced through the lower flank one inch from the drilled hole.

On Monday 26th, several crews cycled to Banff fishing village, some left half way to visit farms in search of eggs – returning with 4 dozen! They encountered very strong head wind on their return. In the evening they went dancing at Macduff and a few stayed the night at the Fife Arms Hotel. At the aerodrome a visiting Warwick was damaged shortly upon arrival, the mid-upper gunner accidentally firing a short burst into the rudder and fin. The young pilot officer was brought before Max Aitken and docked one week's pay.

Originally the Norwegians used to do all the reconnaissance flights but over the past few months the aircrews from 143, 235 and 248 Squadrons had been ordered to get to know the coast. Flight Lieutenant Richard Young and his navigator Flying Officer Geoffery Goodes DFM took off on 27 February in the early morning on one such mission in 'X' 248, patrolling between Utsira and the Naze they strafed a freight train near Naerbo. Young wrote home to Dundee, on 5 March 1945:

'I spoke to one or two of the Norwegians the night previous to my trip, and from them I learnt that only Jerry uses the railway and petrol driven transport. Just before I took off early that morning the pilot who was acting as duty officer said that I might see the train at a certain spot – where he had seen it, but did not attack. When we reached the other side the weather was much too poor to see any landmarks and we were 'groping' our way along the coast when we spotted a lighthouse which gave us a bearing. Just then I saw the telltale trail of smoke and round we went. As we roared in skimming the wave tops, Jerry must have been watching and opened up with light flak. We spiralled up, went over the coast and railway line, and did a circuit around this goods train then dived down and strafed it. A petrol wagon blew up, we went around and took a photograph or two then went in again. I now get called "Taf" Young (Tactical Air Force – who go about shooting up trains) while one Wing Co. prefers to call me the "Scourge of the LNER", all good-natured ragging.'

On Wednesday 28 February, orders were received from the top for local low level formation flying. 18 Group telephoned in the afternoon requiring an immediate strike but this was cancelled due to bad weather. The following day, all aircrew attended a lecture in the morning on 'Escape from Norway' which was given by a young airmen who had just returned. Operations were scrubbed again as force 10 gales were in progress. In the Nissen hutted accommodation scattered around the fields, windows were shattered and corrugated roofing was ripped off where the bolts had rusted during the thaw a month earlier. Parties retrieved the corrugated sheets and fitted them with the help of the service echelons. During February Wing Commander Bill Sise had been awarded a bar to his DSO. The citation for the New Zealander read: 'This Officer has displayed great gallantry in operations against the enemy. He is a brilliant leader whose personal example and untiring efforts have done much to raise his squadron to the highest standard of fighting efficiency.' Other awards were announced in *The Times*, firstly for two Oxfordshire men; Wing Commander Junior Simmonds, who was given the DFC for his work as a flight commander on his previous unit, 254 Squadron, and Flight Lieutenant Basil Quelch who had finished a second tour of operations with 235 Squadron when his DFC was announced. His total operational time with the squadron was three years and he remained associated with the unit until the war ended. Wing Commander Tony Gadd, through his exemplary leadership of 144 Squadron, was awarded a bar to his DFC.

Members of 235 Squadron heard the welcome news that Warrant Officer Ian Ramsay, whose aircraft ditched on 19 October 1944, was safe, although a prisoner of war and in hospital. However, no one had yet been told that another member from 235 Squadron was on the same ward. Flight Sergeant Jock Couttie was two beds down from Ramsay and remained hidden behind screens. Educational activities at Banff had begun in earnest during February, with 19 discussion groups with an average attendance of 20, meeting during the month. Correspondence courses were being taken by an undisclosed number, classes in leather work and dress making had commenced and the libraries were well patronized.

CHAPTER 12

MARCH 1945

In March a crisis arose about the future of the anti-shipping strike squadrons since there was a serious manpower shortage to progress the war in Europe. The fighting was lasting longer than expected and the Air Ministry called for drastic measures, concluding that there was no alternative but to make more use of frontline squadrons there. The Air Ministry had already agreed as a result of War Cabinet pressure exerted in the last half of 1944 not to recruit further from civilian sources until June 1945 and by March 1945 the manpower surplus accumulated in the previous year had been almost completely absorbed. It was apparent that any increase in aircrew would have to come from within the service itself.

Coastal Command's contribution was to be two or three Beaufighter or Mosquito anti-shipping squadrons between April and June 1945, and this was proposed in a letter addressed to Sholto Douglas on 16 March from the Chief of Staff. Portal expressed his readiness to contemplate any alternative cuts that Douglas had to present, on the condition that they resulted in the equivalent reduction in air force personnel. Douglas remonstrated with Portal, saying he could not hope to cut down his first line offensive squadrons as these were stretched to the limit already. The squadrons operating in the Norwegian waters were interrupting troop, equipment and raw material movements from Norway to Germany, but were also causing serious interference with the U-boat operations. This was done by disrupting supplies from Germany to the Norwegian U-boat bases, upon which the enemy was entirely dependent for the continuation of their U-boat campaign against the Allies. Douglas placed a lot of emphasis on the latter aspect of the anti-shipping strike strength in 16 Group with just two Beaufighter squadrons protecting the Thames/Scheldt convoys against enemy action. Indeed, such was the extent of their task that Commander-in-Chief Nore, had pressed Douglas for reinforcements.

Overall figures were supplied to show the efficiency of the anti-shipping campaign during 1944 in terms of merchantmen and naval vessels sunk. The case put forward by Douglas and his team won limited support from Portal, who wrote to the Air Officer Commanding on 3 April: 'I agree as to the importance of the work being carried out in Norwegian waters and the Kattegat by your anti-shipping squadrons and... I have agreed that there should be no reduction in the number of squadrons.' Portal was swayed by part of the argument referring to the strikes on the U-boat supply service.

Nevertheless, not all staff on the board, even the senior staff at Coastal Command headquarters, were entirely certain of the value of maintaining a shipping strike force against the other traffic between Norway and Germany. In order to settle the question a meeting was convened by the Admiralty in Admiralty Arch on 11 April to which Air Staff and Coastal Command representatives were invited. A document, made available by the Economic Advisory Branch of the Foreign Office and the Ministry of Economic Warfare was produced. It reviewed in detail the effects of Coastal Command's anti-shipping offensive in Norwegian waters, and gave a full breakdown of the tonnage sunk and damaged by direct attacks and mine-laying. It provided the German overall tonnage position in separate categories of shipping and the hours engaged by vessels to complete round voyages, and the fall in Norway's imports and exports. The conclusion was that the various forms of anti-shipping attacks, including minelaying had in combination achieved results out of all proportion to the number of vessels sunk. Another result was a significant change in Norway's contribution to the German war effort, with a marked reduction in the enemy's ability to wage war from Norwegian bases. The Ministry of Economic Warfare footnote was:

'The combination of all forms of anti-shipping attacks, their continuity and extent to which they were pressed home, have achieved results which, in view of the limited forces engaged and the tactical difficulties to overcome, could hardly have been anticipated.'

It was decided at the meeting that Coastal Command's offensive off the Norwegian coast should continue. Douglas's request for additional fighter escort for his anti-shipping aircraft was granted, with promises of the services of not one but two additional Mustang fighter squadrons from Fighter Command. At last all the necessary strength was available and had come together with just a few weeks left before the war ended in Europe.

Meanwhile, the operational aircrew and ground personnel at Banff, Dallachy and North Coates were getting on with the job, totally unaware of the fact that the value of their work had been called into question by Portal and other senior staff members. Coastal Command anti-shipping operations were extended as far as Skaw with merchantmen now seldom seen underway by day in the Leads off west Norway. Targets had to be hunted for. The addition of the second Mustang squadron enabled the Banff and Dallachy wings to do these searches with a fighter escort.

In the opening week in March HP836 belonging to 333 Squadron was lost over the North Sea without trace.

Nevertheless, the wing could celebrate something as the long awaited installation of drop-tanks and tiered rockets and the brighter weather gave Group Captain Aitken's squadrons a chance to intervene in the Skagerrak and Kattegat by day which was being visited at night by Liberators and Halifax squadrons. LAC Alec Rix of 8235 Service Echelon recalls the modification:

'The Mosquitoes were not fitted with drop-tanks but just four rocket rails to each wing. The Chief Technical Officer, Wing Commander Richings, received orders to relocate them. We worked continuously day and night to install the wing drop-tank fittings and relocate the rocket rails in pairs of two under each wing. All the parts had been sent to RAF Banff by de Havilland for the three squadrons, in order for them to achieve a greater range. 8235 Service Echelon managed to complete the task of converting all of 235 Squadron Mosquitoes in two days and one night's continuous working. A few days later Wing Commander Junior Simmonds arranged for all the squadron ground personnel to see the gun camera footage of the attack [7 March], which greatly assisted in maintaining the high morale on the station.'

1 March saw aircrews practicing R/P firing at the Macduff range. Four unusual aircraft joined the circuit, and the next day Short Stirlings from Transport Command brought in 100-gallon drop-tanks just before dusk in readiness. The Australian aircrew stayed the night and found a bottle of South Australian Hamiltons wine in the mess which was promptly opened and consumed. The morning was taken up with 'air tests' and the afternoon saw R/P practice, formation, evasive action and escape training. It was not all

work however, the RAF Banff hockey team journeyed to Aberdeen on Saturday 3 March for a match and stayed the night at Gray's Hotel and danced at the 'Palais de Danse' as they had 48 hours off.

Modifications were made on site, commencing on the 4th. Once completed 143, 235 and 248 Squadrons were ready to operate again with a greatly increased range. The day before, after waiting all morning, 21 Mosquitoes with 11 Mustangs had been airborne at 14.15 hours, searching between Marstein and Røvaersholmen, but the patrol was aborted. On 4 March extensive training began for all squadrons for the next three days. An unfortunate accident occurred during the daily inspections while refuelling was under way. An electrical starter trolley was plugged into a power supply which ignited, causing extensive fire damage to a 143 Squadron Mosquito. Wing Commander Christopher Foxley-Norris air tested PZ412 on 143 Squadron's strength. This was shortly followed by flight tests on 6 March, with two 100-gallon drop-tanks and eight 60lb lead rockets; Group Captain Max Aitken was flying 'R' 248 mentioning that it was 'A very ropy aircraft' when filling in his flying book. Aitken later joined the men and women in watching the gun camera footage from the past four months in the station cinema.

A Rhombus flight was curtailed on 6 March, owing to adverse weather conditions on the Norwegian coast, the Hudson landed at Banff together with a 38 Group Halifax. It was requested by the AOC of 18 Group to double check the weather forecast and a Dallachy aeroplane was ordered to carry out a patrol and report on the weather on the outward route. Beaufighter 'A' 404, piloted by Flying Officer McCallan, took off at 11.19 hours and flew at an average height of 400 feet and, despite considerable jamming, sent a full weather report to base: 'Washout, weather unfit' was heard at both aerodromes. At Banff the air was crowded in preparation for the 'big do' with aircrews doing air tests or R/P checks on their Mosquitoes. During the evening many went to see the film *Meet the People* before turning in.

On Wednesday 7 March Dallachy dispatched two Beaufighters at 06.37 hours on a reconnaissance, making landfall at 08.52 hours. On their outward route they were asked to report on the weather in the North Sea between 58.00N and 59.00N and 01.00W-00.00E; they encountered rain and landed at 11.38 hours. Two aircraft took off from Banff at 07.33 and 07.42 hours on a weather sortie to establish the depth and intensity of a warm front known to be lying off the Skagerrak. It would then be decided if it could be negotiated by a large formation. Another single 333 Squadron aircraft, 'N' 333 piloted by Lieutenant Commander K Skavhaugen, took off at 07.40, made landfall off Utsira and searched 13 locations north and south without any sightings. He touched down at 11.15 hours, while Flight Lieutenant 'Lucky' Luckwell in 'D' 248 swept between the Naze and Utsira returning at precisely the same time.

After the weather recce, Skagerrak was on. The respective crews were up at 06.00 hours. Talk in the mess over breakfast was of their long trip, some were a bit apprehensive while others were shooting a line. The crews were briefed thoroughly and given the latest intelligence by a naval officer, one or two questions were asked by the pilots about releasing the drop-tanks or rocket hang-ups. The various squadron commanders gave their aircrews a 'pep' talk on flying discipline and flying generally. It was noted that Aitken couldn't wait to go!

Between 10.35 and 10.45 hours a force consisting of 35 rocket-firing Mosquitoes (using the 25lb APRP 'J' type head with the 1B double-tired rocket projectile system which allowed enough space for 100 gallon [454 litre] under-wing drop-tanks) and a further nine acting as anti-flak (which were armed with just machine guns and cannon), took off led by Wing Commander Roy Orrock in RS628. The photographic aircraft was flown by Flight Lieutenant William Jones and his navigator Flying Officer A J Newell.

They rendezvoused with 12 Mustangs off Peterhead, flew over 'The Ron' and set course for the Skagerrak and Kattegat at 10.51 hours for the position a convoy (A) was known to be in. On the outward trip eight aircraft turned back; Foxley-Norris in RS625 experienced the same problems with faulty drop-tanks when trying to jettison them, one knocked a large hole in the fuselage, and the other seven aircraft returned with generator trouble. The crews had clear skies for once, just as the Met Officer had forecast at the final briefing.

A sharp-eyed Mustang pilot spotted a lone aircraft in the distance, and a section went to investigate. However the aircraft, a Junkers 88, made off when chased. Alfie Lloyd, a 235 Squadron navigator, recalls:

'The navigation on this trip was rather unusual – once out of Gee cover I began getting consul fixes and passing them to Orrock's navigator on the Aldis lamp in morse code. In spite of all the hazards it worked well.'

Two Fraserburgh-based Warwick aircraft took off at 11.44 hours to provide support on the outward trip. One Swedish vessel sighted was thought to be *Emenuel* though the lettering was obscured. They then began sweeping the wing's withdrawal route.

At 13.05 one merchantman was spotted at 58.37N-10.51E but thought to be neutral. Four minutes afterwards a convoy (A), consisting of eight heavily laden self-propelled barges (Marine Fahr Prahmen), 200-300 feet long, and in position 58.30N-1040E was spotted travelling at six knots, and dispersed in three columns with Vp.1605 *Innsbruck* of 256 tons as escort from Horten. It was sailing to Kiel. A second convoy, (B) at 58.32N-10.39E, was also travelling south and was spotted by 'Weaver 1', a Norwegian outrider; it consisted of one laden merchantman led by a destroyer travelling at eight knots, and four other unidentified vessels. The merchantman, *Mar del Plata*, was flying barge balloons and had left Oslo fjord with the German destroyer *Z14*, commanded by Kapitän C Richter-Oldkop, and torpedo boat *T16*. A third convoy consisting of four unidentified vessels was noted at 58.25N-10.40E. 'Weaver 1' then confirmed these two sightings and Orrock selected the former to attack. He called up the formation with 'All aircraft target as indicated by green marker, repeat green maker'. It was very hazy over the chosen target with the sun just obscured as the various sections of the strike force prepared to attack the designated target (A). At 13.10 hours, two sections (totalling six Mosquitoes) of 235 Squadron, designated as anti-flak to suppress enemy gun fire, were first in. They swooped down from 2,000 feet, opening up with cannon and machine-gun fire which silenced some of the light flak positions on all eight barges and smothered Vp.1605 *Innsbruck* as her 88mm and 20mm guns tried to ward them off. *Z14* and the *T16* gun crews commenced firing. The remaining rocket-firing Mosquito force followed seconds later; they peeled off from the main formation and went straight in to attack. In a crowded sky Mosquitoes singled out their designated craft in one of the three columns. Some aircraft had rockets that failed to fire; one had all eight misfire but they pressed home their attack with cannon and machine-gun fire, scoring hits all over one of the barges.

Light flak peppered the sky from the remaining firing positions on the barges while accurate heavy flak came from *Z14* and the *T16* aimed at the Mosquitoes as they fired their load and got out low through these bursts of flak. Five of the heavily leaden self-propelled barges were burning. A 248 Squadron navigator wrote afterwards 'R/P's seen to go straight through one which had lost its way and was smoking from stern to the forward section.' *F-200*, *F-218* and *F-285* sank, the same destiny befell the flakship Vp.1610 *Innsbruck* of 256 tons which exploded after rockets had penetrated her engine room. All her crew perished. Individual aircraft went round for a second run with just cannon and machine guns. The RAF Film Unit Mosquito DZ592 piloted by Flight Lieutenant William Jones, made passes at 1,000 feet while Newell filmed the attack, obtaining some excellent footage for the newsreels. Shortly afterwards two Mosquitoes were seen to collide one and a half miles from the target: 'R' 248, piloted by Flight Lieutenant Richard Young and Flight Lieutenant Jeff Goodes DFM was in front of Australians Flight Lieutenant Harry Parkinson and his navigator Flight Lieutenant Ken Jackson, who had just completed their attack. A split second later both 'R' 248 and 'O' 235 collided on breakaway, slamming together. Flaming plywood spiralled into the sea leaving a wisp of smoke and burning wreckage, no survivors surfaced in position 58.32N-10.39E. An extract from Ken Jackson's diary reads: 'It was a grim sight almost in front of us. No hope of survivors.'

The force then swung to port, setting course for base on a five-hour trip. Once all the remaining aircraft were back on the ground, results on the barges were assessed: 72 dry hits, together with 13 underwater. It was decided that a search would be fruitless for the two missing crews. Wing Commander Roy Orrock reported: 'There were eight gun barges going south with an escorting flak ship. I decided to attack the eight as they seemed more important and were obviously well laden.' Group Captain Max Aitken was flying HR366 on this operation, and wrote in his book: 'First entry into the Skag, clobbered 8 TLCs.' The station commander had Corporal Joyce Trovey type a letter to each of the four squadron commanders: 'Will you please congratulate your ground crews on the magnificent way in which they worked to get the strike wing serviceable for today's effort. The keenness and good will shown by all ranks has been an inspiration to everybody on the station.' After talking to the intelligence WAAFs the crews had two eggs and bacon in the airmen's mess and a quantity of beer in the officers' mess.

The next day Aitken flew in a 248 Squadron Tsetse to Northolt to give Air Officer Commanding Sholto Douglas a firsthand account of the Skagerrak operation, adding 'Unfortunately two of our aircraft collided over the target and were lost.' These four crew members were posted as 'Missing in Action' and telegrams were dispatched to their families. A few aircrew from both squadrons in the evening raised a glass to 'Taf' Young, Jeff Goodes, 'Syd' Hawkins and Eric Stubbs at the Seafield Arms run by the owners Mr and Mrs Maitland. One or two of the aircrew stayed on after the 9.30pm closing time to sample Mrs Maitland's excellent cooking. A station dance was held though some aircrew weren't too happy about attending, amid talk that both Hawkins and Stubbs were due to have been on leave but it was cancelled for the 7 March jaunt.

Five days after the attack, due to a clerical error, Flying Officer Syd Hawkins' wife Grace Hawkins received a letter from the Air Ministry informing her that as they could not recover Mosquito 'O-Orange' RF596 the cost of the aircraft had to be met by her! A month after this Skagerrak operation on 3 April, a letter was received at the Air Ministry in Whitehall from neutral Sweden, stating that a quarryman from Vajern had found the remains of a uniform jacket on 25 March on the Stoken Rocks near Vajern. The report read:

'In one of the pockets the following items were found:
1. One (1) lock of Hair
2. One (1) chain and amulet and 2 identity discs, the latter inscribed
   GB153224 OFFICER E STUBBS CE RAF
3. One (1) clothing card.'

These items where flown back in a BOAC Mosquito from Stockholm and then sent to

London for identification. Shortly afterwards Grace Hawkins and her newborn baby daughter who was five weeks old when her father died, travelled on a slow train from Somerset to London after a written request was received by her from the Air Ministry to help them identify the items. This took place in a section within Selfridges department store in Oxford Street, and a senior RAF officer offered his condolences. It also transpired that Flying Officer Eric Stubbs' body was found by the quarryman but was pushed back into water.

A strike wing wife remembers the pleasures and pressures of those days:

'We lived off the base in a room at the Fife Arms Hotel in Macduff, let to us by the landlord, a Mr Keith. Life continued, as wartime life did, always on a knife's edge. George was off on shipping strike sorties most days, or training, and was under incredible stress. He did his best not to show it as he wanted our fleeting times together to be as happy as possible – walking along the cliffs near the aerodrome, sometimes taking a picnic if the weather was fine or going to the bakery in Castle Street in Banff for tea and cakes. The places varied in quality. A meal was a shilling or one of the hotels did a three-course meal for five-shillings (25p) if we had any money left. I knew the extent of the pressure he was under when he could not find the escape hatch in his nightmares. George was flying from Banff on an experienced squadron. I would wake from sleep some nights to hear George shouting indignantly "Get lower, tighten up", and other instructions. Some tossing and turning would follow this, then he would fall asleep in complete exhaustion.'

On 8 March Wing Commanders Jackson-Smith and Foxley-Norris made individual searches between Utsira light and Utvaer Light. Utsira lighthouse, which lies on a hill on the north-west side of the island, is the only place in Norway where twin towers are to be found on a lighthouse site. The towers were adapted to the landscape so that their lights were the same height. The tower without a lantern room was used as a flak position by the Germans. Utvaer lighthouse, which remains on Utvaer island was also overflown. After delegations from the Admiralty the Norwegian government in exile agreed for the introduction of attacks on lighthouses and these were authorised in February and commenced at the beginning of March and continued throughout the month. Approved attacks had the required effect in keeping vessels in fjord anchorages for long periods awaiting weather and sea conditions for a safe passage without beacons. These attacks were not without casualties: 333 Squadron lost two aircraft – HR262 in a spoof minelaying operation (named operation 'Chuck'), and 'N' 333 while attacking navigational aids.

On 11 March Lieutenant Andvig led four aircraft, two from 248 and two from 333 Squadron, making landfall near Egersund where they dropped their defused 500lb bombs, registering hits on a tanker and a destroyer. Lighthouses at Hesteskjaer, Bjornsund and Flatflesa were hit. Five aircraft flew out with Lieutenant Knut Skavhaugen in 'Q' 333 passing the island groups, towards the approaches in Haugesund. They tackled Nordhein to Salhus with unfused bombs while hitting adjacent navigational aids at 15.44 hours. 'Q' 333 strafed Nordhein and Kjehl beacons and 'W' 248 Salhus beacon just north of Bergen. Mosquitoes 'X' 248 and 'N' 333 hit further specified targets near Haugesund. Lieutenant Rolf Almton, with his navigator Per Olaus Hjorthen, broke away north in 'N' 333 which was last witnessed half a mile away by 'X' 248, near Øyasundet.

On Monday 12 March, Captain Håkon Wenger took off at 07.06 hours, hunting for the disappeared 'N' 333 but nothing was found. Wenger then continued to search the

Norwegian coast, returning at 12.10 hours. In May 1945 the dead body of navigator Hjorthen was discovered in the aircraft's rubber dinghy at Obrestad. Fifteen lighthouses were put out of action using this tactic but with the lengthening hours of daylight in west Norway the Banff wing had discontinued these strikes by 31 March.

18 Group confirmed a wing strike should be carried out in the Skagerrak and Kattegat and all available aircraft at Banff were detailed for the job. Ray Harrington recalls:

'While those of us on this sortie were eating our pre-op lunch a crowd of local students in fancy dress burst in through the door hoping that we could contribute to the charity they were collecting for but we could not because we had deliberately emptied our pockets of all British money. It was quite bizarre.'

Between 12.50 and 13.02 hours 44 Mosquitoes rose into the air for a similar raid to the one six days earlier; 36 were armed with rockets and eight were acting as anti-flak, armed with cannon and machine guns. All carried the 100-gallon drop-tanks. The fighter leader was Flight Lieutenant Bob Golightly in 'H' 333, accompanied by the RAF Film Unit Mosquito DZ592. Wing Commander Junior Simmonds led the formation, which was joined over Peterhead by 12 Mustangs. After forming up they set course at 13.18 hours from Peterhead. The force wandered about between 15.42 hours and 16.47 hours over the Skagerrak and Kattegat. With the escorting Mustangs positioned on the starboard side, both forces were flying at zero feet, through low mist, which only cleared near the target area. They then climbed to 100 feet.

At 15.42 hours with 10/10 clouds over the Kattegat, the strike leader ordered the formation to climb to 5,000 feet choosing to patrol over it! The Mosquitoes and Mustangs, having just turned their noses towards home again after an eventless patrol in Skagerrak and Kattegat, descended rapidly from 5,000 feet at the mouth of Oslo fjord and followed the Norwegian coastline for ten miles until Kristiansund. Twenty miles south-east off Lista at 16.45 hours Flight Lieutenant Jimmy Butler leading White Section spotted some aircraft passing in front of him at 800 yards. Visibility was bad, making it hard to identify them; he had in fact come upon eight Bf109Gs from 13 and 14 Staffel JG5, from Lista and Kjevik. One of their Bf109Gs had crashed on take-off at Lista, the pilot escaping with minor injuries. The Germans were outnumbered by a superior force.

The Allied force jettisoned their rocket projectiles to increase their speed as the wing was intercepted at 16.47 at 57.40N 06.02E. One minute earlier an air battle commenced with Green and Tonic Sections having been bounced by three Bf109Gs which were now being dealt with. Squadron Leader Pete Hearne gave the order for the pilots to drop their long-range tanks and then turn to starboard across the Mosquitoes and climb to 3,000 feet; Hearne spotted two enemy aircraft amongst Green Section turning in ever-decreasing circles, one with its undercarriage down. This was a Bf109G pilot who kept on firing repeatedly as he countered Butler's turn in his Mustang. Butler did a steep climb, turning as the enemy passed. A dogfight ensued and eventually after doing a series of turns he managed to get behind a 109, firing a three second burst at 200 yards and at 3,000 feet. Smoke emitted from the starboard side as his No. 2 Squadron Leader Hill then hit the 109 which went into a steep dive to get the hell out of there, and Butler pursued it to 1,000 feet, giving it another few rounds. The 109 continued in its spiral but Butler was forced to disengage as five 109s singled him out. Taking evasive action, he dived for sea level, levelling out at 30 feet with tracer from his attackers hitting the water off his starboard wing, then he saw a Mustang crash behind him. He broke upwards and realised that White 2 was missing. Mustang KH444, flown by Hill, had been shot down in the mêlée. A colleague flying Green 2, Pilot Officer Avery, was shot up in the first bounce, getting shell splinters in his back which made the journey to Peterhead very uncomfortable. On touching down it was found that his aircraft had been hit five times by 20mm and 13mm cannon.

With the escort split by the dogfights, nine Mustangs managed to reform and escort the Mosquitoes back to base. The remainder diced with the enemy aircraft. Flight Lieutenant Alan Shirreff had his reflector bulb fuse at the critical moment when lined up on a Bf109G; Squadron Leader Pete Hearne, Tonic leader, got onto the tail of the enemy aircraft with its wheels down (flown by Oberfeldwebel Theodor Stebner), which was repeatedly attacking a Mustang from Green Section. Hearne followed it around three tight orbits to starboard, and fired two short bursts in succession from 150 yards, seeing rounds strike the starboard wing root on the second burst, until the aircraft straightened out for a few seconds. The 109 then began another steep turn to starboard. Opening fire Heane got a one and a half second burst from 300 yards, black smoke came from the engine and it immediately rolled over, diving towards the sea. The Luftwaffe pilot, Stebner, jettisoned the Galland hood but did not bail out. His body was later retrieved and buried at Havstein, Trondheim.

After the engagement, Hearne recalled when having lunch with Wing Commander Christopher Foxley-Norris: 'Even with the wheels down it didn't cramp this pilot's style. Dispatching it in a turning fight expediting 160 rounds of ammunition.'

Six Mosquitoes from 248 Squadron were also pounced upon during this engagement. Norwegian Lieutenant Terje Gudmund Gulsrud, flying at 200 feet saw three Bf109s at the same height, which immediately broke to starboard. 'G' 333 followed one of them, piloted by the Staffelkapitän Oberleutnant Hans Schneider (0410780), who was shooting accurately and taking chunks out of a Mosquito rear fuselage. Gulsrud observed these rounds hitting the Mosquito, and fired a long burst of cannon and machine-gun rounds, from 150 yards to 75 yards, setting the Bf109G-6 alight. Schneider turned, and dived down towards the sea. When last seen in the haze the enemy aircraft was on a northerly course emitting thick black smoke. Oberleutnant Hans Schneider subsequently died when his aircraft crashed. He was last reported by his fellow fighter pilots firing at a Mosquito with another on his tail. Gulsrud, from 333 Squadron was credited with one victory. At the end of this combat Gulsrud caught sight of a Mustang in difficulty and turned back to escort it, but was unable to make contact by radio-telephone or using hand signals.

235 Squadron pilot Ray Harrington remembers this trip:

'I think this was one of the more scary trips. Having had a thoroughly uneventful patrol in very low visibility, we found eight 109s on the way out. I had been assigned as fighter cover, and after seeing tracer rounds whipping past my port wing, I did a low high speed turn to follow my No. 1 Terje Gulsrud in 'G' 333 who engaged a single 109 and shot it down. Suddenly I found myself entirely alone in the murk and decided to get out quick. We arrived back before the rest, much to Wing Co. Jackson-Smith's contempt!'

The air battle was spread out over a wide area and at various heights. Two sections from 248 came under concentrated attack, resulting in damage to Flight Lieutenant R Smith's AFC aircraft. Two Australians, Warrant Officer Raymond Moffat of Queensland and Flying Officer Bruce Abbott from Homebush West, New South Wales, flying Mosquito 'Q' 248, followed the leader's call to climb to 3,000 feet but were engaged by the experienced Leutnant Neumann of 14/ JG5 and his wingman. Neumann got within range of cannon and machine-gun firing, saw the bright explosions of the cannon shells on 'Q' 248 and shouted 'Pauke, Pauke' (a hit scored on an enemy aircraft). The Mosquito, known as 'Cautious Queenie', rolled away, dispatched into a watery grave. Neumann had avenged his two comrades.

Two Mosquitoes from 143 Squadron turned to counter an attack, but disengaged because the visibility was down to 300 yards. The Mustang pilots recorded one destroyed and one probable, although later Norwegian SIS agents confirmed two 109s from 14/JG were shot down. Records show that eight Bf109s from Kjevik aerodrome had spotted the Mustangs as they passed in front at the same moment Butler saw them, and they mixed in with 13/JG5 based at Lista. Two Bf109Gs were damaged in forced-landings after this engagement. One pilot was Oberfeldwebel Willi Hein (Wr. 0462339). All the Allied aircraft returned to Banff except the RAF Film Unit Mosquito DZ592 which touched down at Peterhead at 18.20 hours.

With three days of good weather, squadrons were released for training, but unfortunately while doing an air test on 13 March Flight Lieutenant R Haywood of 19 Squadron ran into a squall and hit the ground, dying instantly.

On 17 March five Mosquitoes took part in further operations against navigational aids and carried out reconnaissance patrols. A Norwegian crew, Fenrik Løken and Sergeant Engstørm in 'E' 333 reported seven merchantmen at anchor in Ålesund, and the weather over the target area was suitable for a strike against these vessels. It would be a very difficult undertaking though. Five hundred miles from Scotland, Ålesund was one of the most heavily defended ports in Norway, in the charge of HKaa III/976 (Heeres Küstenartillerie Abteilung) commanded by Major Miersch together with MKB 2/505 (Marine-Küsten Batterie) and a Luftwaffe flak unit Btt 304/III. Ålesund was therefore surrounded by four coastal batteries and anti-aircraft emplacements, twelve 88mm, thirty 37mm and a great number of light machine-gun emplacements. Every serviceable Mosquito set off at 13.45 hours, 11 each from 235 and 248, nine from 143, and two from 333 Squadron, with an escort of 12 Mustangs. Because the attack would now be expected, the plan was to make landfall south of Ålesund. At 15.52 the force flew over Sula. It approached Storfjord, which looped round to the north, and climbed over the mountains behind the town to attack, led in by Wing Commander Roy Orrock in 'K' 248. Orrock reported: 'All went according to plan and eventually there were the merchantmen ahead of us, offering more potential targets than we had dared to hope for.' Using cannon and rockets five merchantmen were hit. Three with a total tonnage of 6,839 tons were sunk. Squadron Leader Bill Clayton-Graham said: 'Two ships were lying in the inner harbour and four more were just outside as we came in over the hills.' Squadron Leader Robbie Reid said of the concentrated attack: 'There was certainly plenty of flak meeting us, but everyone seemed to be scoring hits with rockets.' The force scored 32 hits on one vessel – 14 below the waterline; another is recorded to have received 37 hits, all but six below the waterline.

On the waterfront the vessels were reported to be unloading. *Iris*, the former Norwegian *Herøy* of 3,323 tons, (which was sold in 1939 to Flensberg, and renamed, with flak towers attached) was at anchor awaiting a cargo of munitions before sailing back to Germany. *Iris* disappeared within five minutes of being hit.* *Remage* of 1,830 tons took a salvo of rockets and began taking on water, flooding one of the holds. Her crew worked desperately and other vessels laid up in the harbour came out to assist, but the damage was comprehensive. *Remage* sank in Valderøyfjord shortly after the

---

*Today the wreck lies at 20 to 30 metres at Aspøvågen in fairly good condition on her starboard side with ammunition littering the seabed.

strike.* The *Log* of 1,684 tons had arrived in Ålesund on 14 March, and was waiting for a southbound convoy. The flak battery onboard put up defensive fire though this was soon silenced. A further two ships were damaged: *Stanja* and *Erna***.

Unfortunately a miscalculation in the range-finding that day meant that a few rockets missed their intended targets and hit several buildings on the shore front, resulting in three Norwegian civilians being killed and 16 wounded, some of whom later died. Five buildings in the city were destroyed while a further five suffered extensive fire damage. Ship and shore batteries had put up a heavy barrage as the aircraft attacked, and two aircrews failed to return. As Flying Officer William Ceybird DFC and his navigator in 'F' 143 attacked a merchantman alongside the quay, flak burst on the both sides. His aircraft was seen to crash into the sea, but although a wing aircraft circled the area for a few minutes, it saw nothing. Both of the crew lost their lives.*** The Mosquitoes gathered into loose formation and headed for base; all had returned by 18.03 hours, just after the Short Stirlings had delivered more long-range drop-tanks. The strike leader Wing Commander Roy Orrock was forced to ditch his aircraft. He recalled this in 1989:

'Half way through my attack, just as I fired my rockets, I became aware that my starboard engine had been hit so, on completion of the attack, I feathered the propeller and handed over the lead to my number two. Almost immediately, I realised that the port engine had also lost power so that I would be compelled to ditch. The sea was pretty calm, we feathered the port propeller, turned parallel with the sea lanes and put down a bit of flap, about a third I guess, jettisoned the rescue hatch and held her off as long as possible. The first impact was quite gentle, but that was just a bounce. A moment or two later came the main impact with considerable deceleration. The aircraft assumed the vertical, nose down position and sank rapidly. Before I could extricate myself from my harness and the armoured back of my seat, which was now on top of me, we were well under water. Bobbing to the surface it became apparent that it had been typical Mosquito ditching. The aircraft had broken in two around the hatch where the dinghy was stowed and the rear section was still floating with the inflated dinghy attached to it. We climbed in, separated from the rear section, paddled clear and tried to take stock of the situation.

'We were only a mile or two from what looked like an island, but our attempts at paddling were not very successful. Eventually the rear section of the aircraft sank; a light snow had started to fall. The first indication that we had been spotted was a formation of Bf109s making passes over us. After they had gone, we renewed our attempts at paddling – more to keep warm than anything else. A fishing boat appeared from the direction of the shore. It reached us and came along side and we were helped aboard by the sole occupant, an elderly gentleman. I needed a smoke, a cigarette was hastily made using a scrap of newspaper and the Norwegian's black pipe tobacco, it was the most beautiful cigarette that I have ever smoked. Although we had lived alongside the Norwegian reconnaissance crews for some months, the only Norwegian I had learnt was a drinking song. I had with me a phrase book and found the phrase I wanted: 'Land me where there

---

*In 1988 the reserve propeller was salvaged by divers and donated to the Ålesund museum.
**In July 1946 *Erna* of 865 tons was sailed back to Britain and renamed *Empire Comforth*.
***In 1972 the wreckage of Mosquito 'F' 143 was discovered by Jan Olav Flatmark and other divers just outside Ålesund. They reported the finding to the British Embassy in Oslo and in 1974 Mrs Joan Wreford, the widow of William Ceybird went to Ålesund for the first time. She visited the crash site and attended a memorial service over the spot were 'F' 143 lies.

are no Germans.' My attempts at pronouncing the translation left him looking bewildered so I thrust the book under his nose with my finger on the place. His response was to indicate that he had left his glasses ashore and he could not read without them. At that point another vessel was approaching fast with uniformed Germans aboard. Our saviour made us put out our second cigarette and I thrust upon him my emergency kit and the Norwegian money I had on me. We were transferred across to the other boat and after a short trip we were landed on a pebble beach on one of the islands. I recall that the welcoming party ashore looked old for soldiers and more frightened of us than I hope we were of them. We were led up a footpath from the beach and passed a small group of civilians on the way and had the impression that there were two children with them, I also winked at one lady and tried to whistle my Norwegian drinking song.

'We spent the night at an anti-aircraft position on the island. Next morning a boat, manned by German Naval soldiers, collected us and took us to Ålesund, both of us were thrown into the back of a truck; we dusted ourselves down and stood up in the open back truck with two guards sat near the tailgate. While we were standing a funeral went by. I gathered by the shouts and signs that it was for some civilians who had been killed during our attack. I never trusted anything our captors told us while I was in their hands, but I had to face up to the fact that such an accident was not impossible. After all we had attacked over the town and any undershoots could well have caused unintended casualties. That moment did not, and will never, sit lightly with me.

'I do not know how long we were in Ålesund. I was in a cell with no windows so day and night merged into one. Once we were let out to speak to some inexperienced interrogator, who spoke no English, and once or twice for short walks around a compound. After about three days we were taken to a railway station to be put on a train for Oslo. The train on which we were placed was full of merchant seamen, survivors from the vessels we had pranged. Although delighted at this evidence, we hoped the rifles that our guards carried were as much to protect as to threaten us. The train set off on its slow journey south.'

The day after Orrock's ditching two Mosquitoes were ordered to attack navigational aids in the Stadtlandet area. Flying at 400 feet Flying Officer Jefferson in 'X' 248 together with 'N' 248 also looked for any visible remains of Orrock's aircraft where it had ditched the previous day. Suddenly they were bounced by ten Messerschmitts. Both instantly increased speed and made out to sea, two enemy aircraft momentarily engaged them but the outcome was inconclusive, and they landed unscathed. Both crews reported white smoke rising from Ålesund 10 miles long.

This sudden vacancy for a commanding officer of 248 Squadron was swiftly filled by Squadron Leader Jackson-Smith DFC. He was promoted to the rank of wing commander forthwith by Group Captain Max Aitken. Jackson-Smith was an experienced pilot having fought from the first days of the war flying Blenheims with 235, and managing to rejoin the squadron in 1944. Everyone on the base respected him, for when leading a formation the crews knew Jackson-Smith was courageous but not foolhardy. He was a welcome addition to any group in either mess. His last flight for 235 Squadron was on 20 March flying into the Skagerrak. Forty aircraft took part led by Wing Commander Foxley-Norris in 'Y' 143. Pilots of escorting Mustangs were flying at 50 feet in bad visibility because of the sea salt which was building up on the windscreens – a danger of low flying over the sea; 'Forced to increase altitude due to sea spray breaking over aircraft' had to return to base. Earlier Squadron Leader Robbie Reid aborted a Ranger patrol after his drop-tanks failed to release.

During the evening, Group Captain Aitken wrote a letter to Wing Commander Roy Orrock's parents in Hampshire, from which this is a brief extract:

'I am writing as a good friend of Roy's; he was leading the wing attack on Ålesund harbour, and carried out a most damaging attack on the enemy shipping. He was heard to say that he was in trouble and would probably have to ditch. He was perfectly confident on the wireless and handed over the lead to his number two. Three minutes later he said he would definitely have to ditch. Thirty seconds later he touched down on the sea and made an excellent ditching. One of the wing circled and saw Roy and his observer get out and one of them climbed into the dinghy, the other holding on prior to getting in. At the time enemy aircraft were sighted and the wing had to leave. I am afraid this will be a great blow to you as it is indeed to us for he was a brilliant and fearless leader. I feel sure however that he will be all right though it may be some time before we hear anything.'

Two days later, an air-test was taking place over the airfield in preparation for the next operation when a propeller reversed pitch during unfeathering. The Norwegian crew reacted quickly although losing height rapidly, but the 333 Squadron Mosquito crashed south-west of the aerodrome. The pilot, Lieutenant R Leithe died in the crash; the navigator, Sub-Lieutenant Skjelanger was thrown clear from the wreckage. The next day single aircraft flew out on searches between 06.00 hours to 11.00 hours. In the mid-afternoon, 46 Mosquitoes with ten Mustangs as escort took off at 15.33 hours bound for Stadtlandet, with Wing Commander Foxley-Norris as strike leader in Mosquito 'Y' 143. The force split up at 16.50 hours. Twelve from 235 Squadron, armed with rockets and cannon, left the main force to carry out a solo effort flying on a southerly course. The remaining force went northwards. Lieutenant Mehn-Andersen acted as outrider, flying just ahead of the 12, and greeted by haze near Vaeroya, successfully guided Squadron Leader Robbie Reid with his four sections by navigating over the haze-free mountain tops by using Very cartridges.

At 17.10 eight 248 aircraft left the northbound formation to attack vessels near Måloy, led by Squadron Leader Robinson in 'F' 248, with three Norwegian aircraft acting as fighter escort. A vessel was seen alongside the quay, and intense light flak was experienced from both ends of Måloy. Robinson decided it was impossible to attack owing to the placement of the vessels and steepness of neighbouring mountains. The formation then set course eastwards looking for vessels *Dalsfjord* and *Rovdefjord*, but after eight minutes they headed for home. The last aircraft landed at 19.57 hours.

Wing Commander Christopher Foxley-Norris led the remaining 15 by Svinøy and continued to Teiganes. The *Lysaker* of 1,400 tons was moored at Sandshamn, Sunnmøre, whilst on a voyage from Tromsø to Oslo with general cargo. It was formerly the Belgium merchantman *Ramscapelle*, which was renamed *Lysaker* in Oslo during the 1920s. At 17.23 hours ten attacked with cannon and rockets. The Mosquitoes were up against flak from the merchantman and the shore. Flying Officer 'Bert' Graham in 'K' 143, went in to attack. When his cannon and bullets were striking around the *Lysaker*, he fired his rockets and then pulled away sharply. Salvoes went into the merchantman, which was now taking on water. 143 Squadron scored at least 15 wet and 17 dry hits. A single Mosquito was squeezed out of the strike, the young American pilot Lieutenant Dymek instead found a warehouse, hitting it with rockets and cannon, unfortunately the rockets over shot, but strikes were seen with cannon. Individual aircraft then came in for a second run, strafing with cannon and machine guns, all scoring strikes. Foxley-Norris attacked with machine guns only.

Bursts of flak came up from concealed shore batteries. 37mm shells exploded catching Pilot Officer McCall and Warrant Officer Etchells who were flying 'R' 143. They went spinning into the water near Svinøy. After the attack a dinghy bobbed to the surface but there was sadly no sign of survivors. The starboard engine of a second aircraft, 'W' 143, was hit by return fire, it burst into flames and lost height rapidly. Flight Lieutenant 'Lapper' Lowe and Flying Officer Ray Hannaford made a successful ditching one mile off shore. Flight Lieutenant D Simpson reported: 'Wreckage and dinghy sighted, no trace of survivors.' Hannaford remembers: 'Just after ditching I found myself sitting on the seabed still held in my seat by the Sutton harness which I undid and then I floated up to the surface.' A local family, the Strands, instigated a rescue in a fishing boat. Within ten minutes of being on board they were consuming fried bacon and Scotch whisky. Ashore on Gjaerdsvika island near Ålesund they waited for the Germans to arrive. The Germans duly appeared and transported them to the mainland. Both were shown blood smeared blankets over half frozen bodies and told 'This is what your friends did to our friends.' Afterwards Lowe and Hannaford were separated, each being interned in individual huts on the quay at Ålesund harbour. The recovery of their aircraft began and several searched the wreckage. Intelligence later learnt from SIS agents in Norway that they had both been taken prisoner and were being sent to northern Germany via Denmark.

A third crew in 'V' 143 had an uncomfortable ride home after rocks got into the engines when taking evasive action, it was escorted back to Sumburgh by 'N' 143 and a Warwick. Shortly after touching down pieces of rock, as large as the palm of a hand, were taken away. Flying Officer Smith returned on one engine with the remaining aircraft which landed between 19.17 and 19.46 hours, except for three who landed at Sumburgh.

A small local steamer, *Romsdal* of 139 tons, on her normal route with passengers and local mail was wrongly attacked. The machine guns had a devastating effect on the people in the crowded steamer and unfortunately three passengers were killed. Two people on a fishing vessel called *Norden* returning with the day's catch were also killed.

The next strike was at Dalsfjord at 17.20 hours, led by Squadron Leader Robbie Reid in 'W' 235. 235 and 333 Squadrons escorted by five Mustangs found the German vessel *Rotenfels* of 7,854 tons moored at the southern end of the fjord, with a cargo of ammunition protected by one flakship. In the face of exceptionally heavy opposition the strike leader ordered the attack over the radio. The aircraft increased speed into a shallow dive, pilots lining up the target. Suddenly Reid took a direct hit, diving straight in 50 yards beyond the *Rotenfels* at mast height and the Mosquito exploded. Flying Officer 'Syd' Gordon watched from 'H' 235 just as it did so and a pall of smoke hung in the air. Everyone streamed in scoring hits with rockets and strafing the vessel. A large explosion was seen on the bridge and superstructure and the merchantman began to burn. As they wheeled out, Squadron Leader Bill Clayton-Graham, commanding 'A' Flight, took over the leadership and along with Mehn-Andersen they headed out to sea via Voldsfjord and Hareidlandet; setting course for home. They landed at 19.32 and 19.41 hours respectively. The *Rotenfels* was left on fire with many dead or dying. In 1960 a memorial stone was erected and unveiled in commemoration of Squadron Leader Robbie Reid. Flying Officer Alexander Turner's body was washed ashore and later buried in Stavne Cemetery.

Flight Lieutenant William Jones in the photographic Mosquito was airborne on the 23rd to follow 23 Beaufighters on a strike, supported by 12 Mustangs and two Warwicks. The Met forecast was ten miles of clear air, however there was trouble with the VHF on one aircraft, and consequently no instructions were received from the strike leader. By 14.55 hours the visibility was very poor with hazy conditions. The strike leader steered a course overland to Ålesund and sighted a single merchantman and a tug. At 15.58 hours, over what was taken to be Ålesund, the leader called up on VHF 'Attack, attack', but navigators were unable to confirm their location and lost formation in the confusion. Jones thought they should abort. At 62.18N-03.40E several Beaufighters attacked a small boat that was obviously not the intended target, Jones followed them down in an attempt to obtain camera footage of this attack at mast height. Shortly afterwards the formation headed out to sea for home. Flight Lieutenant William Jones recorded his thoughts on the cine camera report afterwards, now held at the Imperial War Museum Annex: 'The whole effort in my opinion was a shambles and the vessel should not have been attacked.'

There was some relief from flying however. On one occasion it was drinks all round! Foxley-Norris recalls a visit to a Banffshire distillery:

'A memorable occasion! An organised visit to the neighbouring Grants distillery. Max decided to conduct this operation himself with suitable support. All went well until the end of the tour, we gathered for a farewell drink at the Director's table. Before each of us was a half tumbler of dark liquid, which proved to be whisky of over 50 years of age and of quite incredible smoothness and strength. Our guide assured us that it would not be sacrilege to dilute it, which we proceeded to do from the apparent decanters of water before us. Too late we realised that they too contained an equally ancient and powerful whisky, but from white wood casks rather than oak, and therefore colourless. This was the local villagers' traditional jest and they had gathered outside to get a lot of free and innocent enjoyment from watching the distinguished guests attempting to re-enter their motor vehicles.'

On the morning of 24 March, a single aircraft was dispatched to fly a search. Flight Lieutenants Joseph R Williams and Tom Flower were bound for Utsira and Utvaer, taking off at 11.40 hours in 'Q' 235 HR434. Nothing was heard until a report was received from the Royal Navy that a Mosquito had been shot down. HR434 had sighted the wake of a surfaced U-boat. U-249 a type VIIC U-boat commanded by Kapitänleutnant Uwe Kook, a large impressive man, had set sail from Bergen on 21 March, resurfacing at 04.55 three days later making about nine knots near Skjelanger. At 13.20 hours, a single aircraft was spotted approaching by those on watch, the U-boat opened fire as the Mosquito made its run in, but then Williams released his eight rockets and let fly with cannon and machine guns. Effective defensive fire caught 'Q' 235 in the starboard engine and momentarily it seemed to stop under impact and plunged forward, crashing into the water at 13.24 hours before the entrance to the harbour of Fedje. Steam was coming from the U-boat and one sailor lay wounded. The submarine *Dolfijn* witnessed their fate and her Captain J B M J Maas immediately ordered the submarine to submerge and set course towards the scene hoping that U-249 would assist with the aircraft wreckage and survivors, but the U-boat withdrew into Fedjefjord.

The pilot Williams escaped through the hatch from 'Q' 235 and bobbed to the surface; he was subsequently rescued by U-249's crew and pulled onto the deck, once below in the submarine Oberleutnant Uwe Kook, as a gentleman, treated the downed Mosquito pilot well after capturing him. Unfortunately Flower perished in the crash. Slightly damaged, the U-boat set course back towards Bergen, requesting an immediate escort. She entered Bergen at 19.00 hours and docked at 19.10 where an ambulance and Red Cross members waited for the wounded men. Kook then resumed his patrol, and at 20.00 hours, 11 Flotilla Group signalled him that an escort vessel was in position ready to receive the British flyer. Vp.1703 *Unitas*' task was to protect the U-boats arriving and departing from Bergen. Its guard position was by Hillesøy, and it was here that the exchange took place. Leutnant z.S.d.R. Deilke gently brought Vp.1703 alongside the U-boat, and Williams boarded. The following day *Unitas*' captain slackened speed and docked in Bergen. Armed guards escorted Williams away from the pier to his death – shot by Germans. It later emerged that a German Roman Catholic priest from southern Germany serving in Norway was condemned to death by court martial because he had ardently protested against the shooting of Flight Lieutenant Williams. It is uncertain when the priest died as these documents together with the log of Vp.1703 were either destroyed or captured by Russian forces in 1945. Both Williams and Flower are remembered at the Runnymede Memorial at Englefield Green near Windsor, Berkshire. Oberleutnant Uwe Kook died in 1968.

Reg Flower, a cousin of Flight Lieutenant Tom Flower relates how he heard of his death:

'We were due to meet up together at Elgin cinema as we were stationed near each other. I was a wireless operator/air gunner with 10 Squadron operating Halifax bombers, but at the time I was instructing at Lossiemouth. Tom never arrived so I telephoned the base and spoke to a pilot in the officer's mess to find out where he was. I was told he had been on ops that day and had not returned.'

Also on 24 March the Dallachy 404 Buffalo Squadron flew their last Beaufighter sortie. Squadron Leader Christison of 404 led a successful strike to Egersund harbour but was shot down, as was Flying Officer Aljue. All losses hurt the squadron but it was even worse when the man who 'brought it' was an old hand, someone who had risked everything for so long and seemed unstoppable. Christison, from Quebec, had won a DFC and Bar in Coastal Command, and was on his second tour. 144 and 455 Squadrons, which were also participating in the strike, each lost a Beaufighter. The strike was witnessed by Abram Kjell Sordall, who lived four kilometres north of Egersund:

'The 24th was rather a warm day for the time of year. The farm my family lived on was at Fotland, which lay on high ground with views southwards; though the town itself was obscured there were further views of the surrounding hills and fjord. It was in one of these adjoining fields, which belonged to a teacher, that there was a large stone which we as children used to play around, though the teacher often feared we would fall off and injure ourselves. That afternoon he cycled off into town and seeing the way free we climbed onto the stone. After a while we heard the steady drone of aircraft engines some way off out to sea, which made us very uneasy as we had strict instructions from our parents to run for the shelter if any allied aeroplanes should appear. But we decided to stay, wondering what direction they were flying in. Suddenly the oldest, whose name was Morten, pointed out to sea and said "Look at those gnats." They were heading in our direction, and then disappeared from view. A few minutes passed then the air exploded with a tremendous roar of aircraft engines as they came in from all directions, cannon and machine guns firing, with replies coming from German flak emplacements. We children tumbled from the stone and ran like hares to our respective houses. My feet hardly touched the stairs leading to the cellar, but the rest of my family were not there. Explosions could be heard outside, and being brave I crept upstairs. I looked outside and to my amazement the grown-ups were watching these aircraft swooping down firing. Following the tracer rounds, we could also track the replies coming from the harbour machine-gun emplacements at the same time and likewise from the 37mm/88mm battery from the mountain at Tengareid where the Germans were protecting the big camp at Selettebo.

'Suddenly, flying very low at 200 feet, an aircraft passed over us, the German flak fell silent, and another aircraft approached from the left which caught our attention. Looking southwards towards the town it crossed before us on a westerly course, a burst of black smoke appearing near the tail section. The silhouette of the pilot could be seen in the cockpit, and he turned his head as if looking behind him at the streaming black smoke. The aircraft suddenly exploded into a ball of flames that drifted south trailing black smoke and came to rest at Lauvnes. The air around us was quiet once more, as if a magician had made it disappear. Fires had started burning in the wooded area and were soon extinguished with the aid of local farmers. Then a woman ran up the hill towards us, clearly shaken by the experience of this attack, and worried that her chimney would fall down as it was in need of repair. It shook when aircraft passed over it firing so she had spent her time during the attack holding onto the chimney so that it would not fall down.

'For weeks after this attack we children would come across cannon and machine-gun cartridges and fragments of the aircraft in the fields and woods. We learnt from our teacher who had cycled off earlier that he had jumped off and spent the time behind a wall at Vingard. I discovered in later years that two aircraft had been brought down, one at Lauvnes, and the other close to the flak battery at Grone Haugen. Three vessels were sunk, an E-boat, the merchantman *Thetis* and the Norwegian merchantman *Sarp*. This vessel had a cargo of oats on board which the crew battled to save; they made for shallow waters in an attempt to beach. Casualties on board included the pilot and the captain who were killed on the bridge. On the shore an elderly woman in a house near the attack was killed, while a man died and his wife was injured when they were hit by machine-gun rounds as the Beaufighters strafed a flak battery next to their house.'

The local fire brigade journal account reads:

'At 18.10 hours about 30 aircraft came in from the sea and started to shoot up the vessels in the harbour, the air raid warning sounded at 18.15 hours. Our crew were ordered to meet on the wharf with two motor pumps and fire hoses. On arrival we could see that some of the vessels had been damaged and one was on fire. Inland there were two large fires caused by two aircraft which fell to flak, along with a few small fires along Egersund harbour coming from buildings. Three houses close by had been hit with cannon and machine-gun fire and left damaged, with large holes in the brick work; luckily none had been set on fire by these strays. Our equipment was not put to use.'

25 March would be a busy day for the strike wing. Two aircraft from 333 Squadron flew out on separate searches just after dawn at 06.20, touching down at 11.00 hours. A single Mosquito, 'R' 248, became airborne at 06.45 hours, making landfall at Utsira at 08.06, but Warrant Officer Bill Parfitt flew over Haugesund, Bømlofjord and Fengfjord without a sighting. Parfitt swung round and set course for base from Utvaer light, touching down at 10.30 hours. At 08.40 Lieutenant Nodeland sighted a tanker of 6,000 tons and two other vessels in Norangsfjord. Both 19 and 65 Squadrons were put on stand-by at Peterhead. After a quick briefing at 13.34 hours at Banff, 12 235 Squadron aircraft took off on a solo effort, ten armed with 60lb rockets and two with delayed-action 500lb bombs. Wing Commander Junior Simmonds in 'R' 235 acted as

the strike leader with his navigator Flying Officer Murphy, bound for Norangsfjord. They were accompanied by two 333 Squadron aircraft and eight Mustangs from 19 Squadron, led by Captain Håkon Wenger in 'Q' 333, who handed over the escort to Lieutenant Andvig in 'H' 333 at 15.14 hours. Sixteen minutes later Wenger made landfall and turned to fly south-east over Gurskøy, probing the Norwegian fjords and Inner Leads. The 235 Squadron Mosquitoes shadowed Lieutenant Andvig. Then, at 15.43 hours, Wenger sighted three merchantmen and one laden tanker. Two were stationary, one a 3,000 ton merchantman and a laden tanker of 6,000 tons which were berthed next to each other. 'Target in position in Norangsfjord at 62.12N-0638E' came over the intercom. The force changed course after Andvig had called up Simmonds and led them, firing off green Very cartridges. Andvig headed for Norangsfjord, and then did a steep turn, joining the rear of the force which had changed into battle formation ready for the attack.

At 15.47 hours, nine Mosquitoes in quick succession hit the tanker and merchantman in a line astern strike with steep cliffs around the fjord making quick breakaways. Pilot Officer Ray Harington in 'J' 235 made a solo effort against the vessel close to the eastern shoreline, diving from high level at 4,000 feet. Raked heavily by cannon and hit by rockets, the merchantman nevertheless stayed afloat; some of 'J' 235's eight rockets hit the mountain just above the vessel, showering those onboard with rocks. Flying Officer Pennie's aircraft was hit by flak in the starboard wing, tearing a large piece away. The crews were all back at Banff by 18.08 hours that afternoon, after an operation lasting four and a half hours.

Wing Commander Jack Davenport, as operations controller, planned a second strike after intelligence had been received by 18 Group that a German tanker was reportedly sheltering near Sognefjord. Since the fjord was relatively close to Herdla the sortie would require 13 Group fighters to accompany them. The Mosquito formation of 24 was made up from 248 and 143 Squadrons, with 248 led by Wing Commander Jackson-Smith and 143's proceedings directed by Squadron Leader David Pritchard. They took off from Banff at 13.44 and set course for Fraserburgh to meet their fighter escort from 65 Squadron, which was flying their new Mustang IVs and led by the experienced Wing Commander Pete Wickham. These 12 Mustang IVs began taking up position to the port, starboard and rear of the Mosquito formation while heading for southern Norway, having been briefed to sweep from Utvaer Light, Vadheim and Askvoll. Two 333 aircraft acted as outriders. At 15.58 hours Lieutenant Commander Skavhaugen, the navigator in 'G' 333, gave instructions on the course to Askvoll, and minutes later Flying Officer Bobbett DFC sighted the mast and funnel of the merchantman *Tyrifjord* which had been sunk by the wing on 19 September 1944. Despite a prolonged 20-minute search, the target tanker could not be located.

The alerted Luftwaffe put 30 fighters into the air. Fw190A-8 (737935) was badly damaged on take-off but the remainder set off north to intercept the strike force. They were directed by the radar on the island of Fedje, between Bergen and Sognefjord, to meet the strike force opposite Sognefjord. Mosquitoes were crossing out over the Norwegian coast at 3,000 feet when Bobbett sighted eight Fw190s, which altered course to tail them. Four minutes earlier enemy fighters were seen heading in from the south trying to get into position to fire at the strike force. Between them the Mosquito crews counted 20 to 30 enemy fighters. Ten darted for the main Mosquito force. Squadron Leader Wickham shouted a warning to the strike leader Jackson-Smith then called on VHF: 'Leader to all aircraft, increase speed, check fuel and head for base'. The Mustangs flying 'top cover' at 5,000 feet jettisoned their drop-tanks and dived to engage the enemy fighters. The two groups of about 60 aircraft began their aerial combat just off the Norwegian coast at 61.30N/05.00E, north-east of Ytterøyane, when four enemy aircraft were caught by Yellow Section.

Fanrich Friedhelm-Büchler, flying Fw190-A8, latched onto a Mosquito, sending streams of cannon and machine-gun fire into the fuselage. Presto 4, a Mustang flown by Flight Lieutenant Brad Bradford in turn got the Fw190 in his gun sight. After a number of rounds hitting the Fw190-A8 its pilot, Büchler, broke to port and Bradford closed in. Badly hit Büchler headed back towards Herdla nursing his crippled plane. With the airfield in sight he thought he was safe but suddenly after a malfunction Büchler got rid of the hood and bailed out low, falling into space then splashing down at Marøy. His aircraft (350184) subsequently crashed into the water near some coastal cliffs. A passing Norwegian fishing boat rescued him.* It was only four minutes since the first Bf109s were observed and the first enemy fighter had been shot down. Some altered course and followed the Mosquitoes, which increased their speed to 340 knots, the Fw190s did not appear to gain. A single Mosquito from 248 Squadron was seen to turn to port towards the enemy. 'V' 248 with Flight Lieutenant A McLead and Warrant Officer N Wheeley was intercepted over Vilnesfjord; a short dogfight took place as both men constantly tried to look over their shoulder while trying not to fly straight and level for more than a few seconds. Meanwhile a pair of Fw190s, now at 400 feet, sent tracer arcing into the plywood skin. The Mosquito caught fire, pitching straight into the water, and exploded in position 61.15N/04.45E. Twisting and turning aircraft filled the sky, and Warrant Officer 'Rocky' Howells claimed an Fw190 that crashed into the mountains.

Squadron Leader Wickham was involved in a long dogfight with the experienced pilot Oberleutnant Werner Gayko, Staffelkapitän of 9 JG5, before both broke off the engagement. At the time it was inconclusive but having observed hits on the nose of the Fw190A-8 (0737935) Wickham claimed it as damaged. Gayko subsequently experienced serious engine problems, and was forced to ditch north of Bergen. He managed to reach his dinghy and was picked up by a fishing boat. In his logbook Gayko recorded: 'Opened the 1945 bathing season.'

During another engagement involving a dozen Fw190s, Squadron Leader Grahame Stewart, the commanding officer of 65 Squadron, became detached from his section and embroiled in a mêlée with two Luftwaffe pilots. The first was Oberleutnant Fritz Kohrt, commanding 12 Staffel of JG 5, flying Fw190A-8 (732075), who had made a name for himself on the Russian front. It was a lengthy combat with each pilot trying to gain the advantage. Kohrt's number two was Leutnant Eberhard Lemmel, who was newly qualified, having graduated the previous November; he had only been at Herdla a few weeks, and had been lucky to be rescued from the sea by a Norwegian fishing boat after his engine failed on 25 January. Lemmel stuck to his leader like glue, trying to provide some protection for Kohrt. Lemmel describes the events of the day:

'We were scrambled from Herdla to engage a large attack force under the direction of the radar on Fedje Island. I was flying Fw190-8 numbered Blau 4 and flew as number two to my Staffelkapitän Oberleutnant Fritz Kohrt. We were being directed by System "Y", which meant I was unable to transmit on the radio. When we became engaged in combat a Mustang pilot shot down Kohrt, but in the battle I had manoeuvred into a favourable position behind the Mustang and shot it down in turn [Stewart]. The aircraft flew straight into the sea and I returned to Herdla.'

---

*Fanrich Friedhelm-Büchler's Fw190-A8 was found near Marøy in April 1984 by two young scuba divers and subsequently 50% of the aircraft was recovered.

Squadron Leader Stewart was not recovered after being shot down, and no one else from the squadron had seen him go into the sea. He may have had a momentary lapse as he recovered after shooting down Oberleutnant Fritz Kohrt, and so been off his guard. It is quite possible that Flying Officer Dave Davis and Grahame were firing at the same aircraft. Kohrt's Fw190A-8 crashed into the water north of Bergen. Dave Davis put in writing:

'Saw enemy at 2,000 feet and climbing, I dove to attack from 3,000 feet but lost my wingman, who could not keep up. Went at five flying in line astern, picking on one, and the others turned on me. Leaving myself open to attack I went after him. I got a three second burst in on the way down from astern closing to 600 yards, the enemy Fw109 going straight into the sea. All the while the other three were following me down firing. I observed their cannon round striking the sea around me. I then climbed vertically, turned to port to 4,000 feet, rolled over onto my back and dived down again and darted for home. They could not follow me.'

Squadron Leader Wickham witnessed wreckage floating on the surface and Davis was officially credited with one Fw190 destroyed. Grahame Stewart had become a sitting target, and was flying at a relatively low speed and a low level when Lemmel shot him down. Having no time to bale out he would have died instantly on impact with the sea. This was just two months after the former CO of 65 Squadron, Squadron Leader Ian Strachan was reported missing. Kohrt was also reported as missing in action. Stewart's aircraft, KH732, was Lemmel's first Mustang kill, and crashed into the sea at 15.57 hours. Upon landing at Herdla, Eberhard Lemmel recorded: 'Abshüsse, 25.03.1945. 1 Mustang, 15.57 uhr, im höhe 700 metre, angriff von hinten oben. Zeuge.' (Engagement 25 March. 1 Mustang, 15.57 hours, my height 700 metres, attacked from behind with witnesses.)

The Mosquitoes landed back between 17.29 and 17.48 hours and the debrief began. Lieutenant Commander Knut Skavhaugen's aircraft, 'G' 333, was seen by 'D' 143, which was in turn attacked. The Fw190s chased Skavhaugen around, then fired into Mosquito HR141 which dived straight into the water. Warrant Officer Johnston in 'A' 143 landed at 17.46 and reported: 'After the attack by enemy aircraft one Mosquito was seen to go straight in the drink and blow up at 61.15N-04.50E. Another aircraft on fire went down in 61.21N-04.45E.' The Mustang escort claimed three Fw190s destroyed and two damaged, with the loss of two Mosquitoes and a Mustang. The Germans in all lost five aircraft.

So ended a tragic day. It was Palm Sunday 1945. The combat report for Squadron Leader Pete Wickham's shooting down of Oberleutnant Werner Gayko reads:

'I was leading Presto squadron escorting 22 Mosquitoes out from Banff on a shipping strike. The Mosquitoes wandered about southern Norway for half an hour, then turned for home at 3,000 feet; with my section I was 6,000 feet above the leading Mosquitoes. Just as we were leaving the coast I saw 17 Fw190s (short nosed) at 3,000 feet ahead and coming towards us. I warned the Mosquitoes, dropped my tanks and dived to attack. The 190s went left and right, about five coming round onto my tail and the rest turning for the Mosquitoes. I turned into the 190s behind me, and then dived for the Mosquitoes who had ten 190s on their tail. Two then broke right as I began to catch up. I gave them a squirt for good measure, seeing no hits. I carried on after the remaining 190s and two more broke right and then two left. I went after No.1 whilst my No. 4 shot down the No.2. I scored hits on the nose and right wing of the 190 who was jinxing. The enemy aircraft fluttered down in a right hand turn towards the sea and both my No. 2 and myself thought he was finished – however he recovered and a long dogfight ensued; neither my No. 2 nor myself could out turn him, my ASI was reaching 105 mph and after ten or twelve minutes, I broke off the engagement. This enemy aircraft was, I think, the leader and was extremely good and aggressive. These enemy aircraft were on the whole the best drilled and most aggressive I have yet met. One of the two Fw190s had two enormous cannon mounted under each wing.'

On 26 March Feldwebel Herman Jäger from 10./JG5 who had a month previously bailed out, also lost his life when he crashed into the sea just outside the village of Leira on Tustna, north of Kristiansund. Jäger remained in his aircraft, Bf109G-6 (412398) and his body was never recovered. On the same day, 26 March, Flight Lieutenant Johnny Foster took over as squadron leader of 65 (East India) Squadron at RAF Peterhead.

Three days before the end of the month Flight Lieutenant Alexander brought a Liberator from Leuchars to the 'Mossie Boys" aerodrome. Individual aircrews from the squadrons then began fighter affiliation. The Liberator and its crew stayed for a fortnight before returning to Leuchars.

The month finished with dawn searches which revealed targets lying in Porsgrunn up the Frierfjord on 30 March; it was primarily from this port that German troops and transport from Norway were evacuated. Air Minister Sir Archibald Sinclair MP, arrived at RAF Banff as requests had been made by the Russians to help their Red Army advance into Germany, 'hindering the enemy carrying out the shifting of troops to the east from the Western front, from Norway.' Sinclair was briefed on the strike wing's operations by senior officers in the station headquarters, and then listened to the preparations for the Porsgrunn strike with the intelligence officer Squadron Leader George Bellew stressing that the special hazard that existed in Porsgrunn were the high-tension cables across the waterway. Group Captain Aitken then asked Sinclair to address the assembled aircrew. Flying Officer Ray Harrington of 235 Squadron recalled: 'Sir Archibald Sinclair did his best to put the "shits" up us by describing what a dangerously important job we were doing. A few of us left early and missed quite a lot of the chat show.' A navigator scrawled some of his speech down at the time in pencil, all that is legible today is: 'You're already doing a splendid job, though it is estimated that one division leaves by sea every 14 days from Norway.'

Wing Commander Simmonds led 44 Mosquitoes on the raid at 13.25 hours and Flight Lieutenants Jones and Newell followed in the RAF Film Unit Mosquito. It was a long haul across the North Sea, after picking up the Mustang escort at 13.38 hours, the Mosquitoes, laden with 25lb rockets with the 'J' type head and 100-gallon drop-tanks, set off. After 25 minutes Flying Officer Phil Kilmister and Syd Gordon turned back with engine trouble. An hour later the drop-tanks of the strike leader's aircraft, 'N' 235 were not feeding properly and at 14.25 hours he handed over to his No. 2, Flight Lieutenant 'Bill' Knowles in 'T' 235. Simmonds wheeled around, forced to return home. Flying Officer Norman Earnshaw experienced problems as well, and guided 'S' 248 back to land at 15.34 hours.

The two outriders, Lieutenant Thorleif Heine Eriksen in 'E' 333 and Captain Håkon Wenger in 'F' 333, left the formation at 15.12 hours, flying parallel courses. At 15.45 hours they flew over Porsgrunn, and the navigator in 'F' 333 advised the strike leader that the target was three minutes ahead, as he sighted three vessels along Menstad Quay 1. At 15.47 hours, 'E' 333 located merchantmen between Quays 15 and 16, and sending warning of flak, he opened fire on an emplacement, silencing it with machine-gun fire before the force swept in. Two minutes later Knowles received a call 'Weaver 1 to leader, advise target Porsgrunn quay 15 and 16 watch out for flak.' At 15.50 hours the force orbited in a slight haze over Porsgrunn, and Knowles issued instructions. One section peeled off to attack a merchantman lying alongside Menstad Quay 16, which was located on the east side of the river bank. No fighters troubled the formation and those detailed as escort were able to direct suppression fire against gun positions. The opposition ceased, and Knowles led the remaining sections in. Unfortunately 'N' 143 had drop-tank failure and had to orbit the area. Hitting the remaining moored vessels, which where scattered at intervals along the quayside, Squadron Leader David Pritchard in 'D' 143 reported sighting a two-masted sailing vessel near Quay 27.

The Mosquitoes swooping down, flew so low in on their run in that they crested the wave tops, they then gained height and flew out over the hills. Unfortunately Knowles' aircraft, 'T' 235, struck overhead electric cables on his attack line, and caught fire. It suddenly turned over onto its back and dived at speed into the ground, crashing into a wooded pine area west of Borgaas wireless transmitter station, a short distance behind the quayside buildings. Flying Officer R Holmes wrote: 'Seconds before Bill smashed into the ground he had shown concern for those behind him, warning us on VHF of the existence of the high tension line on shore from the harbour – then the radio went dead.' A young boy arrived seconds after the crash which he had watched from a distance until the flames were extinguished. The aircraft was completely destroyed. He recalled: 'Sifting through the wreckage, looking for souvenirs it was a grisly sight coming across one of the crew's disfigured faces as I moved some plywood. In places the skin was completely gone exposing the skull bone.'

To this day Flying Officer Ray Harrington remembers his astonishment:

'The Mosquito that I was formating on when we attacked Porsgrunn fired his rockets before I decided to, the smoke from them seemed to envelop the aircraft and cockpit so I thought he was hit by flak and on fire! I dived down for my strike, seeing a Mosquito slamming into the ground ahead [Knowles]. My own attack was in progress and I concentrated on that and got off eight rockets and 20mm cannon. Scored eight wet hits and cannon strikes on the superstructure. I got all the rockets off together in a group towards our target.'

Flight Lieutenant William Jones made three passes at 250 feet in the RAF Film Unit's Mosquito DZ592 as the attacking aircraft came in west to east. Twenty-eight rockets hit one merchantman, another was hit by 39 and a third by 60. It was not all one-sided however, Flying Officer Smith had two feet of the rear end of the fuselage shot away, but his faithful Mosquito got him back to Banff. Flight Lieutenant 'Royce' Turner, who had taken part in many shipping strikes, reckoned this one of the best he had ever seen. 'As we went after the merchantmen tied to the quay we could see the plimsoll marks on one. We scored hits with all the rockets aimed at one vessel, and as we came away three separate plumes of smoke were building up to a great height, 300 feet, and was still visible 20 miles out.' Turner had taken out a 40mm flak position on the side of the hill, raking it with cannon, with no resistance.

Flight Lieutenant Don Clause, navigator of Flying Officer Tom Diggory added: 'Another gun position on the side of the hill was firing as they went in near the swing bridge. There were about four positions. I swooped down and sprayed them with cannon, they did not bother later crews as they went in.' Flight Lieutenant William Jones flying DZ592 recorded: 'The only snag was the coating of all the windows and windscreen with sea salt before reaching the target, we had no means to remove this. Flames were seen on the far side but were caused by an aircraft and not by rocket projectiles.'

This strike was made difficult by the proximity of civilian buildings to the harbour, but a warehouse on Menstad Quay full of chemicals was also destroyed by rockets. The Hamburg ship *Scharhorn* of 2,642 tons sank with a cargo of salt. Both Norwegian-owned *Torafire* of 823 tons and *Svanefjell* of 1371 tons caught fire, causing substantial damage, and sank. These were both raised and repaired in the 1960s. The *Gudrid* of 1,305 tons had been loaded with 1,800 tons of railway track while berthed at Menstad and was also damaged in the attack, killing one member of the crew. After the attack Wenger in 'F' 333 called up the force and took over as lead aircraft, having seen the strike leader's aircraft go in, and the Mosquitoes followed him northwards around Skein. The exhausted crews landed between 18.36 and 18.51 hours after a round trip of five hours thirty minutes. The body of Flight Lieutenant William Knowles DFC, originally from Portugal, together with that of his navigator Flight Sergeant Lawrence Thomas was retrieved from the smouldering wreckage of 'T-Tommy' and shortly afterwards buried in a joint grave in Skein Cemetery.

After this strike most of 235 Squadron ended up on a long bus ride to Aberdeen for a 'mild piss up' in the Caledonian Hotel in memory of Knowles and Thomas, and the group then caught the train back from Aberdeen station, alighting at Ordens Platform and walking back to their billets in the early hours. Their missions for the day had not yet finished however. Flying Officer Joe Barnett heard a sheep having trouble lambing in a field adjoining the camp. He jumped over a hedge and gave the sheep the benefit of his farming experiences in Australia. When he left both sheep and lamb were doing very well and bonding.

In the course of March 12 wing strikes were made with six escorted strikes involving more than 40 Banff aircraft. During these daylight operations aircraft were lost mostly through enemy action. A letter of 27 March written to Sholto Douglas and Max Aitken said that on one occasion the Luftwaffe sent 45 fighters to intercept a Mosquito formation. Douglas observed that among these a proportion were the latest Fw190-D which had a maximum speed of 453mph. This was at least 45mph faster than the Fw190-A variant and 40mph faster than the MkVI Mosquito used by Coastal Command. Douglas sent a note to Portal, copying in Air Marshal Sir Roderic Hill, and requested a third long-range Mustang squadron:

'At present we have on call two squadrons which is hardly sufficient in view of the scale of opposition. I realise of course my demands conflict with those of Bomber Command, but I feel that, in view of the weakness of the air defence of Germany, the withdrawal of one Mustang squadron from bomber escort work would not seriously affect the success of bomber operations, whereas its addition to the squadrons in the north would make all the difference to my anti-shipping strikes.'

Portal's reply was sympathetic, but he stated that there was no chance of Coastal Command being allotted another Mustang squadron. The reason given was that the advance of the Allied armies into Germany was so rapid that 2nd TAF was having difficulty finding landing grounds and only the Mustangs with their long range could cover the advanced spearhead of land forces.

During the evening of 31 March, in true air force tradition, the Banff officers' mess was ransacked and raided by 65 and 19 Squadron personnel hedge-hopping all the way from Peterhead to let off steam.

CHAPTER 13

THE WAR DRAWS TO A CLOSE

The war in Europe was drawing to a close with the western and eastern armies pressing Germany from all quarters and the possibilities of new airborne and naval weapons had been destroyed by heavy Allied bombing. Field Marshal Bernard Montgomery's land forces progressed into Germany having crossed the Rhine with the American 12 Group commanded by Omar Bradley. The Russians were surrounding Berlin and fighting in its suburbs. For Coastal Command's 18 Group, April, the last full month of the war in Europe, was to prove the most productive. Following the orders received from Group earlier in the month to attack lighthouses and beacons, by the end of March 15 lighthouses had been put out of action by these combined operations, although the effect on the enemy shipping was difficult to detect. With the approach of summer, the strategy was abandoned at the end of March.

The first operation in April saw early morning searches by 333 Squadron and 235 Squadron, trying to gather intelligence. Lieutenant Andvig, in 'G' 333, flew over Flatflesa, Kvitholmen and Hesteskjaer. Lieutenant Plyhn searched from Oslofjord to Lindesnes in 'F' 333, reporting vessels in Tønsberg, Sandefjord, and Larvik. Plyhn also checked the situation in Porsgrunn. Flying Officer Moffett in 'V' 235 explored Jøssingfjord and Flekkefjord. From the report given by Lieutenant Plyhn, Sandefjord was chosen as the target on 2 April. Mosquitoes were to hit the dry dock there. This was one of the few anchorages left to the Germans where they could carry out repairs. Thirty-six Mosquitoes armed with 25lb rockets, 12 each from 143, 235 and 248 Squadron, plus four acting as anti-flak from 143, and two outriders from 333 Squadron, took off just before 14.00 hours to strike merchantmen moored in the entrance to Oslo fjord. The Film Unit Mosquito accompanied the force to capture the proceedings, and 12 Mustangs gave top cover from 65 Squadron.

Major Håkon Wenger and his navigator Sergeant Hagbarth Hein Hassen in 'K' 333 went ahead of the main force at 18.00 hours. Nine minutes later they made landfall. At 18.13 'K' 333 notified the strike leader Wing Commander Jackson-Smith, in 'G' 248, to alter course for Tønsberg. Following the Norwegian's instructions they successfully swept in over Hjetnesskogen and Stubåsen rising over the swathes of green pine forests. Flight Lieutenant Bob Golightly in 'O' 333 said on VHF, 'formation on course to attack target.' Wenger had found nine ships near the Famnaes shipyard. One was the tanker *Kattegat* of 6,031 tons, which had run aground in Sandefjord on 10 November 1944 after a pilot error on board. *Kattegat* was now in dry dock for repairs. She had been scuttled by the Germans in April 1940 and was raised by the Norwegians and renamed *Bodø*. After their capitulation that summer the tanker reverted to German control under the original name *Kattegat*. Wenger led the force in and the aircraft seemed to take the defences by surprise at first, but not for long – they had flown into the concentrated flak defences of HKAA II/981(Heeres Küstenartillerie Abteilung) commanded by Major Müller, and MKB 7/504 (Marine-Artillerie-Batterie). The *Kattegat* bore the brunt of the initial attack, which then followed on to the other merchantmen. The strike wing scored over 30 hits on the *Kattegat* in dry dock, which was subsequently seen to explode by a Norwegian crew. Despite this it was later repaired and re-entered service as *Sandar* under the Norwegian flag. The Germans had been using the vessel to house ammunition.

In the Famnaes shipyard for repairs was the merchantman *Concordia* of 5,154 tons into which Wing Commander Christopher Foxley-Norris let fly a salvo of rockets from 'A' 143. His wingman tackled *William Blumer* of 3,604 tons. The German-controlled *Hektor*, 5,742 tons, which was moored in the open fjord together with the *Belpamela* of 3,165 tons, (the latter capable of carrying steam locomotives), was hit by three Mosquitoes from 235 Squadron and Flying Officer Ray Harrington recorded four dry and four wet hits. The *Espana* of 7,465 tons was severely damaged near Famnaes shipyard, with two others, *Maurite*, 1,569 tons and *Irania*, 2,249 tons. It was now early evening and the Mosquitoes had set ablaze four vessels out of the nine anchored in this fjord, using 262 rockets. After the attack the formation was guided out by Mosquito 'O' 333 which came under spasmodic ground fire at Nøtterøy. Golightly with his navigator Flying Officer Frank Hawthorne made a wheels up landing at base at 21.50 hours. Flight Lieutenant John Milsom's aircraft, 'P' 248, also received damage while another crew from 248 Squadron made for neutral ground, landing safely. A pilot from 143 Squadron recalls events from his diary:

'Easter Monday 1945! It was decided to repeat the type of operation which had been so singularly successful at Porsgrunn on the previous Friday. A weather recce aircraft was sent up the Skagerrak and Sandefjord was chosen as the target. At about 11.00 hours everything was being laid on, by 11.30 we were being briefed by Wing Commander 'Jacko' Jackson-Smith, and again midday saw us starting up. I lay in the grass beside Mosquito 'O' 143 – 'O' Orange. Whenever I flew as fighter escort I always took this aircraft. The armourer was asking me if I had enjoyed evensong at the camp chapel on the previous Easter Sunday evening. The sun was glistening on the silver surface of the 100-gallon drop-tanks; the sky was only broken by a few odd bits of cumulus. Eventually the first people began to taxi out, I jumped in and started up. Together with my No. 2 we joined the last few aircraft so we could conserve fuel. Flight Lieutenant Bert Graham, with his navigator Malkin, was my No. 2. We quickly took up position on the starboard rear of the formation, as always I had a last look at Banff as we passed over on the 'setting course run' towards the east. As we went over the moorlands Peterhead loomed up, in the brilliant sunshine. The Mustangs looked like a swarm of bees. They joined us and on we flew with the midday sun on our right. As on Friday we entered our lane up the Skagerrak, one leader being Flight Lieutenant Bob Golightly, the other Captain Håkon Wenger who took the formation in towards the coast. Again we made an excellent crossing through the flak-free lane. Then we cut across country to Sandefjord. In the intelligence library, Lieutenant Plyhn, a Norwegian friend of mine, had told me just whereabouts his house lay in Sandefjord. The leading squadron 248 went in using machine guns, cannon and rockets to damp the flak and was closely followed by 143. I flew above and out to the right of them, and a little behind. Bert Graham was 200 yards line astern of me. As we approached the target I became painfully aware that the third and last wave of aircraft, 235 Squadron, were three miles behind the rest. I circled over the target trying to miss the light flak. Then I came right back to see 235, being led by Squadron Leader John Barry, go through successfully. I flew about 1,000 yards out from them on their right approaching a little ahead of their leading three. Coming into the target for the second time one vessel had a gun firing so I gave him a burst, and broke away only to see a shore-based position pumping stuff over the two vessels. This crossfire needed damping down so I took the job of squirting these flak gunners and their multiple 40mms. They immediately stopped.'

As the force turned for base a thick mushroom of black smoke was visible 40 miles away. A navigator with 235 Squadron, Geof Hinde recalls:

'Coming up to the target the whole formation climbed to make the attack, feeling very naked after hugging the sea for so long. There was a curtain of flak exploding at 500 feet at the entrance; it was awe-inspiring to look at but then we were suddenly diving steeply. My driver, Pilot Officer Pete Pennie DFC, opened up with cannon and machine gun until the strikes were seen on the bridge and superstructure, at which time the rockets left the rails dipping towards the waterline. An aircraft on our left erupted in flames after a hit on the engine. Pennie then made a violent breakaway from the target and sped out to sea. We had recorded a strike on the vessel in the floating dock. Six dots then appeared between us and the open sea which looked like Bf190s but I then identified them as Mustangs to our relief.'

On 3 April, 404 RCAF Squadron's remaining aircrew arrived on the station and began converting to fly the long-range Mosquitoes. Those officers not flying were entertained by Nina Countess of Seafield, who more or less ran her neighbouring castle at Cullen as an extension to the officers' mess.

The Swedish Government made an official complaint to the Air Ministry, London because one of the Banff wing's Norwegian aircraft, 'G' 333, had fired on a Swedish trawler at 06.00 hours. Cannon shell cases found on the ground afterwards were marked 'R.H. 1943' which was a common marking on British ammunition. Commander-in-Chief Sholto Douglas offered an apology. On 4 April the same aircraft was involved in another incident whilst on daily reconnaissance. Making landfall south of Utvaer Light it swept along the coastline towards the Skagerrak, then off Sweden. Lieutenant Heine Eriksen, the pilot, sighted a target of 12 freight wagons and engines near Stomstad, Sweden. Eriksen came in with cannon and machine guns giving it a short burst, as the crew believed that they were still in enemy airspace over Norway. They resumed their search and there was more to report at 08.25 hours. After encountering light flak from shore positions, they sighted two merchantmen of 2,000 tons off the west side of Sandefjord, opposite Famnaes shipyard. The aftermath of the attack by the wing on 2 April became apparent, the tanker in the floating dock was completely burnt out, while the dock appeared to be heavily damaged and a vessel was also on its side with its paint blackened. After almost an hour and a half of probing Eriksen swung around over the western inlet among the skerries known as Havnholmen, and set course for base. Flight Lieutenant Milson in 'R' 248 flew an independent search between Vigrested and Varhaug.

While on a training flight two Norwegian aircraft sighted and attacked two U-boats just miles off the Scottish coast. Sergeant Thuen went down on the leading boat firing cannon and scoring hits. The second received cannon fire from 'Q' 333, piloted by Second Lieutenant Ure. Both were claimed as slightly damaged. In fact there was a U-boat in the area. Kapitän Ralf Jürs, commanding U-788 was operating off the Moray Firth, although concentrating on the Peterhead area.

On Monday 5 April, the Norwegians were briefed to hunt for vessels and U-boats in the Skagerrak and Sognefjord area and from Orestad to the Naze. A single aircraft from 248 squadron, 'R' 248, was also airborne and the pilot, Fight Lieutenant John Milsom, strafed a freight train with ten wagons as it was coming into a station, the locomotive blew up sending a shower of debris into the air which embedded itself into the plywood as the Mosquito flew through it, damaging the starboard mainplane. Milsom coaxed the aeroplane across the North Sea landing safely. Before the next sortie took place a lecture on flak was given in the morning by a major attached to Bomber Command for all crew. Briefed at 13.00 for a trip to the Kattegat this would be a round trip of over 1,000 miles. Wing Commander Junior Simmonds DFC led a force out at 14.00 hours consisting of 39 aircraft, with 12 Mustangs drawn from Peterhead arriving overhead at 14.38 hours. Crossing the Danish coast at 16.26 hours, the force turned south at zero feet led by Major Håkon Wenger in 'E' 333. As the Mosquitoes sped past they caught glimpses of Danes waving madly; horses galloped away, ploughmen in one field waved enthusiastically and a solitary German soldier dived for cover into a nearby ditch. As the final section passed over he was seen dusting himself off. The strike leader turned south, altering course ten miles from the Isle of Anholt on Wenger's command, and turning towards the Kattegat. The leading section sighted a convoy of six vessels at 16.35 hours travelling at 10 knots in position 5634N/1150E south-east of the Isle of Anholt. 'N' 333's pilot called up Simmonds on VHF: 'Leader do not attack smaller convoy under size', but Wenger's voice was too distorted to be understood. The force climbed to 3,000 feet, passing over the targeted first convoy and turning to port, while the Mustangs rose to 5,000 feet to give top cover. Sweden was in sight. Instructions were given accordingly. All the Mosquitoes dived across the vessels with rockets and cannon firing down to 400 metres. Light flak and small arms fire peppered the sky. During the attack 'U' 235, flown by Pilot Officer Laurence Arthur and Francis Richardson, pressed home their run as low as they could but hit the mast of a trawler and dived straight into the sea, breaking up 100 yards from the vessel, with no trace afterwards of survivors. At debriefing it was mentioned that the perspex screens on the Mosquitoes were heavily salted and this may have been the cause for Arthur's misjudgement. One report reads: 'Upon reaching the target the snag was the heavy coating of salt on the screen all around, impairing our aiming.' Numerous hits were observed on the targets leaving six burning furiously and the *Helmi Söhle*, a flakship of 453 tons, and the fishing vessel *Stutthof* of 299 tons sunk.

Major Wenger, who had taken command of 333 Squadron on 23 March, became a casualty during the engagement having strafed a multiple 40mm position with cannon. The return fire had seriously damaged his port wing and propeller. Wenger radioed Junior Simmonds that he was making for Sweden but having flown into the Swedish sector RF724 was pounced upon by Swedish fighters and forced to land at Thorslanda airport near Gøtenburg. His navigator Hanssen destroyed all the documents onboard while Wenger made a belly-landing. On the way back across the Danish coast spasmodic firing was encountered. A 235 Squadron Mosquito took evasive action while avoiding flak from a moored vessel in the harbour at Noykobing Mors, Western Jutland; as it dropped into the slipstream of the lead aircraft, one of the propellers became deformed. The crews' attempts to regain control were unsuccessful as they were so close to the ground. Flying Officer Ray Harrington and Flight Sergeant Bert Winwood decided they stood a better chance of crash landing in Denmark as they were unlikely to reach Scotland. At 17.50 hours over Jutland with glycol streaming from it, 'F' 235 belly-landed in a field.

Flight Lieutenant Alfie Lloyd witnessed it:

'Squadron Leader Barry and myself were flying level at 50 feet off the deck, with 'F' 235. Suddenly they went in, crashing at a rate of knots. We swung round and swept over the aircraft, one crew member was getting out through the hatch, then we were gone.'

Flight Lieutenant 'Wally' Webster observed 'F' 235 belly-land in a field on his starboard side; watching Harrington's misfortune Webster nearly hit a windmill.

143 Squadron was being led by Squadron Leader Tommy Deck back across Denmark when one of its Mosquitoes, 'Z' 143, strafed a German barracks. The Mustangs were also crossing the Danish coast at zero feet when they were caught by small arms fire. Veteran pilot Flight Lieutenant Jimmy Butler leading White Section was seen to pull up. His aircraft, KM137, burst into flames leaving a smoke trail and went straight into the sea 100 yards off the coast at 17.53 hours. It is presumed Butler was killed; his loss was a real blow to the Peterhead-based squadrons. Suddenly glycol started leaking out of one of the Merlin engines. 'W' 248 pilot Flight Lieutenant Jack Cooper requested assistance, then feathered the engine. Flying Officer Norman Earnshaw in 'S' 248 passed the VHF distress message to the escorting Warwick which helped Cooper back, landing at 19.49 hours. A 235 Squadron Mosquito had its starboard door and windscreen raked with small arms fire. Once everyone had got back, they had a meal and a few drinks in the messes, then just after midnight supper with a few WAAFs. The remaining few got to bed at 02.00 hours.

Shortly after this operation intelligence proved that the vessels set on fire by the Banff wing had been carrying German soldiers, 200 bodies were recovered by Swedish vessels with an estimated 900 troops lost who had been bound for Germany. Major Håkon Wenger and his navigator Sergeant Hagbarth Hein Hanssen soon returned to Scotland from being interned in Sweden, and rejoined 333 Squadron.

Days later Squadron Leader Barry from 235 Squadron set out on a reconnaissance trip to Sognefjord, searching for U-boats. The Met Officer had forecast bad weather on their return and they were detailed to land at Sumburgh in the Shetlands. Barry arrived north of the target area at Solund, then carried on to Askvoll, sighting a wreck from a previous strike. All the anchorages proved negative at the end of their patrol area, and they set course for Sumburgh at 220 knots. The next major action would be in four days time. Squadron Leader Clayton-Graham recollected: 'So few vessels remained available to the Germans that we were able to memorise their names, a few had been damaged by us and Dallachy and were repaired and put back into service only to be struck again.'

CHAPTER 14

WHAT HAPPENED TO 'F' FOR FREDDIE?

When RS619 'F' 235 had crash-landed in a flapless landing at about 140mph at Tandrup Mark, the crew left the aircraft through the top hatch to find both propellers behind them up a gentle rise and glycol still dripping from the port nacelle. A few Danish farm workers leaning on pitchforks looked on impassively and showed no particular enthusiasm when Harrington pointed to his wings and said 'Jar har RAF' in Norwegian, read off a dog-eared language card from his battledress pocket. Although not specifically under any known orders to do so, the crew decided to set fire to RS619 and destroyed any operational evidence in true Biggles style which was much appreciated by the Danes. Attempts were made to fire the machine which refused to burn despite hay under the wings and a Very cartridge fired into an open engine nacelle. Attempts to drive holes into the underside of the fuselage to form a 'brazier' merely resulted in the fire axe bouncing back vigorously off the laminated timber! Eventually a parachute was pulled in the cockpit and set on fire with the Very pistol.

Congratulating themselves on the absence of soldiers, Ray Harrington and Bert Winwood started towards two friendly looking people walking down the field towards them. Suddenly the countryside in front of the Mosquito was raked with machine-gun and cannon fire as the fire found the ammunition containers. The two Danes were a farmer and his wife (Folmer and Anna Lutzhoft) who spoke good English. They walked back up the hill with them and the crew asked them if they might 'borrow' some old clothes and pose as farm workers. The suggestion was politely turned down due to the ever present risk of reprisals since the meeting would undoubtedly have been observed by some who did not necessarily share their antipathy of the occupying Germans. Harrington and Winwood hastily conceived a plan to pinch a boat and work their way eastwards along the Limfjord to the Kattegat and thence to Sweden.

However, the plan began to seem less of a 'doddle' and they were both thankful to accept Anna Lutzhoft's offer of a haystack overlooking a small waterway to the north, the loan of a pre-war Shell motoring map and some food brought out to them from the farmhouse in the late evening. Hidden in their somewhat itchy haystack both peered out across the waterway and marvelled at the large group of evening strollers, apparently looking straight at them – could they really see them in their smelly bower? Inching around the back of the stack they saw a plume of black oily smoke rising hundreds of feet into the still, cool evening air. RS619 said goodbye and every German for miles around appreciated the gesture! Eventually the evening strollers drifted off in the gathering dusk and they shivered in the keen spring air and felt lonely, wondering above all how their families would receive the inevitable Air Ministry telegram saying Harrington and Winwood were 'missing on operations' over enemy territory. Both resolved to get out of the area as soon as possible.

Unbeknown to them they were becoming the subjects of interest of various sorts of people, not least the German garrison at Snedsted, a mere six miles away to the north-east, whose telephone conversations were being monitored by the local headmistress, and also two members of the local resistance who knew of their landing at Tandrup farm and were making plans to get the crew away from the area and into safe hands.

At 21.15 inside the haystack both heard footsteps outside approaching and whispering in English. Emerging quietly they found a young man in a light raincoat who introduced himself as Richardt Dam-Jenson and with him was Ehrnfred Østergaard, both members of the local Resistance. Harrington and Winwood were overjoyed to make their acquaintance. They led them some five miles along field tracks, ditches and culverts and under bridges to a churchyard at Bedsted. Here they hid behind the stone-wall of the graveyard until midnight when they returned with a taxi fuelled by gas and some civilian clothes which both donned over their uniforms. Peter Neilsen the taxi's driver knew the moves of the local German commander well as the taxi was often used by the major. They cowered in the dark recesses of the back of the vehicle and although Peter knew perfectly well the major was not in, asked at the headquarters if he was wanted that night. The guards at the road control, having seen the taxi stop at the headquarters, waved them on with a friendly 'Alles gut' and Peter made for Skjoldborg about 12 miles away via minor roads, farm tracks and even someone's kitchen garden in order to avoid any further contact with guard posts on main roads.

At Skjoldborg they met Richardt's family who ran a local store and Peter's wife gave them a good hot meal. Now at 2.30 hours both were pretty well exhausted having been walking in sloppy flying boots over all sorts of ground. At 4.00 hours they were led to the vicarage and graciously received at virtually no notice by the Pastor, Dahl Hansen and his wife, Annemarie, who was nursing a young child, and were given the most comfortable bed in the world! Next morning the maid had to be consoled in finding two tramps soundly asleep in her immaculate room and the Pastor had to explain them away without creating suspicion. Later that day, after having eaten six fried eggs each, they where conducted to accommodation more appropriate to scruffiness – the hayloft above a piggery. This haven was short-lived due to the attempted Resistance sabotage of a troop train passing on a nearby line which had not gone to plan. Their host, Henry Christensen, had to divert the troops leaving the train before he was able to get help from the local Resistance leader who insisted upon their taking their uniforms off and getting into a taxi before the farm was searched. Henry concealed the uniforms effectively in the hayloft. Both went by taxi to Thisted, a major garrison town heavily populated by German troops who manned the coastal defences which ringed the country. They were taken to the local outfitters and given new suits of clothes by the proprietor, a Resistance leader, and supplied with identification cards made with pictures resembling them cut from a family album.

Despite their manoeuvring, they were only 15 miles from the crash site and were glad to pass over the long bridge over Vilsund to Nyøbing, Mors. As they crossed the bridge they tried to look unconcerned as the guards examined the fake identification cards. (Harrington and Winwood learnt after the war that these guards were Russians serving in the Wehrmacht.) Put up in the Markvardsens Hotel, exclusively used by the Resistance (now a commercial building) the crew met local officers including the military leader Colonel Ejby Nielsen who ordered new photographs to be taken so they could be issued with new identification cards. Harrington and Winwood were now able to wander about the town and harbour and saw German flak ships with stencils of twin-engine aircraft on some of their superstructures and funnels, while others were cleaning their weapons. They also saw a cellar full of weapons dropped by the Royal Air Force which were stored in prime condition ready for immediate use. On or about the sixth day – 11 April – they boarded a ferry to pick up the railway to Åalborg from Skive accompanied by another Resistance escort. The train was fairly full with civilians and some soldiers were travelling in their carriage. Kept apart, standing in the central passage and trying not to catch anyone's eye, Bert Winwood had a nasty moment when he offered a woman a vacant seat and she refused to sit down! At Åalborg the station was very busy – reminding them of Waterloo – with military and naval personnel hurrying to catch trains. Both were glad to reach the forecourt to follow the escort who walked off rapidly down a road opposite. He suddenly stopped to strike a match which didn't seem to light, turned on his heel and went quickly in the opposite direction. A passing cyclist quickly parked his bike and fell in step with them, announcing himself as a friend. At the mid town office of lawyer Svend Andersen and the escort Knud Neilsen (alias Jakob) they wished them both well and quietly left. Svend Andersen took them to his flat in the north-west suburbs where he lived with his wife and daughter, aged about 12 – a delightful family. The rear balcony of the flat overlooked the Luftwaffe base north-west of Åalborg and the front window overlooked the Gestapo Headquarters across the road. Svend suggested they keep a low profile. Harrington and Winwood were guests for about seven to eight days before they had to hare off with ready packed bags, when Svend came rushing in saying a Resistance man had been picked up in town carrying arms in a cart and constituted a security risk if he were made to talk by the Gestapo.

They hung around in the flat for about an hour before they were called and taken to a Resistance man's flat where they were put up for two days, They were then taken to a summerhouse somewhere on the Limfjorden and here they met up with leaders from northern Åalborg who drove them to Strandby, about eight miles north of Frederikshavn and 25 miles south of Skagen at the northern tip of Denmark. Here they stayed with a local schoolmaster and his wife. The Aaen family comprised Granddad, Grandma, Herluf and Asta and 11 offspring. They were all engaged in fishing except Herluf who was also busy organising passage for refugees to Sweden. He took orders from a certain Carl Pedersen, a provisions store owner in Åalborg who was responsible for export arrangements (of escapees and others). The airmen assembled every night for about eight nights running with seven others (two of whom were German soldiers who helped the Resistance) before creeping down to the quayside one very dark night in the early hours of 24 April. Here they boarded the fishing vessel FN264 *Maagen*, skippered by Andreas Larsen of Strandby who stowed them behind sliding panels in the athwart ship's lockers. They moved off at 3.00 hours and at dawn both were allowed on deck to find a calm sea in mid Kattegat and a larger boat alongside. Her name was the *Merkur*, flagship of the Danish Help Service operating out of Gøtenborg. They were put ashore around midday.

Unlike RAF and USAAF crews who had force-landed and were interned, Ray Harrington and Bert Winwood were treated as refugees from Europe by the Swedes and after being medically examined by the Swedish Immigration Authority's doctor they were driven to the British Consulate, debriefed and sent on to Stockholm by train, arriving on 28 April. Reporting to the British Embassy they were given money to buy clothes and waited for transport back to the UK. On the night of 1 May they assembled with other RAF and civilian personnel at Brömma Aerodrome where Junkers 52 of Deutsche Lufthansa were parked on the apron next to BOAC aircraft! Boarding a Dakota of the Swedish AB Aerotransport, which ran a service between Brömma and Leuchars, Scotland, both were landed in the early hours of 2 May. Fortunately the next of kin had received letters from the Air Ministry on 31 April saying they were alive and in the hands of the Resistance.

The remains of 'F for Freddie' were removed from the crash site within 48 hours by the Germans.

CHAPTER 15

U-BOATS RUN THE GAUNTLET

While waters were being heavily mined by both Coastal and Bomber Command, during the first three months of 1945 RAF aircraft had flown 720 'Gardening' (minelaying) sorties. Their 3,240 mines had sunk nearly 70 vessels, for 137,764 tons, and damaged a further 32 for 71,224 tons, which necessitated constant minesweeping by the German flotillas to keep the inner lanes free. However, Allied naval specialists had predicted that a very tough fight versus the new U-boat lay ahead. The Admiralty forecast extremely serious Allied merchant shipping losses after the British Admiral Max Horton made a proclamation to the effect that he considered Coastal Command and Allied naval forces were currently worse of as regards the means of pinpointing and annihilating U-boats, than they had been since the beginning of the Second World War. This declaration in fact, was misleading and gave a false impression, causing two senior staff officers to write in protest to the First Sea Lord Andrew Cunningham.

The true position was that during the spring of 1945, the U-boat flotillas were forced to forsake their eastern Baltic bases and evacuate to the western Baltic and Norway areas because of the Russian advance. The RAF could easily reach them there. Intelligence reported more than 70 U-boats moving towards the Kattegat on their way to Norwegian bases. The passage to Norway had been impossible during the first three months of 1945, due to the constant threat from the air and the mines, which resulted in the U-boats travelling on the surface. The U-boats plying through the Skagerrak and Kattegat now lay open to the full force of the Banff wing's long-range, rocket-projectile Mosquitoes which were about to mount strikes in accordance with a directive given by Prime Minister Winston Churchill and President Roosevelt at their meeting on Malta between 30 January and 2 February 1945: 'Intensification of the RAF air campaign against U-boats in Norway and German surface shipping supplying those bases.'

On 9 April, Group Captain Max Aitken and Wing Commander Jack Davenport (Aitken having recently consulted with the Commander-in-Chief Sholto Douglas about a large anti-U-boat operation), put the plan together. A Met flight from Banff, flying over the Skagerrak area at 12.00 hours, reported back 10/10ths cloud down to sea level. Flight Lieutenant Royce Turner flew over the top of the cloud base; it remained the same. Moving to another area the visibility was five to seven miles of varying haze. The Mosquitoes lined up along the taxiways, then turned and rose off the ground, staggering into the air with rockets and 100-gallon drop-tanks at 14.30 hours in the afternoon. With his navigator Flight Lieutenant Matt Southgate DFC in 'V' 248, Squadron Leader Alec Gunnis DFC of 248 Squadron was leading 31 Mosquitoes with two 333 outriders and the RAF Film Unit Mosquito DZ592, all formed up over Banff in tight formation and set course over the countryside at 14.50 hours. At 15.00 hours they picked up the Mustang escort over Peterhead, although part of the escort failed to reach the assembly point owing to the haze. Heading out over Peterhead Bay they saw fishing boats tied up, a few men waved as they sped away, bound for the Skagerrak. The formation crawled its way through the sea fog with visibility under 200 yards. At 15.54 hours 'C' 235 seemed to be in trouble, and together with 'A' 235 as escort in position 57.34N-

04.20E, they set course for base. A message was heard from 'C' 235 pilot Flight Lieutenant Phil Davenport saying 'I am OK' at 16.01 hours. Flying Officer Johnny Rendell in 'A' 235 turned on a reciprocal course to rejoin the main force. Flying Officer Norman Earnshaw and his navigator Flight Lieutenant H Jamieson called up Gunnis saying one of the engines was overheating, they headed back landing at 16.32. 'T' 248 also experienced problems and detached itself from the formation and made for home.

By 16.55 hours the sea fog had cleared, and they flew into clear blue skies. The Norwegian outrider left the formation sighting three fishing boats. The formation turned south into the Kattegat searching for potential targets. Seconds later at 17.22 hours the strike leader, flying on a course of 180° at 2,500 feet sighted two wakes at 200 yards apart on the starboard side and turned the formation at 17.23 to approach them out of the sun. At 17.25 hours Gunnis ordered 12 Mosquitoes from 143 Squadron to dive on the vessels. Squadron Leader David Pritchard called 'They're U-boats!' Pritchard then ordered one section to attack the leading target and the second to attack the rear target. By this time Gunnis and 248 had overflown the target being the leading squadron, but the strike leader ordered the nine aircraft of 235 which were further behind, to follow 143 into the attack. On this day two U-boats were moving northwards up the Kattegat, close to the Swedish coast both having sailed from Kiel on 6 April; they were making about 15 knots heading for Horten in Oslo fjord. In the lead was U-804, a type IX U-boat from 33 Flotilla in position 57.58N/11.15E commanded by Oberleutnant Herbert Meyer. She was fitted with a schnorkel and had completed two tours. One was on 12 June 1944, when the boat had come under fire north-west of Bergen from Lieutenant Jacobsen of 333 Squadron. U-804 later sank the *Fiske*, a destroyer escort on 19 July 1944. Behind her was U-1065, a type VII commanded by Oberleutnant Johannes Panitz which was on her initial cruise in position 57.48N/11.26E just north-west of Gøtenborg.

143 Squadron went down firing cannon, machine guns and over 70 rockets at the two U-boats, which disappeared under spray and smoke. 235 Squadron followed up with the same treatment. 4,170 rounds of tracer ammunition were fired on the leading U-804 and strikes were observed on the conning tower and the whole length of the hull – 99 hits observed altogether. Crews fired their rockets at ranges of 800 to 200 yards with many wet and dry hits. U-804 put up plenty of flak, and was seen suddenly to submerge then resurface for ten seconds, her bows rising slightly at a 10° angle. Gunnis had taken 248 Squadron around the two targets and seven Mosquitoes detached themselves and attacked U-1065, which was awash aft of the conning tower and angled at 15°. Immediately after the 248 Squadron aircraft struck at 17.30 hours, large explosion debris was flung into the air slightly damaging four aircraft. Seconds later there was a flash and a sheet of flame after which U-804 sank stern first. As U804 exploded the Mosquito from the RAF Film Unit caught the full force of the blast, DZ592 was thrown into the air by the explosion and turned over on its back and spun into the sea from 1,000 feet. No survivors were seen. Flight Lieutenant William Jones and his navigator/cameraman Flying Officer Allan Newell had both perished.* Eleven other members of the RAF Film Unit lost their lives on operations during the war. Squadron Leader Bill Clayton-Graham DFC recalled the tragic loss of DZ592 when interviewed:

---

*At the end of the Second World War, Flying Officer Allan Newell's widow Iris Newell, of Notting Hill, London, showed the Jones family around Pinewood studios in Buckinghamshire, where the RAF Film Unit was stationed, meeting Anthony Squire (son of Sir John Squire, the poet) a wartime pilot who had served with Coastal Command flying Sunderland flying-boats. Squire was making and directing a documentary entitled *Ship-Busters* which had been commissioned by Air Chief Marshal Sir Sholto Douglas because, as he said: 'Not enough is known by the public or members of parliament of the work carried out by the anti-shipping strike squadrons', using the reels of camera footage shot by the aircrews including those of Jones and Newell.

'Squadron Leader Alec Gunnis, an excellent flight commander with our sister, unit, 248 Squadron, led the wing. An RAF Film Unit Mosquito, which was attached to Banff, came with us. I was coming round for my second attack, my navigator, Ginger, and myself saw the Mosquito going in extremely low. As it passed U-804 the boat exploded and it and the aircraft disappeared completely. Our aircraft had been hit by pieces of the boat during our first attack.'

The second U-boat U-1065 was attacked at heights between 500 and 200 feet, eight dry hits were observed just aft of the conning tower, and two wet hits just below the conning tower, although many results were unobserved because of smoke and spray. 2,250 rounds of tracer were used on U-1065 with 68 hits being seen in total. After the first section of 143 Squadron struck, an explosion was observed, the flying debris causing some damage to aircraft. Panitz turned U-1065 to starboard onto a course of 090°, leaving a large oil slick and after the attack by the remainder of 143 and 235 Squadrons U-1065 turned onto its side and disappeared stern first. The submarine left a large patch of oily brilliant greens and reds with debris and bodies as well as yellow dinghies on the surface. Some aircrew reported survivors in the water, waving. Unfortunately the strike leader Gunnis was unable to attack because a drop-tank failed to release and he just orbited the area.

The defenders put up sufficient flak to cause a further three to make for Brighton (code word for Sweden). At 17.40 hours 'K' 248, with one engine smoking and 'B' 248 with one engine feathered, informed Gunnis they were going to neutral territory together with one aircraft from 235 Squadron. There were no survivors from either boat. Fifty-six men lost their lives in U-804, one of whom was Kapitän Leutnant Ruprecht Fischer, commander of U-244, travelling as a passenger. Forty-five died in U-1065. At approximately 17.34 hours the remainder headed back to Banff, touching down between 19.50 and 20.00 hours. An Australian Flying Officer H Parkinson and his navigator Flying Officer K Jackson inspected their charge, Mosquito 'H' 235, at one of the dispersal hard standings quite near the messes only to find 14 large holes in the fuselage and wings, some of which a man could have squeezed through! Both said a quick prayer thanking Geoffrey de Havilland for building such a wonderful aircraft. Squadron Leader Gunnis received a bar to his DFC, while Flight Lieutenant Angus McIntosh received the DFC in May for participating in this operation. McIntosh belly-landed his Mosquito, he and his navigator Thorogood hung on as the Mosquito careered towards the flying control tower. The duty control officer was standing on the balcony when he saw the crippled aircraft slewing towards his insecure position, so he chose to jump clear. The 248 Squadron Mosquito passed the tower, but the young officer broke his leg.

Of the three aircraft which had turned for Sweden after the action against the two U-boats, Flight Lieutenants MacIntyre and Flight Sergeant Smith in 'K' 248, and Flying Officer Mogridge and McQuarrie in 'B' 248 landed unhurt at Satenas aerodrome. The third aircraft 'Z' RS598 was caught in the flying debris damaging both engines. Flying Officer C Parkinson and his navigator Flying Officer 'Jimmie' Halley nursed their Mosquito along carefully monitoring the engine temperatures. Speed and altitude were dropping rapidly, Parkinson was giving it as much trim as possible. Parkinson had no option but to go 'straight in', attempting a wheels-up landing, as he would be unable to make another attempt to go around. They touched down in Sweden with a jolt, their harnesses restraining them in their seats. Suddenly, the remaining engine failed, causing the Mosquito to swing quite violently towards the milling propeller and sending the aircraft careering across the perimeter track outside the main runway. The nose section and both main undercarriage members were knocked off on hitting obstructions. A barbed wire fence together with razor wire was also picked up along the way and the tail unit was ripped off.

Inside the cramped cockpit Parkinson and Halley had had a bruising ride across the field. Undoing their harnesses, both quickly scrambled clear through the emergency hatch. The fuselage fuel tanks had ruptured but fortunately there was no fire. Not realising this, both crewmen ran across the field with an assortment of broken legs and ankles! Shortly afterwards the Swedes set the Mosquito alight, still with its gun camera in place.

Mosquito 'Z' RS598 was not on the Banff strength but belonged to the station flight at Sumburgh, and was serviced at Banff by 8248 Service Echelon. It was used by Sumburgh as a hack between there and Wick. The high winds en route made the Ansons of 1693 Flight unsuitable. For this maximum effort sweep 8248 SE had quickly fitted rocket rails onto 'VV-Z' RS598 and 235 Squadron borrowed it for this operation. Station headquarters at Banff received notice from the Air Ministry after this operation that all crewmembers were safe after landing in Sweden. An immediate message was sent from 18 Group to the Air Ministry reading:

'Air Ministry 10 April 1945. Understand three Mosquitoes landed Sweden (Brighton) yesterday, crew believed to be: Flying Officer Parkinson, Flying Officer Halley, Flying Officer Mogridge, Flying Officer McQuarrie, Flight Lieutenant Shaville, Flight Lieutenant McIntyre. Request you endeavour to extradite them as soon as possible owing to shortage of operational crews. From 18 Group Coastal Command.'

Flying Officer Jimmie Halley recovered from his wounds but walked with a stick for the remainder of his life after this incident. While these attacks were taking place, Flying Officer Rendell of 235 Squadron was searching for the force having turned back to help a fellow squadron member who had reported engine trouble 90 minutes earlier. After Davenport had told Rendell that he could make it back Rendell tried to rejoin the wing. At the same time as the attack on the two U-boats, he came across a third 20 miles to the south-east. This was U-843, a type IXC/40 commanded by Leutnant Oskar Herwartz; she was a Deschimag, a Bremen-built boat, and was commissioned on 24 March 1943.

On 19 February 1944 U-843 set out for the Indian Ocean to take part in the operations of the 'Monsoon-Gruppe', a detachment of German U-boats operating temporarily out of Japanese occupied harbours. On the way U-843 stopped a Portuguese and a Spanish steamer, the latter was carrying an Englishman who was taken on board U-843 as a prisoner, and then transferred onto U-178 bound for France. On her second war cruise in the Indian Ocean a US Navy Liberator, B-8 flown by Lieutenant Krug Junior, had attacked her on 10 April 1944. The crew could not repair all the damage themselves and the U-boat headed for Batavia where U-843 docked on 11 June 1944.

The U-boat came home from the Indian Ocean leaving from Djakarta, Indonesia on 10 December 1944. In the Indian Ocean at approximately 500 miles south of the Cocosis Islands, the U-boat was refuelled by U-181. Herwartz and his crew rounded the Cape of Good Hope unharmed. U-843 took the Iceland passage and stopped over in Bergen on 2 April 1945. There was a sick member of crew on board, the surgeon on U-843 had operated on him during their passage to Norway and he was transported by ambulance to a hospital near Kaapstad. From Bergen U-843 sailed to Stavanger entering on 5 April and then to Kristiansand. On 8 April she left Kristiansand and dived.

Submerged she proceeded to Skagen. There the U-boat surfaced and sailed southward along the mine-free lane. At 17.22 hours U-843 was discovered by Mosquito 'A' 235 at 57.58N and 11.26E, outside Lasö awaiting a small convoy. The U-boat opened fire as 'A' 235 came out of the sun at 17.23 hours attacking with 25lb rockets, cannon and machine-gun fire, scoring two possible underwater hits with its eight rockets. Herwartz took evasive action but did not submerge. Rendell swung 'A' 235 around for a second attack opening up with cannon and machine guns from the opposite side, and met with far less gunfire; aiming for the conning tower and hull it attacked for a third time.Thick grey smoke and steam began to pour from the hull. It was still smoking on the surface when Rawlins flew off at 17.25 hours. On board the U-boat Herwartz and his men thought they could save her but the boat suddenly sank off Skagen, Denmark. Thirteen crew out of a compliment of 58 saved themselves by jumping into the water. A nearby German vessel took on board Franz Benter, Mathias Eriches, Alfons Haedke, Johann Herschbach, Oskar Herwartz, Theodor Kamp, Jakob Loser, Wilhelm Nurk, Alfred Rogge, Heinz Simon, Werner Sturznickel, Friedrich Wilhelm and Georg Wosnitza. By means of signals they tried to contact the trapped crew as U-843 was lying at a depth of 40 metres, but they got no reply. The vessel put the submariners ashore at Kiel and the commander of U-483 tried to have her lifted but in those dying days of the war the Kriegsmarine objected. In the three U-boats a total of 144 German submariners had died.* At the time Rendell could not prove he had sunk U-843 and it was not until the HMSO publication entitled *Strike Wings* by Roy Conyers Nesbit was published that he found out that he had done so. The former navigator of 'A' 235, Rawlins wrote in his logbook: 'Found and attacked U-boat in N. Kattegat – after end of war U-843 reported as sunk.'

U-boat Captain Oskar Herwartz, commanding U-843, recalls sailing through the Kattegat in April 1945:

'The Norwegian passage was considered extremely dangerous (we had received orders about the threat of these Mosquitoes in October 1944) and during daylight hours the RAF Mosquitoes kept a close look-out on those waters, knowing every boat leaving Germany passed that way. Some of our U-boats were lost on that run because we could not dive under air assault owing to the whole area being sown with minefields. At this date we knew they used new rockets, whose full blast we would no doubt get since they could be used effectively against a U-boat in the act of diving. These rockets once fired left a hole three inches across and no submarine could stand up to that. They were more accurate than an ordinary bomb.'

Maintenance and repairs were being carried out at dispersals around the aerodrome on aircraft which had participated in the U-boat attack in the morning. An engine fitter found a piece of metal six inches long, coming from the U-boat, lodged in one of the engine nacelles of Flight Lieutenant Harry Parkinson's Mosquito. On 10 April

---

*In 1957, after U-843 was lifted from the bottom by two vessels of Bugsier in Hamburg on the order of a Norwegian merchant, the U-boat was then brought to Sweden. On inspection it appears that she was sunk owing to a single rocket entering just below the waterline in the aft, it remained unobserved after the attack because at the time nobody was there. Many cannon shells pierced the conning tower. In Sweden she was searched and some items displayed in Hönö Fishing Museum. After 12 years when Herr Oskar Herwartz entered U-843, the remains of the crew were still inside; they were identified as far as possible and officially laid to rest in Gøtenborg with full military honours. U-843 was then scrapped. Among the findings were the board journals, kegs of beer, and a notebook that once belonged to a crewmember. Photographs taken by a German war photographer Leutnant Karl-Emil Weiss travelling back with U-843 from Batavia, Singapore to Germany, were found in excellent condition.

Squadron Leader Barry flew out on a cloudy morning at 11.31 hours searching Sognefjord and Vindafjord, then onto Volsvik. Hampered by low cloud he turned for home landing at Sumburgh at 14.28 hours. 'G' 333, flown by Lieutenant Terje Gudmund Gulsrud searched between Lindesnes and Fredrikstad sighting five merchantmen berthed in Porsgrunn. Continuing to Leirvik and Sandefjord, he sighted five vessels at Tønsberg. Finally at Fredrikstad at 10.58 hours Gulsrud turned for home, and one and a half hours later he touched down at Banff. 18 Group received a copy of the crew's report and intelligence reports from SIS transmitters near Porsgrunn, assessing the enemy's strength. All serviceable merchant vessels were employed in transporting German troops to their Fatherland. An early reconnaissance observed four merchantmen between the floating dock and swing bridge on the north side of Skienselva, near Borgestad railway station. The aircraft encountered light flak.

Wing Commander Jack Davenport planned the operation's two separate wing strikes; the Mosquitoes to Porsgrunn, and the Dallachy wing to Fedefjord just north of Lista. In the afternoon the Mosquitoes were readied and armed. All through lunch the station commander Group Captain Max Aitken talked of salmon fishing and grouse shooting – it made one quite hungry. Afterwards those not on operations with 235 Squadron went to Whitehills by bicycle. Pre-strike briefing at the operations complex was led by Wing Commander Junior Simmonds; the objective was to sink merchant vessels seen anchored at Porsgrunn. Aitken joined in reminding his crews of the regulations against attacking small ships, and if they had any doubts about the size of it, the attack was not to be carried out. Simmonds would lead the force in 'W' 235. Forty aircraft armed with rocket projectiles took to the air and within three minutes had formed up at 1,000 feet. Flying Officer Murphy kept an eye out for stragglers. Mustangs from Peterhead provided escort. One of Simmonds' pilots was Flight Lieutenant Phil Davenport, Wing Commander Jack Davenport's brother. Flying Officer Sid Gordon recalled:

> 'We flew out in Vic formation, in sections of three and four, and line abreast we kept close together just above the swell between 40 and 50 feet. Nearing the target we changed to battle formation. We were warned at the briefing to watch out for fighters, shortly after we started the attack in came the blue/grey 109s. I was giving my pilot Phil Kilmister warnings over the intercom of the impending enemy fighter attack after he fired off our rockets.'

Fenrik Løken and his navigator Sergeant Engstørm, in 'H' 333, were responsible for guiding the force onto the target flying over Lyngør. Unfortunately they were slightly off course to the north of Porsgrunn and when the target was abeam, at 17.32 hours Løken radioed Simmonds briefing him of the current situation and the formation wheeled right onto a southerly heading. Batteries fired in their direction as they did some tight turns approaching from the northwest for a diving attack. The first wave consisted of nine aircraft in three Vics; all sections pressed home the attack at 17.34 hours despite the threat of flak and impending enemy fighters, of which seven were sighted as they attempted to intercept the Mosquitoes in the target area. Simmonds ordered the force to keep together and continue the shipping attack. Bert Graham served with 143 Squadron:

> 'When we first went in there was a fair amount of flak but it had completely faded out on the second trip, 235's anti-flak aircraft must have done a good job. At least two of the largest merchantmen had big fires building up, and we got a further salvo of rockets into one of them. A factory on the quay was ablaze.'

A young German soldier describes the evacuation:

'We moved towards an old hulk the tarred timbers of which might be able to ward off a few blows. We hadn't quite reached it when the massive crackle of an anti-aircraft barrage burst all around us, fired by the coastal defences we had glimpsed earlier. This was my first experience of such a barrage. The falling fragments alone were capable of no small damage.'

The force sank four vessels: the German merchantman *Kalmar* of 964 tons and the Norwegian *Dione* of 1,620 tons, together with the *Nordsjø* of 178 tons, and *Traust*, of 190 tons, a further three suffered damage during the strike. Escorting Mustangs flying at 5,000 feet found they were at the same height as seven fighters of 16. /JG5 who lay in wait, then suddenly the Bf109Gs dived towards the Mosquitoes. 16. /JG5 had formed in the autumn of 1944, and was posted to Rygge near the Oslo fjord. It was on its first operation from this base against the Banff wing. These fighters were scrambled quickly intercepting the Mosquitoes and their escort at 17.33 hours. They were led by an experienced pilot Leutnant Adolf Gillet, the Staffel commander, who had just taken over from Leutnant Vollet. The latter had returned to Germany for conversion onto the jet fighter Me 262.

Gillet's pilots made determined attacks in their Bf.109G-14s, and the escaping Mosquitoes, with throttles open, had to follow the contours of the countryside to evade the enemy fighters between trees and the brightly coloured houses. Flying below 50 to 30 feet for 20 minutes with the enemy fighters just behind demanded heavy concentration from both pilot and navigator and dogfights ensued as Banff aircraft got caught. More fighters tried to intercept the force off Lista but each time the escorting Mustangs drove them away from the main force. Flight Lieutenant Sims flying with 65 (East India) Squadron recalled:

'I picked out one enemy aircraft flying to port of the formation and got onto his tail; at 450 yards I gave him a short burst from my machine guns. Owing to the salt spray having crystallized on my windscreen I had difficulty in keeping him in my reflector sight. I fired two more short bursts, still from dead astern, he jettisoned his drop tank and smoke and oil began streaming out. I pulled alongside the Luftwaffe pilot and was about ten yards away. He took no evasive action, his aircraft appeared to be going very slowly with smoke still emitting from his engine. I then had to take quick evasive action as tracer whizzed past my port wing. I did a low high speed turn as three of his friends were fast approaching astern, and dived down out to sea, as I was by myself. Afterwards I saw the enemy aircraft turn away to port very slowly and it was still going down.'

For Staffel commander Leutnant Adolf Gillet the spiralling air battle was fatal; the German fighter was attacked and crashed into Leirvik harbour. Some Norwegians subsequently rescued him from the cold water. Another Mustang managed to pick off Leutnant Heinz Schüler, who was luckier. A small charge dispensed with the canopy and a figure dispatched himself from the aircraft. The parachute blossomed. Two more Luftwaffe pilots, Uffz Heinz Scoppert and Uffz Willi Voltmer lost their lives. It was not a one-sided fight, however, for two strike aircraft were lost out of 35. RF590 crashed at Svarttjendalen killing both occupants while three miles away RF505 flown by Australian, Flight Lieutenant Phil Davenport and his English navigator Flying Officer 'Ron' Day of 235 Squadron, had heard the yell on the radio 'Bandits three o'clock!' but were committed to the attack. Mastheads and flags flashed by on their right as they then broke away towards the late afternoon sun and home. Davenport realised the Mosquito was not responding and flying over a sea of pine trees sighted a lake, which he thought a better option than baling out. Davenport switched off both engines and swooped down onto ice in Langen Lake. One Mustang was also lost, piloted by Flight Lieutenant 'Brad' Bradford who was last seen leading his section into attack. During the air battle Bradford was dispatched by Leutnant Schneider and KH685 went straight in, leaving Bradford little time to escape. Repeated calls by Flight Lieutenant Sims were not answered. On the return flight at 18.00 hours in position 57.40N/07.00E the Mustangs were bounced by six Bf109Gs and a series of inconclusive air battles took place without loss.

Here are three recollections of this strike. The first is by Flight Lieutenant Phil Davenport on his crash landing:

'At this stage of the war my brother, Jack, was the wing commander at 18 Group Headquarters. He actually planned the operation and he said it was directed solely against vessels which were held to be carrying significant war supplies and transporting German soldiers. The flight crews were briefed to avoid unnecessary damage to shore installations. We were flying No. 1 of the right hand Vic and so were part of the first wave. On the final turn into attack it was necessary, on our side of the wave, to throttle back and extend some flap to remain in formation. It was at this stage that the enemy fighters were reported coming in on our side of the formation. I do not recall seeing enemy aircraft but have the impression that there was considerable flak from the ground as we dived to attack the vessels. Our first indication of damage was when RF505's nose dropped away and a recurring requirement for nose-up trim indicated elevator damage. Subsequent failure of our radio and intercom system indicated damage in the fuselage. From my excellent navigator Ron Day, or from a witness who watched our dive, I later learnt both engines were trailing smoke. The elevator trim condition indicated that there was limited time before control was completely lost and we were looking to jump over a valley when Langen Lake appeared.

The Mosquito levelled out and crashed and bounced sideways along the ice. The aircraft yawed to the right side forward as it went into the water. For the crash Ron Day had positioned himself to be able to release the overhead escape canopy at the critical moment. To do this he had to loosen his harness and this probably caused him to receive the head injury and concussion when the equipment behind him was thrown forward which put him in hospital. Peat-covered water flowed around and over us. When the Mosquito sank, my legs trapped me and for some moments I was resigned. But then I was free, paddling desperately to the top. Ron surfaced before I did and blood covered his face. Subsequently the pressure release for the aircraft's dinghy allowed it to inflate and come to the surface and we climbed in. It is unlikely that we would have reached the shore because of the cold if, Fohannes, Gudmund and Per Grini had not been there to pull us out. From their presence we had a sensation of relief, warmth and friendly care, which, in contrast to the shock and cold, was immense. The Norwegians eventually were able to take us to a cottage, carrying us at a run across an open field. Inside, the benevolent effects of dry clothes, warm blankets and hot drinks stopped our shaking from cold and shock. Sometime after dark the Norwegians became tense and told us the Germans were outside. Late that night the Germans took us across the mountains – first, one at a time by pony cart and a small car, and then we were transferred to another car which took us to Lunde. At Lunde we were both examined by Doctor Bjarne Heggelund and the next day were taken to Oslo.

What surprised me was the second question during the interrogation "Are you Wing Commander 'Jack' Davenport's brother"? They had all the gen, how many squadrons, the numbers, who commanded who, I was astonished.'

Norwegian Gudmund Hegland remembered his and his brother's rescue of the two airmen on 11 April clearly:

'As the Mosquitoes headed back, we two brothers were working on our father's farm in the meadows. The weather was still clear and warm at 4.30pm, when suddenly engines could be heard, the deafening sound came nearer and a formation of aircraft came low over Rønningen Hill heading west, within a few minutes one broke off turning starboard. It lost height rapidly heading towards Langen Lake, which was covered in thick ice, although in places this had thawed out and cracked. The propellers milled round glinting in the afternoon sun, and the engines were spluttering. With the landing gear lowered they touched the ice, but their speed was a little too fast and they were catapulted into the air again. Then as they slammed into the ice the landing gear was torn away and the plywood tail section broke off, pulling the eight-ton machine to the right. It then scraped across a further 300 feet towards a gap in the ice where the formerly pristine RS505 disappeared into the hole, sinking out of sight.* A grey Mosquito roared over taking a wide 360° sweep of the area. Fohannes and I, together with Per Grini had taken to the icy waters in a small wooden boat with Fohannes rowing while Per tried to plug a leak and scoop out water. I guided the boat through the broken ice toward the bright yellow dinghy with two young men inside. Dark smoke could be seen near Høydalen, a hill four miles away, where another crashed aircraft, RF590 was burning. Per could speak only a few words of broken English and understood that there were no more crew within the aircraft. Tying a rope to the dinghy it was towed back toward the shore. Five of us then ran for cover amongst the trees, then across an open field towards the brick red cottage to warmth and safety. Once inside a large fire was lit, for the comfort of the shivering crew. After a while we moved them to Glettungstå where others could help us. Ron Day had head injuries and was given first aid, both were taken care of with warm clothes and food being provided and we asked if they wished to have some alcohol but this was refused. Some hours later the Germans came and led them away.'

Ron Hawkins of 143 Squadron took part in the Porsgrunn strike on 11 April, and recounts the loss of the Norwegian crew flying RF590:

'On the way out Junior, the 27-year-old commanding officer of 235 Squadron was leading when off the southern coast of Norway one of our Norwegian friends informed the leader he was too far east of the target area which initialled a slight detour making our ETA [Estimated Time of Arrival] a little later. As the formation arrived over the target area no flak bursts appeared but they soon woke up to us being there, and it was fairly thick. As we flew out of the target area after the successful attack on anchored merchantmen, warning shouts could be heard

---

*In 1946, Halvor Holte lifted the Mosquito RF505 out of the lake from its resting place at a depth of 54 metres and brought it ashore. The engines, canopy and other parts were removed and taken into storage. Helge Törnes retrieved the Bell and Howell camera, which was in pristine condition but in 1976 when Törnes tried to develop the 20 feet of film he was unable to get any results. Today one of the engines and the Bell and Howell camera is in a local museum.

through my earphones of enemy aircraft ahead. With no accompanying Mosquito on my starboard I spotted a 109 at 10 o'clock, which banked to the right to come in on our tail. I followed his progress as far as I could until he disappeared around our stern. (Visibility was very poor out of the stern due to the shape of the canopy.) The strike leader then came over the radio telling everyone to close-up and throttle back. Seeing the enemy aircraft my pilot increased speed after being informed of its position astern a Norwegian crew behind. Their Mosquito appeared on our portside with the ensuing Bf 109G about 200 yards astern of him, cannon and machine-gun fire were striking the engine and centre section, tearing into the plywood structure of this aircraft. You could see both the pilot and navigator working hard together, they just could not shake the 109 off their tail. After a very short time his port wing dropped and he went straight down into the pine trees and exploded. A mushroom plume of dark smoke rose into the air, both were killed.'

Shortly after this attack on Porsgrunn a report was given by Stockholm radio by an eyewitness: 'The noise was terrible – cannons and machine guns spitting death, while rockets sliced through the sides of vessels like a knife through butter. Nearly all the vessels were sunk.'

North Coates near the coast of Lincolnshire had been the birthplace of the first Coastal Command strike wing using Beaufighters in 1942. Three Beaufighter squadrons combined at North Coates, 143, 236, and 254; the wing was specifically formed to deal with the enemy's convoys off the Low Countries, which were always well covered by escort vessels and flakships and well within reach of fighter protection. Two of the original squadrons, 236 and 254, still operated out of the base in 1945. Mosquito MkXVIIIs were in action with 254 Squadron with crews from 248 Squadron's 'C' Flight. The first action occurred on 12 April when Mosquito 'A' 254 fired 57mm shells at a U-boat, supported by a Wellington of 524 Squadron. Mosquito 'B' 254 pumped off some rounds the next day and on 16 April 'D' 254 attacked a U-boat using schnorkel without results. The North Coates Mosquitoes ran into bad weather on 17 April and aborted the operation, but on the following day two Mk XVIII Tsetses came across five Type 23 U-boats, but before they had time to pounce they had dived and two rounds narrowly missed their intended targets. The Mosquito XVIII Tsetses completed 18 operations during the month of April, often flying in conjunction with 91 Squadron.

Away from operations at Banff, a highlight in the evening for the personnel was watching *Thanks for the Memory* with Bob Hope on 12 April, and two days later there was a performance of *Going My Way* starring Bing Crosby during which the heating failed. Corporal Joyce Trovey said:

'In mid-April 1945 some of the aircrew on the Mosquito units had very worn flying boots and other equipment and were told by the station adjutant 'Buster' Mottram that no replacements could be supplied by the Air Ministry because of a shortage. After a further telephone call to the Air Ministry, Max Aitken told them that if new equipment was not found immediately it would be headline news in his father's newspaper. Crates arrived the following day at Portsoy railway station on a freight train.'

On 17 April 235 Squadron personnel were released from operations, and made the best of an enjoyable day off. Many cycled to the outlying villages near the aerodrome. A dance was being held in the town hall in Macduff. One of those attending was Flight

Lieutenant Ken Parkinson who received a call from his pilot, saying that they were down for an early trip in the morning. On 18 April, Flight Lieutenant Ken Parkinson and Harry Parkinson took off at 04.00 hours having been woken four hours early, to provide fighter escort for Royal Navy destroyers returning from the Norwegian coastal waters. They provided air cover until 08.30 and returned to base. All available crews were assembled in the operations block. Bryan Woodier remembers:

'We were briefed for this strike on 18 April, intelligence had been received that some large Type XXI electro U-boats had left Kiel harbour and they would be in range for us to strike the following day.'

The next day Wing Commander Junior Simmonds of 235 Squadron led the sweep. Twenty-two aircraft took off at 13.33 hours, 11 from 235 Squadron, four from 143, five from 248 and two of 333 Squadron, together with an escort, and probed into the southern waters of the Kattegat, under strict instructions not to attack any other surface craft other than U-boats. Having observed several inviting targets suddenly an M-class minesweeper was seen, steaming towards them, behind her were four U-boats on the surface in line astern enroute from Kiel to Horten. Simmonds spoke to the crews at 16.30 hours, and the force attacked from east to west; the boats were 200 yards apart. 235 Squadron saw four U-boats; the lead U-boat saved itself and crash-dived. The M-class minesweeper and the two remaining U-boats received the brunt of the attack. In the second boat was Oberleutant Franz Säck, commander of U-251, a type VIIC of 769 tons which had completed six of her nine war cruises under Heinrich Timm with the Arctic Flotilla in 1942-43 before a long re-fit at Trondheim in June 1943; it was to be her last cruise. As she tried to turn to port in an attempt to escape, three 143 Mosquitoes hit the U-boat with 24 rockets and cannon fire, and made a second cannon run. She was badly damaged and not able to submerge and ten dinghies appeared aft alongside her. She then disappeared in position 56.37N/11.51E with her compliment of 39 crew; only four survived. 235 and 248 Squadrons now attacked the last two boats. The third U-boat U-2502, a type XXI under the command of Leutnant Heinz Franke was slightly damaged, and although stationary after the attack, she later reached Horten. U-2335, on her first operational cruise took hits to the conning tower before she submerged, managing to limp into Kristiansand South with this extensive damage.

In one of the 248 Squadron aircraft RF615 was Flying Officer Norman Earnshaw who was quoted in a copy of the *Lancashire Evening Post* saying: 'We took on the last U-boat in the line and got at least four cannon hits on the conning tower. Large pieces of the boat were flying through the air as we passed over and we could see the escort vessel burning as we came away.' The M-class was a mass of thick black smoke, burning furiously amidships listing to port with explosions at the stern. Two Mosquitoes from 235 Squadron were damaged; one made for Sweden, the other was hit by flak on the journey home across Denmark when they strayed across a heavily defended bridge. Their starboard engine received concentrated rounds. Flight Sergeant Allan Mackenzie and Frank Relfe were unable to feather the engine and the Mosquito spun into a vicious dive. RS612 crashed in flames south of the town of Lemvig. An escorting Mustang pilot, Flight Lieutenant G Pearson, reported engine trouble; barely able to stay aloft he coaxed KH695 down with a dead engine belly-landing at Getterøn, near Varberg on the west coast of Sweden. He later returned to his unit after being interned in Sweden and was subsequently awarded the DFC. Squadron Leader Bill Clayton-Graham, strafed a steam locomotive as he passed over Denmark with a two second burst of cannon and machine-gun fire, but was unable to see the results. The U-boat U-2335 surrendered at Kristiansund on 9 May, the boat was later disposed of by the Royal Navy in operation 'Deadlight' and was sunk by gunfire on 28 November 1945 north-west of Bloody Foreland.

The last moments of Mackenzie and Relfe in RS612 are recalled by Mr J Helme, who kindly wrote to Flying Officer Ray Harrington of 235 Squadron after the war giving details of the two men's deaths:

'Their aircraft came down in flames south of the town of Lemvig. People from the village arrived quickly at the crash site to find the pilot Flight Sergeant Allan Mackenzie's charred corpse, who had suffered an agonising death having been burnt alive, the navigator Flight Sergeant Frank Relfe was severely wounded and they managed to carry him and the charred remains of McKenzie to the local hospital where Dr Andres Christensen was the Danish senior surgeon. He concentrated on Relfe who was suffering with severe injuries to the spinal cord, and his thigh-bones had been crushed. This was a terrible situations, and he died the same evening. Dr Christensen arranged for the bodies to be put into coffins at the hospital and they were decorated with masses of flowers. The Germans permitted the Danes to bury the airmen, however their permission lasted for just two hours. The Danes were then forced to hand the coffins over to the Germans.'

Burgomaster Nielsen arranged for them to be buried in Struer, the Germans then exhumed the bodies on 20 and 21 April 1945. It was not until 16 June 1945 that both were returned to Struer. Relfe was buried in a joint grave with McKenzie on the hillside cemetery of Struer churchyard in Denmark.

Another former 603 Squadron pilot was also in difficulties after this strike. Flying Officer Bryan Woodier, who landed in Sweden, recounts what happened after he confronted one of the U-boats:

'We attacked across the sun east to west firing cannon, machine guns and rockets, I then went low over the target in a shallow dive. There was a loud bang accompanied by intense vibration. The cockpit immediately filled with dense glycol fumes thick enough to obscure the instrument panel. I felt for the feathering buttons and fortunately pressed the right one! The starboard propeller feathered and the glycol began to clear, looking across to the starboard propeller about 12 inches off one of the blades had been removed. Flying Officer Arthur Jones, my excellent navigator, gave me a course for Halmstad, Sweden and then called up Junior our WingCo, telling him what we were going to do. Thirty minutes later we landed at this small grass aerodrome. After one night in Halmstad, the Adjutant Commander Nilssen escorted us by train to Falum, where we were given some money to buy civilian clothes and accommodated in a large house together with a number of Bomber Command crews who were awaiting repatriation. We caught up with one of our Mustang escort pilots Stuart Pearson who also landed on the west coast of Sweden with engine trouble. After a week we transferred to a hotel in Stockholm for two nights, a brief visit to the British Embassy then shortly afterwards we flew back to Scotland in a BOAC Dakota. Then we travelled to London for our debrief.'

CHAPTER 16

MOSQUITOES DESTROY GERMAN AIRCRAFT FROM II & III/KG 26

Two days after the attack on U-boats on 21 April, aircrew were briefed for a Rover/U-boat patrol at 02.10 hours on Saturday morning. They then waited for updated intelligence. The 42 Banff Wing Mosquitoes, consisting of 16 from 143, 11 from 235, 11 from 248, and four from 333, finally took off, crossing the Danish coast in late afternoon heading for the Kattegat and escorted by 24 Mustangs. This formation was led by Wing Commander Foxley-Norris, commanding officer of 143 Squadron. As the force flew over Denmark they encountered spasmodic incoming enemy fire. Flight Lieutenant Wally Webster, piloting RF753, was caught, recording damage on the portside, nose and ammunition chutes. Unhappily, when the force entered the target area, it proved to be unexpectedly blanketed by mist and heavy rain and only a few small vessels were spotted, not justifying an attack. They then searched the enemy coastal waters on the North Sea for some while and Foxley-Norris gave the frustrated call over the radio-telephone for the wing to turn home, which they set course for. At 19.50 hours the leader of the Mustangs sought permission to press ahead as they had a big party laid on in the Peterhead mess that night, Foxley-Norris agreed and the fighters accelerated ahead. In bad weather, with rain, a cloud base under 600 feet and poor visibility at 200 feet suddenly the Mosquito pilots saw a large force of aircraft approaching on a more or less reciprocal course at 20.30 hours. Eighteen aircraft were in six Vics of three in line astern 150 miles off the Scottish coast. Seconds later shouts of Junkers went out over the radio-telephone.

The two KG26 Staffel involved were deployed from Bardufoss in Northern Norway, to Sravanger-Sola, this being the German airfield in Norway closest to Scotland. Around 18.00 hours the 6./KG26 of II Gruppe with nine Ju88A-17s led by Staffelkapitän Oberleutnant Friedrich Ebert, followed by the 7./KG26 III Gruppe, with nine Ju 188A-3s led by Staffelkapitän Haptmann Fritz Gehring. Although KG26 had been making a series of attacks on convoy JW66 which had left the Clyde on 16 April bound for Russia, today's deployment was for flying an armed reconnaissance sweep along the north-east Scottish coast. Landfall was to have been made at Peterhead where the first wave comprising of nine Junkers 88s of II./KG26 would fly northwards up to the Orkneys, and half an hour afterwards the nine Junkers 188s of III./KG26 had orders to sweep for coastal shipping, southwards down the Firth of Forth. These unfortunate German crews came across one of the most formidable allied aircraft in the De Havilland Mosquito. Wing Commander Christopher Foxley-Norris gave the order 'Attack! Attack! Attack!' In the ensuing battle it did not matter which Mosquito attacked, all were capable. There was some return fire but no casualties. The enemy aircraft turned for home. Flight Lieutenant Keohane said: 'As soon as we saw the markings, we went into attack. They were right down on the water. I let one 88 have a burst, and its starboard engine caught fire. He tried to climb away, but just stalled and went flop into the sea.'

Squadron Leader Alec Gunnis recorded that the sea was ablaze with aircraft: 'Five times I had a Ju in my sights and each time another Mosquito crew mixed in and shot it down before I could draw a bead.' A Warwick from Fraserburgh returning from covering the strike, was flying ten miles away; its pilot called up the force and said, 'I say boys an 88 has just passed me at 50 feet with the gates [throttles] wide open going like hell for home' which caused great laughter. During this short fight it was easy to suddenly find a friendly aircraft firing at another Mosquito as Squadron Leader John Barry recalled: 'We took rather a dim view of one crew who was firing quite madly out of the cloud which was almost on the deck, I screamed "Who the bloody hell is firing out of the cloud at me?" Needless to say we were in good spirits when we got home.' His fellow pilot Warrant Officer Coggie Cogswell remembers: 'I lined up a Junkers 188 but the return fire by the gunner was accurate and I banked away as I did not wish to end up in the drink.' Two 333 Squadron crews also had success. Firstly Lieutenant Thorlief Eriksen and his navigator Second Lieutenant Johan Hansen-Just flying 'L' 333 and secondly Flight Lieutenant Bob Golightly and Flying Officer Frank Hawthorne in 'E' 333 who recalls: 'We approached from the port quarter, bright flashes emitted from the Junkers machine-gun positions, Bob returned fire with a three second burst and these ceased, firing again it exploded at 15 feet above sea level. Debris embedded into the plywood as we took avoiding action.' Flight Lieutenant Wally Webster wrote: 'Hit one in the starboard engine – caught fire and dived into the sea – lined up a second but guns wouldn't fire – fired off rockets but missed! Found out later the air pressure pipes had a slow leak – enough left for one burst.'

For 143 Squadron this was a record day of operations, its maximum effort involving 92 hours of operational flying. Air Chief Marshal Foxley-Norris recalled:

'Mosquitoes were pushing and shoving like housewives in a bread queue to get at their unfortunate targets. When we finally got home and debriefed, we were to everybody's satisfaction credited with destroying nine, and we reckoned a lot more were damaged before they staggered up into the cloud cover. There was naturally great rejoicing at Banff and much welcomed publicity that Coastal Command did not often get. My DSO, coincidentally, came through at about the same time which called for extra drinks in the mess.'

It was getting dark when the Mosquitoes got back and all were all fairly short of fuel having been up for six hours. Flight Lieutenant Webster landed with a damaged port tyre which burst and his charge, RS574, swung off the runway upon landing.

In this one-sided fight 28 men lost their lives. The Staffelkapitän of 6 Staffel of KG26, Oberleutnant Friedrich Ebert and Oberleutnant Dombrowski leading II./KG 26 on this mission were amongst those that perished. The others were; Karl-Heinz Küchenmeister, Siegfried Berndt, Georg Bollwinkel, Heinz Schaller, Gerhard Schäfer, Otto Bauer, Hubert Hoppe, Richard Gattner, Kurt Langendorf, Stephan Schmädicke, Hans Holländer, Werner Jorden, Hurbert Traub, Karl Walldorf, Ewald Wolkenhoff, Heinz Reale, Alfons Pallek, Johannes Stumpf, Koglin, Helmut von der Höh, Willi Flesch, Harald Reimer, Zimmermann, Herbert Kunze, Behrend, Weyhrauch. One of the crews lost was from III./KG 26 but all the aircraft were Junkers 88s from II./KG 26; a shortage of serviceable Junkers 188s in III./KG 26 meant that one of the aircraft lost by II./KG 26 was crewed by personnel from III./KG 26.

Mosquito 'A' 143 HR405 piloted by Flight Sergeant 'Wiggy' Wiggmore and his navigator Flight Sergeant Ron Hawkins had become separated from the main force while flying on this sortie, and flying over Denmark he spotted a German staff car with its occupants; driver, officer, and a Norwegian Forester Hoope. Hoope had been forcefully requested to show the Germans the crash site of Liberator 'N' 206 from

Leuchars which had been shot down by an enemy night fighter. Flight Sergeant Ron Hawkins recalls their encounter:

'We could see the Kattegat ahead when I sighted a staff car flying a Swastika flag at about 2 o'clock passing through a wooded area below. I advised my pilot and he banked the aircraft round reducing height in the process and opened up with cannon and machine guns. The car ground to a halt, and all four doors spewed out men. It happened in seconds, so quickly that we do not know whether we hit them or not, but after narrowly missing the pine trees we turned for home. I recall that on nearing the Scottish coast we passed low over a large convoy heading north. The main force eventually arrived back, needless to say there was quite a large party in the messes.'

At Coastal Command headquarters Commander-in-Chief Sholto Douglas enjoyed himself by telephoning up Fighter Command 13 Group and offering fighter escort to their Mustangs when and if required. The Mustang leader was ticked off to say the least. That evening scenes in the officers' mess were really good, with bigger lines than ever being shot, led by Squadron Leader Alec Gunnis. Elsewhere celebrations were going on, and David Findlay Clark recalls the wing's triumph with them blowing off steam even if it was three in the morning!*

'On this night, we where awakened from our sleep by the church bell sounding in a marked erratic fashion. The first assumption was that we had been invaded by Germans; we had not. We had been invaded by a band of drunken aircrew from the 'drome who had just returned from a highly successful and totally victorious operation. They had decided that the town should know and the ringing of the church bell was sure the way to inform them. In due course, the police and RAF Military Police intervened to put paid to the one-note carillon. They also put the dampner on some casual swimming in the huge emergency water supply tank which had sat with its wire mesh covering undisturbed for three years or so at the foot of Institution Terrace. Throughout all the celebrations there was a notable lack of choral restraint even when the Whitecaps [RAF police] appeared but this tended to die down as first the bell ringers, then the swimmers, and finally a simple bunch of post-graduate-standard drinkers were winkled out of the Royal Oak in Bridge Street.'

On 22 April 404 Squadron flew its first armed operational sortie in one of their Mosquito MkIVs crewed by Flying Officer A Catarano and Flight Lieutenant A E Ford in RF851. At 09.26 hours on reconnaissance, they spotted a BV138 anchored off Kjevik and commenced a strafing run using cannon and machine-gun fire, destroying the BV138 flying boat and a nearby He115 floatplane at their moorings in Kjevik. The BV138 exploded, sending a plume of smoke to 500 feet which was visible 40 miles away as they made for home. On 24 April Mosquitoes returned early from operations after they encountered thick fog off Skaw. By the last week of April it was clear that the German war organisation was rapidly disintegrating, no vessels had been sighted in

---

*After the war in 1969 Foxley-Norris was Commander-in-Chief Royal Air Force Germany and Commander NATO 2nd Tactical Air Force, at the Joint Operations Room in Maastricht in Holland which was internationally staffed. One staff member was Hans Geisemann, a very gallant Luftwaffe pilot and one of their great anti-shipping aces in the Mediterranean. Another was the British officer Bob Golightly who had been at Banff with the Norwegian squadron and participated in the action on 21 April 1945. Golightly and Geisemann became good friends and one evening while talking Giesemann said, 'Do you know once I lost an entire wing in one action, two actually got back to base but they were so badly shot-up they crash-landed'.

the lower half of the North Sea and virtually no movement was detected on the Norwegian coast though wing sweeps continued almost daily. Fearing a last stand in Norway it became important to scour the sea around Denmark.

During time off in April, airmen and women would go in the evenings to Banff, Portsoy and Macduff on the bus for the dancing, the beer, the whisky and that rare delicacy white pudding and chips. It was a new experience. Alec Rix with 8235 Servicing Echelon remembered:

'When the good weather came we considered ourselves lucky to be within easy reach of pleasant cycle rides, you could ride off into the hills and enjoy the countryside calling at the various farms and small holdings to buy a dozen eggs here and there so that we could take home several dozen to our relatives in the south. [Because of rationing egg supplies were limited to one egg per fortnight, though supplies were not guaranteed.] This pursuit was known as "going egging". Dancing in the airmen's mess was popular as invitations were sent out to local girls and coach loads from the local area would arrive. While a special treat on our day off with 8235 would be to have tea at the Crown Hotel in Banff as the proprietor Helen Weir was most friendly and generous and made us welcome. This was a favourite gathering place for all ranks. You could have a high tea with scones, cakes and real butter for two shillings and six pence. Other activities we enjoyed were swimming in the sea near the aerodrome or at Tarlair Baths, in Macduff amid a sheltered bay formed in amongst the rocks. At high tide the pool would fill with sea water, it was a popular place for those on the station. Because of the long daylight hours on double summertime during the war the daylight in the north of Scotland extended beyond midnight. You could be cycling back from Portsoy or Macduff and see service personnel playing tennis.'

Squadron Leader Bill Clayton-Graham remembers the local fishermen:

'The fishermen at Macduff were fantastic, if they were out at sea, they would remain there until we returned, sometimes for up to six hours in case a crew had ditched. We used to drink with them in the local Seafield Arms – and could they drink! One night two others and myself where invited aboard a fishing trawler for a 'night cap' around 11pm. The next thing we knew we were out in the North Sea, so we spent the night on board, we went back to camp with enough fish for the whole officers' and NCOs' mess, the cook's face was a picture.'

WAAF Agnes Shayler recalls: 'Our social life was great! At one party the MT section invited the signals section. One MT driver was very merry she climbed onto a table and then dived into a fire bucket. Boy did she have a headache!'

A large proportion of the fighter pilots of 19 and 65 Squadrons from Peterhead caught the train to Aberdeen on Friday 27 April after the local newspaper *Aberdeen Bon-Accord and Northern Pictorial* ran a front page feature on the two units the day before. This was used to full advantage in the local public houses and The Aberdeen Hotel whenever they where getting unpopular. All those concerned crawled home in the early hours. On the last day of the month at Banff one of 143 Squadron's officers was caught by a WAAF NCO under the covers cosily in bed with his WAAF batwomen making love on his off duty morning. Her squadron leader explained to Group Captain Max Aitken that Sergeant Walkley, while making her routine rounds, discovered this officer and his WAAF in a compromising position. The squadron leader's face went puce, blushing with embarrassment when Aitken asked the NCO to be more explicit.

'Sir – they were in bed together, and unclothed.' Sergeant Walkley interrupted 'this officer was actually making love to this girl.' 'One of my WAAFs?' Aitken replied 'That's what they're here for isn't it?'

CHAPTER 17

MAY 1945 – THE FINAL DAYS

Hitler's suicide on 30 April 1945 in his bunker in Berlin was the supreme sign that peace was close at hand. The Allied forces had a choke hold on the Germans in central Europe. The Germans were still in control in only two countries – Denmark and Norway. But it was only in Norway that fanatical Nazis had an opportunity to prolong the war a little more.

The campaign therefore increased in the early days of May 1945, trying to prevent the German forces from reaching or departing from Norway. RAF Photographic Reconnaissance revealed a build-up of various tonnage of merchantmen in the Kattegat, many of the vessels enroute from Norway, and unloading in Denmark with a steadily growing north-bound movement of equipment, consisting of U-boats, and other naval units, to Norway. Commander-in-Chief of Coastal Command Sholto Douglas decided that the Banff Mosquitoes should carry out a last crushing co-ordinated strike with the Dallachy and North Coates squadrons. The Beaufighter wings were to cover the Kattegat/Kiel Bight area, which saw the Dallachy wing move first to Thornaby in Yorkshire then onto North Coates in Lincolnshire where the crews joined up with 236 and 254 Squadrons. An airfield was made accessible to the two Beaufighter wings as a refuelling stage on the outbound trip or the homeward flight. In the absence of any Luftwaffe fighter opposition due to chronic fuel shortages, the strike wings were able to pursue their hunt over the whole of Kattegat Sound and Belts and even into the bays and harbours.

A further Mustang fighter unit arrived at RAF Peterhead. 234 Squadron would carry out escort duties, as agreed between Portal and Douglas. Flight Lieutenant Bert Graham was detailed to carry out a 45-minute rocket-projectile demonstration in 'A' 143 on the 1 May with Wing Commander Paddy Burns flying as observer. On 2 May crews on the available list from the five Mosquito squadrons rose early at 04.15 hours, briefed to search for U-boats known to be travelling north in the Kattegat. Taking off at 06.15 hours, and subsequently at 08.55 hours, 35 Mosquitoes, led by Squadron Leader Tommy Deck DFC flying RS501, with an escort of 24 Mustangs found two U-boats on the surface, in line astern, half a mile apart, in position 57.29N/11.24E. Five miles to the north-west was an M-class mine sweeper, 'M' 239.

Deck ordered an immediate attack and five of 143 Squadron dived on the leading boat U-2359, firing 38 rockets, scoring at least 12 hits, plus cannon damage. Two others of 143 hit the second boat with 16 rockets scoring two hits, and then four Mosquitoes attacked with cannon raking the whole length of the hull. 248 Squadron, led by Squadron Leader Luckwell, in 'L' 248, went into the mêlée battering the second boat with rockets and cannon. He was followed by 235 Squadron, with Flight Lieutenant Geoff Mayhew DFC leading, flying 'A' 235, who also attacked the second boat, scoring between 8 and 16 rocket strikes. U-2359 was seen to sink after debris had been thrown into the air, leaving an oil patch and wreckage. Some of the U-boat men were seen to escape into their dinghies, but pilots reported 12 being pulled down with the boat as it sank. Oberleutnant Gustav Bischoff commanded U-boat U-2359, a type XXII of 235 tons which belonged to 4 Flottille. U-2359 had not made any combat patrols and was sunk on this passage from Kiel to Horton in Oslo fjord. The second U-boat, another type XVIII, was also damaged.

The minesweeper 'M' 293 of 235 tons became the target for Squadron Leader Barry of 235 Squadron having been forced out during a steep turn in towards the U-boats. The gunners aboard 'M' 239 were pumping up fire in all directions. Barry tore in, catching some concentrated fire, his No. 2, Flying Officer Johnny Rendell and his navigator Flying Officer Ron Rawlins received the same medicine as shells caught their aircraft. Rendell radioed Barry 'Bordeaux 26 – Brighton' and their damaged aircraft headed for Sweden after going in for a second run on the 'M' 239. As the attendant minesweeper received concentrated cannon fire from the attacking Mosquitoes the return fire diminished, there was now spasmodic gun fire from 'M' 239 and it was left burning. It later sank. Rendell managed to land at Satenas but the Mosquito was a total loss, luckily the crew unhurt. With the first pictures of the Jewish prisoners in Belsen concentration camp having been published in the national newspapers the day before, the escorting Mustangs from 19 and 65 Squadrons strafed the German seamen in their dinghies taking out some of their pent-up anger of the atrocities reported by the journalists. Squadron Leader Barry circled round searching the sky for other Mosquitoes but had become separated and headed home alone through the Skagerrak, turning south of Lista and opening the throttles to 250mph and landing back before the main formation. Stockholm radio reported that night that: 'Out of 82 men on board 60 are dead with 15 injured'. In the early evening the duty adjutant received a telephone call from Ray Harrington phoning from Leuchars – it was a great relief to know he and Bert were alright.

On 3 May the North Coates Wing had been briefed to attack anything on sight. Beaufighters with their Mustang escort hit a number of worthy targets in the Kiel area and were credited with sinking three merchantmen, a flakship, a Type XXI U-boat in the Belts and damaging two other surface craft, for the loss of one Beaufighter and crew. After the sortie they landed in south-east Holland for the first time, the next day they took a course over the Kattegat hitting merchantmen, and four U-boats with cannon and rockets, before landing at North Coates. With the improving good weather in northern Scotland patrols took off from Banff, the last being flown at 16.30 hours. Having been detailed to attack any vessels escaping Kiel harbour, two experienced ship-busters Wing Commander Jackson-Smith, and Squadron Leader Clayton-Graham both found nothing worth attacking as the Mosquitoes crossed Denmark. Turning eastwards they ran into heavy thunderstorms and turbulence, with almost nil visibility at 19.00 hours, and set course for Banff. This was to have been the last operational sortie, but Group Captain Max Aitken telephoned 18 Group headquarters. Speaking, briefly to Sholto Douglas the outcome of the conversation was that another strike would take place on 4 May 1945. This final strike would be led by Wing Commander Christopher Foxley-Norris. The crews were briefed early – an unpleasant item from the intelligence officer was that not far from the wing's return route was Ålborg airfield which reconnaissance photographs indicated was occupied by several hundred Luftwaffe fighters. The crews did not know about the fuel shortage. Squadron Leader Clayton-Graham noted: 'Quite a few of the chaps left the room to use the WC after Bellew had put the wind up them, although most of us were seasoned ship-busters the last thing we needed was a gaggle of 190s chasing us back to base.'

Mosquitoes swarmed into the air, eight from 404 'Buffalo' Squadron, whose rocket-firing aircraft were taking part in their final sweep. Over 40 Mosquitoes from the remaining squadrons made up the strike force, 18 Mustangs from 19 and 234 Squadrons had taken off at 13.15 hours. Two Warwicks from Fraserburgh were in attendance in the air while in the sea below were the two high speed launches based at

Fraserburgh harbour, both were covering the wing's withdrawal route. This armada set off at 13.20 hours. A lone E-boat was attacked north-east of Denmark and promptly sunk at 15.35 hours after being engaged by 404 and 333 Squadron aircraft. The weather and visibility were excellent. As they crossed the Danish coast 20mm and 37mm flak punched the sky while in hamlets flags were flying. Aircrews sensed the end was near, the force came out to the north of Kiel. Ten minutes had passed when Foxley-Norris saw immediately in front of the force four Narvik class destroyers. The force continued on its course towards the destroyers, when suddenly navigator Flight Lieutenant Paddy Tuhill shouted over the radio-telephone to his pilot Foxley-Norris: 'Three o'clock, about 12 miles.' Two large merchantmen and two frigates and one flak ship in a small convoy were east of Aarhus Bay (500 miles from their base) on the west coast of Denmark. The formation banked to starboard and split into sections to attack in line abreast on a heading of 230° true. Foxley-Norris led. The convoy put up a heavy flak barrage. As the Mosquitoes made their first attack two Mustangs KH818 and KH674 collided, killing Flight Lieutenant Davidson (Tonic 3) and Flying Officer Natta (Tonic 4), both went into the sea. A quick sweep over the area revealed no sign of them in the water. The Mosquitoes hit them with all their armament and many wet and dry hits were observed. Its cargo was of food supplies and 700 tonnes of ammunition. The merchantman *Wolfgang L M Russ* caught fire immediately, rockets penetrating the main hold and it then exploded, ten minutes after being hit, and sank. Eight members of her crew survived and one of the escort vessels went down. K1's crew were picked up together with those onboard the flak ship which was carrying more than the full complement. Fifty-five from the flak ship were picked up alive. They left the second merchantman, the Danish *Angamos* of 3,540 tons badly damaged and K3 suffered 16 fatalities. Crewmen tackled fires in the stern, ammunition store and crew accommodation. Flight Lieutenant Gerald Yeats said:

'Gunners aboard an escort ship kept firing back at us, so we had to keep going at them. When I pulled out I could see the masthead coming straight at us and ducked automatically. I'd misjudged the height and there was a large bang as we passed over the escort ship. The aircraft was vibrating badly as we climbed away to assess the flak damage.'

Yeats then rejoined the force. The wing turned north for home and immediately sighted a small cargo vessel, the German *Gunther Russ* of 998 tons on a northerly course. This was attacked by those aircraft with ammunition remaining and they left it burning. As Yeats and his navigator Flight Lieutenant Tommy Scott DFC broke away from this final strike the fuselage panels started vibrating in the slipstream. Not knowing what had caused the damage the 22-year-old pilot just concentrated on keeping it flying. Mosquitoes jostled to photograph the damage they saw. RS504 had hit the top section of K3's timber mainmast, tearing the Mosquito's plywood construction from the nose cover to the bomb bay and gutting the aircraft. The nose cover housing the 0.303 Browning's machine guns and 20mm cannon bays were ripped open as were the cannon breeches in the forward part of the bomb bay; the port engine's inner cover had also been wiped off. Both hoped it would see them back safely. The WT lead navigator Flight Lieutenant Ray Simmons of 143 Squadron sent a report that the strike had been successful. The formation then crossed out over Denmark, but unfortunately while crossing the Mariager fjord at 16.13 hours German anti-aircraft fire caught a 234 Squadron Mustang IV 'G' 234; Pilot Officer P J W Bell was hit in the arm. His Mustang KH860 went straight down, but regaining control he managed to make a belly-landing near Hornum. He escaped the wreckage and was taken to Logstor hospital. He reported that his aircraft was 'riddled by bullets'.

Flying Officer Schofield's and Flight Lieutenant Yearwood's aircrafts were both hit fairly badly by light flak but they managed to reach Scotland. Almost as everyone landed the war officially ended. The damaged Mosquito 'Z' 248 touched down normally and Yeats taxied to the squadron's dispersal area and shut down the engines. Their ground crew examined the gutted forward section of RS504 finding the cause of the devastated fuselage a shattered four foot long mast-top fixed under the cockpit housing and still complete with K3's pennant with Iron Cross insignia. Luck was on their side as none of the flying controls, fuel cocks or electrical circuits were wrecked. Flight Lieutenant Angus McIntosh said: 'We all went to look at the damaged Mosquito which had been towed in front of one of the blister hangars and we wondered how Yeats and Scott managed to get back to the aerodrome. It was a bloody awful mess; an acknowledgment to the strength of the aircraft.'

Three Mosquitoes touched down in Sweden due to severe flak damage, one – RS568 flown by Flight Lieutenant Douglas Thorburn DFC of 235 Squadron – was to be the last fatality suffered by the Banff strike wing. With one engine shot away Thorburn attempted to land on the remaining engine when suddenly it cut out at Getterön at 15.50 hours. Thorburn's machine struck a wall, his navigator Warrant Officer Crocker managed to get clear through the escape hatch, with two broken legs and a head injury but his pilot was not so fortunate. As the aircraft caught fire Thorburn was burnt to death. Crocker was sent to Varberg hospital and recovered from his injuries. The sad news was passed onto his parents, Brigadier Stephen Thorburn OBE, MC, and Henrietta Thorburn MBE, of Layer-de-la-Haye, Essex. His former master at Eton in Berkshire was also told of his tragic death and a service of remembrance was held. The young Flight Lieutenant Douglas Thorburn's remains were recovered and buried in Varberg Church New Cemetery on the south-west coast of Sweden. The second aircraft also from 235 Squadron, was RS623 flown by Flying Officer W Moffatt and Flight Lieutenant C Hardy which landed at Satenas at 16.00 hours, damaging the undercarriage in the process. The third, RS501 landed at the airfield of the SAAB aircraft factory at Trollhättan, the crew, Flight Sergeant W Shewry and his navigator Flight Sergeant J E Hornby, both unhurt. Of the three aircraft, two were scrapped. RS501 was sold to AB Svensk Flytjänst in 1946 for target towing duties. The Mosquito was eventually scrapped.

No more strikes were dispatched from Banff. The operation on 4 May 1945 proved to be the final anti-shipping strike of the war to be flown by the RAF Banff wing, Coastal Command. Group Captain Max Aitken DSO DFC who had flown on the first day of the war in Europe, had also flown on this last strike with permission from Sholto Douglas.

General-Admiral von Friedeburg now proceeded to Field Marshal Montgomery's headquarters to negotiate a separate surrender on Grand Admiral Doenitz's behalf. He had been appointed Hitler's successor on 30th April. Montgomery agreed to accept the surrender of the North German area on condition that Holland, Denmark and the German Fleet were included and that no weapons or vessels be destroyed before the surrender, which was to take effect from 08.00 hours 5 May, 1945. At 23.05 hours in the evening the Admiralty signalled Headquarters Coastal Command that surface vessels were not to be attacked unless 20 miles off the Norwegian coast. Operational flying on the 5th was cancelled. The Commander-in-Chief Sholto Douglas dispatched a signal to all Coastal Command groups and stations on 5 May, the day after Montgomery had reported the unconditional surrender of the Germans. Marked immediate and personal from the AOC C-in-C, it read:

'In spite of surrender of German forces on the continent there is yet no indication that they contemplate surrender in Norway. We may therefore expect the continuance of intense U-boat operations from Norwegian bases. All ranks must realise that for Coastal Command the war goes on as before. We started first we finish last. I call upon all squadrons for a great final effort against our old enemy. It falls to Coastal Command to strike the final blow against the enemy's one remaining weapon.'

The likelihood of a peaceful solution in Norway increased when the Germans capitulated in Denmark on May 5. On the same evening General Dwight D Eisenhower, the Allied Supreme Commander, sent a telegram to the Resistance headquarters in Norway giving detailed instructions to be passed on to the Germans about how to make contact with the Allies. This message was duly communicated to General Böhme and Reichskommissar Terboven, the military and civilian commanders in Norway. In the early hours of 7 May, at 02.41 hours the German High Command signed capitulation documents in the Western Allies' headquarters in Reims, France. The signing was repeated the following day at the Russian Red Army headquarters in Berlin, to come into force at midnight on 8 May. In Norway, the news spread like wild fire. As dawn broke on 7 May flags fluttered in the breeze for the first time in years, although the Norwegians had reservations as to how the Germans might respond. Finally at 14.55 hours on 7 May 1945 the order went out from Coastal Command Headquarters that no further anti-shipping operations were to be carried out. At 15.00 hours bodies were crammed round wirelesses, at Banff, everyone listening to Winston Churchill as he broadcasted that the cessation of hostilities in Europe would take effect at 24.00 hours that night. By dusk that evening spontaneous celebrations had begun. On the eve of peace the closely knit strike wing got the sad news that Doug Thorburn was killed on their last operation of the Second World War. In Norway at 21.10 hours General Böhme received an order signed by Generalfeldmarschell Wilhelm Keitel, the chief of OKW, instructing him to prepare for surrender of all units of the army, the Luftwaffe, SS, police and other organisations in Norway. At 22.00 hours Böhme broadcast to the Norwegians that German forces in Norway would obey orders. The Milorg were fully mobilised and some 40,000 armed Norwegians quickly began to take charge.

The war in Europe was over at last and people could breathe freely once more. In the three months from September 1944 to December 1944, the Banff Mosquitoes sank 23,582 tons of shipping, shared in the sinking of two others, and damaged eight vessels of just over 10,000 tons. By the end of the Second World War German controlled shipping had been almost completely destroyed – this alone was a considerable achievement. Loss of life in the last nine months for those who participated in the anti-shipping strikes with the Banff strike wing was a total of 107 known aircrew died, 18 aircrew interned after landing in Sweden, nine prisoners of war, and two evading capture.

VE (Victory in Europe) Day at Banff saw operations continue. Whereas it brought the end of hostilities for much of the Allied Air Forces, 18 Group aircraft continued doing sweeps off the Norwegian coast. Nevertheless, festivities began and continued at a pace throughout the night. Two Short Stirlings arrived with 100-gallon drop-tanks. The crews included a number of Australians who caught a lift to Dallachy for some liquid refreshment. A group of RAF officers arranged to lift the rum kept in the Intelligence Section for after wing strikes and drink it dry. But the three officers found they couldn't drink eight gallons of rum, so reinforcements had to be sent for. One of the reinforcements, a WAAF corporal, decided that on such an auspicious occasion rum could be imbibed quite harmlessly like water. Two hours later she woke up at the sick quarters and found a doctor pumping some out of her system with a stomach pump. For the next 48 hours highlights at Banff were squadron leaders having baths in ale in the officers' mess, an epidemic of shirt tearing and tie cutting, setting fire to one of the messes using Very cartridges and telephone calls to the local Banff and Portsoy fire brigade to douse the flames. Flight Lieutenant Ron Hawkins of 143 Squadron briefly recalls VE-Day:

'We all had a whale of a time when VE-Day arrived at Banff. Outside the officers' mess everyone piled furniture into an enormous mountain. It was then lit with a huge cheer, one over-enthusiastic officer had to be restrained from throwing a photo flash canister on the flames which would probably have blinded everybody around if he had succeeded.'

VE-Day was officially observed on Tuesday 8 May. Those in their living quarters were awoken at 07.00 hours, and personnel living off the base arrived by 08.00 hours. On the station festivities started with a 100% attendance for Church Parade, all turned out in their best blues. At 09.00 hours there was a short Thanksgiving Service in No. 2 hangar. The hymn 'All people that on earth do dwell' was sung with great gusto by the congregation. The station commander Group Captain Max Aitken then read the lesson, Luke Chapter 1 verses 68 to 75:

'Blessed be the Lord God of Israel, for he has visited and redeemed his people, and has raised up a horn of salvation for us, in the house of David as he spoke by the mouth of his holy prophets from of old, that we should be saved from our enemies, and from the hands of all who hate us; to perform the mercy promised to our fathers, and to remember his holy covenant, the oath which he swore to our father Abraham, to grant us that we delivered from the hand of our enemies, might serve him without fear, in holiness and righteousness before him all the days of our life.'

The remainder of the day was free for non-essential personnel, quite a few listened to Winston Churchill's speech at 15.00 hours on the wireless. In the evening there was an RAF Banff dance. On the station peace time routine started the following day (Wednesday) but it was treated as a half day. A training programme was devised for all the squadrons on the basis of five aircraft doing 20 hours flying a day and concentrating on gunnery and rocket-projectile practice. During the day on 10 May, photographs where taken of the Banff wing aircrew and commanding officers against the backdrop of three Mosquitoes in front of one of the main hangars. The sun finally appeared in time for these celebrations and replaced the grey skies. A victory bonfire was lit at 23.00 hours, which Aitken started, but the highlight of the evening was the burning of dummies of Hitler and Göring. Many personnel fired off fireworks and Very pistols over the next few hours. Finally the night ended fittingly with the official tossing of Max Aitken into the water tank by the Canadians; he was later to be found paddling across in the *Victory Ship*, made from 100-gallon drop-tanks launched in the emergency fire tank, and being heckled by members of the various squadrons. Flight Lieutenant Jimmy Thomas fell in to a fire lit earlier by Aitken, but being so drunk he didn't even smoulder! Despite some slight hangovers the Banff wing photographs were taken the following day of ground staff and ground personnel.

As the celebrations continued across Western Europe a Sunderland flying boat landed at 16.30 hours in Oslo harbour with the first allied military mission, comprising four officers. It delivered the instructions for capitulation to General Böhme and the surrender was arranged during the course of the night. At midnight all German forces surrendered their weapons, and at 07.00 hours on May 9 Vidkun Quisling and many other ministers turned themselves in at Oslo's main police station. No. 38 Group was participating in operation 'Doomsday'. Aircraft from this group had flown to RAF Peterhead to commence the sortie in Stirlings and Halifax aircraft. Tasked with flying in the 1st Airborne Division to Gardemoen aerodrome, 50 km north-east of Oslo, they reached the capital that same day with other detachments landing in Stavanger and Kristiansand. One stores aircraft attempted to land at Banff on the return flight but as the wheels touched the runway the pilot received word their charge was to divert to Kinloss. The Banff squadrons were asked to provide 'fighter escort' for a naval force comprising three cruisers and four destroyers and seven mine sweepers, which were taking Crown Prince Olaf the King of Norway back to his native land as far as Oslo, an operation coded 'Kingdom'. In this flight were six 235 Squadron Mosquitoes, and when they came off the patrol Flight Lieutenant Geoff Mayhew DFC, led them over Stavanger/Sola and beat the airfield up. On 14 May, Crown Prince Olav arrived in Oslo aboard a British cruiser. Accompanying him was a 21-man Norwegian government delegation led by ministers Sverre Støstad and Paul Hartmann. The rest of the Norwegian government and much of the London administration followed on the troop transport ship *Andes*.

On 11 May Mosquitoes became involved in a search for two Short Stirlings which had gone missing. One was thought to be carrying Air Vice-Marshal Sir James Rowland Scarlett-Streatfield CBE CDG of 38 Group at the time. The search continued until 15 May. Meanwhile other strike crews searched in vain for a ditched American B17 Flying Fortress, a square search was carried out but there was no sign of any survivors. Anti U-boat patrols were ordered by 18 Group after new intelligence revealed that a U-boat was still attacking allied shipping on the 21st. Two aircraft of 248 Squadron and a pair from 143 Squadron searched between Svinøy and Terningen, small craft were sighted, eight E-boats but no U-boat. Two Mosquitoes from 235 then searched between Ytterøyane and Kristiansund. These activities only occupied a quarter of aircraft available. Many unofficial flights took place under the heading 'air test' or 'training flights' as air and ground crews expressed a wish to see Norway now the hostilities had ended.

Flight Lieutenant Basil Quelch DFC, was detailed to fly down to Benson, Oxfordshire and pick up Mosquito DZ618. Quelch and his navigator Flight Sergeant Corder became Coastal Command's 'Public Relations Flight' and began operating straight away using Banff as base. Flight Lieutenant Cogan brought in a Liberator to the base and with the help of Flight Lieutenant 'Wally' Webster transported 12 passengers to Leuchars the following day, 23 May, for an investiture being held by Sholto Douglas for two Norwegian pilots, Major Wenger and Major Anderson who were being awarded two well earned DFCs. Sixteen passengers returned the day after with Flight Lieutenant Wally Webster assisting a different pilot, Flight Lieutenant Alexander. On two consecutive days, 25th and 26th, the 'Coastal Command Public Relations Flight' was airborne. Flight Lieutenant Basil Quelch DFC, filmed and photographed the German *Prinz Eugen* and *Nürnberg* near Denmark while under British naval escort to Wilhelmshaven. Getting this footage required some exceptional flying by Quelch and navigational skills by Corder. Both received a letter of congratulation from Wing Commander Tom Wisdom at Coastal Command's Northwood headquarters.

Gradually, the spirit of the station changed. After the exhilarating and often very traumatic experience of participating in a long war there now came a mood of gloom. 25 May 1945, was red letter day as on this day half of the anti-shipping squadrons received orders that they were to disband. The squadrons concerned were 143, 144, 236, 404 and 455. No reason seems to be given as to why these squadrons were singled out, but four out of the five had been created since mid 1941. The remaining squadrons continued on peacetime duties.

June 1945 began with a rapid rundown of Coastal Command with 143 Squadron disbanded and quickly renumbered as 14 Squadron, retaining its Mosquito fighter/bombers. Liberators continued to land at Banff, taking part in fighter affiliation. Personnel from 404 Squadron did a tour of Norway landing near Oslo, in two Liberators prior to their repatriation so that they were able to see for themselves the awful havoc which they had helped to wreak on the Kriegsmarine. Commonwealth units from the strike wings saw personnel immediately recalled home and the once powerful Mosquito/Beaufighter strike force was decimated. The New Zealand unit, 489 Squadron, after eight months at Dallachy arrived for conversion onto Mosquitoes on the 16th, and 14 Squadron departed escorting 18 Spitfires from Dyce as far as Kristiansund, along with 12 Mosquitoes from 333 Squadron. The remaining Mosquitoes provided individual escort and ASR aid to RAF fighters flying to Norway as part of operation 'Apostle'. Activities at RAF Banff now centred around the recreation ground and sports field. Cricket commenced and several games were played against the New Zealanders by a combined RAF team from the remaining squadrons.

Hockey matches were also played by the young WAAFs. The New Zealanders also showed a great interest in tennis and undertook matches against the Portsoy Tennis Club whilst the aircrew were acquainting themselves with the Mosquito. Local flying took place and rocket practice continued at buoys moored off the shore at Portsoy. The beginning of July 1945 saw flying training cease. 235 Squadron commanding officer Junior Simmonds heard on 9 July that the squadron would be disbanded forthwith. They held a final farewell dance on 20 July in the officers' mess for all ranks. The decision to disband was sad news for many people, on and off the airfield. Countless numbers of friendships had been made between both the airmen and women at RAF Banff and between the people on the airfield and the civilians in Banff and the surrounding villages. There followed a spate of smaller scale celebrations as villages and pubs gave parties to honour the airmen who had been regular visitors to their communities and who had found friendship with the locals.

August approached and rumours were rife as to the future; the Far East beckoned. 235 Squadron pilots and navigators logged ferrying trips to various destinations throughout mid-June, including: Church Fenton, East Fortune, Hawarden, Abingdon, Finningley, North Weald, North Creek, Cranwick and Reading aerodromes. Meanwhile the squadron slowly began to lose some of its aircrews, who were posted to 544 Squadron for special training at RAF Benson, in Oxfordshire. Many of these crews failed to pass the 37,000 feet decompression chamber test. On their arrival at Benson they tried to bring the 'Banff Coastal' spirit to the airfield but despite colourful renderings of many unsuitable songs their popularity slumped and they beat a hasty retreat from the officers' mess to the White Hart public house in Nettlebed. In Banff the New Zealand squadron continued flying and armament training ready for a move to the Pacific, though it shared the same fate as most of the other anti-shipping squadrons and was dissolved on 1 August 1945. Several impromptu farewell parties and dances took place in the Drill Hall on the station. The aircrew flew their rocket-firing Mosquito aircraft for their final flight to East Fortune, and were then taken back to Banff by road. These aircraft where either destined for match wood or some would be sold to other countries. Before leaving, the members of 489 went to take part in a local swimming gala at Macduff's Tarlair open air pool and saw recent new arrival, Flying Officer Ian Shaw, distinguish himself by winning the 150 yards freestyle against a class field.

A detachment of Supermarine Sea Otters of 279 Squadron led by Flight Lieutenant Scott arrived at RAF Banff from Thornaby while earlier Hurricanes from the same squadron had came in from Fraserburgh. Sea Otter sorties began on 28 July, searching for an out of control local fishing boat. Another flight on 31 July by two Sea Otters failed to locate a reported crash near Arbroath. Domini HF885, piloted by Squadron Leader Anon, landed at Banff, transporting two members of 235 Squadron to and from Turnhouse on 30 June, finally departing for Hutton Cranwick. August saw two 279 Squadron Otters assisting colleagues from Thornaby. A Fleet Air Arm Hellcat and Barracuda went missing off the coast near Drem airfield and Warrant Officer Grange and Campbell searched along the coast in extremely poor weather conditions, with cloud down to sea level, finally landing at Drem. The Sea Otters eventually left, posted to Tain.

The former strike wing airfield was now put on a care and maintenance status and the remainder of August was quiet, the only sound being that of Mosquitoes, and the odd Sea Otter from Tain. A Beechcraft Traveller made an emergency landing due to bad weather, one of the last aircraft to make landing at Banff. With the war in Japan declared over in August, the station held a VJ-Day dance and V-Victory signs were painted onto the headquarter's windows. Those personnel still left said their goodbyes to locals and celebrated at Whitehills where the beer was flowing freely. Operations had finally ended. Soon the airfield had a forsaken look about it. The removal of all aircraft and the reduction in personnel had an immediate effect on Banff itself. The five remaining aircrew from 235 Squadron had to fly the allotted Mosquitoes, eight to Wroughton, eight to St. Athan, and four to Edzell.

Warrant Officer Coggie Cogswell from the disbanded 235 Squadron recalled:

'I had to take my "D-Dog" with great reluctance off with Harry Pepper for Wroughton via Church Fenton. Then four days later "L -Leather" came with me to the same place and they were left in the fields to rot. In June 1946, while I was at No. 2 Ferry Pool, demob was nearing and I guess that aircraft types and aerodromes were soon becoming just memories of happy bygone days. One thing I'm pleased of – I flew "D-Dog" (RS618) again on 6 June from Wroughton to Hamble to be delivered to the French Air Force.'

The end of RAF Banff was in sight. The personnel now numbered 77 compared to the height of the conflict when the airfield was home to some 3,300 officers, airmen and WAAF personnel and some 250 locally recruited civilian staff. At the close of the Second World War it was the biggest Coastal Command station in Britain with over 150 Mosquitoes. At the beginning of 1946 only two of the nine core strike squadrons remained: 248 and 254 Squadrons. 248 moved to RAF Chivenor on the Devonshire coast and 254 to Langham. By the end of May 1946 the two strike squadrons formed a wing at Thorney Island. 248 Squadron flew its Mosquitoes for the King's birthday parade over Southsea on 13 June 1946 at 250 feet together with 811 (Mosquito), 813 (Firebrand), and 813 (Firefly) from the Royal Navy, with Admiral Sir Geoffrey Layton taking the salute. In the same year anti-shipping strike wing aircrew courses were transferred to No.6 OTU at RAF Kinloss, run by former 235 Squadron commander, Simmonds. Six months later 248 was re-numbered as 36 and 254 became 42. In July 1947 235 Squadron was reintroduced as a Sunderland Flying Boat Operational Conversion Unit, subsequently taking part in the Berlin Airlift before disbanding.

In Norway, RAF officers spent ten months in search of RAF aircrew. These officers were members of the Missing Research and Enquiry Service, an organization set up by the Air Ministry soon after the war, which was under the overall command of Group

Captain E F Hawkins DSO who, with officers, began search operations throughout Western Europe. Under the command of Squadron Leader H Scott and afterwards Squadron Leader E Houghton and with another six officers they worked in extremely dangerous situations; in subzero temperatures and ice covered roads covering thousands of miles. As a result of their efforts the total number of Allied airmen lying in cemeteries in Norway was approximately 500 in 1947. According to records only a very few remain 'unknown'. The largest concentration is at Sola Cemetery; Stavanger Cemetery; Mollendahl Cemetery, Bergen; Stvane Cemetery, Trondheim (where there are up to 137 graves); Vestre Gravlund, Oslo; and Rosseb Cemetery, Haugesund. The ground was consecrated before the aircrew burials were carried out. Houghton was astonished to find the largest proportion of the aircraft and men lost were from the anti-shipping strikes along the coast borne mostly by 18 Group Coastal Command.

Before the closure of the Banff airfield local MP for Banffshire Mr William Duthie requested that it remain open in the House of Commons. Nothing happened. It finally closed after just over four years existence, but was then reopened, and renamed Royal Naval Station Banff; an observation post and a single storey hut were built on the site situated near the main intersection of the runways. Royal Naval aircraft from the Fleet Air Arm based at Lossiemouth used the newly established ORS range (Optical Recording System) which consisted of an undisclosed number of cylindrical concrete markers as target practice for simulated bombing runs, although no rockets were fired or bombs dropped.

CHAPTER 18

POST WAR – BANFF

In January 1946 the Home Secretary, as chairman of the Cabinet Airfields Committee, requested that Banff be de-requisitioned in the future. Ten months later the airfield reverted to Seafield Estate, although the ORS range continued to be used. With the steady reduction of airfields throughout Britain the MP for Banffshire kept up a steady barrage of letters for eight years to the Air Ministry and Admiralty requesting that it stayed open because of the local economy. Highlights for locals were: the return of Wing Commander Junior Simmonds DFC in a Sea Otter in August 1946; four months later the Air Ministry Film *Ship-Busters* was released, with Wing Commander Tony Gadd, a 'Coastal' veteran of many raids, playing a leading role. Music was by Leighton Lucas who wrote the music for *Target for Tonight* and later *The Dam Busters*. Local and national reviews described the film as 'thrilling and authentic'; and lastly, in mid 1947, Spitfire XIXs of 82 Squadron beat up the former airfield while the unit were completing a survey of Scotland. Flight Lieutenant Shepherd's RAF Kinloss Mountain Rescue team used the airfield in 1948 whilst helping local farmers. In August 1952, during a review of reclassification of Royal Naval air stations, it was decided to put Banff in reserve and at 12 months notice to commission in the event of war. The state of maintenance was to be minimum; a resident caretaker was employed for its security.

A Dakota of 18 Group Communications Flight involved in 'Exercise Mainbrace' on a regular visit to remote Coastal Command squadrons in Northern Scotland, the Shetlands and Norway, made a brief landing whilst carrying mail and supplies. In October, two T2 hangars and the WAAF site were made available for occupation by the RAF but were then requisitioned by the Ministry of Food and Department of Agriculture for Scotland. December saw the Director of Naval Air Training submit to the Air Ministry that there was a definite possibility that Banff may be required as a satellite to Lossiemouth and the closure of Banff was deferred. Discussions continued in the corridors of Whitehall as a working party contemplated its future. Finally in November 1953 it was to be relinquished but Lossiemouth had become the naval fighter and strike school and it would continue operating the range. William Duthie protested in the strongest possible terms suggesting that it should be brought back into service so that the influx of service personnel, together with the civilian employment on the base could help the area financially and be beneficial to the health of those living in the area. It was also suggested that a branch of the de Havilland Company might relocate, though no firm proposal was received.

The demolition crews moved in shortly afterwards. Most of the dormitory huts and other buildings of the camp were demolished. In 1954 the re-allocation of the airfield for agricultural use began. Some buildings were retained, including: the control tower, three T2 hangars each with 16,200 square feet, two occupied by the Ministry of Works, one blister hangar, WCs, ablutions, small store room, and Nissen huts. With considerable concern over unemployment in this area of north-east Scotland the Department of Health for Scotland and Scottish MPs continued to push for action to be taken. A special measures award made through the Development Commission to encourage large scale industry was awarded to the area, but none was forthcoming. The local Banffshire Council converted the station hospital into a refuse collection centre. The Earl of Seafield, through Seafield Estates, pressed for an early decision to release all of his land back into his possession. No compensation had been paid to the land owner to date although the compensation payable in this case was estimated at £9,000 under Section 2(1) (b) of the Compensation (Defence) Act, 1939. RNAS Banff was finally derequisitioned on 28 November 1954, excluded from the release were the ORS range and the hangars used by the Ministry of Works. The former airfield saw brief action in exercise 'Sea Enterprise' during August and September but a month later a quick clearance of the hangars not required by the Admiralty began.

The airfields main type T2 hangars were demolished and the blister hangars removed, one found its way to a local farm a short distance from the airfield. It is still in use today showing scars of those bygone days. Over the years, the rest of the buildings have disappeared, and some now are hidden among the acres of woodland that dominates part of this sprawling site. Today the airfield is teeming with wildlife and vegetation and the countryside is at peace now. Long may it remain so.

27 November 1969 saw the disbandment of Coastal Command at St Mawgan. Air Marshal Sir John Lapsley CB, OBE, DFC, AFC took the salute. Amongst the onlookers were many former strike wing men and women – Coastal Command was no more. In 1971, the former station commander Sir Max Aitken returned to this corner of Scotland. He was invited to open the new £800,000 Banff Academy School. He had not been back since 1945 and even the pouring rain did not dampen Aitken's enthusiasm on arrival at Aberdeen Airport. The waiting reporter was bombarded with eager questions about what he expected to see. 'What about the town? Is it different?' and most nostalgically of all 'What about the airfield?' The following day saw Sir Max Aitken and Lady Aitken open the school and he recalled memories of wartime life at RAF Banff, known locally as Boyndie, and gave sound advice to the pupils. He recalled: 'A great thing up at Boyndie was to establish and maintain morale and the people of Banff and Banffshire did it for us. Their hospitality was magnificent. Their kindness knew no bounds.' He mentioned 'they had to put up with 3,300 airmen, we all frequented the pubs in the town and in the Kirk.' In particular he mentioned the late Rev Dr D Findlay Clark, then parish minister, and the former Chief Constable George I Strath, both of whom had helped form this special relationship with the Boyndie 'drome. Aitken was presented with a carved paper weight in Portsoy marble and Lady Aitken received an embroidered teacloth, the work of the pupils.

One year later in March 1972, four RAF Harriers made a momentary appearance whilst adopting RAF Kinloss and a satellite at Milltown for exercise 'Snowy Owl' using camouflaged hides amongst the airfield's woodland. June 1976 saw the culmination of more than four year's work by a group of flying enthusiasts who decided to renovate the former wartime base, with thousands of man hours devoted to bringing the airfield up to Civil Aviation Authority standards. Ten months earlier, approximately one-third of the main runway was 'licensed' after shifting tons of rubble, which had accumulated on the runways since the based closed. The control tower, an empty shell, was refurbished with power for use as a clubhouse. Access roads were reopened. On 6 June, it officially reopened for flying as Banff Airfield. During the reopening the Mosquito RS712 of the Strathallan (now owned by Kermit Weeks in the USA) flown by Neil Williams took part in the ceremony producing a memorable display and Sir Max Aitken paid another sentimental visit. Developers Osprey Aviation planned a 6,000 feet runway with traffic control, engineering and charter facilities. Light aircraft continued to fly from the club but planning regulations stopped the £300,000 regeneration of the airfield. Shortly afterwards all flying ended. One of the sounds heard at Banff now is the roar of go-karts which utilise a section of the perimeter track used by the Banff and Moray Kart Club. Former Formula 1 drivers and world champions Damon Hill, and Michael Schumacher have raced around the track.

Sir Max Aitken died in April 1985 and numerous former Coastal Command men and women paid their respects. Two years later a group of Scottish aviation historians got together with the desire to see a permanent memorial on or near the site of the airfield, remembering its history and the servicemen and women based there during six months of the war. This newly formed organisation became known as 'The RAF Banff Strike Wing Memorial Trust'. A former Banff pilot, Group Captain Angus McIntosh DFC, was nominated memorial trust chairman as he had served with 248 Squadron during the war. They began raising money steadily by staging events, with donations given by the general public and war veterans that served on the station. The organisation received great assistance in their work for the provision of the memorial from officials in the planning department of the district council and the roads department. A fitting tribute in granite stone to the men and women who served in the Banff Wing was finally put in place and dedicated two years later alongside the A98 trunk road, near Ordens junction. The ceremony on September 28, 1989 saw Group Captain Bill Sise DSO DFC perform the unveiling and among those present at the ceremony was Lady Aitken, widow of the late Sir Max. To set the seal of success on more than two years of planning a flypast by the only flying BAe Mosquito in Europe was arranged. Tony Craig the pilot of the aircraft recalls:

'David Morgan, one of the trustees of The RAF Banff Strike Wing Memorial Trust phoned and asked could I do a flypast at a memorial they were erecting for some servicemen and women, I accepted with pleasure and it was going to be near the disused airfield of Banff, on the coast some 60 miles from Inverness. The date of the flypast was 28 September 1989, just a day or two after the RAF Leuchars Battle of Britain display. David Morgan arranged free fuel courtesy of the station commander at RAF Kinloss. I know nothing is free, but it was a quid pro-quo for the flight. So payment in kind was in place and hotels and hangarage requested. The best way into the heart of Scotland is on the deck heading due north. The only snag with that is Air Traffic don't have those sort of codes for their flight plan, and they can't see you on radar and further more the CAA do not approve. I checked the weather, could be a problem with cloud on the hilltops, collected maps, flying suits, co-pilot Steve Watson, and went to the Mosquito. As the wheels went up and locked away first time, I climbed steeply and kept the speed low at 120mph. A fly by at Hawarden followed the one at Warton. I couldn't see many people on the ground, but no doubt, lots heard it over fly. Then freedom at last! We headed for Scotland, on the deck and due north. It is not like flying BAe 125, with no electronic equipment. Just a compass and a hand held map. If it rains hard you cannot see out and the rain gets through the canopy and drips onto your kneecaps. No nice seat in a cabin and no toilet. Therefore, life is a bit spartan. You live by looking out, seeing where you are going and watching for and avoiding other aircraft. No comfort of airways, radar control or navigation assistance. The Lake District slid by on the right. Sellafield was then visible on the coast. Gave that a wide berth but saw the smoke lying across our track. I had an impulse to hold my breath as we went through the smoke plume. Criffell, near Dumfries could then be seen slightly left. The skyline ahead was clear of cloud. We squeezed through the air route corridor between Glasgow and Edinburgh and headed for the Highlands and the string of lochs. Flying low over lonely Loch Ericht to the south west of Dalwinnie. I first saw it in my RAF days flying Lightings. We headed north-east to Aviemore and beyond to Forres and Kinloss airfield. At Kinloss, there was a marvellous welcoming party. David Morgan greeted me at the foot of the ladder. The commanding officer met us as well and I had a duty photograph taken in front of the Mosquito. Late in the afternoon, after checking into the hotel, David Morgan collected us and we set off for Banff and the War Memorial for a quick look. It was to be a star-studded event. A much bigger and more important occasion than I had imagined all those months ago at the first telephone call. The memorial had been erected in a layby on the A98. The old airfield was to the north up a rise, and the land fell away to the south, with the line of the road just about east-west. There were no houses or villages. Just cows, wheat stubble or grass. As I looked around the immediate air space, planning my short solo spot after the flypast, to the south was Knock Hill, 1,400 feet high. We had a sneak preview by lifting the edge of the tarpaulin and then went off to a big hotel in Banff to meet some of the warriors who were gathering in anticipation of tomorrow's ceremony. There were AFCs, DFCs, DSO and Bars, and much talk of anti-shipping strikes at 50 feet below radar. Fifty means the same as 'I'll only be two minutes, dear!' 200 feet equals five minutes and 500 feet to ten minutes. Consequently, that 50 feet quoted stuck in my mind. That night I refused more drinks than I can remember! We briefed in the morning with a Nimrod crew and by telephone with two Buccaneers from Lossiemouth who were all in the ceremonial flypast. We were to meet at Knock Hill at 2,000 feet 15 minutes before ON time.

'The flypast went well, it was difficult to mix a Nimrod SAR with two Buccaneers and a Mosquito at 200mph. I either had the radiators open and lost speed or closed and got too hot. The flypast was over in minutes; I was left alone in the cold grey sky above a huddle of people in the layby and a farmer's field full of cars. I flew the Mosquito through three passes to the north of the layby. The crowd would be looking over the memorial towards the aircraft and beyond up the slope to the disused airfield of Banff. On the north side of the road the last pass was to the west so I could wing the Mosquito through a 270° tight turn in the west and around the crowd to come in from the south up the rising ground. Over the parked cars, aiming for the trees, I caught a micro-second's glimpse of the granite monolith and flashes from the cameras, and it was complete. I headed north over the boundary of old Banff and out of sight over the horizon. We flew over Macduff for nostalgic locals and headed off for Aberdeen and pointed south.'

On Sunday 7 May 1995, on the 50th anniversary of VE-Day, a small gathering took place at Banff of servicemen and women who had served at the former Royal Air Force station. A church service and march past took place, at Banff Parish Church, officiated by Reverend Stewart D Jeffery. With its remaining funds the The RAF Banff Strike Wing Memorial Trust gave a gift to the former St Mary's Parish Church – the church to which the former Banff strike wing paraded on special occasions. Group Captain Angus McIntosh presented a 'Book of Remembrance'. The book is contained in a display cabinet crafted by Richard Brockbank of Findhorn.

Occasionally the deserted airfield does get used for 'exercises' by the Armed Forces, one such circumstance saw Special Operations' Hercules C130 and Chinooks coming from Mildenhall, off loading men and kit for a night assault on enemy installations and their headquarters in the old flying control tower on this former Coastal Command base.

A national memorial was unveiled to Coastal Command in Westminster Abbey on 16 March 2004 by HM Queen Elizabeth II. Many former anti-shipping strike crews attended this moving ceremony. Navigator, Flight Lieutenant Ron Simmons, ex-143

Squadron said: 'I survived but 50 percent of my original fellow aircrew didn't. That's why I'm here – to remember.'

Today part of the former strike wing base at Boyndie is a wind farm. The landowner, Seafield Estates, sought terms of interest from a number of wind farm developers in May 2001, Renewable Development Company was selected as the preferred developer in August of that year. A mast to monitor wind was requested in November through Aberdeen Council, at which time the proposal entered the public domain. Environmental assessments were carried out by Aberdeen Council. Various consultations and discussions with the local community were held together with presentations of the projected wind farm. A planning application was submitted in July 2003 after which a public exhibition was held. Consent for the wind farm was granted by Aberdeenshire Council in July 2004. Ground work began in June 2005. Seven 2MW wind turbines were delivered to the site and erection of the towers began immediately in spring 2006. Power was first generated on 27 April 2006 at a cost of between 10-15 million pounds. It is estimated that the wind turbines at Boyndie will generate sufficient electricity for 8,500 homes, equivalent to all the homes in Banff, Portsoy, Whitehills and the neighbouring rural areas.

CONCLUSION

This was the offensive part of Coastal Command's work; the continuous attack on the coastwise shipping in the Norwegian area by 18 Group, disrupting the enemy's trade with Norway. The anti-shipping strike offensive had resulted in a reduction from 8,500,000 tons of cargo in and out of Norwegian ports in 1944, to less than 500,000 tons per annum by the end of February 1945. The other consequence would have been to divert many of the enemy's forces away from the main operational theatres in protecting his ever diminishing merchant shipping thus in a direct sense giving the Allies a military advantage. Sir Arthur Harris C-in-C Bomber Command said his bomber offensive benefited by the tying up in ships and coastal defences of thousands of flak batteries, and by the deployment of Luftwaffe fighter units as convoy protection. The deployment of Fw190s in Norway towards the end of the war lessened the pressure on Allied land operations in Europe, as the aircraft had proved its worth in the ground attack role. The Battle of the Atlantic was aided by Coastal Command's labours in north-west European waters by pinning down German naval vessels, especially destroyers, in a purely defensive function. By having to replace sunken or damaged merchantmen the Germans were also losing construction materials which could have been utilised in naval vessels, and the shortage of steel plate particularly during 1944, was a major constraint on U-boat construction. In 1940 Coastal Command lost roughly 27 aircraft for every merchantman sunk, but by 1945 the ratio was one for one. The efficiency had obviously improved. This was due to a number of factors, including rigorous training and extremely experienced crews devoted to their task. Armament had improved with the use of rocket projectiles and cannon, and they were able to sink and counter flak at the same time. While the cost of mounting the anti-shipping campaign was heavy, with serious losses of aircraft and aircrew, the offensive was fully justified.

The former Commander-in-Chief of Coastal Command from 1944-1945, Lord Sholto Douglas said of their work during an interview in September 1964:

'There were strike squadrons of Beaufighters when I first joined the command and later I had four squadrons of Mosquitoes – the Banff wing under Max Aitken. Two more Mosquito squadrons were added (to those already operating) as the command replaced the slower Beaufighters. While rockets replaced torpedoes.

'I always admired their work. Their job was to attack enemy surface craft with bombs, rockets, and cannon fire; this in turn meant diving down to a very low altitude, with the gunners on the ships firing at you at point blank range; the job needed a great deal of courage and determination.

'Also, in Norway the weather closed in very fast. During the time of attack they were under heavy point blank gunfire from ship and shore heavy armament, imagine doing this with snow and sleet in the middle of the fjord, or off the rugged Norwegian coast with waves leaping up to cut you into the sea. Many such attacks in fact did end with aircraft going into the sea.'

Extracts above courtesy of Mrs Susan Griffith.

POEMS

Over the years since those days in September 1944 to June 1945, many veterans have made a pilgrimage back to the now deserted aerodrome and I am fortunate at being allowed to reproduce a selection of their poems.

No weeping now!   By J R Walsh

I went back to the lovely Glens, and the empty sky,
I saw gaunt elms, heard calling rooks – how time had passed me by.
Grass grown on the runways, where hangars stood there were rusting
   ploughs;
The dispersal points were empty – just starlings and grazing cows.
The watch office stood deserted,
Or maybe the ghosts of men stood and watched as I remembered,
For I had said, "I'll come back again."
The windsock stood in tatters, forlorn in the cold damp air,
Then I thought, "What does it matter? There's nobody to care!"
Old Nissen huts with rotting timbers and sagging floors;
Not a voice to break the silence, just the wind and creaking doors,
Then I recalled they were once billets, full of life and the noise of men
   and women;
The crackling roar of Merlins,
Or the whispering scratch of a pen.
So I stood quite still to listen; was there a message for me?
In the shadows would they remember me; had they left me a sign to see?
If they had it was too elusive, made dim by the veil of years;
Moreover, I recalled all the purpose and courage until my eyes were blurred
   by tears.
I turned away, downhearted, this wasn't the field I had known;
Not the brave bold home of my memoirs; fool I was – for the years had flown.

(Written on his return to former RAF Banff in 1976)

Banff Base Revisited 1974   By Mr Sharp

Not much remains I recognise, and yet, this is the very place,
Where thirty years ago or more, great dramas were acted out,
Still faintly visible 'neath moss and grass, a runway – now trodden on by
*   sheep and cows,*
And here and there some bricks, mortar and broken concrete floors,
The sad remains of Nissen huts and mess,
How quiet it is – naught but flocks and herds remain, they just stare,
How can they know what happened heretofore, where those mighty Merlins
*   rang their war songs,*
That bore aloft the vengeance of an island race,
Those sea grey, green awesome silhouettes, noise filled the air as they tightened up,
Against the rising or shrinking brightness
But, was that a laugh I heard from someone near, or was it a squeal of brakes
*   from a ghostly craft lifting off,*
Its jovial load departing only to be posted missing?
Or was it from the lane nearby that skirts the farm and fir, where men
*   and women, linked by uniform and love, forget Form 540, operations,*
*   and sweeps, try to laugh and be gay, talking of peace?*
It's only a wild bird,
Sadly I turn away, tears roll down my cheek, I mourn those now departed,
Perhaps one day we shall remember them?

LAC Eddie Mackin, below with his pet Alsatian, wrote a poem for the April 1945
235 Squadron Magazine *Chocks Away* about the de Havilland Mosquito:

Fulfilment

The wooded hills have felt the axe, where trees
Fast bound to earth, moaned softly to the sky
Of evil lot who had not wings to fly,
And shed their autumn tears upon the breeze.
I found their stumps, and sat on one of these;
But hardly had I sat when sounded high
Approaching thunder, while up went the sigh
Of dying things that could not appease.
Then spoke the earth, roots writhing in her breast –
"I held them down; they rose at man's behest.
Came they with axes, saws, and other things,
And worked apace to give my children wings."
The lone Mosquito swooped, exultantly . . .
I drew my breath at loveliness set free.

19 GROUP COASTAL COMMAND DEPLOYMENT AS AT 1ST SEPTEMBER 1944

Base	Unit	Aircraft Type	Establishment	Strength	Available	Remarks
Mount Batten	No. 10 (RAAF)	Sunderland III	12	13	9	
Pembroke Dock	No. 201	Sunderland III	12	12	9	
Pembroke Dock	No. 228	Sunderland III	12	12	8	
Pembroke Dock	No. 461 (RAAF)	Sunderland III	12	12	9	
Chivenor	No. 172	L/L Wellington XIV	15	14	10	
Chivenor	No. 612	L/L Wellington XIV	15	18	15	
Chivenor	No. 304 (Polish)	L/L Wellington XIV	15	16	10	
St. Eval	No. 53	L/L Liberator V and VI	15	18	9	
St. Eval	No. 224	L/L Liberator V and VI	15	20	11	
St. Eval	No. 547	Liberator VI	15	20	11	
St. Davids	No. 502	Halifax II	15	14	8	
Dunkeswell	No. 103 (USN)	Liberator (PB4Y)	15	15	11	On loan
Dunkeswell	No. 105 (USN)	Liberator (PB4Y)	15	16	14	On loan
Dunkeswell	No. 110 (USN)	Liberator (PB4Y)	15	17	15	On loan
Dunkeswell	No. 115 (USN)	Liberator (PB4Y)	6	6	3	On loan
Predannack	No. 179	L/L Wellington XIV	15	15	8	
Portreath	No. 235	Mosquito VI (Cannon)	20	18	12	
Portreath	No. 248	Mosquito VI (Cannon)	16	14	11	
Portreath	No. 248	Mosquito XVIII (6 pdr)	8	8	2	

18 GROUP COASTAL COMMAND DEPLOYMENT AS AT 1ST JANUARY 1945

Base	Unit	Aircraft Type	Establishment	Strength	Available	Remarks
Banff	No. 143	Mosquito VI (RP)	20	19	16	
Banff	No. 235	Mosquito VI (RP)	20	22	9	
Banff	No. 248	Mosquito VI (RP)	16	13	5	
Banff	No. 248	Mosquito XVIII (6 pdr)	8	6	2	
Banff	No. 333 (Norge)	Mosquito VI	10	9	6	Mosquito flight
Dallachy	No. 144	Beaufighter X (RP)	20	21	13	
Dallachy	No. 404 (RCAF)	Beaufighter X (RP)	20	18	10	
Dallachy	No. 455 (RAAF)	Beaufighter X (RP)	20	19	10	
Dallachy	No. 489 (RNZAF)	Beaufighter X (Torp)	20	20	9	
Leuchars	No. 206	L/L Liberator VI	15	16	7	
Leuchars	No. 547	L/L Liberator VI	15	15	7	
Milltown	No. 225	L/L Liberator VI and VIII	15	17	5	Re-equipping
Stornoway	No. 58	Halifax II	15	14	9	
Stornoway	No. 502	Halifax II	15	12	4	
Sullom Voe	No. 210	L/L Catalina IVA	12	10	3	
Sullom Voe	No. 330 (Norge)	Sunderland III	9	9	2	
Tain	No. 86	VLR Liberator V	15	15	4	
Tain	No. 311 (Czech)	Liberator V (RP)	15	15	4	
Woodhaven	No. 333 (Norge)	Catalina IB	3	2	1	Catalina flight
Sumburgh	No. 1693 Flight	Anson	6	8	5	

18 GROUP COASTAL COMMAND DEPLOYMENT AS AT 1ST APRIL 1945

Base	Unit	Aircraft Type	Establishment	Strength	Available	Remarks
Banff	No. 143	Mosquito VI (RP)	20	18	16	
Banff	No. 235	Mosquito VI (RP)	20	20	14	
Banff	No. 248	Mosquito VI (RP)	20	22	18	
Banff	No. 333 (Norge)	Mosquito VI (RP)	10	9	7	Mosquito flight
Banff	No. 404 (RCAF)	Mosquito VI (RP)				Converting to Mosquitoes
Dallachy	No. 455 (RAAF)	Beaufighter X (RP)	20	22	13	
Dallachy	No. 489 (RNZAF)	Beaufighter X (Torp)	20	20	11	
Dallachy	No. 144	Beaufighter X	20	19	12	
Leuchars	No. 206	L/L Liberator VIII	15	15	4	
Leuchars	No. 547	L/L Liberator VI	15	14	6	
Milltown	No. 224	L/L Liberator VIII	15	17	8	
Stornoway	No. 58	Halifax II and III	15	15	6	
Stornoway	No. 502	Halifax II and III	15	15	7	
Sullom Voe	No. 210	L/L Catalina IVA	12	10	4	
Sullom Voe	No. 330 (Norge)	Sunderland III	9	8	2	
Tain	No. 86	L/L Liberator VIII	15	15	8	
Tain	No. 311 (Czech)	L/L Liberator VI	15	15	8	
Woodhaven	No. 333 (Norge)	Catalina IVA	3	3	–	
Sumburgh	No. 1693 Flight	Anson I	6	7	5	

APPENDIX 4

LOSS LIST

This appendix was compiled with the help of The Commonwealth War Graves Commission, Marlow staff. Below is a list of all known aircraft and aircrew killed, or injured (including those who escaped via an occupied country or landed in neutral Sweden) while on operations flying with or as part of the Coastal Command Banff Strike Wing between September 1944 and May 1945.

Date 1944		Pilot or Crewman	Navigator	Aircraft Code	Sqdn
1.	14.09.44	Fg Off J M A Baribeau (POW)	Flt Lt C H Taylor +	O	404
2.	14.09.44	Flg Sgt D E Reeves (Rescued)	Flt Sgt G Ogilvie (Rescued)	D	144
3.	19.09.44	Flt Sgt R E C Hossack +	WO B C Wicks +	L	144
4.	02.10.44	Fg Off E R Davey +	Fg Off L E E Robinson +	Q	404
5.	02.10.44	Fg Off G A Long +	Fg Off F M Stickel +	E	404
6.	13.10.44	Flt Lt G E Nicholls +	Fg Off A Hanson +	K	248
7.	19.10.44	WO N M M Martin +	WO I L Ramsay (POW)	F	235
8.	21.10.44	Fg Off R S Driscoll +	Fg Off A Hannant +	I	248
9.	28.10.44	Fg Off J T Ross +	Fg Off F L Walker +	P	235
10.	28.10.44	Flt Lt A E Lusk		FK759	251
		FO A W Campbell		FK759	251
		FO W T E Legg		FK759	251
		FO J Mason		FK759	251
		WO F H Swinson		FK759	251
11.	04.11.44	Fg Off H L Powell +	Fg Off N L Redford +	L	235
12.	08.11.44	Sgt Ritcher +		HB882	315
13.	17.11.44	Fg Off Jenner (Rescued)		Q	281
	17.11.44	Flt Lt Hyde (Rescued)		Q	281
	17.11.44	Fg Off Temple (Rescued)		Q	281
	17.11.44	WO E Roberts W/Op +		Q	281
	17.11.44	Flt Sgt Dixon (Rescued)		Q	281
	17.11.44	WO Moffatt (Rescued)		Q	281
14.	05.12.44	Fg Off R Gilchrist +	Fg Off W Knight (Injured)	P	143
15.	05.12.44	Flt Lt L N Collins +	Fg Off R H Hurn +	G	248
16.	06.12.44	Flt Lt J Schmdit +		HB833	315
17.	06.12.44	Flt Sgt M H J Graham (Rescued)	W/O I G Clark (Rescued)	R	489
18.	07.12.44	Fg Off W N Cosman +	Fg Off L M Freedman +	O	248
19.	07.12.44	Fg Off K C Wing +	Plt Off V R Shield +	Z	248
20.	07.12.44	Fg Off A Czerwinski +		E	315
21.	13.12.44	Wg Cdr R A Atkinson +	Fg Off V C Upton +	R	235
22.	16.12.44	Fg Off K C Beruldsen +	Plt Off T D S Rabbitts +	S	235
23.	16.12.44	Flt Lt J Kennedy +	Fg Off W Rolls +	R	248

	Date	Pilot or Crewman	Navigator	Aircraft Code	Sqdn
24.	21.12.44	Plt Off W D Livock +	Flt Sgt G L West +	HR284	248
25.	23.12.44	Plt Off T Lubicz-Lisowski +		J	315
26.	26.12.44	Fg Off E J Fletcher +	Fg Off A J Watson +	G	235
27.	31.12.44	Flt Lt J F Lown +	Fg Off C J Dayton +	U	248
1945					
28.	09.01.45	Flt Lt D B Douglas +	LAC G P Robbins +	HR159	235
29.	11.01.45	WO M Day +	Flt Sgt J Roddis +	C	144
30.	11.01.45	Flt Lt J Moreton +		B	279
		Plt Off F Bentley +		B	279
		Fg Off G Gallway +		B	279
		WO A Goodall +		B	279
		WO G Mansfield +		B	279
		Flt Sgt W Bryan +		B	279
		WO W Sandercock +		B	279
31.	11.01.45	Flt Sgt P C L Smoolenaers +	Flt Sgt W W Harris +	M	143
32.	15.01.45	Cdt M J M Guedj +	Flt Lt J E Langley +	K	143
33.	15.01.45	Flt Sgt G A Morton-Moncrieff +	Flt Sgt C Cash +	D	143
34.	15.01.45	Lt F E Alexandre +	Plt Off J A McMullin +	V	143
35.	15.01.45	Flt Sgt F Chew +	Flt Sgt S W Couttie (POW)	A	235
36.	15.01.45	QM K Sjolie +	QM J S Gausland +	R	333
37.	25.01.45	Flt Lt D S L Crimp +	Fg Off J Bird +	F	248
38.	24.01.45	Lt L R Bacon +	Fg Off W W Miller +	RF603	248
39.	29.01.45	Sqn Ldr I D S Strachan +		N	65Flt
40.	20.02.45	Flt Lt Hussey +		FB199	19
41.	07.03.45	Fg Off S C Hawkins +	Fg Off E Stubbs +	O	235
42.	07.03.45	Flt Lt R G Young +	Fg Off G V Goodes +	R	248
43.	11.03.45	Lt R Almton +	Sub Lt P Hjorten +	N	333
44.	12.03.45	WO R W Moffatt +	Fg Off B A S Abbott +	Q	248
45.	12.03.45	Sqn Ldr M R Hill +		KH444	19
46.	13.03.45	Flt Lt R Haywood +			19
47.	17.03.45	Fg Off W J Ceybird +	Flt Lt N Harwood +	F	143
48.	17.03.45	Sqn Ldr R Orrock (POW)	Flt Lt Wilding (POW)	–	248
49.	22.03.45	Lt R Leithe +	Sub Lt N Skjelanger (Injured)	K	333
50.	23.03.45	Sqn Ldr R Reid +	Fg Off A D Turner +	W	235
51.	23.03.45	Plt Off K McCall +	WO J A Etchells +	R	143
52.	23.03.45	Flt Lt H H Lowe (POW)	Fg Off R Hannaford (POW)	W	143
53.	23.03.45	Flt Lt J R Williams +	Flt Lt J T Flower +	Q	235
54.	25.03.45	Lt Cdr K Skavhaugen +		G	333
55.	25.03.45	Flt Lt A McLead +	WO N Wheeley +	V	248
56.	30.03.45	Flt Lt W Knowles +	Flt Sgt L Thomas +	T	235
57.	05.04.45	Plt Off L E Arthurs +	Flt Sgt F G Richardson +	U	235
58.	05.04.45	Major H Wenger (Sweden)	Sgt Hanssen (Sweden)	E	333
59.	05.04.45	Fg Off R Harrington (Escaped)	Flt Sgt W Winwood (Escaped)	F	235
60.	05.04.45	Flt Lt J Butler +		KM137	19

Date	Pilot or Crewman	Navigator	Aircraft Code	Sqdn
61. 09.04.45	Flt Lt W M O Jones +	Fg Off A J Newell +	DZ592	138 Wing
62. 09.04.45	Fg Off C Parkinson (Sweden)	Fg Off J R Halley (Sweden)	Z	1693 Flight
63. 09.04.45	Fg Off A N Mogridge (Sweden)	Fg Off McQuarrie (Sweden)	A	248
64. 09.04.45	Flt Lt H A Sharville (Sweden)	Flt Lt P B McIntyre (Sweden)	N	248
65. 11.04.45	Wg Cdr P Davenport (POW)	Fg Off R Day (POW)	RF505	235
66. 11.04.45	Sub Lt J W Løken +	Sgt S H Engstørm +	H	333
67. 19.04.45	Flt Sgt A R Mackenzie +	Flt Sgt F A Relfe +	?	235
68. 19.04.45	Fg Off B Woodier (Sweden)	Fg Off A Jones (Sweden)	?	235
69. 19.04.45	Flt Lt S Pearson (Sweden)		KH695	65
70. 02.05.45	Fg Off A J Rendell (Sweden)	Fg Off R R Rawlins (Sweden)	RS620	235
71. 04.05.45	Flt Lt J Davidson +		KH818	19
72. 04.05.45	Plt Off B M Natta +		KH674	19
73. 04.05.45	Plt Off P J W Bell (POW)		KH860	234
74. 04.05.45	Flt Lt D Thorburn +	WO L W R Crocker (Injured)	RS568	235
75. 04.05.45	Fg Off W Moffatt (Sweden)	Flt Lt C Hardy (Sweden)	RS623	235
76. 04.05.45	Flt Lt W Shewry (Sweden)	Flt Off J E Hornby (Sweden)	RS501	143

INVENTORY OF AIRCRAFT

Listed are the de Havilland Mosquito Mark VIs known to be have been on strength with the Coastal Command Banff Strike Wing from September 1944 through to July 1945. This is by no means a comprehensive inventory. I am grateful to Alan Webb of the de Havilland Mosquito Museum for his help in compiling this record.

**500 de Havilland Mosquito VIs were delivered between
June 1943 and December 1944 by Standard Motors, Coventry**

Code	Sqdn(s)	Outcome
HP858	333	SS 08.07.50
HP887	235	Sold 09.02.49
HP904	333	SS 16.07.47
HP910	333	SOC 29.07.46
HP918	235	SOC 12.10.45
HP922	248	Ditched returning from Flekkefjord 31.12.44
HP967	1FU/235	Shot down attacking convoy off Kinn 04.11.44
HP981	235	Sold to Turkey 1946
HP982	235	SOC 04.09.45
HP984	235/333	Missing 15.01.45
HP988	235/248	Served with 464 Sqdn
		Undercarriage collapsed 06.07.45
HP989	235	Sold 04.07.47
HR116	333	Sold to Turkey 1946
HR118	235/333	Crashed Lossiemouth due to engine fire 22.02.45
HR120	248	Crashed into sea attacking convoy off Norway 05.12.44
HR121	235	SOC 04.07.47
HR122	235	SS 29.06.47
HR125	235	Hit by flak, ditched 19.10.44
HR127	235/248/235	Missing from attack on vessel 16.12.44
HR128	235/248	Served with 8 OTU SS 17.01.51
HR129	235	Sold to Turkey 26.09.47
HR130	235	SS 3.09.47
HRI35	235/248	Sold to Turkey 05.09.47
HR136	235	Sold to Turkey 29.09.47
HR137	235	SS 19.11.53
HR141	333	Pres shot down by Fw190 off Flado Islands 25.03.45
HR156	248	Hit by flak, ditched 16.12.44
HR157	235	Sold to Turkey 06.10.47
HR158	248	Served with 54 OTU
		Czech Air Force 08.02.47
HR159	235	Dived in ground, Banff
		Ailerons jammed 09.01.45
HR160	235	Served with 8 OTU dived into ground

Code	Sqdn(s)	Outcome
		Witland, Carmarthen 04.05.45
HR261	248	Sold to Turkey
HR262	333	Missing mine-laying off Karmsund 11.03.46
HR279	333	Sold to Turkey 04.07.47
HR282	235/248	Damaged by flak
		Crash-landed near Banff 26.12.44
HR287	235	Sold to Turkey 17.04.47
HR288	248	Served with 8 OTU/132 OTU
		Sold to Turkey 15.05.47
HR289	248	Served with 8 OTU/132 OTU
		Sold to Turkey 03.05.47
HR298	235	Hit HR136 on take-off, belly-landed at Banff
HR299	235	SOC 30.08.47
HR303	248	Served with AAEE
		SOC 19.06.46
HR366	235-MA-01	Sold to Turkey 29.09.47
HR367	248	Sold Czech Air Force 24.04.47
HR405	143/14	Sold November 1946
HR411	235/248	Sold to Turkey 30.06.47
HR414	143/14	Sold to Turkey 08.11.46
HR433	235	To Armée de l'Air 14.08.47
HR434	235	Missing 24.03.45
HR436	143/14	Sold 12.11.46
HR569	333	Hit mast, crash-landed 22.02.45 NFD
HR579	235	Sold 23.02.49
HR604	143/14	Crash-landed 04.12.45
HR632	248	Missing shot down by e/a 12.3.45
LR340	248	Missing from patrol 13.10.44
LR347	248	Sold 1947
LR362	248	Served with 464/305 Sqdn SOD 20.08.47
LR363	248	Crashed Sumburgh 04.11.44
LR377	248	Served CGS/1 OFU
		Sold to Yugoslav Air Force as 8095
LR378	248	Served 54 OTU Sold to Fairey 29.09.47

52 de Havilland Mosquito VIs delivered by de Havilland Hatfield, March and April 1945 under Contract No. 555

Code	Sqdn(s)	Outcome
SZ959	248	Collided with RF581 25.01.45

250 de Havilland Mosquito VIs delivered by de Havilland Hatfield, May and June 1945

Code	Sqdn(s)	Outcome
PZ232	333	Served 107/305 26.02.47 DBR
PZ251	CvXVIII/248	Shot down by flak Haugesund 21.10.44
PZ252	CvXVIII/248	Served 254 Sqdn SOC 25.11.46
PZ300	CvXVIII/248	Served 254 Sqdn 03.05.45 DBR

Code	Sqdn(s)	Outcome
PZ301	CvXVIII/248	Served 254 Sqdn Sold 31.12.46
PZ346	CvXVIII/248	Shot down 07.12.44
PZ379	143	Sold 22.10.47
PZ382	248	Served 21 Sqdn Sold 21.02.49
PZ387	143	Armée de l'Air 22.07.46
PZ412	143	Hit by flak, ditched 23.3.45
PZ413	143/248/143/ 248/489	Served 132 OTU/ To RNZAF 23.01.48 as NZ2381
PZ415	143	Flak damage, force-landed Sweden 02.04.45
PZ417	143/14	Served 21 Sqdn undercarriage collapsed 23.02.45
PZ418	143	Hit wall Sumburgh 05.12.44
PZ419	143	Shot down Leirvik 15.01.45
PZ435	143/14	Served 16 Sqdn SOC 26.12.46
PZ438	143	Shot down Leirvik 15.01.45
PZ439	143	Served 16 Sqdn & 21 Sqdn dived into ground 01.07.46
PZ441	143	Armée de l'Air 01.08.46
PZ442	143	Shot down Leirvik 15.01.45
PZ443	143	Sold 16.06.47
PZ445	143	Swung on landing in snow Undercarriage leg collapsed Banff 22.01.45 DBR
PZ446	143/14	To RNZAF as NZ2395
PZ450	248	Served 253 Sqdn SS 21.02.49
PZ460	143	Shot down Leirvik 15.01.45
PZ466	143/14	Sold 22.07.47
PZ468	CvXVIII/248	Served 254 Sqdn SOC 26.11.46
NT223	333/334	RNorAF 1945
NT224	248	Shot down 07.12.44
NT225	248	Served 254 Sqdn Sold 20.11.45

300 de Havilland Mosquito VIs delivered between December 1944 and May 1945 by Standard Motors, Coventry

Code	Sqdn	Outcome
RF587	248	SOC 24.04.47
RF590	333	Shot down by flak Porsgrunn 11.04.45
RF595	248	To RNZAF 16.8.48 as NZ2396
RF596	235	Crashed into sea after attacking a convoy
RF597	235	To RNZAF 27.1.48 as NZ2383
RF599	235	Force-landed Sweden
RF601	248	Hit by flak, crash-landed Banff
RF602	235	Armée de l'Air 28.06.46
RF603	248	Aileron detached while on R/P training, hit tail-plane, broke up in air crashed on Macduff Golf Course. 24.02.45
RF605	248	Engine caught fire crashed 18.05.45 DBF
RF606	235	Shot down 30.03.45
RF607	235	Engine cut after sortie failed to return
RF608	143/14	–
RF609	248	SOC 8.10.46
RF610	248/APS Acklington/ 1 OTU	Yugoslav Air Force 04.09.52 as 8114

Code	Sqdn(s)	Outcome
RF612	248	Spun into sea 25m south of Plymouth 23.08.45
RF613	248	Force-landed in Sweden 02.04.45
RF615	248	Sold 12.03.46
RF617	235	Crashed into sea attacking convoy 05.04.45
RF618	143/248/16/14/21	Undercarriage collapsed Germany 30.08.46
RF620	248	Sold 17.01.51
RF621	248	Sold March 1947
RF622	143/14	Broke up on impact north-east of Sylt 6.12.45
RF623	248	Czech Air Force 5.06.47
RF624	248	Armée de l'Air 16.05.46
RF625	143	Crashed into sea attacking an M/V 23.03.45
RF640	143/14/25	Undercarriage collapsed Sylt 6.02.47 Not repaired
RF641	248	SOC March 1947
RF643	333/248/489	Czech Air Force 08.02.47
RF645	143/14/25/14	Scrapped 12.11.52
RF646	143/14	Armée de l'Air 14.08.47
RF647	333/334	Crashed into Larviks fjord 2.07.45
RF724	333	Belly-landed Sweden 5.04.45
RF725	333/334	Damaged 26.10.45 Not repaired
RF753	235	RNZAF 28.01.48 as NZ2379
RF764	333/334	Damaged 30.11.45
RF769	333/334	Sold
RF777	404/132 OTU	Czech Air Force May 1945
RF786	235	Armée de l'Air 5.09.46
RF787	333/334	–
RF822	235	Armée de l'Air 1946
RF823	235	Czech Air Force December 1946
RF826	248	Undercarriage collapsed St Athan 5.07.46
RF827	333	Crashed 1m south-west of Banff 22.03.44
RF828	333/334	Armée de l'Air 6.07.46
RF831	333/334	–
RF832	333	Armée de l'Air 1946
RF836	333	Armée de l'Air October 1946
RF838	404/132 OTU	Czech Air Force June 1947
RF839	404/489/?	Undercarriage collapsed 24.06.46
RF842	404/489	Armée de l'Air 12.07.46
RF844	404/489	Czech Air Force 19.05.46
RF845	235/404	Armée de l'Air 28.10.46
RF848	404/489	Armée de l'Air 27.06.46
RF849	404/489	RNZAF as NZ2386 1948
RF850	404/132 OTU	Armée de l'Air 28.05.46
RF851	404	Armée de l'Air 12.09.46
RF852	404/489	Armee de l'Air 9.05.46
RF853	404/204 AFS	Sold 1949
RF854	235/404	Armée de l'Air 03.07.46
RF855	404	DH Hatfield 26.11.46
RF856	404	RNZAF as NZ2366
RF857	404/489	Armée de l'Air 24.05.46
RF858	404/?	Dived into the ground Dorking 21.05.45
RF859	404	Armée de l'Air 1947
RF873	404/333/344	RNorAF

Code	Sqdn(s)	Outcome
RF874	404/333	RNorAF
RF876	235/334	–
RF877	235/248	Sold 1949
RF879	404	Undercarriage collapsed East Fortune 1946
RF880	404/489	Armée de l'Air 4.07.46
RF881	404/489	Armée de l'Air 9.07.46
RF882	404	RNZAF as NZ2388
RF883	235	–
RF884	248	Sold March 1947
RF890	404/204 AFS	Undercarriage collapsed Brize Norton 27.04.50
RF893	489/6 OTU	Sold 1950
RF895	235	Armée de l'Air 10.10.46
RF897	143/14	Israel 1948
RF905	333/334	RNorAF

109 de Havilland Mosquito VIs delivered between October 1944 and January 1945 by de Havilland Hatfield

Code	Sqdn(s)	Outcome
RS501	143	Hit by flak in Kattegat force-landed Sweden 04.05.45
RS504	235/248/36	To RNZAF 18.08.47 as NZ2363
RS505	333	Missing over Porsgrunn 11.04.45
RS506	235	To Armée de l'Air 09.09.47
RS508	248/36	SOC 22.10.47
RS509	333/235	Sold 11.07.47
RS519	2 GSU/248	SS 14.10.54
RS523	333/235	Ditched off Leirvik 15.01.45
RS524	333	Missing
RS562	248	Crash-landed Sweden 09.04.45
RS564	248	To MoS 09.02.49
RS565	235	Sold 22.07.47
RS568	235	Kattegat engine cut, force-landed Sweden 04.05.45
RS574	235	To Armée de l'Air 18.08.47
RS575	235	Hit, dived into Dalsfjord 23.03.45
RS606	143/4/14/107	SOC 14.02.47
RS607	143/16/14	SOC 20.08.47
RS610	248	To RNorAF 18.08.47
RS612	235	Hit the mast of vessel, crashed into Kattegat 05.04.45
RS616	235	To Armée de l'Air 03.11.47
RS618	235	To Armée de l'Air 23.07.47
RS619	235	Crash-landed in Denmark 05.04.45
RS620	235	Landed in Sweden after a/s/s in Kattegat 02.04.45
RS621	248	To Armée de l'Air 12.07.46
RS622	248/36	SS 10.11.54
RS623	235	Force-landed in Sweden on one engine 04.05.45
RS624	143/13 OTU	Undercarriage retracted in error Driffield 19.07.48 DBR
RS625	143/248/143/14	SS 19.11.53
RS626	143/248	Collision over Skagerrak 07.03.45
RS627	143	Swung on landing hitting snow bank 01.02.45
RS628	248	Ditched off Storholmen 17.03.45

Code	Sqdn(s)	Outcome
RS629	248	Forced landing after engine vibration 04.02.45 DBR
RS631	248	Engine cut, crash-landed in Sweden 09.04.45
RS632	235/11	SS 09.01.51
RS633	248	Missing, shot down by e/a 70m W of Solund 25.03.45

KEY

DBR	Destroyed Beyond Repair
Pres SD	Presumed Shot Down
SOC	Struck off Charge
SOD	Sold/Destroyed
SS	Sold for Scrap

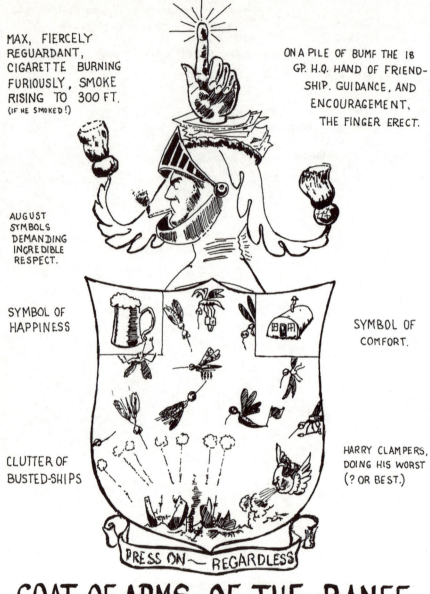

MAX, FIERCELY REGUARDANT, CIGARETTE BURNING FURIOUSLY, SMOKE RISING TO 300 FT. (IF HE SMOKED!)

ON A PILE OF BUMF THE 18 GP. H.Q. HAND OF FRIEND-SHIP, GUIDANCE, AND ENCOURAGEMENT, THE FINGER ERECT.

AUGUST SYMBOLS DEMANDING INCREDIBLE RESPECT.

SYMBOL OF HAPPINESS

SYMBOL OF COMFORT.

CLUTTER OF BUSTED-SHIPS

HARRY CLAMPERS, DOING HIS WORST (? OR BEST.)

PRESS ON ~ REGARDLESS

COAT OF ARMS OF THE BANFF STRIKE WING

This cartoon was drawn especially for the *Somerset Herald* by George Bellew, MVO, who was the base's IO. The original was used as a prize in a raffle among the station personnel and won by Squadron Leader Vernon Smith (*via Tom Wilkinson*).

GLOSSARY & ABBREVIATIONS

Ac	Aircraft
AC	Aircraftman/woman
Adj	Adjutant
AFC	Air Force Cross
AHQ	Air Headquarters
AFU	Advance Flying Unit
AOC	Air Officer Commanding
AG	Air Gunner
Arm	Armourer
ASS	Anti-Shipping Strike
AU	Anti-U-boat Strike
AVM	Air Vice-Marshal
Bordfunker	Radio Operator
Beobachter	Observer
Bordschütz	Air Gunner
Brighton	Codeword used for neutral Sweden
Bristol	Company
BV	Blohm und Voss
CAS	Chief of Air Staff
CB	Commander of the Order of Bath
CBE	Commander of the Order of the British Empire
C de G	Croix de Guerre
C-in-C	Commander-in-Chief
CIU	Central Interpretation Unit
CMG	Companion of the Order of St Michael and St George
CO	Commanding Officer
Col	Colonel
Condor	FW 200 (also known as Kondor or Kurier)
Cpl	Corporal
DC	Depth Charge
De Havilland	Aircraft manufacturing company
Det	Detachment
Deutsche Levante-Linie	German Shipping Company
DFC	Distinguished Flying Cross
DFM	Distinguished Flying Medal
DSO	Distinguished Service Order
Ditch	Force-land in the sea
Dry hit	Above the waterline
E	East
E-boat	Torpedo Boat
Eiserne Kieuz	Iron Cross
Eismeer	Polar Sea Company
Experten	Ace
FAA	Fleet Air Arm
Flakship	Armed Trawler or Whaler (*Vorpostenboote*)
Flak	Flieger Abwehr kanonen/

	German Anti-Aircraft Fire
Flensburg	(FuG 227) German Air Interception homing device
Flt	Flight
Flt Lt	Flight Lieutenant
Flugzeugführer	Pilot
Feldwebel (Fw)	Flight Sergeant
Fern	Long Range
Fg Off	Flying Officer
Flieger	Aircraftman
Flying Control	Control Tower (Watch Office)
Flt Sgt	Flight Sergeant
Führer	Leader
FW (Fw)	Focke-Wulf
Gardening	RAF codeword for minelaying
Gee	Navigational aid
Geschwader (Gesh)	Group (five Gruppen)
Geschwader	Commodore
Grp	Group
Gp Capt	Group Captain
Gruppe	Wing (five Staffeln)
Gustav	Nickname for Bf109G
Hack	Aircraft used for communications or recreational purposes
Hauptmann (Hptm)	Flight Lieutenant (Flt Lt)
HE	High Explosive
Heinkel	Company
Heinrich	German transmitter introduced to jam Gee
HSL	High-Speed Launch
IFF	Identification Friend or Foe
Inj	Injured
Jagdgeschwader (JG)	Fighter Group
Ju	Junkers
KBE	Knight Commander of the Order of the British Empire
KCB	Knight Commander of the Order of the Bath
Kriegsmarine	German Navy
Küstenfliegergruppe	Coastal Reconnaissance Wing
LAC	Leading Aircraftman/women
LL	Leigh Light
Lt	Lieutenant
Leutnant	Pilot Officer (Plt Off)
Leutnant zur See (LtzS)	Sub Lieutenant
Luftflotte	Air Fleet
ME	Middle East
Me (Bf)	Messerschmitt
M-class	Minesweeper *(Minensuchboote)*
MIA	Missing in Action
MAS	Missing at Sea
Major (Maj)	Squadron Leader
MC	Military Cross
Merchantman	Cargo carrying vessel
Met	Meteorological
Minensuchboote	Minesweeper
MT	Motor Transport

MTB	Motor Torpedo Boat
N	North
Nav	Navigator
Nm	Nautical Miles
OA	Priority signal sent by Allied aircraft which indicated that they were under attack or about to be attacked
OBE	Order of the British Empire
Ob	Observer
OCU	Operational Conversion Unit
Oberfeldwebel (Ofw)	Warrant Officer (WO)
Oberleutnant (Oblt)	Flying Officer (Fg Off)
Oberstleutnant (Obstlt)	Wing Commander (Wg Cdr)
OTU	Operational Training Unit
Outrider	Norwegian aircraft that went ahead of the main force searching for targets
P	Pilot
Plt Off	Pilot Officer
PIU	Photographic Interpretation Unit
POW	Prisoner of War
PR	Photographic Reconnaissance
PRU	Photographic Reconnaissance Unit
RAAF	Royal Australian Air Force
RAF	Royal Air Force
RAuxAF	Royal Auxiliary Air Force
RCAF	Royal Canadian Air Force
Ritterkreuz	Knights' Cross (award for bravery)
Rottenflieger	Wingman
RNZAF	Royal New Zealand Air Force
Rover	Search
R/P	Rocket Projectile
S	South
Schwarm	Four aircraft tactical formation
Service Echelon	Major maintenance or repair on squadron aircraft usually carried out within the main squadron hangar
Sgt	Sergeant
SIS	Secret Intelligence Service (British)
Sperrbrecher	Boom defence vessel heavily armed Would precede convoys in order to explode mines or draw off enemy submarines
Stab	Staff or Headquarters
Stabsfeldwebel (Stfw)	Senior Warrant Officer
Staffel (St Kap)	Squadron; commanded by Staffelkapitän
Snort	U-boat air breathing tube
SoC	Struck off Charge
Sqn	Squadron
Sqn Ldr	Squadron Leader
SS	Sold for scrap
Tsetse	Mark XVIII (De Havilland Mosquito)
TTA	Trawler Type Auxiliary *(Vorpostenboote)*
Torbeau	Torpedo-carrying Beaufighter
Ultra	British decrypts of German Enigma encodes
Unteroffizier(Uffz)	Sergeant (Sgt)

USAAF	United States Army Air Force
VHF	Very High Frequency
Vp	*Vorpostenboote*
Vorpostenboote	Trawler Type Auxiliaries (Flakship)
W	West
WAAF	Women Auxiliary Air Force
WOpAG	Wireless Operator Air Gunner
Watch Office	Control Tower
Werk Nummer (Wk Nr)	Serial Number
Wet hit	Below the waterline
Wg Cdr	Wing Commander
W/O	Warrant Officer
Wop	Wireless Operator
+	Killed

BIBLIOGRAPHY & SOURCES

Books, articles and official publications
Banffshire Journal (Scottish Provincial Press), Article on '9 January 1945 Air Crash', 1945
Bon Accord, Article on Peterhead Mustangs, 1945
Burrows, David M. *489 – An Unofficial History of No. 489 Torpedo Bomber Squadron RNZAF 1941-1945*, New Zealand 2006 (Limited Edition)
Clark, Dr Findlay, *One Boy's War, Banff*, Aberdeenshire Council, 1997
Cook, C, *Seventh Heaven*, Key Publishing Limited, Lincolnshire, 1996
Goulter, Christina G M A, *Forgotten Offensive – Royal Air Force Coastal Command's Anti-Shipping Campaign, 1940-1945*, Frank Cass, London, 1995
The Daily Mail, Weather Report for NE Scotland, London, 1945
1939 Electoral Register Banffshire – Aberdeen City Archive, Town House, Broad Street, Aberdeen, AB10 1AQ
Foxley-Norris, ACM C, *A Lighter Shade of Blue*, Ian Allan, 1978
Franks, Norman, *Dark Sky, Deep Water*, Grub Street, 1999
Franks, Norman, *Search Find and Kill*, Grub Street, 1995
Gordon, Ian, *Strike and Strike Again*, Banner Books, Australia, 1995
Guevremont, Stéphane, *Deadly Duo: No.404 Squadron (Buffalo), R.C.A.F. and the Rocket Projectile, 1943-5. In Canada's Air Force: A Global Perspective; Proceedings of the 8th Annual Air Force Historical Conference in Cornwall, Ontario, 18-21 June 2002*, pp. 57-92. Winnipeg, Manitoba: Office of Air Force Heritage & History, 2003
Imperial War Museum Annex, *Various Newsworthy Items on the Banff Wing*, Sept 44 to May 45
Isle of Wight County Press, Article on Wg Cdr Roy Orrock DFC, Hampshire, 1945
Isle of Wight County Press, *Leirvik attack Monday 15 January 1945*, Hampshire, 1945
Lancashire Evening Post, Article on Norman Earnshaw, 1945
Nesbit, Roy Conyers, *The Strike Wings – Special Anti Shipping Squadrons 1942-45*, HMSO London, 1995
RAF Hendon Museum, *RAF Banff – Airfield Construction Drawings*, 1942
Sem & Stenersen A/S, *Flyalarm (AirAlarm) – Luftkriegen over Norge 1939 – 1945*, Norway 1991
The Sussex Express & County Herald, Article on Don Rogers, 1944

AIR 28/182 RAF Dallachy National Archives London

War Diaries – Allied

143 Squadron	AIR27 979	Public Record Office, Kew, London
144 Squadron	AIR27 983	Public Record Office, Kew, London
235 Squadron	AIR27 1444	Public Record Office, Kew, London
248 Squadron	AIR27 1496	Public Record Office, Kew, London
RAF Banff	AIR28 49	Public Record Office, Kew, London
Coastal Command	AIR15	Public Record Office, Kew, London

German War Diaries

KTB Westküste 1944	The Norwegian Armed Forces, Bergen, Norway
ULTRA intercepts U249	National Archives and Record Administration, Maryland USA
Canadian Record of Service	National Archives of Canada, Ottawa, Canada

INDEX